Neighborhood Rebels

CONTEMPORARY BLACK HISTORY

Manning Marable (Columbia University) and
Peniel Joseph (Tufts University)
Series Editors

This series features cutting-edge scholarship in Contemporary Black History, underlining the importance of the study of history as a form of public advocacy and political activism. It focuses on postwar African American history, from 1945 to the early 1990s, but it also includes international black history, bringing in high-quality interdisciplinary scholarship from around the globe. It is the series editors' firm belief that outstanding critical research can also be accessible and well written. To this end, books in the series incorporate different methodologies that lend themselves to narrative richness, such as oral history and ethnography, and combined disciplines such as African American Studies, Political Science, Sociology, Ethnic and Women's Studies, Cultural Studies, Anthropology, and Criminal Justice.

Published by Palgrave Macmillan:

Biko Lives!: The Contested Legacies of Steve Biko
    Edited by Andile Mngxitama, Amanda Alexander, and Nigel C. Gibson

Anticommunism and the African American Freedom Movement: "Another Side of the Story"
    By Robbie Lieberman and Clarence Lang

Africana Cultures and Policy Studies: Scholarship and the Transformation of Public Policy
    Edited by Zachery Williams

Black Feminist Politics from Kennedy to Clinton
    By Duchess Harris

Mau Mau in Harlem?: The U.S. and the Liberation of Kenya
    By Gerald Horne

Black Power in Bermuda: The Struggle for Decolonization
    By Quito Swan

Neighborhood Rebels: Black Power at the Local Level
    Edited by Peniel E. Joseph

Black Power Principals
    By Matthew Whitaker (forthcoming)

Neighborhood Rebels

Black Power at the Local Level

Edited by
Peniel E. Joseph

NEIGHBORHOOD REBELS
Copyright © Peniel E. Joseph, 2010.

First published in 2010 by
PALGRAVE MACMILLAN®
in the United States—a division of St. Martin's Press LLC,
175 Fifth Avenue, New York, NY 10010.

Where this book is distributed in the UK, Europe and the rest of the
world, this is by Palgrave Macmillan, a division of Macmillan Publishers
Limited, registered in England, company number 785998, of Houndmills,
Basingstoke, Hampshire RG21 6XS.

Palgrave Macmillan is the global academic imprint of the above companies and has companies and representatives throughout the world.

Palgrave® and Macmillan® are registered trademarks in the United States,
the United Kingdom, Europe and other countries.

ISBN: 978–0–230–62077–3 (pbk)
ISBN: 978–0–230–62076–6 (hc)

Library of Congress Cataloging-in-Publication Data

Neighborhood rebels : Black power at the local level / edited by
Peniel E. Joseph.
    p. cm.—(Contemporary Black history)
Includes bibliographical references and index.
ISBN 978–0–230–62076–6
    1. Black power—United States—History. 2. African American political
activists—History. 3. Political participation—United States—History.
4. Community power—United States—History. 5. Neighborhood—
United States—History. 6. City and town life—United States—History.
7. African Americans—Politics and government. 8. African Americans—
Civil rights—History. 9. United States—Race relations. 10. United
States—History, Local. I. Joseph, Peniel E.

E185.615.N36 2010
323.1196'073—dc22   2009024203

A catalogue record of the book is available from the British Library.

Design by Newgen Imaging Systems (P) Ltd., Chennai, India.

First edition: January 2010

10 9 8 7 6 5 4 3 2 1

Printed in the United States of America.

Contents

Introduction

Community Organizing, Grassroots Politics, and Neighborhood Rebels: Local Struggles for Black Power in America

Peniel E. Joseph

The period in American and world history popularly known as the Black Power Movement (1954–1975) is undergoing extensive historical reassessment and reevaluation. A new subfield of scholarship, what I have called "Black Power Studies," has produced a series of books, anthologies, articles, essays, and conferences that are actively rewriting postwar American history. These new histories build on groundbreaking scholarly works that, although not exclusively focused on Black Power, thoughtfully examine the era within the broader sweep of American and world history. Perhaps the most striking aspect of these recent works is their efforts to challenge the master narrative of the civil rights era, which portrays Black Power as that movement's evil twin. In that master narrative, Black Power is the figurative and literal embodiment of black rage, anger, and disappointment with the ineffective and glacial pace of civil rights. Black Power enters the historical stage in the bitter aftermath of the civil rights era's *heroic* period, between 1954 and 1965, when the possibilities of racial justice seemed unlimited. Similarly, contemporary historical and popular understanding of the civil rights era places stirring oratory and dazzling iconography at the core of a narrative that neatly explains the rise and fall of the movement for nonviolent social justice. Martin Luther King, Jr., John and Robert F. Kennedy, and Lyndon Johnson represent the stars of this story while Rosa Parks, Fannie Lou Hamer, John Lewis, and Wyatt Walker appear in pivotal supporting roles. Thousands of black sharecroppers, trade unionists, school teachers, students, and ordinary citizens remain largely seen only as extras in the era's unfolding drama. Black radicalism remains largely absent from this narrative, with the

lone exception of Malcolm X who appears in the early 1960s as an angry coun-
terpoint to King's vision of a beloved community and as a portent of the coming
racial storm embodied by Black Power.

In the mid-1960s, Black Power seemingly burst onto the American scene,
scandalizing national politics, triggering a white backlash, dooming interracial cooperation, and pushing impressionable members of the New Left into an
unabated orgy of domestic violence in the name of revolution. Black Power is
most often seen as triggering the demise of the civil rights era, dooming more
promising and effective movements for social justice, and abandoning grassroots
community organizing in favor of jaw-dropping polemics, galloping sexism, and
crude appeals to urban violence and mayhem.

Major new historical scholarship has methodically challenged this view, placing a daunting amount of carefully sifted archival evidence above the autobiog-
raphies, memoirs, journalistic accounts, and first-person recollections that have
dominated interpretations of the era. The most ambitious of these new works
have argued that civil rights and Black Power, far from being mutually exclusive, paralleled and intersected with one another. Both movements grew out of
the ferment of social and political upheaval of the Great Depression and World
War II. Despite tortured debates over strategies and tactics, participants in one
camp often shifted to the other, and certain groups and activists favored both
approaches simultaneously.[1]

Chronologically, these works expand the movement's time frame, locating
its immediate origins in the 1950s when Malcolm X first entered Harlem as a
young local organizer. Placing early Black Power activism alongside the civil
rights struggles' high watermark significantly transforms understanding of each
period. Monumental histories and commemorations of the civil rights period
between the May 17, 1954 Brown Supreme Court decision and the August 6, 1965
passage of the Voting Rights Act have successfully enshrined this epic as the
movement's heroic period, a time of Kings and Kennedys when the forces of good
battled evil in an age of Camelot. In these accounts, Emmett Till's 1955 lynching,
Martin Luther King's role in the Montgomery Bus Boycott, Rosa Parks's iconic
refusal to give up her seat on the bus, and the 1957 Little Rock school desegregation crisis represent the era's first half. The latter half is most often reflected
by the wave of sit-ins across the South in 1960, the rioting at the University of
Mississippi two years later, 1963's tumultuous violence (Birmingham, Medgar
Evers, the Sixteenth Street Baptist Church bombing, and the JFK assassination)
and redemption (the March on Washington), and the passage of the 1964 Civil
Rights Act and Blood Sunday in Selma.

But there is something that is sanitized in these exploits, even as they seemingly acknowledge the era's violence, suffering, and assassinations. All of these
events take place exclusively in the South, ignoring the civil rights era's regional
diversity and denying the very existence of Black Power radicalism. Civil rights'
global reverberations also take a back seat, despite the movement's important role
in shaping American state craft at the height of the cold war. Between 1954 and
1965, Malcolm X led a Black Power movement that exhibited local muscle in New
York City and regional strength in parts of the country and grew to national and

international heights. Early Black Power activists touted racial and cultural pride, pushed the politics of self-determination through bruising and provocative protests, and connected America's domestic movement for racial justice with anticolonial struggles in the third world in defiance of cold war restrictions on drawing such parallels. In their audacious quest for social, political, and economic power, these activists were both deeply inspired by the courage of civil rights activists who risked life and limb in pursuit of democracy and profoundly disappointed in what they believed to be a naive faith in America's capacity for justice. Skeptical of the nation's willingness to extend citizenship to blacks and cynical about notions of redemptive suffering, Black Power activists looked to the third world for a way forward at home. The 1955 Afro-Asian Conference in Bandung, Indonesia, Ghanaian Independence in 1957, and the 1959 Cuban Revolution emboldened African American militants and strengthened their belief that revolutionary ripples in far-off places might resoundingly impact domestic antiracist efforts.

Closer home, Malcolm X's 1957 efforts to prevent a riot in the aftermath of a Nation of Islam (NOI) member's brutal beating made him and the NOI activists folk heroes in Harlem. After only three years in Harlem, Malcolm X had made remarkable political strides that included significantly boosting the attendance and financial strength of the Muslim Mosque No. 7 located on West 116th Street; cultivating a working relationship with James Hicks, managing editor of the *New York Amsterdam News*; and crafting political alliances with a host of local activists and politicians. Two years later, Malcolm X's stature took on national proportions after the broadcast of "The Hate That Hate Produced," a five-part documentary that propelled Malcolm and the NOI to sudden fame. Malcolm's growing iconography during the first half of the 1960s makes him the one Black Power leader whose exploits are discussed during the civil rights era's highpoint.

However, more often than not, Malcolm is pitted as King's foil, a brilliant if misguided foe whose dire predictions of race war represented the pent-up frustrations of the nation's seething black masses. This top-down perspective plucks Malcolm out of the historical context that shaped him and turns him into a messianic figure with little or no grassroots relationship to the black community. Such a perspective ignores the rich activist intellectual, labor, religious, and political organizing traditions and communities that shaped Malcolm. Many of these forces came out to protest the assassination of Patrice Lumumba, the first prime minister of the Democratic Republic of Congo, although Malcolm was forced by the NOI to stay on the sidelines. The 1961 UN demonstration featured dozens of activists, including Maya Angelou and LeRoi Jones, who found a political mentor in Malcolm. By that year, a number of early local Black Power groups, such as the Revolutionary Action Movement (RAM) out of Ohio and Detroit's Group on Advanced Leadership (GOAL), had formed. In June 1963, the same year as the March on Washington, 125,000 supporters marched in Detroit's "Walk for Freedom" in a pro-Birmingham sympathy demonstration keynoted by Martin Luther King and partially organized by Malcolm's allies, most notably the fiery reverend Albert Cleage, who shared the dais with King. That November, Malcolm delivered one of his most important speeches, "Message to the Grassroots," during a conference in Detroit where black militants from across the country sought to craft a more radical political agenda and endorsed the Freedom Now Party's (FNP) efforts at organizing an independent black political party.

The failure of most historical scholarship to take into account the diversity of the civil rights era and the existence of Black Power during an earlier period is compounded by a too-facile break between the good 1960s and the bad 1960s marked by the movement's shift North. Martin Luther King's campaign for slum clearance and open housing, the Watts uprising, and Stokely Carmichael's call for Black Power, all help to explain the demise of Southern civil rights organizing and the coming Black Power revolt. Black Power is most often portrayed as an almost exclusive Northern and urban phenomenon, despite the facts that Carmichael's declaration took place in a small town in Mississippi, that the Black Panther Party's (BPP) roots can be traced to Alabama, and that robust cultural and political organizing at the community level took place in both small (Greensboro and Durham) and large (Atlanta, New Orleans) cities in the South.

The years between 1966 and 1975 represent the Black Power era's *classical* period. The movement's impact is popularly associated with civil disturbances that spread across the United States between 1964 and 1968, marking the late 1960s as a period influenced by riot politics emanating from urban ghettoes in the North. This era is memorialized in the enduring iconography of urban destruction indelibly associated with Northern cities such as Newark and Detroit. Although the 1965 Watts uprising took place in California, it has come to be identified as part of the wave of insurrection that occurred outside of the South. Such a portrait of the 1960s obscures as much as it reveals. Indeed, the civil disturbances most commonly associated with the era can be traced back to racial violence in Birmingham in 1963 at the height of the civil rights movement. Black radicalism's geographical breadth reached beyond Northern cities to encompass virtually every part of the nation. This decade witnessed the movement's rise as a national and international phenomenon that touched every aspect of American society. It also encompassed a series of events, demonstrations, and imagery that comprise the era's still pungent iconography. Stokely Carmichael's June 16, 1966 call for "Black Power" in Greenwood, Mississippi, remains the starting point for the movement's transition into America's national political scene. Historians have neglected Carmichael's evolution from militant civil rights organizer to Black Power revolutionary. Moreover, too little has been written about Carmichael's subsequent role as a national leader and international icon between 1966 and 1968—a period when he became, among other things, a sought-after campus speaker, a prominent antiwar activist, and a target of the Johnson White House and Hoover's FBI; embarked on a whirlwind 180-day trip around the world; and helped introduce the Black Panthers to a national audience.[2]

Carmichael's complex interaction with civil rights activists, maverick attempts to forge international alliances, and thoughtful antiwar activism challenges the master narrative of the Black Power period. This narrative portrays the movement's energies as largely spent by the late 1960s, burned out in a self-destructive whirlwind of fratricidal violence, FBI surveillance, and a tragic turn from the slow, patient "organizing tradition" to a rhetorically grandiose but practically delusional politics that indulged in racially separatist fantasies and placed a premium on style over substance.[3]

Carmichael's activism in Lowndes County, where he spent over one year organizing, belies such a simplistic portrayal. For Carmichael, Lowndes represented a laboratory of creative political experimentation where the movement's goal of securing black political and economic power could be implemented in miniature. Organized in the aftermath of the Mississippi Freedom Democratic Party's dramatic defeat at the Atlantic City Democratic National Convention, the Lowndes County Freedom Movement represented a community organizing project guided by Carmichael's understanding of Black Power. Far from being burdened by angry rhetoric or guerrilla fantasies, the movement in Lowndes proved to be tightly organized, politically pragmatic, and, over time, successful. In Lowndes, Black Power meant local control over the board of education, sheriff, coroner, and taxes. Although the seven candidates who ran for these positions lost the 1966 election, it marked a breakthrough in the county's local history and, more broadly, in the history of American democracy.[4]

Today if Lowndes is remembered at all, it is for being the home of the first BPP and for providing an enduring symbol of revolution that would be adopted by more charismatic militants in Oakland, California. Lowndes provided more than just a launching pad for radicals in a different part of the country. It showed how effective Black Power militancy could be when organizers took time to study the local conditions seriously. Local politics shaped the way in which Black Power emerged in cities and towns across America. In many instances, this proved decisive for the longevity or demise of controversial groups such as the Black Panthers. Most blacks participated in or experienced the effects of the movement through less-glamorous avenues that utilized the era's militancy to coalesce around concrete objectives at the neighborhood level. At their best, militants such as the Black Panthers became local heroes, blending revolutionary rhetoric with a pragmatic focus on alleviating the burdens of racism by offering free breakfast, health clinics, ambulance service, schools, and grocery giveaways. At their worst, Black Power radicals substituted overheated polemics for concrete programs and engaged in galloping sexism that alienated the group—black women—most likely to participate in the grunt work that formed the backbone of community organizing. In short, local conditions and the extent to which militant activists politically adapted to these circumstances indelibly shaped the Black Power Movement.

Black Power profoundly affected the nation's political calculus, perhaps nowhere more deeply than in the local communities and neighborhoods of America. From big cities and sprawling suburbs to rural hamlets and college towns, Black Power's reverberations, although national and international in scope, were felt most practically at the local level.

Recent community and urban studies demonstrate the movement's impact on local community organizing in the urban North and South. More than a quarter of a century ago, in his classic study of the civil rights movement in North Carolina, *Civilities and Civil Rights* (1980), William Chafe chronicled Black Power's evolution in a Southern city. In Greensboro, the birthplace of direct action, Black Power militants initiated community-wide coalitions among high school and college students at historically black North Carolina A&T, campus workers, and poor people "around issues of housing, rent, redevelopment, and jobs."[5] This local pursuit of political power involved more than angry polemics, afros, and dashikis (although these were part of the movement). "The vehicle for achieving this power," writes Chafe, "was to be *community organizing*."[6]

Chafe's insights, in large part, have failed to penetrate subsequent histories of the era. Scholars have been more comfortable portraying Black Power era militants as little more than saber rattlers whose provocative polemics helped to demobilize civil rights activism. Clayborne Carson's *In Struggle* and Charles Payne's *I've Got the Light of Freedom*, two classic histories of Student Nonviolent Coordinating Committee (SNCC), helped to popularize this view. From this perspective, black militants turned their backs on local, grassroots struggles in favor of political posturing, a trajectory exemplified by Stokely Carmichael's meteoric but ultimately ineffective rise as a national figure.[7]

Komozi Woodard's *A Nation within a Nation* (1999) instructively applies Chafe's thesis to Newark.[8] Through a combination of urban and social history, Woodard documents Black Power's practical impact on a large metropolitan center. From the ashes of the city's 1967 urban riot, poet and activist Amiri Baraka (formerly LeRoi Jones) emerged as an effective local organizer and an astute national political mobilizer who utilized Black Power, especially its nationalist and pan-Africanist impulses, to catalyze large sectors of the city's black community. By 1970, Baraka had become a power broker. His support was critical to Newark's black activists, who defined power through community organizing goals, and whose work culminated in the election of the first black mayor of a major northeastern seaboard city.[9] Beyond Newark's local story, the "modern black convention movement," a series of national meetings, mapped out a domestic and international agenda for Black Power activism.

Although Black Power is central to Woodard's history, several recent studies have placed it within the broader sweep of postwar American history. Heather Ann Thompson's *Whose Detroit?* (2001) effectively illustrates Black Power's impact on the city's labor and electoral politics during the late 1960s and early 1970s, paying special attention to the bruising protests, movements, and organizing that culminated in Coleman Young's successful election as mayor in the early 1970s.[10] By 1969, Thompson argues, "black militants became determined to lead the Motor City forward on their own terms." They would do this through politics and protest, merging radical trade unionism, community organizing, and electoral politics in a bold—and in many ways unprecedented—effort aimed at unleashing "a full-fledged grassroots black revolutionary challenge" to Detroit's existing culture of racism and inequality.[11]

Robert Self's *American Babylon* (2003) devotes considerable attention to the BPP's understudied turn toward electoral politics and community activism during the early 1970s. The Panthers' campaign to elect co-founder Bobby Seale as Oakland's mayor captured a central dynamic of Black Power activism in the early 1970s, when local urban activists coordinated efforts to gain political power in a dramatically reconfigured urban landscape. The Panthers' practical efforts to control Oakland's municipal politics illustrate *American Babylon*'s provocative claim that "black power stood in the main currents of American politics in the 1960s and 1970s."[12]

Matthew Countryman's *Up South* (2005) places Black Power's emergence within the context of postwar urban development and contestations over liberalism's political scope, economic breadth, and racial character. In Philadelphia, Black Power activists challenged both white power brokers and the city's liberal black leadership to forge a local movement that borrowed political rhythms from the Southern civil rights movement's "organizing tradition." Philadelphia's local history of Black Power confounds popular and scholarly perceptions of the movement as violent, racially separatist, and politically untenable. Black militants waged creative struggles for community control of schools, welfare rights and antipoverty services, to curb police brutality, and to achieve black elected political power. *Up South* suggests that, although leather-jacketed Black Panthers and other colorful militants populated Philadelphia's Black Power landscape, the political work of less-glamorous grassroots activists had a more enduring impact on the city.[13] Black women played particularly important roles on this score, ratcheting up community-based antipoverty efforts and, in the process, exerting local control over a movement notorious for its masculinist vision of black liberation. Indeed, the "combination of consumerist and maternalist discourse" helped make "the welfare rights movement's emphasis on working-class women's leadership implicitly complementary to Black Power's masculinist ideology."[14]

Kevin Mumford's *Newark* (2007) examines Black Power's impact on the city's municipal politics, race relations, and community organizing. If Black Power is central to Woodard's narrative, for Mumford the movement represented just one of the multiple options pursued by black activists in search of racial, political, and economic empowerment.[15] Beyond Amiri Baraka's high profile, Mumford forcefully argues that "the rise of municipal empowerment proved to be the legacy of Black Power in the post-civil rights era."[16] *Newark* critically examines the legacy of the city's Black Power era politics, concluding that although the movement successfully spearheaded a new black urban political machine, it proved incapable of defending the city's residents against the conservative assault on social services during the 1980s.[17]

Black Power's impact in the South is examined in Kent Germany's *New Orleans after the Promises* (2007). In the Crescent City, a wide range of militants—from welfare rights organizers to reformed, urban street toughs to aspiring politicians—utilized Black Power's ethos of self-determination and community control to gain a foothold in local politics. Ultimately, Black Power activists in New Orleans attempted to transform local democratic institutions in hopes of securing better opportunities for the city's poorest residents. Although Black Panthers and other colorful characters populated this landscape, the most effective organizers often turned out to be black women who used the movement's rhetoric to secure increased social services for their communities.[18]

Documenting the Black Power era's impact on postwar American cities moves the study of urban history beyond "crisis" frameworks that view the post–civil rights era as a period of decline, white flight, urban alienation, and the rise of the underclass toward a complex examination of the way in which black militants helped to reshape the very structure of democracy at the municipal level. If case studies of Newark, Oakland, and Philadelphia are any indication, Black Power activism profoundly impacted the shape of postwar urban America.

Black Power manifested itself in a series of community-based struggles that found beachheads in urban cities, rural hamlets, neighborhoods, and universities across America. Examining Black Power from a community studies framework challenges prevailing wisdom that black militancy represented a retreat from organizing and that black nationalism inspired an emotional racial separatism that triggered the end of interracial alliances and the demise of key organizations (most notably SNCC and Congress of Racial Equality [CORE]). Black Power activism in Atlanta resists easy historical dichotomies that equate militancy with an anti-intellectual anger, and liberal integrationism with a human rights agenda.[19] In the "City Too Busy to Hate," black militants formed dense, complicated networks of neighborhood activists that concentrated on pragmatic issues related to police brutality, good schools, tenants and welfare rights, and expanded social services. Moreover, Atlanta SNCC organizers successfully connected "the Black freedom struggle and the Vietnam War" with the antiwar activism that reverberated nationally.[20]

Black Power in Atlanta proved to be eclectic, ranging from a radical think tank called the Institute of the Black World and a local Panther chapter to a new class of black political leaders, most notably Maynard Jackson, who was elected as the city's first African American mayor in 1973. Although Black Power failed to permanently institutionalize the radical politics envisioned by some of its most ardent proponents, the movement did inspire an impressive combination of "grassroots neighborhood activism, radical Black nationalism, progressive Black electoral activism, and explicitly women-centered activism" that fundamentally transformed the city's race relations.[21]

Welfare rights organizers, tenants' rights activists, and other poor and working people's movements do not fit within the standard portrait of the activism and goals associated with Black Power. However, a common thread linking community and urban studies focusing on Black Power is the prevalence of black women activists who utilized the movement's militant rhetoric in the service of grassroots organizing. According to historian Rhonda Williams, African American women activists at the local level "engendered" Black Power in innovative and unpredictable ways that refute the male-dominated iconography that remains attached to the era.[22] In Baltimore, for example, black women "public housing tenants, welfare mothers, and nuns"[23] utilized the militant rhetoric of Black Power politics to mobilize grassroots efforts to fight poverty, slum living conditions, and poor social services. Female community organizers adopted the language of Black Power militancy in service of community power. Ultimately, black women in Baltimore defined Black Power as a rejection of male authority, rigid ideology, and racial separatism in favor of a militant but flexible political agenda that focused on community empowerment.[24]

In Washington DC, just as in Baltimore, black women attempted to utilize Black Power's militant rhetoric to carve out important spaces for social, political, and cultural activism. As local chapters of CORE and SNCC embraced masculine rhetoric as the next stage of the black liberation movement, African Americans made important inroads as activists and leaders of movements in Black Studies, black consciousness, and welfare rights. In their roles as Black Panthers, welfare-rights organizers, community activists, and feminists, black women in Washington DC sought to expansively define Black Power as a movement capable of promoting community empowerment, racial pride and solidarity, and gender equality.[25] The city's local black political culture during the 1960s shaped its Black Power era politics, where male activists such as Julian Hobson and Marion Barry dominated headlines while their female counterparts such as Gwen Patton and Adrienne Manns organized in relative anonymity.[26]

Poor black women formed the backbone of community-minded Black Power activism in Durham, North Carolina.[27] As part of Durham's Black Solidarity Committee, black women made welfare rights a priority that partly led to a seven-month boycott that protested widespread racial discrimination. Durham's local expression of Black Power challenges "the tendency of both scholars and the public alike to focus on the more sensational aspects of Black Power and on black violence" while ignoring the era's "more lasting and significant aspects" and "projects initiated by women."[28]

If most black women participated in Black Power politics through community-based organizations, smaller numbers characterized themselves as black feminists.[29] While radical black feminists criticized the movement's masculinist ethos and misogyny, others viewed "black feminism" as a "component of the Black Power movement's ideology."[30] The Third World Women's Alliance (TWWA), a feminist activist group led by ex-SNCC worker Francis Beale, deployed its unique brand of feminism as "not simply a critique of Black Power politics but, rather, a *form* of it."[31] Black Power feminism transformed intellectual and political discourses of the early 1970s by expanding the public policy considerations, political goals, and strategic coalitions within African American politics.[32]

Rethinking the Postwar American City

Collectively, this recent scholarship suggests that historians need to reevaluate Black Power's relationship to the development of the postwar American city. This necessitates rethinking the temporal, spatial, and chronological framework of the Black Power era. New scholarship traces the movement's modern origins back to the immediate postwar era, when Malcolm X arrived in Harlem during the same year as the landmark *Brown* Supreme Court decision. Over the next decade Malcolm, through local organizing and national and international political mobilizing, became the leader of a movement for Black Power that paralleled and at times intersected with the civil rights movement's heroic period.[33] Through his base in the NOI, Malcolm forged alliances with local nationalists, elected officials, journalists, and civil rights leaders that helped make him a power broker in New York City politics. Of course, Malcolm operated against a political backdrop that featured a robust community of civil rights activists and local organizers protesting racial discrimination in schools, housing, and employment.

The contours of these Northern black freedom struggles are the focal point of new scholarship intent on unraveling entrenched biases and stereotypes that view black freedom struggles outside of the South as a relatively minor story.[34] Historians Jeanne Theoharis and Komozi Woodard's anthologies, *Freedom North* and *Groundwork*, helped to ignite critical debates over the fundamental significance of black political activism in the postwar era that, until recently, has remained marginalized in the historiography of the civil rights era. Perhaps the boldest challenge to conventional narratives of the postwar era has been offered by historian Jacqueline Dowd Hall. In a provocatively argued and well-researched essay, Hall presented a case for a "Long Civil Rights Movement" rooted in the Great Depression era and extending through to the Reagan administration. Building on earlier historical works that questioned the 1954–1965 framework, Hall issued a clarion call for a more expansive definition of the era that has invigorated historians of the movement.[35]

Thomas J. Sugrue's *Sweet Land of Liberty* (2008) represents perhaps the first major response to Hall's challenge. Wide in scope and richly researched, *Sweet Land of Liberty* documents Northern black freedom struggles from the 1930s to the 1970s. Paying particular attention to cities in Northern states with the highest black populations—Pennsylvania, New York, Michigan, New Jersey, and Illinois—Sugrue presents a well-detailed study of the evolution of black political activism over time. The benefits of this longer view are immediate in conveying the complicated and overlapping contours of black political activism, where radical trade unionists, pan-Africanists, liberals, and conservatives found common ground in broad goals and yet remained embattled around issues of strategies and tactics. In Sugrue's narrative, Black Power, rather than appearing sui generis in the mid-1960s, emerges from an earlier generation of radical protest.[36] Yet, like most histories, *Sweet Land of Liberty* portrays Black Power as a historical phenomenon that comes to light only in the heat of the 1960s politics.

The Long Black Power Movement

Black Power activists connected domestic antiracist struggles with international anticolonial movements, advocated racial and cultural pride, and preached a message of radical self-determination whose wide-ranging implications included community control of schools and neighborhoods, Black Studies programs and departments, business ownership, the Black Arts, self-defense and armed struggle, and community services to the poor and the incarcerated. The period from mid-1960s to the mid-1970s represents the most visible manifestation of this movement—an era when afros, dashikis, African and Muslim names, black history books, as well as talk of race war, race relations, and racial identity dominated much of America's national conversation and reverberated around the world. However, the immediate period before this highpoint, from the *Brown* decision to the passage of the Voting Rights Act in 1965, comprises more than just a prelude to the actual movement. Indeed, activists such as Malcolm X and Robert F. Williams and the writers Lorraine Hansberry, LeRoi Jones, and James Baldwin deployed the language, style, and passionate demeanor of Black Power activists before the term ever came into vogue.

Black Power's modern roots, in fact, can be traced back to the politics of self-determination, radical internationalism, and racial and cultural pride of the New Negro Movement as well as the iconography of Marcus Garvey. After Garvey's arrest and deportation in the 1920s, the movement survived and in certain cities thrived through the street-corner oratory of sidewalk speakers, the religious nationalism of the NOI, and the cultural organizing of Paul Robeson who almost single-handedly mentored an entire generation of radical black writers and cultural figures. Robeson's political and cultural identification with Africa and the wider third world, friendship with W.E.B. Du Bois, and leadership in the Council on African Affairs served as a bridge between aspects of the New Negro Movement of the 1920s and the postwar freedom surges of the 1940s.[37]

In her evocative study of New York City's civil rights movement during this era, historian Martha Biondi argues that the city's black freedom struggles provide "a backdrop to the Black Power era in the North."[38] In some instances, it was more than simply a backdrop. Rather than seeing Black Power simply as a response to the failure of postwar liberalism, the limitations of the civil rights movements, or a byproduct of institutional racism, a longer historical view recognizes and documents the existence of an indigenous movement for Black Power whose modern roots can be traced back to post–World War I movements for black self-determination. Part of the confusion about Black Power's longstanding roots in twentieth-century America stems from an inability to properly define the movement's relationship to civil rights. Civil rights and Black Power come out of a longstanding, centuries-long black freedom struggle. Rooted in the same family tree, these movements formed separate branches that followed parallel and at times intertwining roads toward black liberation. Yet perhaps because of civil rights' longstanding association with racial integration and the promotion of democracy, it has come to be the catchall phrase for modern antiracist struggles. Thus, even as notions of a "Long Civil Rights Movement" seek to break convention through adopting a more panoramic view of the era, they reinforce master narratives by subsuming Black Power under the all-powerful rubric of civil rights.

If we define Black Power as a movement for radical self-determination, although not one that consistently advocated racial separatism, we uncover previously forgotten historical actors and evaluate longstanding icons and groups from a fresh perspective. On this score, what are we to make of A. Philip Randolph's March on Washington Movement? Was it simply an example of Northern-based black militancy or something more? How are we to comprehend the fact that, as Thomas Sugrue observes, "Randolph insisted that the March on Washington be exclusively black, and he vigorously defended the decision against charges of reverse racism"?[39] How do we explain the political activism of Gloria Richardson in Cambridge, Maryland, during the early 1960s? Richardson's bold belief in self-defense led supporters to characterize her as the "Lady General" of the civil rights movement. The Cambridge Movement attracted militant civil rights activists such as Stokely Carmichael and garnered national media attention. Historian

Sharon Harley argues that Richardson represented a forerunner to Black Power with her audacious call for self-determination and uncompromising belief in racial justice. Scholars Sundiata Cha-Jua and Clarence Lang refute this suggestion, pointedly arguing that Cambridge's militancy illustrates simply the contours of civil rights activism in a border state. Yet Richardson's relationship with Malcolm X, membership in the militant organization ACT, and participation in the Grassroots Leadership Conference complicates efforts to define her and the movement she led. In truth, Richardson operated at the lower frequencies of the black freedom struggles, where activists adopted flexible tactics in pursuit of racial and economic justice. By the early 1960s, Richardson, politically intimate with both Black Power and civil rights activists, found herself increasingly drawn to a kind of militancy most often associated with Black Power activists but adopted just as frequently by community organizers outside of the South.[40]

Despite longstanding assumptions to the contrary, much of Black Power activism took place at the local or neighborhood level. The notion that Black Power militants embraced grassroots organizing seems surprising, especially in light of by now accepted narratives that suggest the exact opposite. Recent scholarship illustrates how Black Power activism encompassed more than the spectacular iconography of the Black Panthers and involved forgotten struggles for bread and butter issues, including welfare and prisoner rights, social services, safe streets, hot lunches, good schools, and safe neighborhoods. Although a national organization, the Black Panthers, perhaps more than any other Black Power era organization, were shaped by local conditions. Adding to its chapters in thriving metropolitan centers such as New York, Chicago, Philadelphia, and Los Angeles, the BPP started chapters in Indianapolis, Cleveland, Baltimore, Winston-Salem, North Carolina, and New Haven, Connecticut. Although these chapters enjoyed varying degrees of success, controversy, and longevity, all attempted to build deep ties in their respective communities at the neighborhood level.[41]

In the 1960s, American cities seemed to be in a full-blown crisis, wracked by shrinking tax bases, loss of industry, white flight, spiraling crime, and urban decay. But where many saw despair, Black Power militants envisioned opportunity, vowing to take control of the democratic institutions that shaped black life in urban cities and rural towns across America.

Neighborhood Rebels chronicles these activities, stretching its gaze from the 1940s to the present. In documenting Black Power's impact at the community level, it aims to tease out the contours of a movement whose complexity is too often lost in flat analysis shaped more by memory than history. Among the questions these chapters ask are the following: how do local histories better explain Black Power's impact on urban cities? What was the relationship between civil rights and Black Power at the local level? How did geographical regions impact Black Power's successes, failures, and overall impact at the local level? How did local conditions impact the transition from civil rights to Black Power in the 1960s? What was early Black Power radicalism's impact in urban centers? How did Black Power activists approach community-level organizing? Ultimately, this book seeks to begin an intellectual dialogue that, through fresh historical research and analysis, chronicles the Black Power Movement's impact at the community or neighborhood level across the United States.

My own chapter takes an unusual look at Malcolm X. Rather than viewing Malcolm as a historical icon, I examine the way in which his early activities as a local organizer in Harlem shaped Black Power politics in local municipalities such as New York City and Detroit. As a local organizer, Malcolm possessed the unusual ability to craft working political coalitions with a diverse range people. From his neighborhood-level base in Harlem out to the wider locales of New York City, Rochester, Detroit, Chicago, Los Angeles, and Oakland, Malcolm viewed the local politics of Northern cities as paralleling the brutal reality of the Jim Crow South. But it was as a grassroots activist that Malcolm came to identify, appreciate, and articulate the rage, hope, and despair of African Americans who lived and operated in the shadow of the civil rights era's high tide.

Patrick Jones offers a fascinating look at the way in which black militancy helped transform Milwaukee's local civil rights struggles. In examining the way in which Milwaukee's local civil rights struggles took on increasingly militant edges during the late 1950s and early 1960s, Jones depicts a transitional period in the city's local history, one wherein calls for direct action and self-determination took on new meaning.

Donna Murch documents the way in which Oakland's local politics shaped the rise of the BPP. Murch places the Panthers within the wider sweep of Oakland's postwar history, arguing that the city's precarious economic climate, pervasive racism, poverty, and police brutality created the conditions that nurtured the Black Panthers. Poor schools, meager job prospects, and a hostile police force ensured that a generation of young blacks coming of age in the early 1960s faced worse prospects than their migrant parents. The young activists who founded the BPP were shaped by these circumstances and, against daunting odds, turned the burden of low expectations into inspiration to organize poor black communities in Oakland.

Black Power's impact on the South has, until recently, gone largely ignored. Simon Wendt explores the politics of self-defense in the South during the civil rights and Black Power era. Rather than viewing civil rights and Black Power as mutually exclusive, Wendt finds areas of intersection and overlap, especially within the politics of self-defense. Black Power's call for armed self-defense, most often associated with Malcolm X and the Black Panthers, found Southern manifestations in the voice of Robert F. Williams. Perhaps most intriguingly, local militants in the CORE and the Deacons for Defense, although not advocating for the third-world revolutionary struggles promoted by Malcolm X and Williams, adopted tactics of self-defense to help protect civil rights workers in the South.

Atlanta's Black Arts Movement is the focus of James Smethurst's evocative look at the movement's cultural politics in a New South city. From the Atlanta University Center to grassroots initiatives to city-sponsored arts initiatives, Black Arts activists in Atlanta attempted to redefine black identity while simultaneously reinvigorating local democratic institutions. Black Arts and Black Power organizing in Atlanta energized social, political, cultural, and intellectual networks to promote electoral power, institutional building, and the vitality of the arts in transforming the lives of everyday black folk.

Kent Germany's portrait of Black Power in New Orleans uncovers historical parallels between 1960s era activists and grassroots organizing in the aftermath of Hurricane Katrina. By chronicling late 1960s and early 1970s Black Power activism in the Crescent City, Germany illustrates the way in which contemporary black activists in the city echo the militancy and the search for expanding democratic frontiers that marked an earlier generation of organizers.

Black Power's uncanny ability to incite roiling controversy animates Tracy K'Meyer's penetrating discussion of the movement's impact in Louisville, Kentucky. Black Power activists helped transform the University of Louisville in expansive and unprecedented ways, perhaps most notably by founding a Black Studies Department that still exists and by promoting the commitment to racial diversity and social justice as key to a healthy and prosperous city.

Black Power's impact on the urban Midwest remains understudied. Clarence Lang helps to fill this scholarly gap by examining the movement's origins, evolution, and impact in St. Louis. In the Gateway City, Black Power transformed the local CORE chapter and was embodied in the organization ACTION. By the late 1960s, St. Louis' Black Power movement sparked new and vibrant local organizations that ranged from student-based efforts to create Black Studies to Black Arts activism to the paramilitary group the Black Liberators that was inspired by the Black Panthers.

Jeanne Theoharis's eye-opening account of black high school students in Los Angeles provides new insight into the way in which Black Power impacted struggles for educational equality at the local level. Overshadowed by Black Panthers and the US Organization, black students waged war against an educational establishment that dehumanized and criminalized them. They also found common ground with young organizers of the incipient Chicano Movement and successfully secured modest reforms that brought black history to the curriculum, diversified faculty and administration, and countered stereotypes of young African Americans as anti-intellectual.

Local activists significantly altered the shape and character of Baltimore's Black Power movement. Rhonda Williams' chapter examines the way in which Black Power developed at the neighborhood level in Baltimore through CORE's Target City project and local activists' efforts to reshape communities and city space. In Baltimore, local activists defined the movement as part of an expansive and eclectic vision of social justice that helped to transform the city's activist black community. Ultimately, Baltimore's local history of Black Power activism provides an important ground-level view of the way in which the era's politics shaped community organizing, urban policy, and race relations.

Collectively, these local histories contribute to a larger reevaluation of both the civil rights and Black Power era. Indigenous struggles for education, jobs, Black Studies, the Black Arts, welfare and tenants' rights, freedom of expression, and community control shaped community-wide movements for Black Power. Far from taking a decisive break with civil rights struggles, Black Power militants sought similar goals but interpreted words such as "freedom" and "liberation" in stark contrast to their civil rights counterparts. In certain cities and communities, Black Power activists existed alongside civil rights organizers and even participated in conventional civil rights demonstrations. In other instances, Black Power's appearance in a local community conforms more closely with its mid-1960s eruption on the national stage. A unifying theme of all these chapters is the movement's intense local character, commitment to grassroots organizing, and political pragmatism.

The movement's cast of historical actors, organizational diversity, practical accomplishments, and enduring contradictions take on added dimension and nuance when examined from the perspective of its grassroots participants. Indeed, case studies have revealed new details of the era, perhaps none as striking as the prominent role of black women in cities such as Baltimore, Philadelphia, Durham, and New Orleans. It is becoming increasingly apparent that, like its civil rights counterpart, Black Power's ethos animated thousands of community-based movements around the country. Black high school students from Los Angeles to Philadelphia staged walkouts to demand educational equality even as college students took over campus buildings and demanded Black Studies, while black women in local welfare rights organizations and tenants' rights groups organized around securing increased benefits, social services, and safety. Black nationalists, Pan-Africanists, and Marxists on both coasts and beyond organized conferences, created bookstores, built independent schools, and, in an alliance with black elected officials, helped to create a new generation of urban machine politics. Advocates of the Black Arts founded community centers, theaters, local radio and television programs, as well as dance, mural, and music troupes in virtually every corner of the nation. Major and minor cities welcomed Black Panthers who served free breakfasts, held political education classes, and provided vital legal and community-wide service programs. Prison inmates organized study groups and demanded reform of a system focused more on punishment than on rehabilitation.[42]

This is not to suggest that Black Power's national and international history lacks significance. The insistence on the importance of local history augments and enhances the pursuit of a comprehensive national and global history of Black Power. On this score, emerging case studies chronicling the movement's impact on the local level will provide rich intellectual and analytical resources to properly evaluate Black Power's national and international depth and breadth. Indeed, the local, national, and global character of the era are what make it an epic in world history, and their interconnections and intersections remain vital to a fuller comprehension and understanding of this era. *Neighborhood Rebels* seeks to contribute to this larger historical project by offering a critical examination of the Black Power Movement's impact on key local communities across America. The chapters that follow break new ground in placing the activities of Black Power militants in their community-based settings. They tell the story of the women and men who—at the grassroots level—either participated in or prepared the way for Black Power activism and in the process helped transform American democracy.

Notes

1. Peniel E. Joseph, *Waiting 'Til the Midnight Hour: A Narrative History of Black Power in America* (New York: Owl Books, 2007); ed., *The Black Power Movement: Rethinking the Civil Rights-Black Power Era* (New York: Routledge, 2006); "Black Power's Powerful Legacy," *The Chronicle Review*, July 21, 2006, pp. B6–B8; ed., "Black Power," *Magazine of History*, 22, No. 3 (July 2008); James Smethurst, *The Black Arts Movement: Literary Nationalism in the 1960s and 1970s* (Chapel Hill: University of North Carolina Press, 2005).

2. Joseph, *Waiting 'Til the Midnight Hour*, pp. 124–240; See also Stokely Carmichael and Ekueme Michael Thelwell, *Ready for Revolution: The Life and Struggle of Stokely Carmichael* (Kwame Ture) (New York: Scribner, 2003).

3. Charles Payne, *I've Got the Light of Freedom: The Organizing Tradition and the Mississippi Freedom Struggle* (Berkeley: University of California Press, 1995), pp. 338–390.

4. Joseph, *Waiting 'Til the Midnight Hour*, p. 170 and Hasan Kwame Jeffries, *Bloody Lowndes: Civil Rights and Black Power in Alabama's Black Belt* (New York: New York University Press, 2009).

5. William H. Chafe, *Civilities and Civil Rights: Greensboro, North Carolina, and the Black Struggle for Freedom* (New York: Oxford University Press, 1981), 175.

6. Ibid., 173 (emphasis added).

7. Clayborne Carson, *In Struggle: SNCC and the Black Awakening of the 1960s* (Cambridge, MA: Harvard University Press, 1981); Charles Payne, *I've Got the Light of Freedom: The Organizing Tradition and the Mississippi Freedom Struggle* (Berkeley: University of California Press, 1996).

8. Komozi Woodard, *A Nation within a Nation: Amiri Baraka & Black Power Politics* (Chapel Hill: University of North Carolina Press, 1999).

9. For a more negative assessment of Black Power's impact in Newark see Kevin Mumford, *Newark: A History of Race, Rights, and Riots in America* (New York: New York University Press, 2007).

10. See Heather Ann Thompson, *Whose Detroit?: Politics, Labor, and Race in a Modern American City* (Ithaca, NY: Cornell University Press, 2004).

11. Ibid., p. 81.

12. Robert O. Self, *American Babylon: Race and the Struggle for Postwar Oakland* (Princeton, NJ: Princeton University Press, 2003), p. 218.

13. Matthew Countryman, *Up South* (Philadelphia: University of Pennsylvania Press, 2005), pp. 224–327. Two important case studies, on Detroit and New Orleans, respectively, illustrate that Black Power was critical to shaping the emerging interracial political alliances that took shape in the decade after the passage of the Voting Rights Act; Heather Ann Thompson, *Whose Detroit?: Politics, Labor, and Race in a Modern American City* (Ithaca, NY: Cornell University Press, 2001); Angela D. Dillard, *Faith in the City: Preaching Radical Social Change in Detroit* (Ann Arbor: University of Michigan Press, 2007) and Kent B. Germany, *New Orleans after the Promises: Poverty, Citizenship, and the Great Society* (Athens: University of Georgia Press, 2007).

14. Countryman, *Up South*, p. 273. For histories of the welfare rights movement see Premilla Nadasen, *Welfare Warriors: The Welfare Rights Movement in the United States* (New York, 2004); Annelise Orleck, *Storming Caesar's Palace: How Black Mothers Fought Their Own War on Poverty* (New York, 2006); and Felicia Kornbluh, *The Battle for Welfare Rights: Politics and Poverty in Modern America* (Philadelphia, 2007). See

also, Francis Fox Piven and Richard Cloward, *Poor Peoples Movements: Why They Succeed, How They Fail* (New York, 1979).

15. Mumford, *Newark*.

16. Ibid., p. 199.

17. Ibid., pp. 203, 218.

18. Germany, *New Orleans after the Promises*.

19. Winston A. Grady-Willis, *Challenging U.S. Apartheid: Atlanta and Black Struggles for Human Rights, 1960–1977* (Durham, 2006). (Chapel Hill: University of North Carolina Press, 2006).

20. Grady-Willis, *Challenging U.S. Apartheid*, p. 101. For new scholarship that is reconsidering SNCC's legacy see Barbara Ransby, *Ella Baker and the Black Freedom Movement: A Radical Democratic Vision* (Chapel Hill, 2003); Hasan Kwame Jeffries, "Organizing for More Than the Vote: The Political Radicalization of Local People in Lowndes County, Alabama, 1965–1966" in *Groundwork*, pp. 140–163 and "SNCC, Black Power, and Independent Political Organizing, 1964–1966," *The Journal of African American History* 91 (Spring 2006), 171–193 and *Bloody Lowndes*; Fanon Che Wilkins, "The Making of Black Internationalists: SNCC and Africa before the Launching of Black Power, 1960–1965," *The Journal of African American History* 92 (Fall 2007), 467–490; Wesley Hogan, *Many Minds, One Heart: SNCC's Dream for a New America* (Chapel Hill: University of North Carolina Press, 2007); Leigh Raiford, " 'Come Let Us Build a New World Together': SNCC and the Photography of the Civil Rights Movement," *American Quarterly* 59 (December 2007), 1129–1157. The classic study of the group remains Carson's, *In Struggle*.

21. Grady-Willis, *Challenging U.S. Apartheid*, p. 169.

22. Rhonda Y. Williams, "Black Women, Urban Politics, and Engendering Black Power," in *The Black Power Movement*, pp. 79–103.

23. Ibid., 81.

24. Williams, "Black Women, Urban Politics, and Engendering Black Power," pp. 97–103. See also Rhonda Y. Williams, " 'We're Tired of Being Treated like Dogs': Poor Women and Power Politics in Baltimore," *The Black Scholar* 31 (Fall/Winter 2001), 31–41 and *The Politics of Public Housing: Black Women's Struggles against Urban Inequality* (New York: Oxford University Press, 2004), pp. 187–191. See also, Mumford, *Newark*, pp. 149–169.

25. Anne M. Valk, *Radical Sisters: Second-Wave Feminism and Black Liberation in Washington, D.C.* (Urbana: University of Illinois Press, 2008).

26. Ibid., pp. 115–119.

27. Christina Greene, *Our Separate Ways: Women and the Black Freedom Movement in Durham, North Carolina* (Chapel Hill: University of North Carolina Press, 2005).

28. Ibid., p. 189.

29. Kimberly Springer, *Living for the Revolution: Black Feminist Organizations* (Durham, NC: Duke University Press, 2005); Benita Roth, *Separate Roads to Feminism: Black, Chicana, and White Feminist Movements in America's Second Wave* (Cambridge, UK, 2004); Breines, *The Trouble between Us: An Uneasy History of White and Black Women in the Feminist Movement* (New York: Oxford University Press, 2006); E. Francis White, *Dark Continent of Our Bodies: Black Feminism and the Politics of Respectability* (Philadelphia, PA: Temple University Press, 2001); Duchess Harris, "From the Kennedy Commission to the Combahee Collective: Black Feminist Organizing, 1960–1980," in *Sisters in the Struggle*, pp. 280–305; Valk, *Radical Sisters*.

30. Stephen Ward, "The Third World Women's Alliance: Black Feminist Radicalism and Black Power Politics," in *The Black Power Movement*, p. 120.

31. Ibid., p. 120.
32. For interdisciplinary examples already underway see Beverly Guy-Sheftall, ed., *Words of Fire: An Anthology of African-American Feminist Thought* (New York, 1995); Joy Ann James, *Shadow Boxing: Representations of Black Feminist Politics* (New York, 1999) and ed., *Angela Davis: A Reader* (London, 1999); Cheryl Clark, Margo Perkins, *Autobiography as Activism: Three Black Women of the Sixties* (Jackson, MS: University of Mississippi Press, 2001); Cheryl Clarke, *After Mecca: Women Poets and the Black Arts Movement* (New Brunswick: Rutgers University Press, 2005); Linda Janet Holmes and Cheryl A Wall, ed., *Savoring the Salt: The Legacy of Toni Cade Bambara* (Philadelphia, PA: Temple University Press, 2007).
33. Joseph, *Waiting 'Til the Midnight Hour.*
34. See Jeanne F. Theoharis and Komozi Woodard, eds., *Freedom North: Black Freedom Struggles Outside the South, 1940–1980* (New York: Palgrave Macmillan, 2003); *Groundwork: Local Black Freedom Movements in America* (New York: New York University Press, 2005); Martha Biondi, *To Stand and Fight: The Struggle for Civil Rights in Postwar New York City* (Cambridge, MA: Harvard University Press, 2003).
35. Jacquelyn Dowd Hall, "The Long Civil Rights Movement and the Political Uses of the Past," *The Journal of American History* 91, no. 4 (March 2005), pp. 1233–1263. For a critique of Hall's thesis see Sundiata Cha-Jua and Clarence Lang, "The 'Long Movement' as Vampire: Temporal and Spacial Fallacies in Recent Black Freedom Studies," *The Journal of African American History* 92, no. 2 (Spring 2007), pp. 265–288. See also Peniel E. Joseph, "Rethinking the Black Power Era," *The Journal of Southern History* 75, no. 3 (August 2009), pp. 707–716 and "State of the Field: The Black Power Movement," *The Journal of American History* (December 2009).
36. Thomas J. Sugrue, *Sweet Land of Liberty: The Forgotten Struggle for Civil Rights in the North* (New York: Random House, 2008).
37. Toni Martin, *Race First: The Ideological and Organizational Struggles of Marcus Garvey and the Universal Negro Improvement Association* (Dover, MA: Majority Press, 1986); Ula Taylor, *The Veiled Garvey: The Life and Times of Amy Jacques Garvey* (Chapel Hill: University of North Carolina Press, 2001); Mary G. Rolinson, *Grassroots Garveyism: The Universal Negro Improvement Association in the Rural South, 1920–1927* (Chapel Hill: University of North Carolina Press, 2007); Colin Grant, *Negro with a Hat: The Rise and Fall of Marcus Garvey* (New York: Oxford University Press, 2008); Penny Von Eschen, *Race Against Empire: Black Americans and Anticolonialism, 1937–1957* (Ithaca, NY: Cornell University Press, 1997).
38. Biondi, *To Stand and Fight*, p. 2.
39. Sugrue, *Sweet Land of Liberty*, p. 55.
40. Sharon Harley, "'Chronicle of a Death Foretold': Gloria Richardson, the Cambridge Movement, and the Radical Black Activist Tradition," in Bettye Collier-Thomas and V.P. Franklin, eds., *Sisters in the Struggle: African American Women in the Civil Rights-Black Power Movement* (New York: New York University Press, 2001), pp. 174–196; "The 'Long Movement' as Vampire: Temporal and Spatial Fallacies in Recent Black Freedom Studies," *Journal of African American History* 92, no. 2 (Spring 2007), p. 276; Peter B. Levy, *Civil War on Race Street: The Civil Rights Movement in Cambridge, Maryland* (Gainesville: University Press of Florida, 2003); Joseph, *Waiting 'Til the Midnight Hour*, pp. 88–92.
41. For local histories of the Panthers see Williams, *Black Politics/White Power*; Self, *American Babylon*; Curtis J. Austin, *Up against the Wall: Violence in the Making and Unmaking of the Black Panther Party* (Fayetteville: University of Arkansas

Press, 2006); Paul Alkebulan, *Survival Pending Revolution: The History of the Black Panther Party* (Tuscaloosa: University of Alabama Press, 2007); Judson L. Jeffries, ed., *Comrades: A Local History of the Black Panther Party* (Bloomington: Indiana University Press, 2007); Donna Murch, "The Campus and the Street: Race, Migration, and the Origins of the Black Panther Party in Oakland, CA," *Souls* 9, no. 4 (October–December 2007), pp. 333–345; Jama Lazerow, "'A Rebel All His Life': The Unexpected Story of Frank 'Parky' Grace," in *In Search of the Black Panther Party*, pp. 104–157.

42. See Williams, *Black Politics/White Power*; Countryman, *Up South*; Wayne Glasker, *Black Students in the Ivory Tower: African American Student Activism at the University of Pennsylvania, 1967–1990* (Amherst: University of Massachusetts Press, 2002); Joy Anne Williamson, *Black Power on Campus: The University of Illinois, 1965–1975* (Urbana: University of Illinois Press, 2003); Germany, *New Orleans after the Promises*; Williams, *The Politics of Public Housing: Black Women's Struggles Against Urban Inequality* (New York: Oxford University Press, 2004). See also Fabio Riojas' sociological study, *From Black Power to Black Studies: How a Radical Social Movement Became an Academic Discipline* (Baltimore, MD: Johns Hopkins University Press, 2007).

Malcolm X's Harlem and Early Black Power Activism

Peniel E. Joseph

"We respect authority, but we are ready to fight and die in defense of our lives," Malcolm X once told reporter Louis Lomax.[1] The resolute candor behind these words provides insight into the remarkable political journey, personal travails, and intellectual evolution of Malcolm Little, born in Omaha, Nebraska on May 19, 1925. Malcolm's childhood was defined by the death of his father, Earl Little, a political activist and part-time preacher who followed the black nationalist teachings of Marcus Garvey. Earl's death, in Lansing Michigan in 1931, remembered by Malcolm as a lynching at the hands of local white terrorists, left psychic scars on Malcolm and the rest of the family, straining their financial resources and personal strength. Malcolm's mother, Louise Little, experienced bouts of mental illness that forced her eight children to lead scattered lives bereft of the safety and security provided by a stable family. From this point onward, Malcolm would try to replace the spiritual and physical home shattered by Earl Little's untimely death.[2] Malcolm's memories of the small and large humiliations of poverty would haunt him for the rest of his life. So would images of Earl, strong and fierce, passing out pictures of Marcus Garvey at sparsely attended Universal Negro Improvement Association (UNIA) meetings that attracted blacks in Lansing, brave enough to listen to taboo discussions of racial pride and black power. The fact that family lore attributed Earl's death to his militant crusading made less of an impression on Malcolm than the swaggering, larger-than-life aura of bravado that he exuded while alive.[3]

For a time the big city underworlds of Harlem, Detroit, and Boston served as dangerous havens for the young Malcolm, a boy precocious enough to be voted class president in junior high school and sensitive enough to feel panic and alienation after a white teacher dismissed his dream of becoming a lawyer with a racial slur. The clarifying danger that Malcolm encountered during his subsequent descent into a sordid world of urban crime, drugs, and vice approximated, albeit in a decidedly different manner, the constant threats faced by his father.

But his subsequent incarceration for burglary in 1946 would lead to personal redemption and a political transformation after encountering the teachings of the Nation of Islam (NOI). While a convict in Massachusetts from 1946 to 1952, Malcolm joined the NOI; in doing so, he was, at least partially, following in his late father's footsteps. Organized after the heyday of the Garvey-inspired nationalism of the post-World War I era, the NOI advocated personal dignity, economic self-determination, and organizational discipline in the service of an unorthodox interpretation of Islam as defined by a semi-literate wise man called Elijah Muhammad (né Elijah Poole). While Marcus Garvey relied on the recovery of suppressed historical truths to project a vision of African kingdoms and uplift blacks in America, Muhammad substituted religious prophecy for fact-finding and characterized whites as "devils," created by a renegade black scientist named Yacub thousands of years ago.

The NOI fit comfortably into Harlem's eclectic postwar political milieu, where Communists, black nationalists, trade unionists, liberals, and socialists jockeyed for political power. The NOI dismissed overt political action and impugned standard protests of boycotts, pickets, and marches in favor of an ethos that touted rugged self-determination—in the form of black entrepreneurship, diligence, and community control—as the key to genuine black empowerment. Black dignity would come from African American self-awareness and would be earned through racial uplift strategies rather than "handouts" from white politicians and powerbrokers. Bootstraps rather than ballots served as the NOI's point of departure for black power in urban centers across the nation. Religious prophecy contoured the NOI's message of personal responsibility. Elijah Muhammad's teachings offered black people a chance at redemption if they were intelligent and disciplined enough to follow them. With unconventional religious believers and maverick black nationalists, the NOI positioned itself as a fresh face among a Harlem landscape teeming with militant groups. The NOI's rise coincided with Malcolm's growing involvement with the groups in the mid-1950s. Spotting Malcolm's potential, Muhammad became a father figure who allowed his younger protégé creative space to turn the NOI into an international phenomenon. Named Muhammad's national representative in 1957, Malcolm served as the NOI's chief strategist, main recruiter, and organizational architect. That same year, the FBI placed Muhammad under electronic surveillance that included telephone wiretaps and miniature listening devices.[4]

On the surface, Malcolm X seemed a most unlikely diplomat—an ex-convict, barely five years removed from jail, who now led the local temple of an unorthodox group of Black Muslims. But Malcolm knew the streets of Harlem like few of his contemporaries did, having had past ties with New York City's criminal underworld. His distillation of black America's social, political, and cultural misery would prove to be timely, controversial, and historic. He dissected the legacy of chattel slavery, the impact of racial segregation, and the humiliation of urban poverty with surgical precision, biting wit, and a kind of verbal flair that expertly combined the sacred and the profane. Over time, the audience for Malcolm's speeches grew, stretching from Muslim Mosque No. 7 on Harlem's 116th Street, to jam-packed university auditoriums and giant outdoor rallies.

Impeccably groomed, tastefully dressed, and as well-mannered as he was eloquent, Malcolm's imposing personal appearance (he stood six feet three inches) magnified his growing political stature.

Malcolm X first entered Harlem's consciousness after an outrageous act of police brutality pushed New York City to the edge of racial violence.[5] On April 26, 1957, white police officers brutally assaulted NOI member Johnson X. James Hicks, managing editor of the *New York Amsterdam News,* contacted Malcolm and asked him to mediate sensitive negotiations between law enforcement and Harlem community representatives in hopes of avoiding a riot. Two standoffs took place that evening. The first, outside the 123rd Street police precinct in Harlem, ended after police agreed to move Johnson X to Harlem Hospital. For fifteen blocks, NOI members marched in formation through one of Harlem's busiest thoroughfares—Lenox Avenue—a sight that inspired an even larger crowd outside of Harlem Hospital. After one police official told Malcolm to "get those people out of there." Knowing that the Fruit of Islam (FOI) would follow a precise chain of command that frowned on freelance retribution—but that the rest of the crowd did not, Malcolm declined. "I politely," recalled Malcolm, "told him those others were his problem."[6] Malcolm's broodingly charismatic presence, along with the disciplined actions of NOI members, helped to avoid further violence. With a few words and a gesture to one of his lieutenants, the Black Muslims dispersed, the crowd quickly followed suit, and a major crisis was averted.

Malcolm's deft handling of the Johnson X case showcased his superb political skills and the growing strength of the NOI. Johnson X would be awarded $70,000 from an all-white jury and the Black Muslim phenomenon was officially born.[7] The Johnson case became indelibly attached to Malcolm's growing legend. The black press proved instrumental in this regard, with the *New York Amsterdam News* serving as a key ally in publicizing the Black Muslims as genuine freedom fighters, a sentiment that countered white newspapers' depiction of the group as violent and dangerous. "The *Amsterdam News* made the whole story headline news," Malcolm remembered, "and for the first time the black man, woman, and child in the streets were discussing 'those Muslims.'"[8]

Malcolm received counsel from two of Harlem's most distinguished figures: Lewis Michaux, an activist who participated in Marcus Garvey's UNIA movement, and Carlos Cooks, a local activist who kept the burning embers of Garveyism alive with the single-minded determination of a true believer. Nicknamed the "House of Common Sense and the Home of Proper Propaganda," Michaux's bookstore was a favorite rallying point for Harlem nationalists. Michaux's charismatic presence served as an added attraction. Michaux frequently sported a hat called a fez that made him favor the equally slight Black Muslim leader Elijah Muhammad. Unlike Muhammad, however, Michaux was a confident, rapid-fire speaker whose style had been honed through years of practice on Harlem streets.

Malcolm took control of Muslim Mosque No. 7 in 1954, just as the *Brown* Supreme Court decision transformed America's civil rights landscape, and the early rumblings of the civil rights movement's heroic years paralleled Malcolm's political organizing in Harlem. In contrast to the NOI's emphasis on black self-determination and separate independence, civil rights leaders vigorously asserted the citizenship rights of black Americans. Down south, civil rights activists rebelled against a system of Jim Crow invested with dramatically visible symbols that separated blacks and whites in public life. Civil rights activists and black leaders promoting the virtues, indeed the necessity, of racial integration displayed a stubborn faith in the resiliency of American democratic traditions.

The majority of black activists in Harlem did not share this faith. Harlem's poorest areas featured raw, unfiltered misery that manifested itself in the foreboding shadows of dark alleys, across garbage-strewn sidewalks, and inside tenements where random violence, alcoholism, drug addiction, and hunger shaped the lives of thousands of residents. Malcolm X cast the NOI and the teachings of Elijah Muhammad as a tangible oasis amid a searing urban wilderness.

Martin Luther King Jr. offered a more hopeful vision of race relations in the United States. A series of nationally publicized events during the second half of the 1950s made civil rights a domestic priority, one that had the potential to awaken the nation from its cold war stupor. As Malcolm searched for inroads within Harlem's most vulnerable communities, King emerged as the young leader of the successful bus boycott in Montgomery, Alabama. In short order Gandhian nonviolence became the lynchpin of a new movement that made deft use of King's status as a black preacher and the national recognition of the black church as the headquarters for African American social respectability and community building. Longstanding black militancy in the Deep South coalesced with King's eloquent call for nonviolence, reflecting a diverse political terrain where the competing rhetoric of King and Malcolm X found fertile soil in which to take root and grow.[9] Contemporary media interpretations and subsequent historical narratives would posit King and Malcolm as dueling political leaders engaged in nothing less than an epic political struggle for the hearts and minds of black Americans. In this telling, Malcolm argued for black identity as the soul of a worldwide political revolution, just as Martin countered with prophetic words that imagined a type of beloved community and engaged citizenship that transcended racial divisions.

Such a reading misses the way in which both Malcolm's and Martin's rhetoric and activism infuriated, antagonized, and inspired the other. Civil rights demonstrations bubbling up in the South provided Malcolm X with tangible evidence of mass discontent in the black community and offered poignant examples of black solidarity in service of social and political transformation. Urban unrest in the North revealed to King the depth of black poverty, anger, and despair in ways that impacted his political thought and future organizing.

New York proved to be the ideal city for Malcolm X's political growth and intellectual development.[10] Harlem's aching despair, poignant dignity, and mischievous pride made the neighborhood particularly attractive to the NOI's brand of social reform. In decaying storefronts and trash strewn alleys, open vice-dotted Harlem street corners and random violence, routine poverty, and creeping apathy stalked the lives of Harlem residents.

However, Malcolm was hardly alone in his quest for a revolutionary politics that would transform the black freedom movement. Stressing racial pride, the connection between America and the third world, and political self-determination through bruising and at times deliberately provocative protests, black radicals in the North were simultaneously inspired by the heroic efforts orchestrated by southern civil rights activists and repulsed by the spectacle of racial violence there. By the late 1950s, cynical about American democracy's willingness to protect black citizens, they had formed an unnamed parallel movement led by Malcolm X. This movement, with its varied expressions at the local, regional, national, and global levels, was more than just a mélange of black nationalists, civil rights renegades, and iconoclastic radicals. It was within these radical circles, where cynics and optimists intersected, that Black Power was forged. Collectively, the political struggles waged by radicals in Harlem, Detroit, and elsewhere were early examples of Black Power.

The Local Organizer

Malcolm X spent much of his early political career working as a local organizer in some of Harlem's roughest areas. An uncanny combination of personal brio, rhetorical eloquence, and political brilliance provided Malcolm with the organizing edge needed to stand out on Harlem's competitive street corners. His political instincts favored broad coalitions not often associated with sectarian leaders. Ordinary citizens, upstanding members of Christian churches, and participants leaving rival black nationalist rallies were fair game for Malcolm. The search for new recruits made him dig deep for the singular phrase, historical example, or biographical insight that could turn a curiosity seeker into a member of Mosque No. 7. Patrolling the edges of race-conscious rallies with handbills touting the NOI's call for self-determination became a part of "fishing" expeditions at storefront churches whose working-class constituents were open to aspects of Malcolm's message.[11] "I had learned early one important thing," he later recalled, "and that was to always teach in terms that people could understand."[12] Part of this meant appealing to black women who frequently poured out of Christian church services only to be greeted by bowtie-wearing Black Muslims, including Malcolm X, describing the way in which the NOI offered respect and protection for black women.[13]

Malcolm X's assured public demeanor and private displays of humor enthralled Harlem's leading figures.[14] Through actor Ossie Davis, he developed important relationships with the city's black intelligentsia. Impressed by Malcolm's brilliance and sharp wit, Davis, and his wife Ruby Dee, introduced him to a group of friends and associates that included writers Lorraine Hansberry and Julian Mayfield.[15] Malcolm purposefully brokered alliances with the infamous: individuals who, like himself, were tarnished by reports that linked them with taints that ranged from Communism to black extremism. Davis, along with John Killens and Julian Mayfield, approximated the behind-the-scenes support that Martin Luther King enjoyed in public from movie stars such as Harry Belafonte.[16] Privately, they formed an ad hoc group of advisers who would serve as Malcolm's personal brain trust.

Malcolm's high profile propelled him beyond the NOI's confines into a larger world that introduced him to influential journalists such as William Worthy,

Louis Lomax, and Alex Haley. Worthy, a correspondent for the *Baltimore/ Washington Afro-American*, frequently wrote about the NOI in newspaper and magazine stories marked for their unusual level of depth and complexity. The coverage of Malcolm X by Worthy, one of the most important radical black journalists of his generation, was both professional and political. As a foreign correspondent during the 1950s, Worthy traveled to China, South Africa, and other international hot spots. The soft-spoken reporter's running feud with the State Department over traveling restrictions made him a celebrity among black radicals and civil libertarians in the United States. Worthy and Malcolm shared close political networks that would culminate at the Grassroots Leadership Conference in Detroit in November 1963.

Bespectacled, inquisitive, and erudite, Lomax cut his journalistic teeth exposing the Black Muslims before a national television audience in the 1959 special "The Hate That Hate Produced." The five-part *News Beat* documentary, broadcast during the week of July 13, ignited the civil rights era's first intraracial controversy.[17] Given unprecedented access to the NOI, Lomax, along with an all-white camera crew, filmed never-before-seen aspects of the organization.[18] The documentary pointedly characterized the NOI as a group of idiosyncratic, potentially violent hate-mongers. America's first glimpse of the NOI featured the foreboding image of thousands of Muslims at a Washington, DC rally. The tens of thousands of members filling Washington's enormous Uline Arena provided shocking footage that attested to the NOI's organizational strength. Interviews with Malcolm and Elijah Muhammad bolstered narrator Mike Wallace's claims that the "Black Muslims" represented a dangerous, understudied, and increasingly threatening facet of America's racial life. Malcolm X, addressing an "African Freedom Day" rally in Harlem, underscored *News Beat*'s claims that the Muslim movement had penetrated black America's foremost citadel.[19] Despite the documentary's unflattering portrayal of the group, the publicity proved to be a boon. In short order, Lomax became a national expert on the NOI and would collaborate with Malcolm X on the book *When the Word Is Given*.

Alex Haley would indelibly shape Malcolm's legacy in ways unimaginable at the time. Both Worthy and Lomax (or James Hicks) seemed better suited to tell Malcolm's story, at least in terms of sharing Malcolm's radical political sympathies. Primarily organized and edited by Haley after Malcolm's death, *The Autobiography of Malcolm X* would indelibly transform Malcolm's legacy for a popular audience in small and large ways, fundamentally casting Malcolm as a lost soul tainted by loss of family, a criminal past, and service to corrupt leadership—a soul whose ultimate redemption was found only upon acknowledging the potential for interracial brotherhood.[20]

In general, black newspapers, including the *Afro-American, New York Amsterdam News, Pittsburgh Courier, Chicago Defender*, and *Los Angeles Herald Dispatch*, reported on the growing specter of the NOI when mainstream journalists ignored the group. Malcolm took note, stalking the offices of the *Amsterdam News* and other publications, determined to find a national organ to disseminate the NOI's worldview. As Malcolm's public image gradually took shape in the year after the Johnson X incident, it was partially fueled by the popularity of his syndicated column "God's Angry Men." Malcolm served an ad hoc apprenticeship at the offices of the *Los Angeles Herald Dispatch* during the late 1950s determined to reach the widest possible audience. Trained by the paper's most exacting administrator, he learned the skills that would later help him create the newspaper *Muhammad Speaks*, one of the Nation's most profitable and important enterprises.[21] *Muhammad Speaks* became the NOI's main vehicle for shaping its organizational worldview and spreading a philosophy of militant self-determination. The weekly newspaper hired talented non-Muslim journalists who reported on a wide range of domestic and international racial controversies. With a weekly circulation of over 500,000 by the early 1960s *Muhammad Speaks* proved to be a secular news organ that attracted diverse readers eager to read reports about anti-racist struggles taking place in global cities such as Angola to local metropolises such as Los Angeles to Southern civil rights beachheads in Birmingham.

If newspaper reporters shaped much of the black world for public consumption, powerbrokers such as Congressman Adam Clayton Powell Jr. ruled it. An old-fashioned politician who rose to become Harlem's most important elected official, Powell was a cunning deal-maker, shrewd legislator, and beloved symbol of national black political power. Reports of Powell's womanizing, drinking, and complicated—at times ethically questionable—financial dealings made him a kind of folk hero among Harlemites who reacted to the latest news of his exploits with the glee of witnessing a rakish showman and master entertainer. Malcolm X and Powell bonded over shared reputations as extraordinary political showmen, dazzling public speakers, and unapologetic political mavericks. Malcolm spoke at Powell's Abyssinian Baptist Church in Harlem and the two established an alliance that withstood rumors of dissension over which man wielded more influence over Harlem politics. Mutually providing each other with establishment legitimacy and street credibility, Malcolm and Powell cultivated a pragmatic political alliance that offered both men the promise of new and potentially powerful constituencies.[22]

Malcolm's growing notoriety also led to new scrutiny from the authorities. In 1958, the FBI designated Malcolm a "key figure."[23] NOI plans to establish mosques in the South and throughout the West Coast prompted special concern from Bureau officials.[24] For much of his public political life, Malcolm's every move was under strict surveillance by federal authorities headquartered in Washington DC and New York City's Bureau of Special Services (BOSS) unit, and by international emissaries from the State Department and other agencies during his trips around the world.

Harlem and the Third World

If Harlem was changing during the 1950s, so was much of the wider world. The 1955 Afro-Asian Conference in Bandung, Indonesia, represented a world-historical event. Imagining a world free from the dictates of the United States and the Soviet Union in favor of self-determination by previously colonized nations,

Bandung audaciously promoted indigenous self-rule. Calls for third-world solidarity articulated at Bandung would be echoed by Malcolm X over the course of his career.

Africa represented a key part of the Bandung conference's hopes to reshape the world. Perceived by both American and Soviet interests as a continent vulnerable to cold war intrigues, Africa plotted its own course of independence through indigenous movements for self-determination that gripped the continent. Harlem, with a rich history of black nationalist street speaking and pan-Africanist organizing that stretched back to the New Negro movement of the 1920s, greeted the sounds of African independence with cheers. American officials responded more cautiously, crafting an imaginative strategy for diplomacy in Africa that exaggerated domestic racial progress in hopes of spreading democracy in the region, forestalling Communism, and defending against assertions that Jim Crow practices rendered America unfit to preach democracy to the rest of the world.[25]

The arrival of Ghanaian independence in 1957 suggested that an African renaissance was well underway. Ghanaian prime minister Kwame Nkrumah made dreams of a revolutionary new Africa seem tantalizingly real. Nkrumah's promise to "show the world" that Africans could take the "lead in justice, tolerance, liberty, individual freedom and social progress" seemed especially encouraging given his special relationship with black America, having been educated at Lincoln University in Pennsylvania.[26]

Ghana, for different reasons, mesmerized black radicals and moderates. Radicals viewed Ghana as the potential spark toward a continent-wide insurgency that would ultimately trigger a global revolution powerful enough to meaningfully impact American racism. Moderates adopted a more pragmatic outlook, hopeful that Ghana's newfound stature would pressure the United States into making real and symbolic inroads toward racial progress.

The black press helped to amplify Harlem's and the rest of black America's pan-African impulses by meticulously chronicling the independence movements surging across Africa. Leaders such as Nkrumah became instant icons of revolution and self-determination, touted by radicals and moderates as positive proof of racial progress. Recapping the year's events, the *Amsterdam News* declared 1957 as the "Year Negroes Fought Back" and held independence celebrations in Accra, Ghana, as one of the year's most important events.[27] Nkrumah's trip to Harlem on Sunday, July 27, 1958 served as an unofficial coronation of sorts. Returning to Harlem for the first time since being elected Ghanaian prime minister, a beaming Nkrumah rode in an open car flanked by New York City mayor Abe Stark as 25,000 Harlemites lined the streets.[28]

Harlem both basked in the reflected glory of Nkrumah's rise and received more tangible benefits. Nkrumah personally invited skilled blacks committed to Africa's restoration to help build a new nation. Around two hundred African Americans would respond to this call, leading to the establishment of an expatriate community that included Harlem radicals such as Julian Mayfield and Maya Angelou, and the ninety-three-year-old W.E.B. Du Bois. Malcolm would encounter Ghana's community of expatriates in May 1964, less than two years before the fall of Nkrumah's political kingdom; they welcomed him as a prodigal son returning to Africa.[29]

*   *   *

The World That Malcolm X Made

Civil rights activist Robert F. Williams visibly manifested the political rage to which Malcolm X gave eloquent voice. Malcolm's growing national political stature lent increasing credibility to civil rights renegades such as Williams who defied the movement's nonviolence orthodoxy. Head of the NAACP's Monroe, North Carolina chapter, Williams confronted the local Ku Klux Klan with militant words and deeds. Leading skirmishes against the Klan with armed civil rights activists, debating the merits of self-defense versus nonviolence, and forging alliances with activists across a wide political and ideological political spectrum, Williams became the South's most controversial civil rights activist. Tall, broad-shouldered, and confident, Williams's became a national celebrity in 1959 after a violent assault on a black woman in Monroe by a white man. Reckless words suggesting the need to be "willing to kill if necessary" triggered Williams's six-month suspension and eventual break from the NAACP.[30] Rebuffed by civil rights moderates, including Martin Luther King Jr., as intemperate and ill-advised, Williams turned to Harlem for political support. He found kindred spirits. Activists associated with the Harlem Writer's Guild, the NOI, and others lent Williams their prestige, raised money to support activism in Monroe, and introduced him to new contacts. Harlem activist Mae Mallory helped organize the "Crusader Families," who took their name from *The Crusader,* Williams's mimeographed newsletter. Designed as an effective means to detail events in Monroe unfiltered through the national press, *The Crusader* became a vehicle that distilled feelings of black nationalism, revolutionary internationalism, and radical democracy.

Williams's political activities—like Malcolm X's—although in many ways unique, were, in certain quarters at least, quite common. The previously hidden connections between black radicalism, racial democracy, and African independence movements embodied in the political activism taking place in Harlem and the militancy of Robert Williams down south imbued *A Raisin in the Sun,* Lorraine Hansberry's magisterial play about a working-class black family on Chicago's south side. Hansberry's brilliantly nuanced portrait of black life mesmerized mainstream audiences and critics alike. The play's gritty eloquence made the subjective life of poor Negroes transcendent, elegantly creating a world that was both fiercely personal and poignantly universal. In Hansberry's prose, Jim Crow's shattering impact on black life existed alongside dreams of self-determination that stretched from Chicago's south side all the way to Africa. *A Raisin in the Sun* plumbed the depths of a style of black cultural nationalism that would become associated with a second generation of Black Power militants who took center stage during the mid-1960s.[31] Nationalist themes of robust self-determination and dreams of African independence paralleled the Younger family's efforts to secure the American dream. These pursuits, for many critics at least, overwhelmed *A Raisin in the Sun*'s more radical aspects. A blockbuster analysis of race, democracy, and the very meaning of postwar America, the play elegantly transcended cold war era racial myths and social fictions.[32] If Malcolm X served as the avatar for Black Power during the 1950s, Hansberry represented one of the movement's earliest and most eloquent literary voices.[33]

In the summer of 1959, Malcolm X returned to Harlem after visiting Africa and arrived in the middle of the storm of controversy generated by *News Beat*'s Black Muslim documentary. The visit to Africa, where he toured the Middle East, left Malcolm irrevocably transformed. In Africa to prepare for Elijah Muhammad's planned *hajj*, Malcolm met with Egyptian leaders Gamal Abdel Nasser and Anwar Sadat. Visits to Nigeria, Ghana, Sudan, and Saudi Arabia proved to be eye-openers; from the Middle East, Malcolm wrote dispatches detailing his travels for the *Amsterdam News*. He purposefully declared that "racial disturbances in faraway New York City" made front-page news in Sudan with the express intention of illustrating connections between the American domestic racial crisis and Africa. Penetrating what Malcolm described as a "veil of global diplomatic art" were "hordes of intelligent Africans" unmoved by American propaganda extolling domestic racial progress.[34]

Alternately demonized or ignored by white press outlets and not in complete control over black coverage, Malcolm created the newspaper that would become one of his most important legacies. *Muhammad Speaks* would become the leading black radical weekly newspaper during the early 1960s, offering coverage of civil rights struggles, labor and rent strikes, and political revolutions raging across much of the third world. The paper would prove to be unconventionally bold and sophisticated in its coverage of insurgent racial movements around the world. But Elijah Muhammad's control over the paper would push Malcolm increasingly into the background. Ultimately, *Muhammad Speaks*, with a weekly circulation that exceeded half a million by the mid-1960s, would become a lucrative enterprise that helped institutionalize the NOI in urban centers across the United States.[35]

*   *   *

On Monday September 19, 1960, the Cuban Revolution arrived in Harlem. Led by Fidel Castro, the Cuban delegation descended on Hotel Theresa's stunned owner and operator Love B. Woods. Controversy surrounded Castro's unexpected arrival. The Shelbourne Hotel originally booked by the Cubans accused the delegation of uncivilized behavior even as Castro leveled charges of racial bigotry.[36] His presence in Harlem turned its 125th Street corridor into New York City's most congested area. Harlem residents stood outside of the Theresa in hopes of catching a glimpse of the Cuban leader, as did members of the Harlem Writers Guild who led chants of "Viva Castro" amid the blare of Spanish music.[37]

In many ways Harlem had been anticipating Castro's arrival for almost two years. In the aftermath of the January 1, 1959 Cuban Revolution, black radicals in Harlem had become some of the island's biggest boosters. Members of the Harlem Writers Guild, including John Oliver Killens and John Henrik Clark, helped form the Fair Play for Cuba Committee, founded to provide unbiased coverage of the revolution. Robert F. Williams embarked on two tours of Cuba during the summer of 1960. Leading black writers accompanied Williams on his second trip. Harlem indelibly shaped the past of some participants, such as Harold Cruse, whose intellectual and political awakening could be traced back to the New York Library's uptown branch's Negro History Division (soon to be renamed after its founder Afro-Puerto Rican bibliophile Arturo Schomburg). For others, most notably LeRoi Jones, Harlem would prove crucial to a renaissance in black art and culture. Connections between Harlem and Havana, then, were cultivated at the grassroots level even as they would become enshrined in legend by a meeting between icons.

Malcolm X and Fidel Castro's meeting placed Harlem at the center of cold war intrigues. As they chatted through a Spanish translator, a photographer snapped pictures of the two men sitting on the edge of a bed. The intense conversation included snippets of Malcolm's typically blunt remarks. "I think you will find," said Malcolm, "the people in Harlem are not so addicted to the propaganda they put out downtown."[38] Malcolm and Fidel's conversation served as preparation of sorts for the Cuban leader's upcoming United Nation's speech.[39] FBI surveillance observed Malcolm and Fidel's meeting with intense interest. Publicly Malcolm rejected attempts to connect him to Communism, while maintaining freedom to associate with whomever he pleased.[40] The black press reported Malcolm and Castro's meeting as a bombshell political development while white journalists greeted the entire event as a Communist-orchestrated spectacle.[41] *The New York Times* characterized Castro's visit as a public relations stunt and characterized Malcolm as "a leader of the so-called Muslim movement among United States Negroes."[42]

Castro received a host of dignitaries at the Theresa, including Egyptian president Gamal Nasser, Soviet premier Nikita Kruschev, and a contingent of black radicals associated with Fair Play. Recognizing America's vulnerability regarding Jim Crow, Castro made race the central focus of his visit, consorting openly with black Cuban comandante Juan Almeide—who was flown from Cuba only *after* Castro came to Harlem—to underscore this point. African American radicals, some of whom had witnessed Cuba's march toward racial equality first-hand, relished the unfolding spectacle.

The gregarious Castro, followed everywhere by journalists, photographers, and onlookers, charmed Harlem's black community with his wide smile and effusive demeanor. (William Worthy, who managed to find time to cover domestic and international racial crises, covered Castro's visit from Havana.)[43] Describing Harlem as an "oasis in the desert," Castro was celebrated at the Hotel Theresa while President Eisenhower played host to Latin American delegates at the Park Avenue Waldorf Astoria Hotel. Content to mingle with the "poor and humble people of Harlem," Castro enjoyed a reception hosted by Fair Play that featured enthusiastic African American supporters. He continually stoked controversy through expressions of admiration. "My impression of Harlem is that it's wonderful," he said. "We are very happy here. I think this is a big lesson to people who practice discrimination."[44]

Castro's visit to Harlem provided symbolic evidence of Malcolm X's sophisticated understanding of world affairs. The assassination of Congolese prime minister Patrice Lumumba would accelerate Malcolm and Harlem's political maturation. Following 1960, designated as the "Year of Africa" by the United Nations, the early winter and spring of 1961 brought seasons of discontent with news of the murder of Lumumba and several humiliating episodes wherein African diplomats were barred from restaurants and hotels inside the Washington beltway.[45] Indignation over Lumumba's death provided many young blacks with their first taste of political organizing. Primed by Malcolm X's trips to Cuba and his increasing profile as well as by a resurgence of black nationalist organizing in Harlem, the sociopolitical climate was such that the time for resistance was ripe. Indeed, writer John Henrik Clarke would mark this event as giving birth to a revival of black nationalism not seen since the Garvey Movement's heyday.[46] Appointed Prime Minister in 1960 after two stints in jail related to his political activism Lumumba's spectacular rise and fall illustrated the hopes and impediments confronting African nation-building. In an international arena unfamiliar with African autonomy in foreign affairs, Lumumba's brazen confidence, punctuated by a militant June 30, 1960 Independence Day celebration speech that outraged Belgian officials who deemed the young politician dangerously unsuitable.

Lumumba's assassination at the hands of political enemies, in combination with the previous year's events, had primed Harlem for organized political rebellion. During the second half of 1960s the region's political turmoil, popularly known as the Congo Crisis, was chronicled in the black press and became a subject of frequent, passionate debates as Congo fever gripped a broad segment of the black community. For example, street-corner nationalists in Brooklyn organized a quixotic drive to recruit volunteers to fight in the Congo; the effort ended in a near-riot.[47] The Harlem Writers Guild cabled President Eisenhower demanding American intervention in the escalating conflict, and the *Amsterdam News* published a stream of editorials and news stories documenting America's inconsistent foreign policy in Africa.[48] All of these initiatives failed.

On February 15, 1961, a group of black nationalists, many from Harlem, took over the United Nations. As more than two hundred demonstrators picketed on 42nd Street outside the U.N.'s headquarters, events inside turned violent as dozens of black protesters infiltrated a U.N. Security Council meeting to express outrage over Lumumba's murder. The demonstration quickly turned into a melee that featured fist fights, multiple arrests, and the kind of dramatic political theater that would come to be almost exclusively associated with Black Power groups of the late 1960s such as the Black Panthers. Men and women in black armbands and veils formed their own ad hoc funeral procession inside and outside the United Nations to honor and mourn Lumumba's untimely death.[49] The day's events made international headlines and established Lumumba as an icon of African independence.

Some of Harlem's leading black activists took part in the protests. Carlos Moore, the young charismatic black Cuban, was as usual in the thick of the fray.

So was Harlem's senior Carlos—the incomparable Carlos Cooks. Cooks, a young Afro-Cuban, had served as interpreter during Castro's Hotel Theresa episode and—until his later disillusionment with Cuba's racial progress—was among that revolution's most ardent supporters. Cooks had preserved his allegiance to Marcus Garvey-style Pan-Africanism even when it fell out of vogue, a distinction that once led Kwame Nkrumah himself to personally escort Cooks to a scheduled rally with him, after careless organizers had snubbed the distinguished nationalist.[50] To the casual observer, these men were bizarrely dressed and rakishly behaved kooks. To informed Harlem residents, including Malcolm X, they were part of a community of black street speakers who kept the embers of black nationalism alive even during its lowest point.

Maya Angelou was one of the dozens of black activists who made their way inside the Security Council meeting. Abandoning California to find a new life in the big city, Angelou had found a warm refuge in the Harlem Writers Guild. A single mother whose deep voice matched her tall, elegant frame, she danced, sang, and did whatever else she could to make ends meet. Even the most cynical observer would have envied the sights and sounds of Angelou's New York. Seen through her eyes, Harlem was less of a neighborhood in decline than a community filled with street speakers, food vendors, Black Muslims, nationalists, labor organizers, and children playing stickball in the street.

During the Harlem summers, colorful street speakers would be out in full force. Standing tall on top of semi-sacred stepladders across from Lewis Michaux's legendary bookstore was Benjamin Davis, the black Communist and former City Councilman. The Dean of Marxist Studies, though past his prime as a political leader, still commanded the respect of a community elder. Eddie "Porkchop" Davis, the charismatic Garveyite, mesmerized young men and women with his vast knowledge of African history and black nationalist philosophy.[51] These were Harlem's community of "elders," African American griots who informed, cajoled, and harangued—ready to debate with anyone, anytime, and anyplace.

The protest that took place inside the United Nations, in retrospect, represented Black Power's formal arrival on the national political scene. Malcolm X was conspicuously absent from the day's protest, but his spirit hovered over the entire proceedings. Rumors traced what was now being called a "riot" at the United Nations to an unholy alliance forged between Black Muslims and Communists. Malcolm vigorously denied attempts to link the NOI to the U.N. protest and just as strongly resisted efforts to lure him into denouncing the entire affair. "I will permit no one," Malcolm defiantly explained, "to use me against the nationalists."[52]

Malcolm's need to remain on the edges of the controversy left it to writers such as James Baldwin to defend the actions of the demonstrators and place the events in a larger historical context. In a scathing editorial published in the New York Times, Baldwin characterized the U.N. demonstration as only "a small echo" of the potentially cataclysmic anger spreading around the world. For Baldwin, American democracy's best hopes lay in confronting the social and political reasons behind the protest, a kind of political maturity the nation had not often been able to show.[53] Lorraine Hansberry echoed much of Baldwin's sentiment in a letter to the *Times*. Hansberry railed against "the continuation of intrigues against African American Negro freedom" before apologizing to Pauline Lumumba (Patrice Lumumba's widow) for UN Undersecretary for Special Political Affairs Ralph Bunche (who had publicly apologized for the behavior of the U.N. protesters).[54]

Unable to reveal in public his true feeling about the U.N. demonstration, Malcolm confessed his appreciation in private. At the NOI's Shabazz Restaurant in Harlem, Malcolm conveyed his support to some of the event's leading pro-testers. Malcolm told Maya Angelou, Abbey Lincoln, and Rosa Guy how proud he was and informed them that he had just finished shooting down rumors of Communist conspiracies leveled by the New York police officials.[55] The U.N. demonstration was, in many ways, the culmination of the kind of political orga-nizing that Malcolm had been advocating since he arrived back in Harlem as a political activist in 1954. In spirit and practice, it reflected his political message of radical self-determination, international awareness, and necessity for self-defense. Malcolm's inability to fully participate in an event his presence and preaching helped facilitate illustrated the paradox of membership in the NOI. Prevented from participating in organized boycotts, picket-lines, or political demonstrations, Malcolm brokered alliances with individuals and organiza-tions who found their metier in the very tactics that the NOI largely disavowed.

Despite Malcolm's failure to formally lead protests such as the U.N. demon-stration, activists in Harlem looked up to him as a teacher, mentor, and guide. Malcolm drew similar inspiration from his deepening political and personal ties in Harlem, relationships that would bolster him as he attempted to turn a sec-tarian organization into a cosmopolitan one. While Malcolm's well-publicized overtures to civil rights leaders in 1964 are most often interpreted as a belated attempt to broaden his political and organizational horizons, his past organizing complicates this thesis.

Message to the Grassroots

In 1963, Malcolm raged against the sight of blacks in Birmingham, Alabama, routed by dogs and fire hoses. Barred from formal participation in the era's unfolding events, he lent measured support to southern civil rights struggles while scrupulously maintaining the NOI's policy of non-engagement. Having recently been named head of Muslim Mosque No. 4, located in the Washington DC area, Malcolm addressed the crisis from the nation's capital. In interviews inside Washington's beltway, he excoriated the federal government and black leaders he decried as little more than modern-day "Uncle Toms."[56] Shortly after this speech, the *New York Herald Tribune* reported that Malcolm was planning on going to Birmingham to sort things out personally. Interviewed about these star-tling revelations from the NOI's New York restaurant, Malcolm X backpedaled from the story—which was leaked by Jeremiah X from the Nation's Birmingham temple—claiming he had no plans to visit.[57]

Malcolm's anger over the events in Birmingham was compounded by a fes-tering organizational crisis. His blistering criticism against high-profile targets hid creeping doubts that challenged his religious beliefs and political purpose. The unavenged murder of Los Angeles Muslim Ronald Stokes at the hands of the police made Malcolm openly question the usefulness of the NOI's army of soldiers if potential battles were always to be waged on the enemy's terms. Even as Malcolm upheld Elijah Muhammad's doctrine of divine patience, he confessed that a new generation of Muslims was itching to see "some action."[58] Swirling rumors of financial mismanagement out of Chicago and moral hypocrisy from Phoenix placed him in the middle of potentially explosive truths.[59] Conducting a fact-finding mission that promised to renew his faith at the expense of Messenger Muhammad, Malcolm descended into a web of organizational and personal intrigue.

Its immediate roots sprang from what should have marked a personal and professional high point. In February 1963, Malcolm presided over the NOI's annual Savior's Day Conference in Chicago, a lavish spectacle that brought thousands of the faithful to hear Elijah Muhammad speak. Malcolm chaired the meeting in the absence of the messenger, who remained in Phoenix, too ill to attend. Muhammad's insecure relatives, aware that his appearance seemed to confirm speculation that Malcolm was the dashing prince to Muhammad's aging king, became emotionally charged and threatened Chicago officials. Malcolm's commanding presence, authoritative posture around Muhammad's family, and use of Muhammad's prized Cadillac rubbed already frayed nerves raw.

Malcolm's attempts to address nasty rumors of Elijah Muhammad's infidelities compounded an already overheated situation. The ugly truth—that Muhammad had, in fact, fathered several offspring out of wedlock and mediated rough negotiations with mothers who could barely take care of their children—loomed over Malcolm's secret investigations.

After listening to an earful of complaints and charges of disloyalty against Malcolm, Elijah Muhammad sent him packing back to New York. Forced to retreat, Malcolm attempted to secure his own place amid charges and countercharges that threatened to topple the NOI's empire. He personally met with Muhammad in Phoenix, unveiling a plan that was a double-edged sword. On the surface, Malcolm and Wallace Muhammad, the scion of the royal family, for daring to reject his father's flights of religious fancy in favor of Orthodox Islam, had concocted religious evidence to defend Muhammad's indiscretions. Dispatched from Arizona on a mission to scuttle the rumor-mongering that was now running rampant in the nation's ranks, Malcolm embarked on a high-wire act: making revelations to groups of handpicked ministers as leverage against rapidly unfolding intrigues.[60]

In November 1963, Malcolm delivered perhaps his most important speech, "Message to the Grassroots," from a podium in Detroit, Michigan. Malcolm's ties to the Motor City could be traced to his brother Wilfred X, the leading minister of Detroit's Muslim Mosque No. 1. Malcolm's visit to Detroit brought him full circle. In 1957, he toured the city, giving a series of electrifying speeches that announced him as a fresh new voice of militant protest. In the ensuing years, Detroit served as a political haven whose homegrown activists such as Reverend Albert Cleage, James and Grace Lee Boggs, and Richard and Milton Henry became some of

Malcolm's key political allies, confidantes, and advisors. The city's mosaic of political organizing incorporated trade unionists, militant Christians, socialists, black nationalists, and open-minded liberals into an ad hoc headquarters for black radicalism that welcomed Malcolm X even as they merely tolerated the less-appealing aspects of the NOI's orthodoxy.

A case in point is Malcolm's political alliances with Detroit activist Albert Cleage. Cleage's leadership of black militants in Detroit did not prevent him from sharing a stage with Martin Luther King during the June 23, 1963 Walk for Freedom. A footnote in most historical accounts of the 1963 Detroit's freedom walk reveals the sometimes blurred lines between civil rights and Black Power activism, where a known ally of Malcolm X could co-organize a sympathy march to support civil rights demonstrators in Birmingham. Comfortable appearing alongside King, Cleage was bold enough to be a key organizer of the Grassroots Leadership Conference where Malcolm delivered his electrifying speech. Malcolm's rhetorical jabs—where he chastised civil rights leaders as "Uncle Toms," ridiculed nonviolence as idiotic, and predicted a growing scourge of racial violence—at times obscured the nuanced, practical, and fluid approach to organizing that marked his political activism.

The "Message to the Grassroots" speech laid down the blueprint for a national movement for political self-determination that characterized revolution on terms defined by blacks. According to Malcolm, this required a strong historical perspective unafraid to admit that radical change required equally radical methods. His daring sense of the possible connected domestic racial crises with international revolutions spreading around the world. The talk distilled four centuries of racial oppression through a rhetorical tour de force that touched race and democracy, war and peace, and self-defense and nonviolence. Most often remembered for the biting allegory that argued that America's slaveholding past produced two warring types of blacks—"House Negroes" and "Field Negroes"—Malcolm's Grassroots speech took place against a backdrop of growing divisions within the civil rights movement, racial unrest in the United States, and increasing cracks along the world's racial fault lines.

As the keynote speech to the Grassroots Leadership Conference, Malcolm's "Message to the Grassroots" served as a generational manifesto advocating Black Power during the high point of the civil rights era. In its aftermath, distinguished activists, local organizers, and regional leaders planned to spark a national movement for black political power.

Ballots and Bullets

Malcolm X's exile from the NOI drew him closer to Harlem even as it made its streets palpably dangerous. His suspension, following comments about John F. Kennedy's assassination (he described the event as "chickens coming home to roost"), capped internal tensions within the group that had been festering since at least the late 1950s. Malcolm's aggressive efforts to turn Black Muslims into political activists rankled high-ranking Muslim officials who feared government repression. Muhammad loyalists viewed Malcolm as self-aggrandizing and reckless, a chameleon who longed for the aging leader's throne. Federal surveillance added further layers of mistrust, suspicion, and paranoia to an already tense environment.

In March 1964, Malcolm set out to carve an independent course, the outline of which he had sketched over the previous decade. Harlem would serve as his political base even as he spent more time around the world than in the United States. At a massive rally at Harlem's Rockland Palace, Malcolm promised to organize a national convention to deliberate on forming a political party. Before leaving the United States for a five-week tour of Africa, Malcolm unleashed his most scathing and thoughtful critique of American democracy yet. The "Ballot or the Bullet" speech suggested that the civil rights struggle aspire toward higher political and social altitudes that only a "human rights" movement could hope to reach. Malcolm mapped some of the next decade's most pressing concerns in a speech whose provocative title at times obscured its sophisticated analysis of world events.[61]

The two organizations Malcolm created between March and June 1964—Muslim Mosque Inc. and the Organization of Afro-American Unity (OAAU)—were both headquartered in Harlem's Theresa Hotel and seemed to have the potential to create a mass movement for social and political transformation. Despite support from well-known local activists, a secular political outlook that tied national ambitions to pragmatic local measures, and a modest two-dollar membership fee, the OAAU, the more promising of the two groups, failed to capture the imagination of Harlem and black militants around the nation. Malcolm's inability to engage in the slow, patient, local organizing that helped propel the NOI in Harlem and around the nation during the 1950s clearly marked this failure.

Malcolm's extensive travels overseas left him struggling to maintain organizational control over the OAAU and close alliances in Harlem. Malcolm's final year witnessed promising efforts to speak to multiple audiences, groups, and factions, sometimes simultaneously. The breadth of these pursuits made for jarring portraits, perhaps none more so than Malcolm's sole meeting with Martin Luther King Jr., which took place in the unexpected, but no less appropriate, setting of the United States Senate. During that year, Malcolm aggressively courted African leaders, made overtures to civil rights leaders, and cautiously dealt with white socialists. His absence from Harlem during the July 1964 urban rebellion (the kind of racial conflict he so often predicted) would prove bittersweet. In Cairo, practicing freelance diplomacy when the violence erupted, Malcolm was relegated to releasing press statements explaining his activities overseas while a host of national figures, including King, provided more visible leadership through physical, if not ideological, proximity to Harlem residents.

But Malcolm's tours of Africa were hardly in vain. His diplomatic adventures tapped into long-simmering pan-African impulses whose modern expression combined New Negro rhetorical effervescence with the kind of practical nation-building that dwarfed even Marcus Garvey's outsized imagination. Harlem remained on Malcolm's mind and at the center of his political agenda, even as his political sojourn took him from its street corners.

It is fitting, then, that Malcolm X made his last public appearance in Harlem on February 21, 1965. A premeditated diversion turned the Audubon Ballroom into a jumbled scene of frightening confusion, scattering assassins, and panicked supporters, that concluded with Malcolm's bullet-riddled corpse being rushed to Columbia Presbyterian Hospital. Hailed by black militants in Harlem and the rest of the nation as a bold prophet cut down in his prime, Malcolm would, in death, become an even bigger icon than he had been while alive.

Conclusion

In the popular imagination and most historical narratives, Malcolm X serves as Martin Luther King's most well-known counterpart. Whereas King is celebrated as the national leader of the civil rights movement, Malcolm's leadership is largely reduced to symbolism. King's efforts to desegregate public accommodations in the south, the historic March on Washington Speech, and influence over the successful passage of the 1964 Civil Rights Act and 1965 Voting Rights Act have the cumulative effect of making him the leader of a movement while Malcolm remains the fiery expression of a political mood.

Such a perspective separates Malcolm from the social and political context in which he lived, operated, and died. King served as a national political mobilizer who inspired far-flung local movements, organizations, and individuals toward the civil rights movement's goals of racial reform that included desegregation, equal protection under the law, and voting rights. King's eloquence, creativity, and global stature accelerated civil rights victories and, over time, would resonate around the world. However, his political mobilizing would have been impossible without local groups, organizers, activists, and everyday people, who bled for American democracy during the civil rights era.

Malcolm X served as more than just a symbolic leader for America's black militants. In Harlem, Detroit, Los Angeles, and other cities, Malcolm organized coalitions of early Black Power militants that included civil rights renegades, socialists, intellectuals and artists, and independent organizers. Such activists confronted social miseries such as unemployment, police brutality, crime, and drug abuse through local organizing that took place outside bookstores and bars. As a young activist, Malcolm served at least two political apprenticeships. The NOI imparted mental and physical discipline that honed Malcolm's prodigious mind and allowed him to further develop previously untapped skills. His second apprenticeship came courtesy of Harlem, a city within a city, where legendary street speakers such as Carlos Cooks and Lewis Michaux provided him with insight into black nationalism, political organizing, and institution building. Harlem's political terrain became a lab where Malcolm experimented with organizing methods, collaborated with homegrown activists, and surveyed a national landscape being inexorably altered by civil rights insurgency. Malcolm applied these lessons first in Harlem, and, in time, across the United States and around the world.

Black radicals who unleashed bedlam at the United Nations were just a small part of the constellation of activists who looked to Malcolm as their leader. To many—from the young militants of the Revolutionary Action Movement and UHURU to the more seasoned political veterans associated with GOAL (Group on Advanced Leadership) to civil rights heretics such as Gloria Richardson and the local organizers behind ACT (no acronym just the organization's name)—Malcolm served as a political touchstone, mentor, and spokesman. For others, such as Robert F. Williams and Lorraine Hansberry, Malcolm's activism helped to expand the terrain of their own political and cultural engagement. In essence, Malcolm's radical critique of American democracy broadened an entire generation's political horizons. In contrast to King, years before he became a national figure, Malcolm engaged in street-level organizing in some of urban America's worst areas, where the quest to convey political ideas played out as a kind of trench warfare where combatants included the police, criminals, rival political sects, and apathy.

Civil rights and Black Power emerged during a moment of national racial crisis brimming with momentous expectations. Black Americans found themselves shut out of postwar prosperity they had helped secure during these years. Southern civil rights activists evoked the social justice advocated by black militants during the prewar years but scaled back its social-democratic thrust. Black Power activists took the notion of righting historical wrongs to a new level, promoting self-reliance, internationalism, and cooperation among the race. Despite rancorous debates over strategies and tactics, activists from one camp often switched to another, and certain individuals and organizations often favored both approaches at the same time. Both movements dreamed of redefining American democracy but discovered that there were no easy solutions to America's racial problems. Instead, both settled for exposing rough, unsettling truths about the limits of racial justice and economic equality—in so doing, both helped transform America's racial landscape. The failure to acknowledge Black Power's immediate roots in the postwar freedom struggle and its early fermentation under Malcolm X's leadership perpetuates the mythology that the movement represents nothing more than the civil rights era's destructive, violent, and ineffectual sibling—a horrific doppelganger that practiced politics without portfolio and successfully thwarted more promising movements for social and political justice. Following Stokely Carmichael's declaration of "Black Power" in 1966, a generation of militants proclaimed themselves heirs to Malcolm's personal political activism. Even Malcolm's most ardent admirers tend to characterize him as a man ahead of his time, a prophet unrecognized in his own country and held political hostage by the period's overwhelming allegiance to nonviolence and gradual racial reform. Most fail to recognize that Malcolm had been more than a charismatic militant. He was, in fact, the leader of a national movement for Black Power that took on new dimensions and a mass public expression only after his assassination.

Malcolm X's—and the larger Black Power Movement's—impact, political importance, and historical legacy remain crucial to understanding the full depth and breadth of African American postwar freedom struggles. From his early political development under the tutelage of some of Harlem's leading nationalists to his deft relationship with the media and more enigmatic ties to Adam Clayton Powell Jr., Malcolm proved to be one of the most versatile political leaders black America has ever produced. The national controversy stoked by the NOI catapulted him to undreamed-of political heights and unprecedented opportunities to satisfy his large intellectual appetite. From his first trip to Africa in 1959 to his final visit five years later, Malcolm's interest in world affairs grew equally radical and pragmatic. Meetings with Fidel Castro, Kwame Nkrumah, and other global figures turned Malcolm into black America's unofficial prime minister. Through all of this, Harlem would remain as close to a permanent political base (first through Muslim Mosque No. 7's 116th Street headquarters and later the Hotel Theresa and Audubon Ballroom) as Malcolm would ever have. Chronicling the Black Power Movement's early origins, activism, and political debates and defeats in Malcolm X's Harlem (a world that shaped and was shaped by civil rights activism as well) moves us closer to a more nuanced, complicated, and historically accurate portrait of not simply a man, but the period that shaped his political struggles.

Notes

1. Louis Lomax, *When the Word Is Given: A Report on Elijah Muhammad, Malcolm X, and the Black Muslim World* (Toronto: Signet Books, 1963), p. 24.
2. Malcolm X and Alex Haley, *The Autobiography of Malcolm X* (New York: Ballantine Books, 1999), pp. 3–26.
3. Ibid., pp. 8–9.
4. Malcolm X and Haley, *The Autobiography of Malcolm X*, pp. 230–289; Peter Goldman, *The Death and Life of Malcolm X* (New York: Harper & Row, 1973), pp. 49–91; Bruce Perry, *Malcolm X*, (Barrytown, NY: Station Hill Press, 1992), pp. 160–166, 174–186; Peniel E. Joseph, *Waiting 'Til the Midnight Hour: A Narrative History of Black Power in America* (New York: Henry Holt, 2006); Taylor Branch, *Pillar of Fire: America in the King Years, 1963-1965* (New York: Simon and Schuster, 1998), p. 15.
5. See Goldman, *The Death and Life of Malcolm X* pp. 55–65; Benjamin Karim, *Remembering Malcolm* (New York: One World, 1992), pp. 45–46 and ed., *The End of World White Supremacy: Four Speeches By Malcolm X* (New York: Arcade Publishing, 1971), pp. 2–6, where he claims Malcolm conflated Johnson's name. In his autobiography Malcolm refers to him as "Brother Johnson Hinton." See Malcolm X and Haley, *The Autobiography of Malcolm X*, p. 257; Perry, *Malcolm X*, pp. 164–166, 437; FBIMX 100-399321 (Part 3), "Malcolm Little," April 30, 1958, p. 29.
6. Malcolm X and Haley, *The Autobiography of Malcolm X*, p. 255.
7. FBIMX 100-399321, (Part 3), "Malcolm Little," April 30, 1958, p. 79, quoting Malcolm X from *Pittsburgh Courier*, November 9, 1957; Johnson was awarded $70,000. Perry, *Malcolm X*, p. 166.
8. Malcolm X and Haley, *The Autobiography of Malcolm X*, p. 256.
9. See Timothy B. Tyson, *Radio Free Dixie: Robert F. Williams and the Roots of Black Power* (Chapel Hill: University of North Carolina Press, 1998); Lance Hill, *The Deacons for Defense: Armed Resistance and the Civil Rights Movement* (Chapel Hill: University of North Carolina Press, 2004); Christopher B. Strain, *Pure Fire: Self-Defense as Activism in the Civil Rights Era* (Athens: University of Georgia Press, 2005); Simon Wendt, "The Roots of Black Power?: Armed Resistance and the Radicalization of the Civil Rights Movement," in Peniel E. Joseph, (ed.), *The Black Power Movement: Rethinking the Civil Rights and Black Power Era* (New York: Routledge, 2006); Peniel E. Joseph, *Waiting 'Til the Midnight Hour: A Narrative History of Black Power in America* (New York: Henry Holt, 2006).

10. Robert Caro, *The Power Broker: Robert Moses and the Fall of New York* (New York: Vintage Books, 2000), p. 5.
11. Malcolm X and Haley, *The Autobiography of Malcolm X*, pp. 238–239.
12. Ibid., p. 240.
13. Ibid., p. 241.
14. Goldman, *The Death and Life of Malcolm X*, p. 88.
15. Rebeccah Welch, "Black Art and Activism in Postwar New York, 1950–1965," p. 2. Ph.D. diss., New York University, 2002.
16. Taylor Branch, *Parting the Waters: America in the King Years, 1954–1963* (New York: Touchstone, 1988), pp. 592–593.
17. FBIMX 100-399321 (Part 4), Memo, July 16, 1959, p. 1.
18. FBIMX 100-399321 (Part 4) Memo, July 21, 1959, pp. 1–20.
19. Louis Lomax, *To Kill a Black Man* (Los Angeles: Holloway House, 1968), pp. 65–76.
20. Joseph, *Waiting 'Til the Midnight Hour*, p. 123; Manning Marable, *Living Black History: How Reimagining the African-American Past Can Remake America's Racial Future* (New York: Basic Civitas, 2006), pp. 149–161.
21. Hakim Jamal, *From the Dead Level: Malcolm X and Me* (New York: Warner Books, 1973), pp. 188–189.
22. "brilliant" FBIMX (Part 5), "Malcolm Little," November 17, 1959, p. 45; Invitation to Abyssinian Baptist Church, FBIMX (Part 3) "Malcolm Little," April 30, 1958, pp. 74–75, citing *Los Angeles Herald Dispatch*, August 8, 1957; Karim, *End of World White Supremacy*, pp. 14–15; Goldman, *The Death and Life of Malcolm X*, p. 68; For competition between Malcolm and Powell, see Goldman, *The Death and Life of Malcolm X*, pp. 134–135; Perry, *Malcolm X*, pp. 302–304; and Branch, *Pillar of Fire*, p. 96.
23. FBIMX 100-399321 (Part 21) Sub A, *Pittsburgh Courier*, January 25, 1958 and *Los Angeles Herald Dispatch*, February 13, 1958. FBIMX 100-399321 (Part 4) Memo, July 2, 1958.
24. FBIMX 100-39321 (Part 4), Malcolm Little, October 17, 1958, pp. 1–4; November 19, 1958, pp. 9–10; Jamal, *From the Dead Level* pp. 94–122.
25. Brenda Gayle Plummer, *Rising Wind: Black Americans and U.S. Foreign Affairs, 1935–1960* (Chapel Hill: University of North Carolina Press, 1996); Penny Von Eschen, *Race against Empire: Black Americans and Anticolonialism, 1937–1957* (Ithaca, NY: Cornell University Press, 1997) and *Satchmo Blows Up the World: Jazz Ambassadors Play the Cold War* (Cambridge, MA: Harvard University Press, 2005); Mary Dudziak, *Cold War Civil Rights: Race and the Image of American Democracy* (Princeton, NJ: Princeton University Press, 2000); Thomas Borstelmann, *The Cold War and the Color Line: American Race Relations in the Global Arena* (Cambridge, MA: Harvard University Press, 2001); James H. Meriwether, *Proudly We Can Be Africans: Black Americans and Africa, 1935–1961* (Chapel Hill: University of North Carolina Press, 2002).
26. *Baltimore/Washington Afro-American*, March 9, 1957. Ghana's recruitment efforts rescued one exceptionally high-profile leader from political oblivion. W.E.B. Du Bois, two years before his death, expatriated to Ghana to start his proposed *Encyclopedia Africana* at Nkrumah's personal request. The long delayed project—it had been conceived of as the "Encyclopedia of the Negro"—was planned as a multivolume history that would trace the black presence on several continents and the Caribbean. Perpetually denied funding for this ambitious venture, Du Bois, at ninety-three, became a citizen of Ghana and embarked on his lifelong dream of completing the Encyclopedia. See David Levering Lewis, *W.E.B. Du Bois: The Fight for Equality and the American Century, 1919–1963* (New York: Henry Holt, 2000), pp. 389, 442–449.

27. *New York Amsterdam News*, December 28, 1957, pp. 1, 3.
28. *New York Amsterdam News*, August 2, 1958, p. 1; *Baltimore Washington Afro-American*, August 2, 1958.
29. Kevin Gaines, "African-American Expatriates in Ghana and the Black Radical Tradition," *Souls*, 1, no. 4 (Fall 1999): 64–71;" Revisiting Richard Wright in Ghana: Black Radicalism and the Dialectics of Diaspora," *Social Text* 67, 19, no. 2 (Summer 2001), 75–101.
30. Tyson, *Radio Free Dixie*, pp. 146–148.
31. Historian Komozi Woodard argues that Paul Robeson's elaboration on W.E.B. Du Bois' notion of black culture inspired future Black Arts and Black Power activists, most notably the young LeRoi Jones. See Komozi Woodard, "Amiri Baraka, the Congress of African People and Black Power Politics: From the 1961 United Nations Protest to the 1972 Gary Convention," in Peniel E. Joseph, (ed.), *The Black Power Movement: Rethinking the Civil Right and Black Power Eras* (New York: Routledge, 2006).
32. Of course Black Power nationalists were among *A Raisin in the Sun's* and Hansberry's most vociferous critics. Harold Cruse's dismissive analysis of Hansberry in his 1967 classic, *The Crisis of the Negro Intellectual*, served as a capstone to a discourse imposed by cold war liberals who defined the play and Hansberry's politics on their own terms and set the stage for a hopelessly distorted debate. See Ben Keppel, *The Work of Democracy: Ralph Bunche, Kenneth B. Clark, Lorraine Hansberry, and the Cultural Politics of Race* (Cambridge: Harvard University Press, 1995) pp. 177–214 and 227–229. Over twenty-five years later, former critics, including Amiri Baraka would issue reevaluations, declaring the play to be on "the cutting edge" of the black movement's "class and ideological struggles." See Robert Nemiroff, "Introduction," to Lorraine Hansberry, *A Raisin in the Sun* (New York: Modern Library Edition, 1995), p. xx.
33. Joseph, *Waiting 'Til the Midnight Hour*, pp. 26–28.
34. Marable, *Living Black History* p. 153; FBIMX 100-399321 (Part 21), *Pittsburgh Courier*, August 15, 1959.
35. *Muhammad Speaks* also generated significant amounts of income. Members hawked copies on urban street corners in an effort to meet demanding sales quotas. Desperately competitive, bowtie-wearing Muslim entrepreneurs sank or swam based on the number of papers they sold every week, which they had to pay for in advance, in bundles of fifty newspapers; Black Muslims earned or lost income in accordance with the Messenger's frugally tough discipline that denied them credit. High sales figures were rewarded with fleeting fame in the pages of *Muhammad Speaks* while slackers were verbally chided and at times beaten by Muslim enforcers. For hundreds of thousands of readers unaware of the pressures to meet sales quotas or the punishments doled out to those who didn't, *Muhammad Speaks* offered detailed coverage of the era's unfolding events by employing a skillful group of journalists, including many unaffiliated with the Nation. The paper's coverage of Africa was particularly informative, offering insight into revolutionary movements breaking out all over the continent. Perry, *Malcolm X*, pp. 220–221; Branch, *Pillar of Fire*, p. 260; Karim, *Remembering Malcolm*, pp. 153–154. See also, Von Eschen, *Race against Empire*, pp. 173–174; James Edward Smethurst, *The Black Arts Movement: Literary Nationalism in the 1960s and 1970s* (Chapel Hill: University of North Carolina Press, 2005), pp. 181–183.
36. *New York Times*, September 20, 1960, p. 1.
37. Maya Angelou, *The Heart of a Woman* (New York: Bantam Books, 1997), p. 111.

38. Mealy, *Fidel and Malcolm X: Memories of a Meeting* (Melbourne, Australia: Ocean Press, 1993), p. 42.
39. Ibid., pp. 43–44.
40. FBIMX 100-399321 (Part 6), "Malcolm K. Little," November 17, 1960, p. 20.
41. Van Gosse, *Where the Boys Are: Cuba, Cold War America and the Making of a New Left* (London: Verso, 1993), p. 151.
42. *New York Times*, September 20, 1960, p. 16; September 21, 1960, p. 17.
43. William Worthy, "Writer sees no need to stay out of Cuba," *The Baltimore-Washington Afro-American*, October 8, 1960, p. 1.
44. *The Baltimore-Washington Afro-American*, October 1, 1960, pp. 1, 9; *New York Amsterdam News*, October 1, 1960, p. 35; Worthy, "Writer sees no need to stay out of Cuba," p. 1.
45. Dudziak, *Cold War Civil Rights*.
46. John Henrik Clarke, "The New Afro-American Nationalism," *Freedomways*, 1, no. 3 (Fall 1961): 285–295.
47. *New York Amsterdam News*, (Brooklyn Edition) August 13, 1960, p. 19; August 27, 1960, p. 19.
48. *New York Amsterdam News*, August 6, 1960, p. 4; September 17, pp. 1, 11; October 22, 1960, pp. 1, 35.
49. Angelou, *The Heart of a Woman*, pp. 169–180.
50. Plummer, *Rising Wind*, p. 282.
51. Calvin Hicks, "African-American Literary and Political Movements, 1960's, on New York's Lower East Side," *A Lower East Side Retrospective*, pp. 1–2
52. Joseph, *Waiting 'Til the Midnight Hour*, p. 42.
53. Ibid., p. 43.
54. Lorraine Hansberry, "Congolese Patriot," *New York Times Magazine*, March 26, 1961, p. 4.
55. David Gallen, *Malcolm X As They Knew Him* (Caroll & Graf Publishers, 1992), pp. 31–32.
56. FBIMX 100-399321 (Part 8), Memo, May 13, 1963, pp. 1–2.
57. FBIMX 100-399321 (Part 9), Airtel, May 15, 1963, p. 1; Perry, *Malcolm X*, p. 210.
58. Perry, *Malcolm X*, p. 212.
59. Goldman, *The Death and Life of Malcolm X*, pp. 107–113; Branch, *Pillar of Fire*, pp. 13–20; Perry, *Malcolm X*, pp. 217–225; Malcolm X and Haley, *The Autobiography of Malcolm X*, pp. 318–328.
60. Branch, *Pillar of Fire*, pp. 16–20.
61. Joseph, *Waiting 'Til the Midnight Hour*, pp. 102–103.

2

"Get Up Off of Your Knees!": Competing Visions of Black Empowerment in Milwaukee during the Early Civil Rights Era

Patrick D. Jones

Sunday, February 2, 1958, was a typically wintry day in Milwaukee.[1] Snow covered the ground and temperatures dipped below zero as people went about their business. At about 8:30 p.m. Thomas Grady and Louis Krause, two white uniformed motorcycle patrolmen, stood at the corner of Wright Street and 7th Street, in the heart of Milwaukee's segregated black community, smoking and talking. Grady told Krause he was headed to a string of vacant homes to "arrest some niggers" in order to beef up his arrest rate.[2] As they spoke, Daniel Bell, a twenty-two-year-old African American migrant originally from rural Louisiana, passed through the intersection on his way home. Grady noticed one of the taillights on Bell's car was dark and gave pursuit. Bell pulled to the curb, jumped out of his car and ran. Grady and Krause followed on foot, shouting "Halt!" and firing several warning shots into the air. Unable to catch up with Bell, Krause commandeered a passing car, picked up Grady and continued the chase. The driver stopped just ahead of Bell and the patrolmen scrambled out of the car with guns drawn. Hoping to shake off his pursuers, Bell hopped a snow bank and darted between two homes. Grady, sprinting ahead of Krause, mounted the snow heap while shouting for Bell to stop running. As he closed in on the young man from behind, patrolman Grady extended his right arm and, with the tip of the muzzle touching the fabric of Bell's jacket, fired a single shot into his back. The bullet traveled upward, broke Daniel Bell's neck and entered his head. Grady stopped, holstered his firearm, took off his gloves, and felt Bell's outstretched wrist for a pulse. "I think he's dead," he calmly informed his partner. Krause removed his glove, felt Bell's jugular vein and agreed. Grady then sloughed it off, "He's just a damn nigger kid anyhow."[3]

What happened next compounded the initial tragedy of Bell's death with the injustice of a cover-up. Krause walked to a nearby house where he called the district station to report the incident. Back at the scene, Grady removed a small pocketknife from his jacket and placed it in Bell's right hand. After his return, Krause warned Grady that the blade was too small, so Grady closed the knife, returned it to his coat, and produced a larger one, again laying it in Bell's right hand. The two patrolmen then "dealt with the story they would tell people in charge, officials, on what happened." Police officers and detectives soon arrived and went about the business of documenting what they found at the scene.[4]

According to the story the two officers concocted, Bell fled his vehicle, knife in hand, yelling the curiously self-incriminating, "You won't catch me, I'm a hold-up man!" Grady said that he believed Bell fit the description of a man listed on a recent police bulletin for a string of armed robberies and that he had thus shot him as a "fleeing felon," a critical distinction that, if true, justified the use of deadly force. Later, Grady claimed Bell had lunged at him with the knife in a menacing manner. These fictions, repeated and amplified in police reports, press conferences, and news stories over the next several days, became the official version of events.[5]

For most white Milwaukeeans, there was no immediate reason to question the initial accounts of Daniel Bell's death. Milwaukee's crime rate, while rising, had historically stood well below that of other comparable American cities. Its police department had received national recognition for effectively ensuring a safe, livable environment, ideally suited for families. White news editors, politicians, business leaders, judges, clergy, parents, and citizens often marshaled these facts with pride as evidence of Milwaukee's civic virtue. Yet, at the same time, over the course of the 1950s, a growing number of white residents began to voice unease over the rapid influx of African American migrants to the city and the attendant stress they believed the newcomers placed on housing, employment, city services, and crime rates. Newspaper stories about crime in the inner core were commonplace and sometimes sensational. Many white Milwaukeeans reading about the incident probably accepted the implicit link in the news accounts between race, crime, and Daniel Bell's death that night.

But almost immediately, Daniel's brothers and sister questioned the circumstances surrounding his death. Newspaper accounts emphasized Daniel's criminal record, but according to his sister Sylvia, he was "a really good child... [not] a wild boy, or a drunken boy. He had lots of friends, black and white. He let things roll off his back." Television reports claimed Daniel had a knife, yet he left his own pocket-knife at home on the bathroom sink. And, perhaps the biggest inconsistency to emerge from those early reports was Grady's claim that Daniel attacked him with his right hand; in fact, he was left-handed. The Bells offered a much simpler explanation for Daniel's decision to run from officers Grady and Krause, one that did not trade on deep-seated stereotypes of black male criminality. They explained that none of the Bell brothers could read or write well, a legacy of Jim Crow schools in the South and substandard inner-city schools in Milwaukee. This made it difficult to ride the bus, fill out job applications, and read newspapers or unfamiliar place names. It also precluded the Bell brothers from getting driver's licenses in Wisconsin because the state required a written exam as well as a road test. Even though the Bell brothers could all handle a vehicle safely, they could not pass the written portion of the test. As a result, they had received several citations from the Milwaukee police for driving without a license. In fact, most of Daniel Bell's criminal record consisted of citations for this offense. Bell's brothers and sister believed the situation was clear: Daniel ran to avoid another ticket, hardly an offense that warranted lethal force. Yet, when the family raised these issues at the police station the night of the murder, the exchange degenerated into a shouting match. Frustrated and angry, one of the Bell brothers was heard to ask, "Oh, you think it's open season, like on rabbits? We are going to start shooting a few of you cops." The sergeant on duty allegedly responded, "You can't tell you niggers nothing. Get out of here or I will throw you in jail."[6]

Internally, too, the case was falling apart. Serious discrepancies in the physical evidence at the scene and inconsistencies in the officers' own accounts emerged, calling into question the veracity of their claims. Two African American witnesses came forth who challenged the officers' story and none of the victims of recent inner-city robberies identified Daniel as the perpetrator. Even so, the white district attorney and an all-white inquest panel cleared patrolman Grady of wrongdoing, stating that he "had justifiably shot and killed" Daniel Bell in "the reasonable execution of his duty as an officer making a lawful arrest, and in self-defense." The inquest verdict was a devastating personal blow to the Bell family and a public outrage to many in the black community who had learned through experience that the "official story" was rarely the whole truth. To them, the case symbolized the increasingly desperate plight of African Americans in the city, particularly the migrant working class, and underscored the low value white officials often placed on black life.[7]

The Bell murder case played a catalytic role in the early history of protest politics in Milwaukee during the movement era. The case spurred the first, fitful attempts to organize a community response to the growing frustrations of local black residents, entangled in the complex web of urban racial inequality. Those efforts highlight both the possibilities and limitations of a more aggressive, grassroots approach to racial change during the late 1950s and early 1960s. In addition, these early campaigns afford an opportunity to explore the competing visions of black leadership and community empowerment in one northern city at that time. In the process, this research opens a small window to the roots and contested meanings of Black Power politics.

Brewing Racial Pressures in a Rapidly Changing City

Before World War II, the black community in Milwaukee was small and severely circumscribed, but after the war, the city's racial dynamics changed dramatically. The need for labor in Milwaukee, a major site in the U.S. "Arsenal for Democracy," combined with pressure from the Federal Employment Practices

Commission (FEPC) finally opened up the industrial segment of the economy to African Americans in the late 1940s and early 1950s, even though overall advancement was slow and black workers continued to suffer from widespread hiring discrimination, union restrictions, and unequal wages and benefits.[8] The increased economic might of the city attracted thousands of African Americans, poor Appalachian whites, and displaced rural workers. Following an ebb in black migration during the Depression era, 13,000 African Americans relocated to Milwaukee in the 1940s, an increase of 146 percent. The following decade, the black population again nearly quadrupled to 62,458 and by 1970 105,088 African Americans lived in Milwaukee, a startling increase from the pre-war period. In 1960, African Americans made up roughly 8.5 percent of Milwaukee's total population and topped 10 percent by 1965. Altogether, the black community grew over 700 percent in twenty-five years, rising from less than 2 percent of the population in 1945 to nearly 15 percent in 1970. The majority of these new migrants were under the age of 30. Comparatively high birth rates throughout the postwar period assured a disproportionately young and poor African American population. Tensions were perhaps inevitable in Milwaukee given this dramatic rise in the black population, but white Milwaukee, with its ethnic pride, moral traditionalism, and tendency toward xenophobia, was particularly unprepared to handle this large and rapid influx.[9]

Earlier in the century, a combination of restrictive housing covenants, discriminatory real estate and loan practices, and overt racism established an identifiable 35-block "black district" on the city's near North Side, referred to variously as "Little Africa," "Bronzeville," and in the post-World War II period, "the inner core." By the eve of World War II, the inner core had expanded to a 75-block area that housed more than 90 percent of the city's African American population. The steep rise in black population during the postwar era intensified racial segregation and fueled the further deterioration of housing, health and urban education. The most immediate problem was overcrowding in an already severely stressed housing market. While white homeowners, realtors, banks, and government officials continued to conspire against African American renters and homeowners to maintain strict racial boundaries, the inner core steadily pushed north and west from its original location. Neighborhoods on the frontiers of this expansion changed rapidly as more affluent whites abandoned them for the suburbs. By 1960, the inner core claimed a space six times larger than the square mile it occupied in 1950. Inside that area, greater than 75 percent of the black population lived on blocks that were more than one-half non-white. In effect, the level of segregation in Milwaukee equaled Birmingham, Atlanta, and other southern cities.[10]

The inner core showed numerous and growing signs of stress and strain throughout this period. Though the urban crisis had been developing for many decades, the rapid influx of African American migrants after World War II overwhelmed Milwaukee's black community and accelerated urban decay. Unemployment and chronic underemployment led to increased poverty and rising crime rates. The glacial pace with which new economic opportunity opened for black residents could not keep up with the sheer volume of young new migrants looking for work. African American young adults faced a particularly rough labor market and disproportionately high unemployment rates. Each year, community leaders looked for new ways to battle chronic youth unemployment during the summer months. Housing conditions continued to be grossly substandard, overcrowding being just one of several problems. The inner core's aging structures and a general lack of resources for needed improvements caused entire neighborhoods to decay. Often, what had been a "respectable neighborhood" was slowly replaced by blight. Poor African Americans could afford only the worst housing, while whites consistently thwarted the efforts of middle-class black people to find higher-quality housing inside and outside the core. Many white residents, unaware of the structural bases of poverty and racial inequality, joked that so many inner-core houses were becoming decrepit in the 1950s that there was going to be a shortage of blacks to live in them. With high unemployment and poverty rates on top of poor housing conditions, social problems in the inner core became rampant. And, because Milwaukee's African American community had been historically very small, it had not developed institutions capable of successfully dealing with explosive growth and its attendant challenges. As a result, economic, social, and spiritual decay spread quickly; crime rates and drug use escalated; the presence of police grew; and confrontation simmered. The construction of a highway system between 1960 and 1967 exacerbated these trends by cutting a swath through the heart of the black community, displacing more than 7,000 African American residents.[11]

Social life in Milwaukee was also historically segregated well into the postwar period. While a vibrant black community thrived along Walnut Street—including restaurants, nightclubs, theaters, offices, and stores—African Americans faced blatant forms of discrimination in many restaurants, theaters, health services, recreational facilities, and hotels outside the segregated ghetto. Many businesses used harassment, refusal of service, poor service, and overcharging as mechanisms to discourage black patronage. Interracial couples claimed to face frequent harassment and discrimination. Racial bias could be detected at insurance companies, banks, real estate agencies, public utilities, social welfare organizations, and in law enforcement. Newspapers regularly included stereotyped reporting on African Americans that both mirrored and reaffirmed discriminatory treatment of black people. Even so, black Milwaukeeans worked hard to create a livable community within the walls of segregation through churches, social clubs, literary societies, black-owned businesses, self-help and racial uplift organizations, and newspapers.[12]

One of the by-products of segregation was the rise of a small black middle class. Largely dependent on the African American working class for their livelihoods and caught in a mutual struggle against racial inequality, the black middle class frequently attempted to simultaneously defend the community, as a whole, while distancing themselves from the poor. For instance, when Columbia Savings and Loan, a black-owned bank, aided middle-class blacks to move to transitional neighborhoods along the edge of the expanding inner core, it also helped create a distinct middle-class district apart from working-class members of the community. Similarly, when African American residents went to church on Sunday, they often chose between distinctly working-class and middle-class houses of worship. And, when racial crisis emerged, these leaders were often quick to draw distinctions between their own behavior and that of the rougher, less-polished, migrant working class.

Politically, the growth of Milwaukee's black population and its concentration in a small geographic area held the promise of greater political power as had been the case in other northern cities.[13] By the 1950s, Milwaukee's Tenth and Twelfth wards, which covered large areas of the inner core, had become known as "Negro districts." In 1946, LeRoy Simmons, an African American Democrat, won a state Assembly seat representing the Sixth District and ultimately served four terms. The district quickly became a "safe" seat for both Democrats and African Americans, with Isaac Coggs and later Lloyd Barbee succeeding Simmons as the only African American in the state legislature. Coggs served six terms in the state Assembly and later moved on to the county board. Barbee spearheaded the school desegregation campaign in Milwaukee before entering the legislature in 1964. But election to the city's Common Council and County Board proved much more difficult than capturing one seat in the state Assembly. In 1956, Vel Phillips became the first African American and the first woman to sit on the Common Council, but it took twelve more years before another African American joined her. Voter registration rates remained chronically low among Milwaukee African Americans and black electoral power in the city and state continued to lag well into the 1960s and beyond despite rising population figures. Without a well-organized and mobilized black electoral presence, African American candidates faced significant obstacles to political power. At the same time, white elected officials could feel secure that no political cost would result from neglecting African American concerns and inner-core problems.[14]

Leadership dynamics in the black community did not change much from the prewar era. A small group of middle-class African American professionals continued to speak for the community and curry favor from prominent whites. The National Association for the Advancement of Colored People (NAACP) and Urban League still preferred quiet negotiation, mild political pressure, and acculturation programs for new migrants. This relative political powerlessness was compounded by the fact that black businessmen did not command enough resources to bargain from a position of strength with other economic players, nor did African American workers occupy any significant positions within the powerful local labor movement. But as the new national civil rights consciousness emerged during the mid and late 1950s, the clamor for change, particularly among young people—the working class and new migrants—grew. Internal fissures emerged between old and young, middle class and working class, new migrants and those who had been born in Milwaukee, and between those who thought change was coming at a sufficient pace and those who thought the tempo should quicken. Frustration with the slow rate of racial change gave rise to calls for new leadership, new tactics, and new strategies. The circumstances were increasingly ripe for the emergence of a more aggressive style of black leadership in Milwaukee.

Organizing Community Protest after the Murder of Daniel Bell

The Daniel Bell case was but one, albeit the most tragic, in an increasingly contentious string of incidents between inner-core residents and the Milwaukee
police during the second half of the 1950s. The local media's coverage of most
of these events was sensationalized, ignoring the pervasive racial discrimination and structural inequalities at the root of black frustration and, instead,
heightening white fear of black crime by reinforcing stereotypes about African
American criminality. In 1955, the *Milwaukee Journal* reported that a "mob" of
angry residents attacked white police officers when they arrested a young black
woman. But, according to several prominent members of the NAACP, the group
was attempting to "rescue" the woman from what they perceived to be an unjust
detention. The following summer, the arrest of a young black man incited more
than 400 African American teens to surround two policemen and pelt their
car with stones. Again, media coverage focused on the plight of the two white
officers, portraying local black residents as irrational and menacing, while an
African American minister at the scene described the incident as an example of
police misconduct. And in 1957, following an inner-core crime wave that included
attacks on four white women, overheated media reports of a "gang of Negro rap-
ists" prompted a police dragnet that resulted in the indiscriminate arrest of more
than 260 black men—both middle-class and poor, new migrants and old—and
"pitched an otherwise calm community into turmoil." The incident, which may
have reminded many black migrants of southern lynch law, made clear that most
white Milwaukeeans did not make subtle distinctions of class or status in their
judgments of black people. The cumulative result of these incidents, combined
with persistent inequality and distorted mainstream media coverage, fueled
growing racial tensions throughout the community.[15]

Following the inquest verdict in the Bell case and fruitless negotiations between
the Milwaukee NAACP and police officials, an array of local leaders and black
residents attempted to mobilize a community response; it was the first notable
attempt to do so since the 1941 March on Washington movement. This unified
organizing effort quickly fragmented after an initial mass meeting attracted
450 people. One group formed around the faith-based leadership of Rev. T.T.
Lovelace, pastor of Mt. Zion Church, the largest middle-class black church in
the city. Lovelace had initially called Bell's fatal shooting a "dastardly attack"
and stated that "something should be done...not just as a matter of vengeance,
but justice." But, he quickly reneged laying the bulk of the blame for police-
community conflict on unruly African American migrants, not on systematic
discrimination or individual racism. Lovelace exhorted his followers to "improve
the general behavior of the Negro community" through an "ounce of prevention"
and a healthier respect for law and order. He claimed that black migrants "created in the general populous disgust, shame and fear" and encouraged all black
Milwaukeeans to "quit rioting among ourselves" and "stop slashing each other to
pieces." At a February 25 meeting, an estimated 300 inner-core residents—most
reportedly members of Mt. Zion—agreed to establish the "Institute for Social
Adjustment" to deal with problems facing African Americans in Milwaukee.

According to Rev. Lovelace, the institute would help rehabilitate black people who had violated the law; orient rural and immigrant blacks to the "standards and customs" of a large city; try to get at least 5,000 African Americans to join so that the group could make an impact on local politics; and form a "tavern committee" to deal with black people who became "problem cases" while drinking. In addition, the group drafted a resolution, which they sent to the Milwaukee Police, that suggested that any officer who took the life of a person in a "questionable shooting" should receive a reprimand not less than a form of suspension. Rev. Lovelace unexpectedly passed away from a heart attack on April 14, 1958. With his death, the Institute for Social Adjustment fizzled out, although the vision of black empowerment he espoused continued to play a significant role in community politics, particularly among older residents and some members of the black middle class.[16]

Several moderate black leaders, along with a few liberal white political figures, spoke out through the Lapham-Garfield Neighborhood Council. In 1957, representatives of 62 local civic, fraternal, social, and religious organizations, representing a collective membership of over 5,000, founded an umbrella organization as an outgrowth of concern over the mass arrest of African American men during the North Side crime wave that year. Grant and Lucinda Gordon, mainstays of Milwaukee's black establishment, headed the council. At the group's first public gathering on February 28, 1958, Grant Gordon cited Bell's death as an impetus to action. "If there had been more understanding and trust between our community and the community at large," he said, "Daniel Bell would be alive today." Gordon added, "We cannot bring Daniel Bell back to life, but we can improve our relationships so that this type of incident will not happen again." He called for increased educational, recreational, and employment opportunities for Milwaukee's black population and said the group would work with sympathetic white leaders to develop more adult leadership to work with youth in the area, secure better housing, and obtain representation in city governmental bodies. Mayor Frank Zeidler, a Socialist, also spoke at the gathering and urged greater "mutual trust" as the foundation for improved race relations in the city.[17]

Elsewhere, a group of activists and working-class residents joined together around the leadership of Assemblyman Coggs, Rev. R. L. Lathan, pastor at New Hope Baptist Church, and Calvin Sherard, a local metal finisher at American Motors Company and the founder of The Citizen Committee to Protest the Case of Daniel Bell. At the initial mass meeting, Coggs and Attorney George Brawley suggested that the best way to address their grievances was at the ballot box. "We talk about the poor Negro in the South who doesn't have the opportunity to vote," Brawley said. "What about the poor Negroes in the North? Do you get out and vote when the opportunity comes? If you don't vote to protect yourselves, you have no right to attend this protest meeting or any other meeting to protest anything." Sherard passionately argued that Milwaukee police had shown a consistent pattern of prejudice enforcing the law and flatly encouraged a march or demonstration.

On March 17, 1958, Rev. Lathan publicly announced plans for a "prayer protest" the following Sunday at MacArthur Square in front of the courthouse.

Participants were to meet in the afternoon and then march a short distance to the square to pray for "justice and the good of all mankind." Organizers optimistically hoped to attract 2,000–3,000 community members to the event and stressed that the "pilgrimage" was not restricted to African Americans, but rather was open to "anyone who believes in justice." Assemblyman Coggs endorsed the "prayer protest," stating, "There is no difference between shooting Dan Bell in the back than killing Emmett Till in Mississippi." Following a burst of applause, he added, "and there wasn't much difference in the picking of the [inquest] jury either." "Hats off to Ike Coggs for not pussyfooting," one local resident wrote in a letter to the *Defender.* "Almost everyone is saying it was 'down right murder.'"[18]

The New Hope contingent's proposed "prayer protest" alarmed traditional black leaders who felt uncomfortable with the group's strident rhetoric, confrontational style, appeal to the large working class, migrant population, and overall challenge to their status in the community. Vel Phillips voiced this middle-class unease when she cryptically warned that "lawless elements" might infiltrate a protest march, a claim repeated by a number of African American leaders. Three prominent black ministers paid Rev. Lathan a private visit in an attempt to dissuade him from going forward with the demonstration. The ministers urged Lathan to preserve the dignity of the clergy by confining prayer to its "proper place" within a church and again warned that there might be unfavorable repercussions if a crowd of poor and working-class migrants could not be handled. Following the meeting, Lathan relented and called off the march "in the best interest of both Negroes and Whites" because he feared they might be "smeared" as subversive if they went ahead with the planned protest. Later that spring, after the emotional response and the energy generated by the Bell shooting had died down, Sherard and Lathan held another public meeting at New Hope, featuring Rev. Fred Shuttlesworth—a Birmingham civil rights minister, charter member of the Southern Christian Leadership Conference, and Rev. Lathan's cousin. Shuttlesworth encouraged the crowd to continue their push for racial justice in the urban north and led a group of 50–75 people, including Daniel Bell's sister Sylvia, on a short protest march down Walnut Street.[19]

A new round of after-hours clashes in 1959 again focused public attention on the inner core and the need to develop more effective means to cope with the struggles and stresses of Milwaukeeans living in that area. In response, Mayor Zeidler appointed a committee to study and make recommendations on the "social problems" of the inner core. At the initial meeting, Zeidler told community leaders that he had "long felt that the problems in the core of the city are growing and need faster and greater action than the community has given them." More than 100 public officials, community leaders, specialists, and authorities worked together on the report. On April 15, 1960, the mayor's "Study Committee on the Social Problems in the Inner Core Area of the City" issued its findings, complete with fifty-nine recommendations. The Zeidler Report, as it came to be known, represented the largest official study of the city's African American community in Milwaukee's history and indicated a greater awareness of the area than had previously been acknowledged by the white power structure.[20]

The Zeidler Report relied on statistical data culled mainly from city agencies to make its analysis and mirrored the dominant social scientific thinking of the day. Historian William Thompson has pointed out that the report emphasized the physical and family bases of the core's problems, implying that the root causes "emanated from the Core alone and could be dealt with by measures limited to the Core." It failed to seriously address much more nettlesome external causes, such as white supremacy and institutional discrimination. Instead, the Zeidler Report argued, "Physical rebuilding of the area and acculturation of many of its citizens are the key problems." The authors urged city leaders to inaugurate, in addition to brick and mortar projects, a variety of programs to assist African American migrants make the transition to urban life. In this way, the Zeidler Report embraced the immigration model of ethnic succession put forth the previous year by Harvard historian Oscar Handlin. Handlin argued that African American and Puerto Rican migrants to large northern cities, like previous waves of European immigrants, would ultimately adjust to the demands of urban living and escape the ghetto. As Jack Dougherty has pointed out, though, Handlin's analysis "did not fully consider the powerful economic and political forces that contained black Milwaukeeans within the inner city; it simply sought to adjust the migrants to them."[21]

On issues that black people considered most pressing, the Zeidler Report offered only vague and cautious recommendations. For instance, on education, the committee asserted, "there is adequate educational opportunity available to the residents of the core area. But there is a need to increase the motivation of individuals to avail themselves of the existing opportunity." The report remained silent on the pattern of segregation in Milwaukee's public schools. On employment, the report put forth a statement about ending discrimination that was vague and provided no details about how that might be achieved. Instead, the authors emphasized job training, education, and part-time summer employment for high school students as the primary remedies for the economic struggles of black residents. Finally, on housing, although the report did implicitly acknowledge racial discrimination in real estate and lending practices, it failed to call for an open housing ordinance. The authors proposed, as an alternative, the "Covenant of Open Occupancy," a voluntary agreement by property owners prohibiting racial discrimination in the renting or selling of housing, as well as in panic selling.[22]

Almost as soon as Zeidler received the report, his tenure in office ended. His successor, Henry Maier, inherited the problems of the inner core, but showed little inclination to aggressively attack them. A pro-business, pro-growth Democrat in the Kennedy mold, Maier had spent the previous decade in the state senate. Later, while under fire for his handling of race relations in Milwaukee during the late 1960s, Maier would claim that he had been a leader in civil rights during his days in the senate. Early in his mayoralty, however, he showed little interest in African Americans or in the city's pervasive racial inequality.[23]

A savvy politician and rising star within the ranks of Democratic mayors, Maier may have ignored issues of race in Milwaukee because of politics. African Americans did not make up a significant proportion of the new mayor's base. In fact, although Maier easily defeated Congressman Henry Reuss in the 1960 election, those wards with the largest number of black voters gave him the weakest support. Given the widespread racial prejudice and stereotyped thinking among white Milwaukeeans, it stands to reason that the new mayor might not have been willing to aggressively address the needs of African Americans for fear of alienating key components of his electoral coalition.[24]

If the Bell case and its aftermath alerted Milwaukee to the crisis of the inner core, it also revealed the limits of direct action in Milwaukee during the late 1950s. Those advocating more forceful and aggressive action to achieve racial justice in the city remained a relatively small group. Organizing efforts following the inquest verdict brought to light not only the shallow pool of popular support for direct action, but also the serious divisions among new and old black leaders over the best way to achieve black empowerment. The immigration-acculturation model, so prevalent among whites, also continued to be popular among the traditional African American leadership class. If the Zeidler Report reflected a myopic complacency, and if the new mayor was no firebrand for racial reform, they mirrored much of Milwaukee. While most black Milwaukeeans readily acknowledged the presence of racial problems in the city, many continued to hold fast to the hopeful idea that steady progress through negotiation and accommodation was preferable to confrontation and demand. All of that, however, would begin to change in the early 1960s.

Calvin Sherard and the Politics of Economic Protest

Out of the fractious organizing campaign that followed the coroner's inquest in the Bell case, a small group of African American industrial workers coalesced around the leadership of Calvin Sherard. Born in Atlanta, Georgia, Sherard—the son of a Baptist minister—found inspiration in A. Philip Randolph, the political activist, labor and civil rights leader. "It was his fight for jobs and economics," Sherard remembered. "I felt that that was the foundation [for racial equality], jobs and economics." Following high school graduation, Sherard moved to Cleveland, Ohio, to live with his brother. There, he got "a good job" with American Motors and became active in the labor movement. After a stint in the military during the mid-1950s, Sherard, attracted by the strong industrial economy and vigorous labor movement, settled in Milwaukee.[25]

The old guard's halting, and ultimately failed, efforts to organize a response to the Bell shooting frustrated Sherard and his supporters. Tom Jacobson, a white lawyer who represented Sherard and his organizations during the early 1960s, recalled, "Sherard had some guys and they wanted to go down in flames [after the Bell incident]. They were totally upset by the way blacks were deserting and selling out to whites and undercutting them." Jacobson claimed that the group was particularly embittered that prominent black ministers talked what they called "Negro talk," placing the emphasis on "cleaning ourselves up instead of going out and demonstrating." According to Sherard, "There was no [African American] leadership. When an issue came up where there should've been a response from the Afro-American community, there was no response." He and about a dozen of his coworkers set about creating a new organization, the Crusaders Civic and Social League, to focus on employment discrimination and police-community relations. Although the organization accepted white members, positions of power were reserved for African Americans.[26]

The Crusaders believed that expanded black business ownership and increased African American employment in white-owned businesses were the keys to black success in Milwaukee. They noted that most businesses operating in the inner core were white owned and rarely employed black workers. The Crusaders argued that all businesses located in the core ought to hire from within the local community. By employing African Americans in proportion to the amount of business the store did with black clients, companies would be putting resources back into the community from which they drew the bulk of their profits. The members of the Crusaders, rooted in their labor experience, were convinced that public boycotts and organized picketing were the best strategies to compel previously unmoved white business owners to hire more black workers. In this, they joined a long tradition of "Don't Buy Where You Can't Work" campaigns throughout the urban north stretching back to the Depression era.[27]

Sherard and his men first targeted a popular ice cream parlor on North Avenue, in the heart of the black community. About a dozen Crusaders, fortified by a group of local migrant, working-class churchgoers, picketed outside the store. The nervous owner quickly relented and agreed to hire more African Americans, a small but satisfying initial victory. In May 1960, the group organized sympathy pickets outside Milwaukee Woolworth stores to support the southern student sit-in movement. That same year, Sherard began negotiations with A&P, the inner core's largest national grocery chain, to increase African American employment at three North Side stores.[28]

The Crusaders also continued to fight against police brutality and the unjust treatment of black people by the legal system. In July 1960, three African American sisters appeared before Judge Frank Gregorski after a late-night disturbance. When one of the sisters testified about police brutality, Gregorski interrupted to cast aspersions on her claims. As he did, laughter erupted in the gallery. Gregorski exploded and ordered the bailiff to bring "all the dark people" before the bench, where he promptly fined ten black spectators $100 each for contempt of court, whether they had laughed or not. Once again, a white official had made all "dark people" pay the consequences for the behavior of a few individuals. The Crusaders supported a Milwaukee NAACP media campaign against the judge and led picketers outside his office.[29]

That fall, a confrontation between Milwaukee police and more than 1,100 black youth outside a rock-n-roll concert degenerated into what the *Milwaukee Journal* called "a wild 40 minute fracas." In the end, a hail of rocks and bottles injured five officers and resulted in the arrest of seventeen black youths. Typically, conflicting stories emerged. Police claimed the altercation began when Joseph Baker, a twenty-two-year-old African American man, cursed the police, struck an officer, and then asked the crowd for help. Alvin Moorer, one of the young men arrested that night, disagreed stating, "Police just cut loose and started beating on us." Robert Brill, the theater manager, blamed "all those Milwaukee policemen lined up in front of the theater." The Crusaders organized a mass meeting the night after the incident where three of the arrested African American youths shared their experiences. But, as with the Bell case, Sherard and his men were unable to attract the support of traditional black leaders or mobilize a large number of inner-core residents to the cause, despite widespread frustration at police brutality. In the end, the three men, along with one white youth, received sentences of up to two years in jail. No action was taken against any of the white officers involved.[30]

Frustrated by what appeared to be a pattern of inaction, the Crusaders called another public meeting at Rev. Lathan's New Hope Baptist Church one month later to protest police brutality and to criticize traditional African American leaders. An estimated 200 local people sat inside while a small group of picketers stood outside holding signs that read "Commie Plot to Discredit Police Dept.," "Pro-Communist Meeting," "The Reds Want to Create Race Hatred," and "Calvin Sherard Go Back to New York City."[31] Ali Anwar, the Crusaders' field secretary, told the gathering, "In a crisis you can't find [traditional black leaders] anywhere" and asked, "What are they doing for you?" Sherard slammed police brutality and attacked black civic groups as "nothing but social clubs." He said African American leaders used their "intellect to keep the lower Negro classes in hand" and encouraged community members to "Get up off your knees!" "There's a time for praying and a time not to pray," he explained. "These folks out here are hurting us. Let's go march!" Sherard's call for a new organization in Milwaukee to hear African American complaints of injustice met with enthusiastic applause. The local NAACP, American Civil Liberties Union, and Human Rights Commission, all dominated by more cautious, established leadership, rejected the Crusaders' charges, attacking the group as "irresponsible" and "precipitous."[32] But behind the scenes, some NAACP leaders recognized the growing gap between the organization and the working-class black community and suggested change. During a "very heated board meeting," traditional leaders prevailed over these dissenting voices and further consolidated organizational leadership in the hands of a small group of black elites who contributed large sums to the group.[33]

In a bid to increase their effectiveness and legitimacy in the eyes of local black people, Sherard's group affiliated with the newly created Negro American Labor Council (NALC) toward the end of 1960. The NALC was organized by A. Philip Randolph to pressure the labor movement to take a more active approach to civil rights. Like the original March on Washington Movement in 1941, the NALC restricted membership to African Americans, sought to bar communist infiltration, and vowed to use "pressure tactics" to combat racial inequality. While at the national level the NALC focused on pressing the American Federation of Labor–Congress of Industrial Organizations (AFL-CIO) leadership to adopt a "racial code of conduct" for its unions, local chapters largely defined their own agenda within the broad parameters of the parent organization. "We thought that we would identify with that group to get national recognition," Sherard explained. "So, we changed the Crusaders into the Negro American Labor Council." A Milwaukee chapter of the NALC (MNALC) might even evolve into the new kind of civil rights organization Sherard and Anwar had suggested at the December mass meeting.[34]

The MNALC ratcheted up pressure on three inner-core grocery stores during the summer of 1962. Negotiations with the chain's management had proven fruitless, so MNALC members conducted a two-week picket of the stores. Police arrested Sherard and other picket leaders for "disorderly conduct" during the protest, the first civil rights-related arrests in Milwaukee. Three weeks later, representatives of the MNALC and A&P announced an agreement to increase the number of black clerks, enroll African Americans in the store's management training program, and hire qualified black journeymen in the meat department. Soon thereafter, the organization reached an agreement with another grocery chain, Kroger-Kramble, to hire more black workers. In September, Sherard met with representatives of the Upper Third Street Businessmen's Association to discuss ways to increase black employment along the inner core's main shopping district. The MNALC also sponsored a forum with black businessmen to discuss ways to stimulate support for black-owned business. Sherard emphasized the need for African Americans to enter business on a much larger scale to stem the outflow of money from the community in the form of salaries and wages to white workers who neither lived in the core, nor shopped in its stores.[35]

Meetings and rhetoric yielded minimal concrete results. The MNALC campaign exposed employment discrimination in Milwaukee, but the actual employment numbers in targeted stores were slow to change, which led to charges of tokenism. Ultimately, despite small gains in employment for African Americans at a few inner-core stores, the MNALC could not overcome the considerable obstacles in its path. In addition to underscoring business resistance, the local retail clerk union argued that the MNALC's demands threatened the seniority of its members. Sherard countered, stating, "we are not here to do a wrong, but to correct a wrong. If you had employed Afro-Americans there would be some Afro-Americans with seniority... We are here to correct that."

Though many middle-class black leaders supported the goals of the MNALC, they also opposed their tactics, worried that a developing militancy among newer African Americans in the city might prove explosive. Corneff Taylor, the African American head of the Milwaukee Commission on Community Relations (MCCR), told Sherard that he agreed with the goal of increased black hiring in core businesses but preferred the MNALC work with "established agencies" to increase employment. "If the Negro is to make progress," Sherard replied, "he must assume primary responsibility himself. No agency is going to do it for him." Reflecting years later, Sherard explained, "Afro-Americans at that time who considered themselves middle-class sometimes didn't identify [with working class or poor black people]. They were fearful of the opposition they might get from their Caucasian counterparts so they didn't identify with the grassroots struggle."

There is also evidence that a broader debate within the local African American community over the philosophy and tactics of black nationalism, fueled by a spirited Nation of Islam (NOI) membership drive, may have contributed to MNALC's difficulties in mobilizing local people. During the summer of 1963, as the MNALC's economic campaign peaked, the NOI began a statewide membership drive in Wisconsin, focused primarily on the large black population in Milwaukee's inner core. Dozens of members moved to the city from Chicago, held educational rallies, exhorted from street corners, sold copies of *Muhammad Speaks* at busy intersections, and reportedly converted "hundreds" of new adherents. The drive ignited an energetic debate within the local community about the group's philosophy and aggressive organizing style. The *Milwaukee Star*, the city's African American newspaper, noted that most black residents "readily agree [with the Nation of Islam] that the caucasian [*sic*] has taken them for all they're worth, hung their fathers and raped their mothers." Others appreciated the organization's attempt to build up African American economic power, their accent on race pride, embrace of self-defense, and overall militancy. One local paint sprayer told a reporter, "Muslims are doing more, materially, for the Negro than any other Negro supported organization."

But others criticized the NOI as anti-Christian and violent, and for advocating a philosophy of racial superiority and separatism. "The Muslims are causing nothing but trouble," claimed an inner-core housewife. "They preach race hatred. I am certain nothing ever born of hatred can flourish." While general opposition remained strong, many black Milwaukeeans held a more ambivalent view of the NOI. "Muslimism is a good idea," a local teacher argued. "Don't misunderstand. I am not a Muslim, and I am certain I never will be. However, at least they are making whites aware that the Negro has the potential for insurrection." Then she added, "The Muslims will never reach their true objectives. There are too many objectionable ideas in their laws." *Star* editorialists concurred, writing, "While most of us delight in the strides we as a race are making, we wish to continue as citizens of the United States regardless of our color, and not set ourselves up as something separate or better. Go out and fight for your rights and freedoms as individuals and as a race of people, but in the end, remain in the true fold of free men. Remain an American—a Negro American."[36]

According to Calvin Sherard, this debate intersected with the work of the MNALC. Ali Anwar, one of Sherard's main lieutenants in the group, was an outspoken adherent of orthodox Islam. His name indicated his faith to the public in news articles and on television. Sherard stated that many black Milwaukeeans failed to make a distinction between Anwar's faith and that of the NOI blitzing the community. He recalled that those who criticized the MNALC often employed similar rhetoric against the NOI, calling both groups "separatist" and "anti-white." Ironically, the NOI complained that Sherard's group did not go far enough in advocating black business ownership.[37]

But the greatest obstacle to the group's success came not from white business leaders, unions, moderate black leaders, or even members of the NOI, but from working-class African Americans themselves who failed to honor picket lines. "Some of them didn't have transportation [to another store]," Sherard explained, "some of them didn't agree with us, and some of them just didn't want to drive." By November, an exasperated Calvin Sherard publicly complained that black people were "committing financial suicide on their own community. It's disgusting to see black faces going through picket lines set up to get them jobs." Lola Bell Holmes, the national vice-president of the NALC, visited Milwaukee in the fall to drum up local support, telling one audience, "If [traditional leaders] say [protest] is not the right way, ask them what is the right way. We have waited, knocked on doors and begged. Picketing is the only way. To sit, wait, and pray like our parents did, expecting it to come to them, didn't work. The Negro must move in *masses*." Later, she underscored the link between economic empowerment and racial autonomy, "Give the Negro economic opportunities and you will see the end of the slums. We must have full employment in our neighborhoods so we can end ADC... We are tired of being degraded... When you get economic opportunities then everything else will fall into place." Holmes may have been speaking the truth about power, but without grassroots support, the MNALC faced a tough road to success.[38]

Sherard and his followers continued to picket local stores periodically through 1965 and they played an active role in a broad-based school desegregation campaign spearheaded by Lloyd Barbee and the Milwaukee United School Integration Committee, but Sherard left Milwaukee in late 1965 for Detroit. "[Local people] got satisfied with things by going into stores and seeing Afro-Americans working," he explained years later. "I guess they thought that was the whole show. I got disgusted and moved to Detroit." In Detroit, Sherard worked for Chrysler and continued to be active in the NALC through the UAW Trade Union Leadership Conference.

For a short time, between 1960 and 1963, the Crusaders and the MNALC played a leading role in the city's emerging civil rights movement. Their story offers an important continuity with the fragmented community protest that followed Daniel Bell's death and provides further evidence of a rising activist spirit among some African Americans. This activism pressed the concerns of working-class black people living in the core into the public spotlight and stoked growing pressure both on white business owners to hire more black workers and on traditional African American leaders to be more responsive to the needs of migrants. By appealing to young African Americans and involving them in their protests, the MNALC anticipated the explosive awakening of youth in the local movement during the late 1960s, when demonstrations against segregated public schools, the membership of public officials in a discriminatory fraternal club, police brutality, and—most notably—housing discrimination received national attention. Calvin Sherard's leadership highlighted the interconnection between racial inequality and economic justice. It represented the first attempt by a new generation of black leaders to organize a community-based protest campaign.

These efforts showed that more militant tactics could be effective in generating media attention and at least modest results. They also made the point that black people in Milwaukee wielded collective economic power *if* they could stay unified; in the early 1960s, that remained a pretty big "if." At the same time, the picketing and boycotting of the MNALC also revealed the limits of direct action in Milwaukee during this period. Resistance by white businessmen and union leaders, disinterest from local government officials, internal community opposition from traditional middle-class black leaders, and public apathy, all proved potent obstacles.

To be sure, there were signs of growing anger and frustration within the black community over racial inequality and an increasing desire among many in the migrant working class to develop new leadership that better represented their experiences and aspirations. But in 1961, 1962, and 1963 these issues did not ignite the passions of enough local African Americans to move them to action. Perhaps employment discrimination did not inspire most black Milwaukeeans to take the personal risks necessary for protest politics. It is possible that the charges of "communism" and "separatism" sometimes leveled at the national and local NALC deterred potential supporters. Some working-class migrants no doubt continued to support traditional community leaders who encouraged them to oppose the MNALC. It is also possible that black people in Milwaukee did not believe racial inequality in the local economy was as dire as the MNALC portrayed it. To be sure, many clung to the hope that although the economic situation in Milwaukee might not be great for black people, some progress was being made and more change would come through the traditional mechanisms of hard work and negotiation. Whatever the reasons for its limited success, the MNALC marked a further step from the Bell activism toward new black leadership and a more militant approach to change. Reflecting back, Tom Jacobson concluded, "[the MNALC] were the first demonstrations here in Milwaukee where people really hit the streets and went to jail for their freedom." Sherard was more philosophical in his assessment, "At least we got on the payroll and had a few more jobs in our community... But now we need to own and control the businesses in our community. If we don't, it goes into the hands of people who don't stay there and who don't spend their money there."[39]

Conclusion

The flurry of inner-core organizing that took place in the wake of the Daniel Bell murder offers the opportunity to look closely at the dynamics of black leadership and community empowerment during an understudied transitional period of movement history. During the late 1950s and early 1960s, traditional African American leaders in Milwaukee clashed with a rising set of often younger and more aggressive activists as they each struggled to articulate a compelling approach to racial change. Rather than any single ideology, tactic, or strategy dominating the scene, this period was defined by the contest between competing visions of black empowerment: Rev. Lathan's faith-centered entreaties for moral uplift and self-help; Assemblyman Coggs's belief that organized black electoral power was the best avenue to broader racial change; the NOI's more stringent position on racial autonomy and black nationalism; Calvin Sherard and his followers' emphasis on economic empowerment and protest politics. And, we might reasonably include the willingness of young inner-core residents to clash with white police officers as yet another form of self-assertion and community empowerment. By the late 1950s, it was increasingly clear that if black leaders, new or old, did not develop a politic that spoke to the experiences and struggles of the migrant working class, then some were willing to take matters into their own hands, a prospect that foreshadowed the more explosive racial violence in Milwaukee and other northern cities during the mid and late 1960s.

This research supports the spate of recent scholarship that has pushed back the origins of Black Power well before that term electrified the nation in 1966 and that problematizes simple definitions of the controversial term.[40] Many of the elements that often get lumped together as "Black Power" in that later period of movement history are present in Milwaukee during this earlier phase of activism: race pride; a willingness to more directly challenge entrenched white power; an emphasis on working-class African American experience and collective black economic empowerment; the assertion of black community control over local institutions; some restrictions on white participation and leadership in the movement; and the primacy of black male leadership. What this and other emerging research suggests, perhaps, is that the crux of Black Power is not found in any elusive, single definition, but rather in the debate itself, in the community's willingness to grapple seriously with identity, empowerment, and racial justice. In the end, it seems clear, there were many local variations of Black Power, each rooted in unique local circumstances, contested by local people, and molded through struggle.

Notes

1. The following narrative is culled from the "Facts of the Case" section of a 1983 appeal of a civil suit brought against the city of Milwaukee by Daniel Bell's father, Patrick Bell, Sr. Until 1978, the events surrounding Bell's death remained murky and disputed. According to court records, "In 1978 [officer] Krause went to successor District Attorney E. Michael McCann and revealed that he and Grady had lied about what occurred during the Bell shooting in 1958." Krause's testimony formed the foundation of a renewed inquiry in to the case and the criminal prosecution of officer Grady. On August 29, 1979, Thomas Grady pled guilty to homicide by reckless conduct and perjury in connection with the Daniel Bell inquest. Grady received a sentence of seven years imprisonment and was paroled after serving three years. See, United States Court of Appeals, Seventh Circuit, *Patrick Bell, Sr. v. City of Milwaukee*, September 4, 1984, pp. 10–20. For another overview of the Bell case see, Sylvia Bell White and Joanne LePage, *Her Brother's Keeper: A Sister's Quest for Justice*, an unpublished manuscript in the possession of the author, ca. 2003, pp. 161–176.
2. This quotation is based on the testimony of officer Krause in 1978. Grady denied making the statement but his employment records show that his superiors had criticized him for having too few arrests. A report from his probation officer in 1980 claimed that Grady had admitted making racial slurs during the 1950s. See *Patrick Bell, Sr. v. City of Milwaukee*, p. 11; White and LePage, p. 169.
3. Again, this statement is based on court testimony by Krause and disputed by Grady. See, *Patrick Bell, Sr. v. City of Milwaukee*, p. 11.
4. Ibid., p. 12.
5. White and LePage, *Her Brother's Keeper*, p. 170. According to court documents, Krause contrived the somewhat bizarre, self-incriminating declaration. See, *Patrick Bell, Sr. v. City of Milwaukee*.
6. Sylvia Bell White interview with Patrick Jones, July 23, 2007; See also, *Patrick Bell, Sr. v. City of Milwaukee*, p. 13.
7. *Milwaukee Journal*, February 5, 1958, pp. 1 and 3; *Milwaukee Sentinel*, February 6, 1958, p. 1, pt. 2; See also, *Patrick Bell, Sr. v. City of Milwaukee*.

8. For example, the median household income of all families in Milwaukee during the mid-1960s was roughly $7,000. By contrast, the median African-American household income during the same time period was about $4,000. See, Mark Braun. "Social Change and the Empowerment of the Poor: Poverty Representation in Milwaukee's Community Action Programs, 1964–1972." (Ph.D. Dissertation, University of Wisconsin-Milwaukee, 1999), p. 24.

9. Charles O'Reilly, "The Inner Core—North: A Study of Milwaukee's Negro Community." (School of Social Work, University of Wisconsin-Milwaukee), 1963, p. 2. It is also important to note that this increase, as dramatic as it was, was probably even greater in magnitude than official census data reveals. William Thompson has pointed out that census enumerators were often hesitant to approach African-American homes or apartments, instead relying on estimates from nearby business owners. At the same time, black people were sometimes unwilling to report the actual number of residents in an overcrowded dwelling because it violated city building codes. The Milwaukee Urban League estimated that the true number of African American residents in Milwaukee during the 1940s and 1950s may have been under-reported by 2,000–6,000. See, William Thompson, *The History of Wisconsin: Volume VI: Continuity and Change, 1940–1965.* (Madison, WI: State Historical Society of Wisconsin, 1988), pp. 309–310. See also, Paul Geib, "The Late Great Migration: A Case Study of Southern Black Migration to Milwaukee, 1940–1970." (M.A. Thesis, University of Wisconsin-Milwaukee, May 1993).

10. See, O'Reilly, pp. 70–79; Braun, pp. 31–33.

11. Patricia House, "Families Displaced by Expressway Development: A Geographical Study of Relocation in Milwaukee," (M.A. Thesis, University of Wisconsin, 1968): p. 76; Olson, pp. 66–76.

12. Joe Trotter, *Black Milwaukee: The Making of An Industrial Proletariat 1915–1945* (Champaign, IL: University of Illinois Press, 1985): pp. 39–79; Charles O'Reilly, Willard Downing and Steven Pflanczer. *The People of the Inner Core-North* (New York: LePlay Research, Inc., 1965), pp. 65–80; Thompson, *The History of Wisconsin,* pp. 315–319.

13. In Chicago, for instance, there was a black "sub-machine" that received patronage from the Daley administration in return for political support. In Cleveland, a coalition of whites and blacks led to the election of Carl Stokes, the first African American mayor of a major American city, in 1967. See, William Grimshaw, *Bitter Fruit: Black Politics and the Chicago Machine, 1931–1991* (Chicago, IL: University of Chicago Press, 1995); Adam Cohen and Elizabeth Taylor, *American Pharaoh: Mayor Richard J. Daley: His Battle for Chicago and the Nation* (New York: Little Brown & Company, 2000); Estelle Zannes, *Checkmate In Cleveland: The Rhetoric of Confrontation during the Stokes Years* (Cleveland, OH: The Press of Case Western Reserve University, 1972); Carl Stokes, *Promises of Power: A Political Autobiography* (New York: Simon & Schuster, 1973).

14. Vel Phillips interview with Patrick Jones, January 31, 2000; Gurda, pp. 360–361; Thompson, *History of Wisconsin,* pp. 322–323; Phillips interview.

15. *Milwaukee Sentinel,* January 30, 1955; *Milwaukee Sentinel,* November 3, 1956; See also, "Incidents of Crowd Resistance to Arrests, 1952–55," in "Report on a Survey of Social Characteristics of the Lower Northside Community, by John Teter and students in the appendix of the Milwaukee Commission on Human Rights, *Annual Report,* 1956.

16. "Memorandum on Conference with Chief of Police—Howard O. Johnson," undated, Milwaukee NAACP Papers, Box 2, Folder 16, State Historical Society of Wisconsin;

Milwaukee Journal, February 16, 1958, p. 5; *Milwaukee Journal*, February 21, 1958, p. 20; *Milwaukee Journal*, February 15, 1958, p. 8; *Defender*, March 1, 1958, p. 1; *Milwaukee Journal*, February 26, 1958, p. 8.

17. *Milwaukee Journal*, March 1, 1958, p. 7.

18. *Milwaukee Journal*, March 17, 1958, pt. 2, p. 1; *Milwaukee Journal*, March 18, 1958, pt. 2, p. 1; *Defender*, March 1, 1958.

19. *Milwaukee Journal*, February 16, 1958, p. 5; *Milwaukee Journal*, February 21, 1958, p. 20; *Milwaukee Journal*, March 11, 18 and 21, 1958; *Milwaukee Sentinel*, February 21, 1958; *Defender*, March 1, 1958; *Milwaukee Journal*, March 21, 1958, pt. 2, p. 1; *Milwaukee Journal*, March 24, 1958, p. 10; Sherard interview with Patrick Jones, February 17, 2001; White interview. See also, White and LePage, pp. 177–178.

20. "Statement of Frank P. Zeidler, Mayor, at Meeting on 'Social Problems of the Core of the City,' Thursday, 9/3/59," in *Mayor's Study Committee of Social Problems in the Inner Core Area of the City, Final Report to The Honorable Frank P. Zeidler, Mayor*, April 15, 1960, pp. 1–32.

21. Zeidler Report, pp. 1–32; Thompson, *History of Wisconsin*, p. 371; Oscar Handlin, *The Newcomers—Negroes and Puerto Ricans in a Changing Metropolis* (Cambridge, MA: Harvard University Press, 1959); Dougherty, *More Than One Struggle The Evolution of Black School Reform in Milwaukee* (Chapel Hill: University of North Carolina Press, 2003) p. 60.

22. Zeidler Report, pp. 1–32.

23. Henry Maier would go on to preside as Mayor of Milwaukee for the longest term in city history, an astonishing 28 years. See, Henry Maier, *Challenge to the Cities: An Approach to a Theory of Urban Leadership* (New York: Random House, 1966), pp. 44–45; Henry Maier, *The Mayor Who Made Milwaukee Famous: An Autobiography* (Lanham, MD: Madison Books, 1993), pp. 38–40.

24. *Milwaukee Journal*, June 13, 1960, p. 1; *Milwaukee Journal*, June 14, 1960, p. 1; See also, *Wisconsin Blue Book, 1960*, p. 21; Ralph Whitehead, Jr., "Milwaukee's Mercurial Henry Maier," *City* 6 (1972), pp. 10–20; Frank Aukofer, *City with A Chance* (Milwaukee, WI: Bruce Publishing, 1968), pp. 9–10; Sarah Ettenheim, *How Milwaukee Voted, 1848–1968* (UW Extension, Institute of Governmental Affairs, Milwaukee Office 1970), pp. 24 and 128.

25. Sherard interview.

26. Tom Jacobson interview with Patrick Jones, November 1, 1999; Sherard interview.

27. Sherard interview. On "Don't Buy Where You Can't Work" campaigns, see Cheryl Lynn Greenberg, *"Or Does It Explode?": Black Harlem in the Great Depression* (New York: Oxford University Press, 1991); Martha Biondi, *To Stand and Fight: The Struggle for Civil Rights in Postwar New York City* (Cambridge, MA: Harvard University Press, 2003); Matthew Countryman, *Up South: Civil Rights and Black Power in Philadelphia* (Philadelphia, PA: University of Pennsylvania Press, 2006).

28. Sherard interview; *Milwaukee Journal*, May 29, 1960, p. 8.

29. Sherard interview; Dougherty, *More Than One Struggle*, p. 78.

30. *Milwaukee Journal*, October 29, 1960, p. 1; Flier titled "Mass Rally Defends Negro Youth against Police Brutality," John Gilman Papers, Box 1, State Historical Society of Wisconsin.

31. Interestingly, Calvin Sherard was not from New York and had never lived there.

32. *Milwaukee Journal*, December 6, 1960, pt. 2, p. 2; *Milwaukee Sentinel*, December 6, 1960, pt. 2, p. 1; *Milwaukee Sentinel*, December 7, 1960, pt. 2, p. 9; Interview with Reuben Harpole by Patrick Jones, November 17, 1999; Dougherty, *More Than One Struggle*, pp, 77–79.

33. Eddie Walker to Gloster Current, December 7, 1960, pt. 3, section C, box 166, "Milwaukee, 1959–1960" folder, National NAACP Papers; See also Dougherty, *More Than One Struggle,* p. 79.

34. *Milwaukee Journal,* May 27, 1960, p. 14; *Milwaukee Journal,* May 29, 2960, p. 5; *Milwaukee Journal,* May 30, 1960; On the NALC, see, Paula Pfeffer, *A Philip Randolph, Pioneer of the Civil Rights Movement* (Baton Rouge, LA: Louisiana State University Press, 1990), pp. 214–239; Jervis Anderson, *A. Philip Randolph: A Biographical Portrait* (New York: Harcourt Brace Jovanovich, Inc, 1972), pp. 305–306 and 309–310; Sherard interview.

35. *Milwaukee Journal,* August 4, 1962, p. 9; *Milwaukee Star,* August 25, 1962, p. 1; *Milwaukee Star,* September 1, 1962, p. 2; *Milwaukee Star,* September 8, 1962, p. 1; *Milwaukee Star,* September 22, 1962, p. 1; Sherard interview.

36. *Milwaukee Star,* May 4, 1963, p. 2; *Milwaukee Star,* May 18, 1963, p. 4; *Milwaukee Star,* June 1, 1963, p. 3; *Milwaukee Star,* August 3, 1963, p. 5; Sherard interview.

37. *Milwaukee Star,* June 1, 1963; Sherard interview.

38. *Milwaukee Journal,* October 30, 1962, pt. 2, p. 1; *Milwaukee Star,* November 3, 1962, p. 1; *Milwaukee Star,* November 5, 1962, pt. 2, p. 1; *Milwaukee Sentinel,* December 10, 1962, p. 1; Sherard interview.

39. Jacobson interview.

40. Timothy Tyson, *Radio Free Dixie: Robert F. Williams and the Roots of Black Power* (Chapel Hill: University of North Carolina Press, 1999); Komozi Woodard, *A Nation within A Nation: Amiri Baraka & Black Power Politics* (Chapel Hill: University of North Carolina Press, 1999); Peniel Joseph, ed., "Black Power Studies I," *The Black Scholar* 31 (2001): Peniel Joseph, ed., "Black Power Studies II," *The Black Scholar* 32 (2002); Jeffrey O.G. Ogbar, *Black power: Radical Politics and African American Identity* (Baltimore, MD: Johns Hopkins University Press, 2004); Peniel Joseph, ed., *The Black Power Movement: Rethinking the Civil Rights-Black Power Era* (New York: Routledge, 2006); Judson L. Jeffries, *Black Power in the Belly of the Beast* (Urbana, IL: University of Chicago Press, 2006); Peniel Joseph, *Waiting 'Til the Midnight Hour: A Narrative History of Black Power in America* (New York: Henry Holt and Company, 2006); Christopher Strain, *Pure Fire: Self-Defense as Activism in the Civil Rights Era* (Athens: University of Georgia Press, 2005); Simon Wendt, *The Spirit and the Shotgun: Armed Resistance and the Struggle for Civil Rights* (Gainesville: University Press of Florida, 2007).

3

Black Power on the Ground: Continuity and Rupture in St. Louis

Clarence Lang

Introduction

A sea change is underway in the field of "Black Freedom Studies."[1] Not only have numerous scholars engaged new chronological, geographical, and conceptual frameworks to complicate popular narratives of postwar Civil Rights struggles (1955–1966), but they have also critically reexamined, and rehabilitated, key figures, organizations, and institutions associated with Black Power (1966–1975). Far from simply provocative rhetoric, inarticulate rage, and self-defeating violence, Black Power encompassed a range of concrete, programmatic initiatives geared toward tangible—indeed, political—visions and goals. Yet, historians and social scientists have further to go in recovering these many legacies. While an earlier wave of scholars excavated the "indigenous" character of Civil Rights campaigns, the growing subfield that historian Peniel Joseph has characterized as "Black Power Studies" remains in need of more local treatments that foreground the groups and activists that seeded the soil for the Black Nationalist renaissance of the mid-to-late 1960s and early-to-mid 1970s. As with the Black Freedom Movement writ large, Black Power achieved its successes, experienced its reversals, developed its various strategies, and encountered its myriad opportunities and constraints, on the ground.[2]

Focusing on Black Freedom activism in the border-state city of St. Louis, Missouri, this chapter contributes to the ongoing historical retrieval of localized Black Power struggles, and their genealogies. In one vein, this has an additive significance, for it helps augment a richer synthesis of Black Power. Using St. Louis as a case study of local movement trajectories, this chapter contends that the thesis of movement continuity must similarly be tested on the ground, with scholars paying attention to grassroots movements as they developed and evolved over time, and in response to changing social and economic circumstances. One challenge lay in assessing not only the political and ideological blocs that surged and receded within shifting black activist communities over time, but also the uniquely *generational* schisms that emerged among freedom workers in different historical periods and defined the predominant forms of activism. In places like St. Louis, African American protest over the long haul of the Great Depression, World War II, early cold war, and the high tide of the late 1950s, 1960s, and early 1970s, was defined by historically specific leadership, strategies, constituencies, objectives, and popular understandings of "freedom." Thus, I trace the city's Black Freedom struggle from the 1930s to the 1970s to illustrate that while Black Power was consistent with preceding (and subsequent) efforts, it was nevertheless a distinct historical moment reflecting both continuity and change in the African American experience. Moreover, as the following section discusses, localizing Black Power studies requires establishing the importance of place, and its effects on social (racial) relations and political economy.[3]

The St. Louis Context

Located at the nation's center, St. Louis was a cultural and political transition point between the Northeast, Midwest, and the South, and embodied "a microcosm—often in exaggerated terms—of national trends."[4] The city was typical of a border-state environment; yet, what constitutes a border state is both simple and elusive. At its most basic, the concept identifies the slaveholding states—Missouri, Maryland, Tennessee, West Virginia, and Kentucky—that did not secede from the United States during its Civil War. At the same time, it speaks of other ways in which these states were both southern and conspicuously "non-southern." Their relatively small black populations contrasted with the large numbers of African Americans who resided in the former Confederacy, particularly in its cotton-producing areas. Likewise, the ethno-religious diversity of white border-state residents—the product of European immigration during the late nineteenth and early twentieth centuries—departed significantly from the demographic homogeneity characteristic of most southern whites. Border-state black people participated in regular electoral politics, where the Democratic and Republican parties "shared" a plurality. This differed from mass black disfranchisement and white Democratic hegemony in the South. The breadth and depth of industrial mass production vis-a-vis the South also distinguished border-state cities, as did the uneven civic cultural influences inherited from Dixie.[5]

Located along the Mississippi River, near its confluence with the Missouri River, St. Louis City had been a vital center of steamboat commerce. After the war, it became a rail link between eastern financial interests and the conquered western territories drawn by the Market Revolution into an evolving national economy. The "Gateway City" also became a supplier of finished goods to the West. The city not only developed an industrial base, but also, similar to Chicago and Detroit—two of its midwestern neighbors—housed an active labor union movement. The heterogeneity of its European immigrant population (primarily

German and Irish), and the immigrants' Catholicism, were heavily inscribed in many of St. Louis's civic, as well as religious, institutions. This Catholic presence was even more the case, given St. Louis's colonial Spanish–French origins. Consistent, too, with a border-state typology, the city had small numbers of African Americans: Black St. Louis had grown dramatically following the Civil War, but in 1880 it only comprised 22,000 out of a total city population of 351,000. This factor, alongside Republican–Democratic contestation, had much to do with why black St. Louisans retained the vote even after ex-Confederates redeemed the South. White leaders fostered a public perception of interracial cooperation, and used discourses of racial "civility" to maintain black subordination, with outright brutality as an unspoken corollary. Incorporated into municipal and state patronage politics, St. Louis's emergent black leadership relied on white paternalism to tap political appointments and public employment and services.[6]

Jim Crow permeated St. Louis's institutional life. Missouri state law protected segregated public education and prohibited racial intermarriage; most public accommodations, aside from libraries and public transport, also enforced the color line. The same applied to residential settlement. In 1916, white voters passed the nation's first residential segregation ordinance achieved through a popular referendum. (Just one year later, major race riots erupted across the Mississippi River in East St. Louis, Illinois, similarly emblematic of white resistance to black migration and mobility during the Great War.) While a U.S. Supreme Court decision later nullified the law, it nonetheless set a precedent for private restrictive housing covenants. Thus, while black St. Louisans lived in clusters around the city, their area of settlement and growth became rigidly confined to older, declining areas near the downtown business district and central riverfront. African Americans were equally constricted in local job markets, where they were overwhelmingly employed as domestics and common laborers. Unusual even for African Americans in southern cities, St. Louis's black workers were excluded from the skilled building trades and most professional crafts.[7]

From the Great Depression to the Early Cold War

These conditions generated a range of indigenous black cultural, social, and political institutions, including the Civic Liberty League, and local chapters of the Urban League, Negro Business League, and the National Association for the Advancement of Colored People (NAACP). While ministering to African Americans' immediate needs, many of these organizations also helped ignite popular struggles for racial reform. During the 1930s, black St. Louisans waged community campaigns for more recreational space, schools, and relief and employment. The Colored Clerks Circle, working with the city's Housewives League, led efforts for the hiring of African American delivery drivers and dime-store sales staff. African Americans also comprised a particularly visible and militant core of the Unemployed Councils organized by the American Communist Party, and their involvement in downtown demonstrations and street fights with police helped goad city hall into establishing a formal public relief structure.

Assisted by the Trade Union Unity League, black female nutpickers and rag and bag factory laborers organized a massive, though short-lived, movement for wages and working conditions.[8]

Through the "Popular Front" vehicle of the American Workers' Union, black workers fought for equity in the emerging federal New Deal programs. The St. Louis Urban League, whose Industrial Department was an unlikely hub of radicalism during this period, supported the self-organization of black construction and hotel workers, motion picture projectionists, janitors, and domestics. St. Louis's Negro Workers' Council, created in 1934, challenged the monopoly on skilled work held by white tradesmen of the American Federation of Labor; after 1936, black organizers helped fortify a burgeoning Congress of Industrial Organizations, especially in the steel industry where they had a strategic foothold. St. Louis's branch of the National Negro Congress, though small and dependent on the Urban League, nonetheless was a convergence of black community-based mobilization, left-wing politics, worker self-organization, and industrial union militancy.[9]

The popular upsurge also affected the city's electoral politics. George Vaughn, Jordan Chambers, and David Grant—a young attorney involved in the Colored Clerks' Circle—were among a rising new coalition of black politicos who helped engineer a white Democratic sweep of local municipal offices, including the mayoralty and the Aldermanic Board. By 1937, 60 percent of the city's African American voters had defected to the party of the New Deal. Chambers, elected committeeman of the heavily black Nineteenth Ward, ascended as the city's principal black Democratic boss. St. Louis's decentralized, weak-mayor system of government allowed black ward-level politicians like "Pops" Chambers to exercise far greater power than was possible in machine-run cities like Chicago.[10]

As depression gave way to war and industrial regeneration, the March on Washington Movement galvanized black communities against racism in defense production and the armed forces. Spearheaded by the Brotherhood of Sleeping Car Porters (BSCP), and adopting the vocal anticommunism of BSCP president A. Philip Randolph, the group generally eschewed any association with radicalism in favor of a militant liberal racial reformism. Highlighting the contradiction of maintaining Jim Crow at home while fighting fascism abroad, and using the imminent threat of disruption, the coalition leveraged a presidential executive order and the creation of a Fair Employment Practice Committee (FEPC). Yet, the March on Washington Movement was a grassroots project that continued throughout the war, sustained by active local committees that assumed the weight of actually implementing the federal decree. St. Louis's affiliate, led by Grant and local BSCP President T.D. McNeal, staged several marches to force the hiring and upgrading of black workers at McDonnell Aircraft, U.S. Cartridge, and other firms. As public transport and communications were deemed war industries by the White House, demonstrators also pressed for the employment of black men as streetcar and bus drivers, and picketed the Southwestern Bell Telephone Company for white-collar jobs for black women. By the spring of 1943, March on Washington activists boasted of having won more than 8,000 jobs for African Americans in the city.[11]

The mayor's office, maneuvering to staunch the tide of black militancy, avert the race riots that had erupted in cities like Detroit and Philadelphia, and preserve the city's image of interracial civility, created a race relations commission. But in areas where city hall failed to act, politicized citizens were more than willing. In 1944, a coterie of women associated with the local March on Washington committee, NAACP, and labor union auxiliaries formed the Citizens Civil Rights Committee, which conducted a series of sit-in protests at the segregated lunch counters of the major downtown department stores. Stemming from the women's ties to the Christian pacifist Fellowship of Reconciliation, these were among the earliest sit-in demonstrations in the nation.

Following the war, black activists persisted in their efforts to dismantle American racial apartheid—for instance, lobbying for a permanent national FEPC. Yet, in a postwar climate of heightened U.S.–Soviet rivalry and perceived threats to internal security, "communistic" demands for racial equality invited unwanted attention from federal, state, and local authorities. This is not to say that Black Freedom workers ceased drawing the potent linkages between racial and economic justice. The Civil Rights Congress, active in St. Louis and East St. Louis, engaged in protests against police brutality and black unemployment in 1949 and 1950. In 1952, the St. Louis Negro Labor Council (NLC), similarly connected to a national united front of progressive trade unionists, veteran left-wing organizers, and members and "fellow travelers" of the American Communist Party, gained attention through its lengthy boycott of the city's main Sears, Roebuck and Company store. One of its leading figures, Hershel Walker, was a former Young Communist League member and a veteran of St. Louis's unemployed movement. The early cold war, however, had a chilling effect on forms of black militancy that had been possible during the Depression and World War II. Certainly, the protests of the NAACP and Congress of Racial Equality (CORE) during this period were carried out by a small number of committed activists, who at best achieved short-lived and piecemeal reforms.[12]

Just thirty people walked the NLC's picket line, due in no small part to the fact it had been named in the U.S. Attorney's Subversive Organizations list. The NAACP, CORE, and the Urban League all refused any involvement with the demonstrations, and the council was largely ostracized in St. Louis's black public sphere. Harassed by police, and hounded by charges of subversion from conservatives and cold war liberals, black and white alike, the NLC's national body was forced to dissolve less than six years after its birth. (A similar fate befell the Civil Rights Congress.) Hence, the late 1940s and early 1950s comprised a moment of rupture in the Black Freedom Movement, particularly in the development of its radical flank.[13]

Civil Rights in St. Louis

As bus boycotts in Baton Rouge, Montgomery, and Tallahassee, Florida helped push matters of racial justice to the forefront of the national agenda, Civic Progress, Incorporated—an organization of the city's major industrial and civic leaders—touted a proposal to revise the municipal charter. The plan unwittingly ignited the "heroic" period[14] of postwar Civil Rights struggle in St. Louis. For many African Americans, the proposed new charter's provisions reducing the Aldermanic Board and enlarging the scope of at-large elections directly undermined the electoral strength of a growing black populace. Between 1940 and 1950, 38,000 African Americans had migrated to the city; by 1956, they comprised approximately 180,000, or well over 20 percent of the city's population. Given the charter's silence on civil rights and fair employment guarantees in municipal employment and projects, and given that the city was entering the throes of a protracted downtown-area renewal, the proposal threatened to strip black people of their collective power in public decision making at the very moment they were poised to wield substantive influence at the polls.[15]

At a time when the NAACP was on the defensive in the South, and often recoiled from mass protest in the North for fear of accusations of Communism, St. Louis's branch launched a successful grassroots opposition to the charter's passage, one involving black ward politicians, beauticians, taxicab drivers, unionists, and clergy. It is noteworthy that the NAACP's president at this time was Ernest Calloway, a veteran union organizer and high-ranking official in Local 688 of the powerful International Brotherhood of Teamsters.[16] Calloway, a newcomer to the city, was of the same generation as individuals like Grant and McNeal; yet, he was part of a nascent cohort of mainly younger activists, like Margaret Bush Wilson and William L. Clay, who emerged out of the NAACP's community mobilization campaign.

The anti-charter moment of the late 1950s is also historically significant because it illustrates how early Civil Rights activism, including initiatives outside the South, responded to quality-of-life issues beyond ending Jim Crow accommodations. Victory over the proposal set in motion a modern black mass movement for better jobs and wages, meaningful electoral power, equitable education and housing opportunities, black communal stability amid urban redevelopment—as well as an end to segregated facilities. Local Black Freedom workers articulated this agenda in a comprehensive "Negro Proclamation." At the cutting edge of this activity were two NAACP affiliates—the Job Opportunities Council and the NAACP Youth Council—who often collaborated with St. Louis CORE. St. Louis's unit of the Negro American Labor Council (NALC), subsequently led by Calloway, was also involved in aggressive action against job discrimination.[17]

Cold war liberalism was not the only framework activists employed in response to racist exclusion. Muhammad's Mosque No. 28, which had grown dramatically since the early 1950s, represented a persistent Black Nationalist vision. Spurning the Civil Rights strategy of nonviolent direct action, members of the Nation of Islam (NOI) questioned the desirability of racial integration. Such messages resonated with many black St. Louisans. Some 3,500 people gathered at the city's municipal auditorium in August 1962 to hear NOI leader Elijah Muhammad deliver the apocalyptic prediction that the "rule of the white man over the black man" was coming to an end. Malcolm X, Muhammad's national spokesman, also drew a sizable audience during an early 1963 appearance. An effective organizer, Malcolm had been planting the seeds of a secular Black Nationalist rebirth since the late 1950s.[18]

But the NOI stood at the margins of black protest (and fell out of favor altogether with many black activists after Malcolm's assassination). As the tempo of Civil Rights struggle quickened in the South, the thrust of insurgency in St. Louis similarly became more robust, with CORE at the forefront. Many Youth Council members, hampered by their parent organization, defected from the local NAACP to CORE in the early 1960s. Appeals for a "fair" share of jobs became demands for "full" employment as definitions of black "freedom" evolved. African Americans were negligibly employed in banks, retail stores, and grocery chains; soft drink, dairy, bread, and brewing companies hired them neither as plant workers nor driver-salesmen. Racial inequality also defined the hiring policies of the city's utility companies and major industrial firms. With one in every three black St. Louisans employed in unskilled work or household service, African American families earned an annual income of $3,000 in contrast to $6,000 for whites. Another result of economic disfranchisement was a high rate of black unemployment. Between 1958 and 1964, black unemployment stood at more than 10 percent, with one of every six black youth absent from the formal labor force. The problem was especially acute for black men. Still, the fact that women had an easier time finding work did not mean they were better employed: In 1960, 62 percent of black women in paid labor earned $1,999 or less. Suitably, women anchored most Civil Rights projects, despite the fact that gender equity was not an explicit basis of organization. However, the nature of many jobs campaigns implicitly promoted the expansion of employment available to black women, albeit within the confines of "women's work"—retail, telephone operative, and petty clerical work.[19]

St. Louis's Civil Rights movement reached its peak in 1963–1964, when CORE activists launched mass disruptions at the Jefferson Bank and Trust Company in response to its hiring practices. The campaign assumed the form of a "general strike" against city hall, downtown businesses, and other institutions that deposited their receipts at the bank. CORE, once a small, predominantly white middle-class organization philosophically sworn to nonviolence, changed dramatically as younger, working-class blacks swelled its membership, questioned nonviolence, leaned closer to Black Nationalism than liberalism, and contested for leadership. The increasingly militant character of CORE's civil disobedience, and mass arrests, elicited criticisms from older activists like Calloway and then-State Senator McNeal, who the "Young Turks" dismissed as "Uncle Toms." The dispute revealed the straightforwardness of a grassroots rank-and-file who, facing structural unemployment, had no abiding allegiance to the rules of civility that had governed relations between black and white leadership. Intergenerational schisms also underlay the hostilities. Many of the critics, having come of age during the forties, or earlier, had been schooled in earlier paradigms of militancy that adhered to legal boundaries. For veteran activists, the Jefferson Bank boycotters represented a form of protest they neither understood nor appreciated. Mass protests eventually dented racial apartheid in the bank's employment practices, but this success was contradictory. It splintered local movement forces, exacerbating CORE's internal differences over tactics and goals, and the complexion of the group's leadership.[20]

A major outgrowth of this disaffection within CORE was the formation of the Action Committee to Improve Opportunities for Negroes (ACTION) in 1964, chaired by Percy Green, an ex-gang member and McDonnell Aircraft Company worker. Composed initially of CORE dissidents, the group first came to public attention after Green and Richard Daly, a white member, climbed the base of the unfinished Gateway Arch and secured themselves more than 125 feet above workers, police, and other demonstrators. The highly visible protest, spanning four hours, was designed to draw attention to the exclusion of black workers, by unions and contractors, from skilled work at a federally funded project. ACTION quickly gained a militant reputation for its flamboyant, yet meticulously planned, nonviolent guerrilla theater waged against the local construction industry, and the metropolitan area's other major employers. A purely local organization, ACTION nevertheless informs a broader history of the postwar Black Freedom Movement. Focused primarily on "More and Better Paying Jobs for Black Men," its leadership was characteristic of the ways in which black "freedom" during this period imagined the redemption of a black "manhood" premised on the patriarchal, male-headed household. This paralleled an emergent thesis of cultural pathology that attributed black poverty rates to the dominance of black matriarchy in African American communities.[21]

Like a number of other local groups around the nation, ACTION also constituted a vital bridge between the civil rights movement and what would soon come to be labeled "Black Power." At a time when national organizations such as CORE and the Student Nonviolent Coordinating Committee (SNCC) were adopting the policy that white members should organize anti-racist campaigns in their own communities, ACTION remained stubbornly interracial. Yet, its top leadership positions were self-consciously reserved for African Americans only, under the presumption that black activists deserved to play the central role in their own struggles for self-determination. Members adopted many Black Nationalist flourishes common to the period, including military berets, army field jackets, and dark sunglasses. Influenced by third world revolutionary movements, the organization even established a youth auxiliary known as the ACTION Guerrilla Force. And while adhering to a strategy of nonviolent action, members were not philosophically opposed to self-defense. As a number of scholars have illustrated, this was not atypical of Civil Rights activists. However, it is noteworthy that ACTION's leadership went beyond a pragmatic support for defensive violence, and actually made preparations for the time when revolutionary violence might be historically necessary: Members regularly participated in military training in forest preserves outside the city. When viewed as organizational transition points from "Freedom Now" to "Black Power," indigenous groups like ACTION reveal organic linkages between the two phases.

From "Freedom Now" to "Black Power" in the Gateway City

It is noteworthy that a number of elder activists—mainly cold war liberals who had survived the anticommunist purges of the late 1940s—were put off by what they regarded as black "separatism." Existing organizations like the NAACP and Urban League rejected the concept with equal vehemence. Even senior Black Nationalists like Elijah Muhammad were out of step with their junior counterparts. Although the NOI continued to attract members, it remained tainted by Malcolm's death and its general aversion to political engagement. Not only were the Black Muslims politically suspect, but many younger activists also found them culturally reactionary. Steeped in a nineteenth-century paradigm of Black Nationalism that echoed Western discourses of "civilization" and regarded sub-Saharan Africa as backward, Muhammad publicly lambasted beards and "afro" hairstyles as "germ-catchers." Fruit of Islam members, adhering to strict codes of "respectability" with their clean-shaven faces, closely cropped hair, and conservative suits and bowties, likewise stood in stark contrast to their peers in dashikis, sandals, earrings, and dangling African jewelry. Moreover, at a time when black women were beginning to assert (proto)feminist identities and interests within movement organizations, the NOI held fast to patriarchal ideals.[22]

In St. Louis, as elsewhere, Black Power sprang from numerous changes in the movement's landscape. Foremost were the remarkable, if qualified, successes of Civil Rights activism. These included the attainment of greater black representation on the St. Louis school and aldermanic boards by the end of the 1950s, and T.D. McNeal's election, in 1960, as Missouri's first black state senator. With the passage of a public accommodations ordinance in 1961, activists finally achieved a major goal many had been seeking since 1948. The 1963 March on Washington had powerfully symbolized black demands for full citizenship, and helped yield national legislation that included the 1964 Civil Rights and 1965 Voting Rights acts, and the advent of the federal "War on Poverty."

These reforms exposed, at the same time, deepening racial inequalities. Automation eroded black advances in semi-skilled operative jobs, leading one sociologist to ruefully contemplate, "Who needs the Negro?"[23] Despite the defeat of the Civic Progress-touted charter in 1957, large-capitalist prerogatives had prevailed in directing the path of urban redevelopment. Beginning in 1959, the demolition of St. Louis's central-city black enclave, Mill Creek Valley, displaced some 20,000 black St. Louisans. Many moved north of downtown, or took up occupancy near the central business district in the massive Pruitt-Igoe homes and other federal housing projects. The relocations tightened the spatial containment, and the racialized poverty, of the black community: in 1960, for instance, 70 percent of the city's 214,337 African Americans lived in or near old, decaying housing. White St. Louisans retired to the suburbs of St. Louis County, with private capital and federal welfare programs following them. Because its boundaries had been frozen since 1876 (when voters approved home rule), St. Louis City's government lacked the power to annex economically thriving adjacent communities.

Moreover, bitter experiences of arrests, beatings, church bombings and assassinations—and the unreliable nature of the Kennedy and Johnson administrations as Civil Rights allies—helped to sour younger activists on the idea that they could end racism, poverty, and militarism through American liberalism. They became deeply critical of local anti-poverty agencies like St. Louis's

Human Development Corporation (HDC), which, while supportive of popular participation in principle, resisted genuine popular control. Premised on correcting the defective behavior of the black urban poor, rather than structural racial inequalities, many Johnson-era Great Society programs trained younger black workers for declining or obsolete jobs.

The pervasive influence of Malcolm X, and the inspiring examples of third world revolt and revolution, also conditioned profound strategic, tactical, and ideological transformations among young African Americans. Drawing from the contemporary examples of Malcolm, Robert F. Williams, and formations like the Deacons for Defense and Justice—as well as from a longer history of black armed "self-help," activists publicly (re)asserted and popularized discourses of self-defense. Civil Rights workers also critically reevaluated the place of white organizers in the movement, and formally adopted long-term "community organizing" projects. As part of this strategy, existing organizations, such as SNCC, attempted to expand their base beyond the South, where their activities had been concentrated before the demise of legal apartheid. Further, black radicalism and (inter)nationalism, while certainly present during the early cold war, discovered new mass constituencies as it journeyed from the movement's margins to its center in the mid-to-late 1960s. Thus, when SNCC organizer Willie Ricks and chairman Stokely Carmichael popularized "Black Power" in 1966, they spoke to the particular frustrations, concerns, and idealism of movement activists at a specific historical moment. Further, while individuals such as James Forman, Floyd McKissick, Queen Mother Audley Moore, and Detroit's Reverend Albert Cleage, Jr., attest to Black Power's cross-generational appeal, the slogan nonetheless had its greatest appeal among younger militants.

Yet, as many scholars have noted, "Black Power" lacked real definition, and therefore was broad enough to embrace a wide range of framing processes and diffuse activities. "Negroes" became "Black." The "white power structure," "crackers," "honkies," and "pigs" emerged as negative condensation symbols that sought to explicitly reveal, and delegitimate, the institutions and practices of white racial control. Many black people adopted the "afro" and other African-derived hairstyles and clothing, assumed new names, and engaged in new social practices and symbolism, as in learning Swahili and raising fists in the "Black Power salute." The black urban working-class rebellions that shook most major U.S. cities between 1963 and 1968 spoke even more dramatically to these tectonic political shifts. St. Louis often escaped national attention in the media coverage of "riots" because of the relatively small scale of its disturbances; yet, recovering the many narratives of revolt in midsized and small cities like St. Louis illustrates how truly widespread the phenomenon was. In early July 1964, police, responding to a fight between two siblings, touched off an hour-long civil disorder on the near north side of the city. Officers dispersed a crowd of rock- and bottle-throwing black youth with tear gas, and arrested three people. Thirty minutes after the clash ended, about forty-five demonstrators marched to the nearby Lucas Avenue police district station, whose officers were particularly known for violent treatment of black citizens in their custody. After someone hurled bricks through two station windows, officers drove the protesters away with police dogs.[24]

Scattered neighborhood disturbances again occurred in June 1965, following the shooting death of a seventeen-year-old burglary suspect, Melvin Cravens. The black community reacted in outrage over the news that the youth, unarmed and with his hands cuffed behind his back, had died from a gunshot to the back of the head. In October 1965, nearly 100 black youth ran along Delmar Boulevard—a street which marked the north–south dividing line between black and white St. Louis—smashing automobile and store windows. A similar outbreak occurred in September 1966, following a CORE demonstration at the St. Louis Police Department's downtown headquarters. A group of teenagers, shouting "Black Power," tossed garbage cans in the streets and broke car windshields. One group smashed the plate glass windows of a laundry. Firefighters responding to false alarms were pelted with flying glass and stone, as were uniformed police.[25]

Civic officials prided themselves on the fact that St. Louis did not experience the mass uprisings that shook Kansas City, Chicago, Detroit, and most other major U.S. cities following the assassination of Martin Luther King, Jr. in April 1968. This was not altogether true, for minor disturbances did occur in several black neighborhoods. Yet, several factors intervened on the side of the status quo. Local news media, fearing the spread of disturbances, avoided coverage. Meanwhile, leading members of CORE and the Mid-City Community Congress (discussed below) worked to quell further unrest. Also, St. Louis Mayor Alfonso J. Cervantes—seeking to direct the anger of the black populace, and drawing on the city's culture of "civility"—helped craft an interracial, ecumenical coalition that sponsored what became a 30,000-person eulogy procession and prayer service under the auspices of city hall.[26]

More serious rebellions occurred immediately east of the Mississippi River in neighboring East St. Louis. In early September 1967, SNCC Chairman H. Rap Brown spoke before a crowd of 1,500 people at East St. Louis's Lincoln High School. Following the speech, he gave another, more impromptu presentation atop a police cruiser outside the school. That evening, disturbances erupted in the city's downtown. At least 200 people were involved in white-owned property destruction and looting, as well as firebombings. Several residents were arrested, and a nineteen-year-old was shot to death as he fled police in a stockyard parking lot just outside the city limits. The following day, thirty people marched to police headquarters; looting continued sporadically into the following evening, requiring the intervention of more than one hundred state and city police officers.[27]

But reducing Black Power to black rebellion against police, and other symbols of white authority and power, buttresses its oversimplification as unorganized, violent rage. To the contrary, Black Power had institutional moorings. Certainly, it transformed CORE and ACTION. By 1965, most of St. Louis CORE's mainly white founding members were gone as a result of organizational schisms, both local and national. A year later, the national CORE, like SNCC, formally endorsed a version of "Black Power." In 1966, when the region's Bi-State Transit System purchased a local service car company with the intention of dismantling it, CORE began a boycott. Less expensive than Bi-State fare, and more extensive in its routes, service car companies had served a disproportionately African American clientele. CORE subsequently organized its own network of "Freedom

Cars" to transport black patrons. Negotiations with Bi-State Transit ended the boycott in March. Not surprisingly, the Gateway City became a test site in 1967 for CORE's national program, "Black Power, a Blueprint to Success and Survival," which focused on strategies of black control of community institutions.[28]

ACTION's history committee, chaired by Luther Mitchell, became another vehicle for institutionalizing Black Power. A veteran of Chicago's South Side Community Art Center, Mitchell coordinated the production of weekly questionnaires on African American history, which were delivered along routes in black neighborhoods. At a moment when the Black Studies movement was developing in many college and university communities, residents eagerly consumed the pamphlets, and waited for the answers to run in the following week's edition. These experiences provided the entrepot for Mitchell's involvement in a community-driven mural project that would bring art and history to the public. Working with activists and artists, Mitchell helped oversee the painting of the "Wall of Respect" at the intersection of Leffingwell and Franklin avenues, near the Pruitt-Igoe projects. Initiated in the summer of 1968, the mural featured a color collage of faces that included Jomo Kenyatta, W.E.B. Du Bois, Malcolm X, Martin Luther King, Jr., and Muhammad Ali. Marcus Garvey's famous appeal, "Up You Mighty Race," underscored the images. After its completion, the wall became a popular gathering space for political speakers, organizers, and cultural workers.[29]

Black Power Organized: A Local View

Besides transforming existing groups, Black Power also inspired new institutions, networks, and organizational forms. The opening of the black-owned Gateway National Bank in 1965 simultaneously refuted the endemic racism in St. Louis's banking industry, provided a source of credit and loans for working-class African Americans, and announced the arrival of a burgeoning new black entrepreneurial middle class. The Committee for Africa, also founded in 1965, mainly attracted students and faculty from St. Louis University and Washington University, both private schools. The committee's goal lay in connecting black St. Louisans to other people of African descent, mainly through educational forums and cultural programming, and providing aid to African liberation movements. *Proud*, a monthly publication also established in St. Louis during this period, was consistent with numerous periodicals around the nation geared to audiences of the new Black Nationalism. Similarly, the Association of Black Collegians, which staged building takeovers in 1968 at St. Louis and Washington universities, and Forest Park Community College, was part of a wave of militant black student unions that emerged at historically white institutions of higher learning when, following the urban riots after King's death, African Americans were first admitted in substantive numbers. In St. Louis, as elsewhere, campus-based black insurgency led to the creation of Black Studies curricula and programs, among other reforms.[30]

Southern Illinois University's Experiment in Higher Education (EHE), located in East St. Louis, likewise became a regional hub of Black Studies and Black Arts ferment. The EHE contained the Performing Arts Training Center, helmed by the internationally renowned choreographer and anthropologist Katherine Dunham; and enjoyed ties to poet Eugene B. Redmond, whose Black River Writers Press was central to popularizing the new aesthetic through chapbooks, published fiction, and spoken-word recordings. As scholars like Benjamin Looker and James Edward Smethurst have reminded historians, the Black Arts movement was not confined to the East and West Coasts, but also blossomed in the nation's interior. According to Looker, the Black Artists' Group (BAG), founded in St. Louis around 1968, was particularly illustrative of this point. Heavily influenced by Chicago's Association for the Advancement of Creative Musicians, the collective sought to raise a black social consciousness through multimedia works of poetry, dance, theater, visual arts, and free-jazz music; at its peak in 1969–1970, BAG had over fifty members. Headquartered in a renovated industrial building in the city's declining midtown area, the group staged performances in churches, storefronts, public housing centers, public schools, and sidewalks of black working-class communities, and ran a free youth arts academy.[31]

In some instances, anti-poverty programs provided bases for Black Power organizers. Certainly, the EHE, as well as East St. Louis's Project IMPACT—geared toward cultural and recreational outlets for black youth—were beneficiaries of federal funds. Another was St. Louis's Jeff-Vander-Lou (JVL) Community Action Group, which was formed in 1966 in the heart of the black neighborhood bounded by Jefferson, Vanderventer, St. Louis Avenue, and Natural Bridge Road. The JVL focused mainly on housing rehabilitation, and the corollary opportunities of black employment and homeownership these projects generated. The group also developed a medical clinic. The Mid-City Community Congress (MCC), established that same year, similarly promoted black community control. The MCC's autonomous youth "action arm," the Zulu 1200s, took shape in November 1967 under the leadership of Vietnam veteran Clarence Guthrie. The group's name spoke clearly of an agenda of reconnecting to the African past and raising black cultural consciousness. Its members, operating out of the MCC's Delmar Boulevard office, were involved in initiating the Wall of Respect project and other educational programming.[32]

The Black Liberators, formed in 1968 soon after King's assassination, were perhaps the city's most daring new organization. Charles Koen, the Liberators' founder and "prime minister," had, at sixteen, been chairman of the Cairo Nonviolent Freedom Committee, a SNCC affiliate in southern Illinois. Sometime after graduating from McKendree College, he had moved to the East St. Louis area, where he led school protests. Although new to the area, he had become a spokesman for East St. Louis's Black Economic Union, an umbrella organization made up of antipoverty, youth, and cultural organizations, and the Imperial Warlords and Black Egyptians, two local gangs. An experienced and dynamic organizer, Koen had recruited heavily from the Egyptians and Warlords to build the Liberators, and envisioned the new group as a vehicle for a metropolitan-wide black militant youth alliance. The Liberators, in fact, developed a statewide influence in Illinois, though its actual membership ranged between 150 and 300 people. At the invitation of the Reverend William Matheus, a white ACTION member, the newly formed organization, in addition to maintaining a headquarters near Pruitt-Igoe, used St. Stephen's Episcopal Church as a regular base of operations.[33]

In appearances, the paramilitary Liberators patterned themselves after Oakland, California's Black Panther Party for Self-Defense, which had formed two years earlier. Members sported black berets and leather jackets, held weekly military drills, published a short-lived newspaper, *The Black Liberator*, ran a free breakfast program for children, and worked closely with white antiwar student activists at Washington University. (The Liberators supplied draft counseling to black youth fighting military conscription.[34]) Curiously, female recruits did not belong to the organization, per se, but rather to a women's auxiliary. This fit the group's self-image as a band of warriors, an identity centered largely on a masculinist vision of heroism. The Liberators' platform, a manifesto of radical Black Nationalism, demanded an end to black police violence and capitalist exploitation, and called for black pride and draft resistance to the war in Vietnam. Like the Panthers, they also drew immediate media attention through well-publicized and audacious acts. In August 1968, the Liberators approached the mainly white Franklin Avenue Businessmen's Association about making donations to the group, as well as hiring its members as night watchmen. The protection plan, which the merchants rejected, was both an obvious fundraising ploy and a step toward the group's other goal of supplanting police authority in the black Franklin Avenue area they patrolled. That same month, the Liberators provided an armed escort to the embattled black Congressman from New York, Adam Clayton Powell, Jr., whom they had invited to town for a speaking engagement. A standoff between police and Liberators occurred as Powell attended a rally at the Wall of Respect. As the situation threatened to erupt into gunplay, Powell's aides spirited him away, and the small Liberator delegation dispersed. Police arrested two members on weapons violations charges.[35]

Other black militant leaders, like Green, deemed the Liberators' activities "adventurist," a reckless invitation to a police showdown for which its young, relatively inexperienced rank-and-file were ill prepared. Such criticism reflected more than just the fact that Green was a movement veteran who viewed such tactics as politically immature, or regarded the upstart Liberators as competitors. While Green regarded nonviolence in purely practical terms—and though he had played a role, locally, in the shift to what became labeled "Black Power"— his discomfort with the Liberators' activities speaks to how Black Power initiatives could differ dramatically from their Civil Rights antecedents. It is telling, moreover, that while the Liberators were a source of frustration for someone like Green, they apparently provided a model for *younger* African Americans. The Black Nationalist Party (BNP), which formed in 1969, was a similar avatar of black revolutionary politics. Like the Liberators, the BNP conducted separate community patrols of police. With funding from the city's HDC, the group also ran a short-lived Community Variety Store.[36]

Although organizations such as the Liberators and BNP were regional and local in character, they have broader significance in understanding the crosscurrents of Black Power. For instance, given Koen's preexisting ties to SNCC, one may view the Liberators as consistent with SNCC's earlier, abortive effort to form organizations under the insignia of the Black Panther in Philadelphia and other cities. (This was conceived as an outgrowth of the Lowndes County Freedom Organization, or Black Panther Party, organized by SNCC activists in Alabama in 1965–1966.) It is notable, also, that the Liberators developed at a time when SNCC and the Oakland-based Panthers had been attempting to forge an alliance. To the extent that the Liberators imitated the Black Panthers (who experienced explosive growth in 1968), it suggests that historians cannot evaluate the impact of a national organization like the Panthers simply on the basis of its chapters and known members. Rather, in localizing Black Power, we must also factor in the other numerous community groupings that readily adapted Panther platforms, programs, and stylizations to their specific conditions.[37]

The close ties between the Liberators and Zulus are also historically revealing. At the outset, both organizations shared members and engaged in joint activities. These multiple connections between the Liberators and the Zulus call into question the long-running bifurcation between "revolutionary" and "cultural" nationalists that have characterized descriptions of the encounters between nationally known groups like the Panthers and the US Organization. The Liberator–Zulu relationship supports the arguments, made by historians such as Komozi Woodard and Scot Brown, that the two Black Nationalist "camps" were not as diametrically opposed as the national Black Power narrative—told primarily through the deadly Panther-U.S. feud—suggests. Clearly, real ideological differences existed, as on the question of forming coalitions with white radicals; and police agencies had different evaluations of the respective threat each tendency posed to the status quo. Still, revolutionary nationalists were not dismissive of cultural work, just as cultural nationalists were not glibly "apolitical." In the relatively tight-knit activist community of a midsized metropolis like St. Louis, it was common for Black Freedom workers to participate simultaneously in "political" and "cultural" organizations, including ACTION, the Zulu 1200s, CORE, BAG, and the Liberators. Certainly, this overlap did not necessarily make organizational relationships harmonious—the small geographical space and density of interactions in a small city like St. Louis could in fact exacerbate battles over "turf," and differences of personality and ego among titled leaders. Yet, the frequency and multiplicity of relationships among African Americans here may equally have mitigated the sort of intense intra-movement conflicts that elsewhere turned deadly.[38]

The Black United (Liberation) Front

The Liberators and Zulus were part of a larger bloc of local organizations known as the Black United Front (later renamed the Black Liberation Front). Other members included CORE, ACTION, the Mid-City Community Congress, the Jeff-Vander-Lou action group, and after its formation, the Black Nationalist Party. In the spring of 1968, soon after King's murder, the alliance presented Mayor Cervantes with a fifteen-point mandate calling for upgrades of black municipal workers, city contracts for black businessmen, greater efforts to recruit black police officers, and a massive restructuring of the Model Cities program. That fall, students at the predominantly black Vashon High School rioted after administrators eliminated a prom queen candidate because of her afro hairstyle. Students, and members of ACTION, the Liberators, and Zulus, met with school officials to negotiate a series of student demands, including the adoption of Black Studies curricula and the creation of a student advisory committee.[39]

The mainly male leaders of this local Black Power bloc, however, soon found themselves supporting players in the increasingly militant activity of black women and mothers receiving public assistance and living in St. Louis public housing. Signs of their growing dissatisfaction had been evident in 1967, when nine women and their children staged a ten-day, round-the-clock sit-in at the HDC offices. Having recently completed an HDC training program in electronics assembly, the women were frustrated by their inability to find employment—the result, they claimed, of racial discrimination practiced by McDonnell and fourteen other firms, as well as the HDC's hollow promises of job placement. That same year, sixty demonstrators, the majority of them black women, picketed the offices of the St. Louis Housing Authority, calling for rent reduction, better janitor services and pest control, and greater tenant representation on the housing authority board. These rumblings of discontent had turned thunderous as these women, drawing on their identities as mothers, public housing tenants, and aid recipients, more assertively voiced their right to social citizenship, autonomous households, and lives with dignity. In laying claim to entitlements independent of any male breadwinner, they implicitly rejected masculinist discourses that assigned them a secondary or entirely passive place in the Black Freedom Movement—and projected a new one rooted in "welfare rights."[40]

In May 1968, 200 public housing residents had marched to city hall to dramatize the need for jobs at a minimum wage of two dollars, a reduction in public rents, reforms in Missouri's means-tested welfare system, and the investigation of seventy-six caseworkers accused of unethical practices. Organized by the locally formed League for Adequate Welfare, the marchers walked twelve abreast with the Zulus and ACTION's Guerrilla Force serving as parade marshals. Holding signs with such pronouncements as "Idle Hands, Empty Stomachs, Hot Weather = Riots," demonstrators played on the white public's anxieties about urban rebellion to further goad city officials into action.[41]

The breaking point came in February 1969, though not in the form of a street uprising. When the housing authority announced its second rent increase in two years, more than 1,000 tenants of the city's six public housing developments launched a general rent strike. Their central argument, articulated by leaders like Jean King, was that rents should not exceed a quarter of a family's income. Initially, the protest did not constitute even half of the Gateway City's 7,800 public housing residents; yet, it became the largest of its kind in the nation ever, effectively commanding the attention of housing authority staff, the mayor's office, and even the White House. While the St. Louis Housing Authority faced the prospect of bankruptcy, the strikers picketed city hall. Federal officials, anxious about the directions the insurgency could take, intervened to settle the crisis. Not since the 1930s, when African American women laborers staged strikes in St. Louis's food-processing industry, had black working-class women so boldly demonstrated their autonomy from the male-centered leadership that had characterized most periods of local activism. ACTION, the Liberators, and the Zulus all lent support to the strike, and St. Stephen's Episcopal Church (the stronghold of Matheus, a prominent ACTION member, and a hub of Liberator activity) became the strikers' headquarters. Community organizer Buck Jones, the St. Louis Legal Aid Society, and the Teamsters Local 688 also aided the strikers. A settlement with city officials, reached in the fall of 1969, acceded to the strikers' main demands, which included rent reductions, the establishment of tenant management boards, and better upkeep and policing of the housing developments. Nationally, the rent strike helped influence the passage of the Brooke Amendment to the 1969 Housing Act, which placed a ceiling on public housing rents and provided subsidies for rent reductions.[42]

Black Power activists' involvement in women's struggles for fair public housing rents and adequate welfare payments illustrates the grassroots organizing that defined local Black Power initiatives, which historians like Matthew J. Countryman and Yohuru Williams have described. Consistent with Rhonda Y. Williams's work on black female public housing activists in Baltimore, this episode also contradicts narratives of a Black Power movement that was thoroughly masculinist and anti-woman. This is not to say that male organizers like Green or Koen were pro-feminist, or that they did not idealize the patriarchal, male-centered household (or even that female public housing and welfare rights activists did not harbor the same ideals). The point, rather, is that viewing Black Power mobilizations on the ground reveals that the actual praxis of both were more nuanced than any public pronouncements from national, or even local, figures.[43]

Police and FBI Repression of Black Power Militancy in St. Louis

As is well known in national narratives of Black Power, activists were also targeted by police agencies. The Liberators, arguably the city's most radical Black Power organization, weathered the brunt of this harassment locally. A long history of police abuse in black St. Louis communities directly influenced the formation of the Liberators, and authorities frequently harassed, provoked, and arrested members through discriminatory uses of existing ordinances. Yet, the Liberators' own tendencies toward "adventurism" may have further inflamed the harassment. In early September 1968, a violent series of incidents unfolded after Koen and four other young men were arrested following a dispute with police about an unlaminated license plate. Gunmen fired shots through the front window of the infamous Lucas Avenue police station, where the five had been taken. Gunshots were also fired into the home of Fred Grimes, a black police lieutenant and Lucas Avenue station watch commander. Assailants, too, firebombed the office of a black realtor who served on the Board of Police Commissioners.[44]

In rapid succession, a barrage of gunfire destroyed the window of the Liberators' headquarters, and unknown assailants ransacked their office and set their patrol car ablaze. (A witness later claimed to have seen Lieutenant Grimes fire a shotgun blast through the Liberators' office window.) That same evening, police rounded up twenty-one people affiliated with the Liberators, as well as the Zulus, for questioning. Claiming that the spate of shootings and firebombings was the result of a Liberator–Zulu feud, the president of the police commissioner board, Mayor Cervantes, and Missouri governor Warren Hearnes, endorsed a police crackdown on both groups. The chain of events reached a crescendo on September 13, 1968 when Koen and Leon Dent, another key Liberator, were seriously injured while again in custody at the Lucas Avenue station (Police had arrested them on traffic charges). Dent suffered facial lacerations, while Koen's skull and both hands were fractured. Disputing charges that they had assaulted officers, the two activists claimed that police had beaten them with brass knuckles and clubs in the basement of the station house. A broad coalition of Black Power, student and antiwar organizations came to the Liberators' defense. Congressional hopeful William Clay, a veteran of the Jefferson Bank boycott and the 1957 charter fight, telegrammed U.S. Attorney General Ramsey Clark to investigate the police station incident. In October, Koen, Green, and Joel Allen of the Washington University Students for a Democratic Society (SDS) were plaintiffs in a lawsuit seeking an injunction against the police harassment of local black and antiwar activists.[45]

Public criticism of police actions made the department more circumspect in its dealings with Black Power organizers, but it did not qualitatively change police activities. Nor did the outcry even begin to address the larger campaign of state terror directed at St. Louis's Black Liberation Front by the Federal Bureau of Investigation (FBI). FBI director J. Edgar Hoover had updated his anticommunist crusade in August 1967, when the Bureau launched its Counterintelligence Program (COINTELPRO) to undermine Civil Rights, Black Power, and New Left organizations. Expanded in March 1968, COINTEL operations instigated police raids, arrests, and assassination, bankrolled informants, maintained surveillance of individuals and groups, and fed negative stories about activists to cooperative newspapers. The *Globe-Democrat*, a consistent foe of Civil Rights and Black Power activism, had in fact been one of the five newspapers selected by the FBI to spread propaganda about local and national movement figures.[46]

The Bureau also circulated phony correspondence and seemingly anonymous cartoons to spread distrust and paranoia, and exploit the latent friction within, and between, organizations like the Liberators and Zulus. In October 1968, the FBI distributed an unsigned flyer praising the Zulus and criticizing the Liberators for, among other things, "work[ing] with white college honkies" and dressing like "honkie truck drivers and motersycle cats [*sic*]." The circular, noted an internal Bureau memorandum, "is purposely slanted to give the impression that the Zulus may have had a key role in its preparation although this is not stated." The widely disseminated flyer fed claims by St. Louis police that the two groups were engaged in a war. The FBI similarly weighed the possibility of promoting animosity between the Liberators and ACTION. Observing that the two organizations were drawing closer together, an FBI memorandum, dated January 8, 1969, declared that the Bureau was looking into plans that would "frustrate any strong degree of cooperation" between the groups. However, a succession of costly arrests in 1968, and the indictment of Koen and Dent on charges of assaulting police, had effectively hampered the Liberators' ability to function as an organization by the end of 1969, despite its publicized merger with SNCC the previous fall. The group faded steadily from the St. Louis scene—as did the Zulu 1200s, who were largely defunct by the spring of 1969.[47]

The Bureau concentrated its attention on ACTION, which according to a September 1969 memorandum, was "the only Black group of any significance other than the NOI [Nation of Islam]." FBI documents reveal that by early 1970, the agency was developing a plan against an unnamed white female active in ACTION. Through apparent surveillance, agents learned that her husband, who was uninvolved in the group, was threatened by the woman's close interactions with black men. The Bureau mailed him a phony letter, signed by "A Soul Sister," intimating that his wife had had multiple affairs with ACTION members. The couple soon separated and divorced, and Bureau correspondence noted approvingly that the woman's political involvement waned. In localizing the story of FBI counterinsurgency, scholars may recognize how these operations were symptomatic not only of the harassment of thousands of little-known local individuals and organizations around the nation, but also of the FBI's monitoring of entire black communities. It was not until November 1975 that the U.S. Senate Select Committee on Intelligence disclosed the full extent of these tactics against the progressive social movements of the period.[48]

Conclusion

Considered over time, and on the ground, the Black Freedom Movement has shown a durable continuity. But it has also been marked by change, in terms of leadership, constituencies, dominant ideologies, and strategies and tactics—as well as shifting structures of U.S. capitalism and modes of racial control. As anti-communist harassment during the early cold war, and FBI counterinsurgency during the late 1960s attest, Black Freedom workers have encountered moments of political rupture that disabled radical tendencies while promoting, or at least sparing, others. What is striking about the black radical tradition is not its impermeability to repression, but rather its ability to reemerge at different historical junctures, despite attempts to suppress it.

While Black Power followed numerous antecedents, including a long history of Black Nationalism, it nonetheless represented the agendas of a particular generation who experienced the successes and failures of postwar, popular black struggles. Black Power Studies has expanded historians' knowledge and appreciation of this period of the late twentieth century—the weaknesses and setbacks, as well as the triumphs and enduring legacies. As Black Freedom scholars retrieve more local narratives of Black Power (and their precursors), the richer will be our engagement with past, and present, transcripts of African American resistance.

Notes

1. Clayborne Carson, "Civil Rights Reform and the Black Freedom Struggle," in Charles W. Eagles, ed., *The Civil Rights Movement in America* (Jackson: University Press of Mississippi, 1986), pp. 19–37.
2. Jeanne F. Theoharis and Komozi Woodard, eds., *Freedom North: Black Freedom Struggles Outside the South, 1940–1980* (New York: Palgrave Macmillan, 2003); Theoharis and Woodard, eds., *Groundwork: Local Black Freedom Movements in America* (New York: New York University Press, 2005); Robert O. Self, *American Babylon: Race and the Struggle for Postwar Oakland* (Princeton, NJ: Princeton University Press, 2003); Nikhil Pal Singh, *Black Is a Country: Race and the Unfinished Struggle for Democracy* (Cambridge, MA: Harvard University Press, 2004); Matthew J. Countryman, *Up South: Civil Rights and Black Power in Philadelphia* (Philadelphia: University of Pennsylvania Press, 2006); Jacqueline Dowd Hall, "Civil Rights and the Political Uses of the Past," *Journal of American History,* 91 (2005): 1233–1263; Timothy B. Tyson, *Radio Free Dixie: Robert F. Williams and the Roots of Black Power* (Chapel Hill: University of North Carolina Press, 1999); Peniel E. Joseph, "Waiting till the Midnight Hour: Reconceptualizing the Heroic Period of the Civil Rights Movement, 1954–1965," *Souls* 2 (2000): 6–17; Joseph, ed., *The Black Power Movement: Rethinking the Civil Rights-Black Power Era* (New York: Routledge, 2006); Charles E. Jones, ed., *The Black Panther Party Reconsidered* (Baltimore: Black Classic Press, 1998); Yohuru Williams, *Black Politics/White Power: Civil Rights, Black Power, and the Black Panthers in New Haven* (St. James, NY: Brandywine, 2000); Jama Lazerow and Yohuru Williams, eds., *In Search of the Black Panther Party: New Perspectives on a Revolutionary Movement* (Durham, NC: Duke University Press, 2006); Komozi Woodard, *A Nation within a Nation: Amiri Baraka (LeRoi Jones) and Black Power Politics* (Chapel Hill: University of North Carolina Press, 1999); Scot Brown, *Fighting for US: Maulana Karenga, the US Organization, and Black Cultural Nationalism* (New York: New York University Press, 2003); Bettye Collier-Thomas and V.P. Franklin, eds., *Sisters in the Struggle: African American Women in the Civil Rights-Black Power Movement* (New York: New York University Press, 2001). See also Jeanne Theoharis, "Black Freedom Studies: Re-imagining and Redefining the Fundamentals," *History Compass* 4 (2006): 348–367.
3. See, for example, Theoharis and Woodard, (eds.), *Freedom North*; Self, *American Babylon*; Hall, "Civil Rights and the Political Uses of the Past,"; and Self, "The Black Panther Party and the Long Civil Rights Era," in Lazerow and Williams, (eds.), *In Search of the Black Panther Party*, pp. 15–55. See also Sundiata Keita Cha-Jua and Clarence Lang, "The 'Long Movement' as Vampire: Temporal and Spatial Fallacies in Recent Black Freedom Studies," *Journal of African American History* 92 (2007): 265–288.
4. Scott H. Decker, Jeffrey J. Rojek, and Eric P. Baumer, "A Century—or More—of Homicide in St. Louis," in Brady Baybeck and E. Terrence Jones, eds., *St. Louis Metromorphosis: Past Trends and Future Directions* (St. Louis: University of Missouri Press, 2004), p. 257.

5. V.O. Key, Jr., *Southern Politics in State and Nation* (New York: A.A. Knopf, 1949); John H. Fenton, *Politics in the Border States: A Study of the Patterns of Political Organization, and Political Change, Common to the Border States—Maryland, West Virginia, Kentucky, and Missouri* (New Orleans: Hauser Press, 1957).

6. Clarence E. Lang, "Community and Resistance in the Gateway City: Black National Consciousness, Working-Class Formation, and Social Movements in St. Louis, Missouri, 1941–64" (Ph.D. dissertation, University of Illinois at Urbana-Champaign, 2004), 50; Fenton, *Politics in the Border States*, p. 7.

7. Segregation Scrapbook, Missouri Historical Society Library and Research Center, St. Louis, Missouri (MHS); Lawrence O. Christensen, "Black St. Louis: A Study in Race Relations, 1865–1916" (Ph.D. dissertation, University of Missouri-Columbia, 1972); John E. Farley, "Racial Housing Segregation in the St. Louis Area: Past, Present, and Future," in Baybeck and Jones, eds., *St. Louis Metromorphosis*, p. 200; and Deborah Jane Henry, "Structures of Exclusion: Black Labor and the Building Trades in St. Louis, 1917–1966" (Ph.D. dissertation, University of Minnesota, 2002).

8. Priscilla A. Dowden, "'Over This Point We Are Determined to Fight': African-American Public Education and Health Care in St. Louis, Missouri, 1910–1949" (Ph.D. dissertation, Indiana University, 1997); Paul Dennis Brunn, "Black Workers and Social Movements of the 1930s in St. Louis" (Ph.D. dissertation, Washington University, 1975).

9. Brunn, "Black Workers and Social Movements."

10. David M. Grant Papers, Western Historical Manuscript Collection, University of Missouri-St. Louis (WHMC).

11. Brotherhood of Sleeping Car Porters records, St. Louis Division, Chicago Historical Society (CHS); Patricia L. Adams, "Fighting for Democracy in St. Louis: Civil Rights during World War II," *Missouri Historical Review* 80 (1985): 58–75.

12. "'A Strong Seed Planted': The Civil Rights Movement in St. Louis, 1954–1968" Oral History Collection, MHS.

13. National Negro Labor Council, Vertical File, Archives of Labor and Urban Affairs, Wayne State University; Kenneth S. Jolly, *Black Liberation in the Midwest: The Struggle in St. Louis, Missouri, 1964–1970* (New York: Routledge, 2006), p. 150.

14. Joseph, "Waiting till the Midnight Hour."

15. Ernest Calloway Papers, WHMC; Clarence Lang, "Civil Rights versus 'Civic Progress': The St. Louis NAACP and the City Charter Fight, 1956–1957," *Journal of Urban History* 34 (2008): 609–638.

16. Ibid. See also Lon W. Smith, "An Experiment in Trade Union Democracy: Harold Gibbons and the Formation of Teamsters Local 688, 1937–1957" (Ph.D. dissertation, Illinois State University, 1993).

17. Calloway Papers, WHMC.

18. Negro Scrapbook, Vol. 2, MHS.

19. William L. Clay, "Anatomy of an Economic Murder: A Statistical Review of the Negro in the Saint Louis Employment Field, 1963," pamphlet, MHS.

20. Negro Scrapbook, Vol. 2, MHS; Lang, "Community and Resistance in the Gateway City." See also George Lipsitz, *A Life in the Struggle: Ivory Perry and the Culture of Opposition* (Philadelphia: Temple University Press, 1988); and Jolly, *Black Liberation in the Midwest*, pp. 37–41.

21. Clarence Lang, "Between Civil Rights and Black Power in the Gateway City: The Action Committee to Improve Opportunities for Negroes (ACTION), 1964–75," *Journal of Social History* 37 (2004): 725–754. See also Steve Estes, *I Am a Man!: Race, Manhood, and the Civil Rights Movement* (Chapel Hill: University of North Carolina Press, 2005).

22. Ula Taylor, "Elijah Muhammad's Nation of Islam: Separatism, Regendering, and a Secular Approach to Black Power after Malcolm X (1965–1975)," in Theoharis and Woodard, (eds.), *Freedom North*, pp. 177–198.

23. Sidney M. Willhelm, *Who Needs the Negro?* (Cambridge, MA: Schenkman Publishing Co., 1970).

24. Negro Scrapbook, Vol. 2, MHS.

25. Buddy Lonesome, "Youth—Handcuffed—Shot to Death by a Policeman Here," and "A Shocking Incident" (news editorial), *St. Louis Argus*, June 18, 1965, 1A, 2B; Lonesome, "Rights Groups Oppose Cop Slaying of Handcuffed Youth," *Argus*, June 25, 1965, 1A; Negro Scrapbook, Vol. 2, MHS.

26. Negro Scrapbook, Vol. 3, and "Strong Seed Planted," MHS.

27. Negro Scrapbook, Vol. 2, MHS.

28. Jolly, *Black Liberation in the Midwest*, p. 42, pp. 52–59.

29. "Strong Seed Planted," MHS; and Benjamin Looker, *Point from Which Creation Begins: The Black Artists' Group of St. Louis* (St. Louis: Missouri Historical Society Press, 2004), pp. 26–27.

30. Jolly, *Black Liberation in the Midwest*, p. 120; Looker, *Point from Which Creation Begins*, pp. 85–87.

31. Jolly, *Black Liberation in the Midwest*, pp. 88–89, p. 95; Looker, *Point from Which Creation Begins*, p. 15, 42, 48, 96. See also James Edward Smethurst, *The Black Arts Movement: Literary Nationalism in the 1960s and 1970s* (Chapel Hill: University of North Carolina Press, 2005).

32. Looker, *Point from Which Creation Begins*, pp. 42–43; and Jolly, *Black Liberation in the Midwest*, p. 68.

33. Negro Scrapbook, Vol. 3, MHS; Jolly, *Black Liberation in the Midwest*, pp. 63–64, 72; and Looker, *Point from Which Creation Begins*, pp. 41–44.

34. Looker, *Point from Which Creation Begins*, p. 44.

35. Negro Scrapbook, Vol. 3, MHS; Jolly, *Black Liberation in the Midwest*, p. 75, 163. See also William B. Helmreich, *The Black Crusaders: A Case Study of a Black Militant Organization* (Harper & Row: New York, 1973), p. 174; and Helmreich, "The Black Liberators: A Historical Perspective," in Judson L. Jeffries, (ed.), *Black Power in the Belly of the Beast* (Urbana: University of Illinois Press, 2006), pp. 281–295.

36. Lang, Between Civil Rights and Black Power in the Gateway City; Jolly, *Black Liberation in the Midwest,* pp. 77–84; and Helmreich, The Black Liberators, p. 292.

37. See James Forman, *The Making of Black Revolutionaries* (1972; report, University of Washington Press, 1985); Judson L. Jeffries, ed., *Comrades: A Local History of the Black Panther Party* (Bloomington: Indiana University Press, 2007); Yohuru Williams and Jama Lazerow, eds., *Liberated Territory: Untold Local Perspectives on the Black Panther Party* (Durham, NC: Duke University Press, 2008); and Hasan Jeffries, *Bloody Lowndes: Civil Rights and Black Power in Alabama's Black Belt* (New York University Press, 2009).

38. See Woodard, *A Nation within a Nation*; Brown, *Fighting for US*; and Looker, *Point from Which Creation Begins*, p. xxiii, 47, 82.

39. Negro Scrapbook, Vol. 3, MHS; and Jolly, *Black Liberation in the Midwest*, p. 105.

40. Negro Scrapbook, Vols. 2 and 3, MHS.

41. Negro Scrapbook, Vol. 3, MHS.

42. Ibid. See also Lipsitz, *A Life in the Struggle*, p. 148; Looker, *Point from Which Creation Begins*, pp. 82–84.

43. See Countryman, *Up South*; Williams, *Black Politics/White Power*; and Rhonda Y. Williams, *The Politics of Public Housing: Black Women's Struggles against Urban Inequality* (New York: Oxford University Press, 2004).

44. Negro Scrapbook, Vol. 3, MHS.

45. Ibid. See also Jolly, *Black Liberation in the Midwest*, pp. 163–169; Helmreich, The Black Liberators, p. 283.

46. See Kenneth O'Reilly, *"Racial Matters": The FBI's Secret File on Black America, 1960–1972* (New York: The Free Press, 1989); Ward Churchill and Jim Vander Wall, *The COINTELPRO Papers: Documents from the FBI's Secret Wars against Domestic Dissent in the United States* (Boston: South End Press, 1990), n351.

47. COINTELPRO, Black Nationalist-Hate Groups File, microfilm reels 1 and 2. By 1970, Koen had returned to his native Cairo, Illinois, where he resumed his organizational efforts amid white police and vigilante terror—and continued FBI subterfuge.

48. COINTELPRO, Black Nationalist-Hate Groups File, microfilm reel 3.

4

A Campus Where Black Power Won: Merritt College and the Hidden History of Oakland's Black Panther Party

Donna Murch

The great exodus of poor people out of the South during World War II sprang from the hope for a better life in the big cities of the North and West. In search of freedom, they left behind centuries of southern cruelty and repression. The futility of that search is now history. The Black communities of Bedford-Stuyvesant, Newark, Brownsville, Watts, Detroit, and many others stand as testament that racism is as oppressive in the North as in the South. Oakland is no different.

—*Huey Newton*[1]

Introduction

In 1948 Harry Haywood wrote, "The Negro Question is agrarian in origin...It presents the curious anomaly of a virtual serfdom in the very heart of the most highly industrialized country in the world."[2] World War II and the advent of the mechanical cotton picker resolved this contradiction by spurring the single largest black population movement in U.S. history. In an ever-expanding tide, migrants poured out of the south in pursuit of rising wages and living standards promised by major metropolitan areas.

In 1940 77 percent of the total black population lived in the south with more than 49 percent in rural areas; two out of five worked as farmers, sharecroppers, or farm laborers. In the next ten years over 1.6 million black people migrated north and westward, to be followed by another 1.5 million in the subsequent decade.[3] The repercussions of this internal migration were felt throughout the United States leaving their deepest imprint on west coast cities that historically possessed small black populations. California's lucrative defense industries made the state a prime destination for southern migrants. By 1943, the San Francisco Chamber of Commerce declared the Bay Area, "the largest shipbuilding center in the world."[4] Sociologist Charles Johnson explained, "To the romantic appeal of the west, has been added the real and actual opportunity for gainful employment, setting in motion a war-time migration of huge proportions."[5] Oakland's black population mushroomed from 8,462 residents in 1940 (3%) to an impressive 47,562 in 1950 (12%).[6] A pattern of chain migration continued until 1980, when Oakland reached the racial tipping point with 157,484 black residents, 51 percent of the city's total.[7] The resulting shift in demography secured Oakland's position as the largest black metropolis in northern California.

In two decades after World War II, Oakland's recently settled African American community produced one of the most influential local Black Power movements in the country.[8] First and second generation migrants who came of age in the late 1950s and early 1960s composed not only the leadership, but also the rank and file of large segments of the Black Panther Party (BPP) and other Black Power organizations.[9] In contrast to their parents who entered the San Francisco Bay area at a time of economic boom, postwar youth faced a rapidly disappearing industrial base along with increased school, neighborhood, and job segregation. However, socioeconomic factors alone cannot explain the development of Bay Area radicalism. In response to the rapidly growing, and disproportionately young, migrant population, city and state government developed a program to combat "juvenile delinquency" that resulted in high rates of police harassment, arrest, and incarceration.[10] With its founding in October 1966, the Black Panther Party for Self-Defense (BPPSD) mobilized against this new scale of repression by organizing young people throughout the Bay Area. Within a few short years, the Oakland-based group dropped the words "Self Defense" from its name and expanded into an international force with chapters in more than sixty-one U.S. cities and twenty-six states.[11]

Although the BPPSD is best known for its armed police patrols and embrace of "brothers off the block" as revolutionary vanguard, this chapter argues that its origins lay in black student and campus struggles at Merritt College and University of California, Berkeley (UC, Berkeley). While we often think of Black Studies as the product rather than the catalyst of postwar social movements, in the Bay Area fights over curriculum and hiring in the early 1960s were integral to the emergence of Black Power after Watts. Radical groups like the Panthers reflected not only the problems, but also the ambitions of California's migrant communities who saw schooling as "the primary vehicle for their children's upward mobility."[12] Oral testimony reveals that for many black families greater educational access helped inspire western migration itself. Melvyn Newton, brother of the Panther co-founder Huey Newton, expressed this sentiment most clearly. "We were children of migrants that came here for social opportunity...families...came with the dream of sending their kids to school. I don't know if they necessarily knew what schools were like out here, but they knew what the conditions were like out there."[13] Given the postindustrial restructuring of Oakland's economy and penal system, the need for quality education took on a particular urgency.

Black Migration and World War II

Before World War II, the black community of the San Francisco Bay Area was tiny. In the first quarter of the century, black residents actively discouraged migration, because of limited economic opportunity. World War II ushered in a new era; national defense brought an unprecedented policy and capital investment in the state. The federal government invested more than forty billion dollars in west coast factories, military bases, and other capital improvements. The resulting economic and demographic changes to the region were immense.[14] In 1943, the San Francisco Chronicle summed up this process by announcing, "the Second Gold Rush" had begun.[15] While people fled from regions throughout the south, and brought with them a diversity of experiences and backgrounds, Bay Area war migrants shared some particular characteristics. The majority came from Texas, Louisiana, and Oklahoma with Arkansas and Mississippi contributing lesser numbers.[16] With an average age between twenty-two and twenty-three, they were younger than the resident population and disproportionately female.[17]

In addition to the obvious economic incentives, the San Francisco Bay Area held a special allure for these young migrants. Racial segregation functioned like a palimpsest whose layers grew denser with the passage of time. The recent migration of the East Bay's black community meant that before the population influx spurred by World War II, formal systems of racial control had not yet been consolidated. Black rates of property ownership in California ranked among the highest in the nation, and in contrast to their places of origin, black migrants suffered less physical repression, worked largely outside agriculture, and had greater access to public services.[18] Most importantly, the state's promise of higher quality public education at all levels tapped a persistent, if understudied, motive for black migration throughout the twentieth century.[19]

By 1945, national defense industries had produced more than 600,000 jobs for African Americans and drawn a million black southerners to northern and western industrial centers. Although Bay Area shipyards resisted hiring black workers at the outset of the war, systematic organizing efforts by C.L. Dellums, the local business agent for the Brotherhood of Sleeping Car Porters (BSCP), and other civil rights leaders forced both unions and local employers to hire African Americans.[20] Their campaign provided this newly settled population with unprecedented economic opportunity. In the Bay Area over 70 percent of black migrants found work in the shipyards, and black female employment tripled.[21] Southern migration combined with a changing job structure inaugurated the formation of a strong black working-class movement. C.L. Dellums, a close friend of A. Philip Randolph and uncle to future Congressman Ronald Dellums, remained a touchstone of local black politics in subsequent decades, and his union became one of the most powerful black institutions in the East Bay. However, this era of abundance proved fleeting as postwar demobilization led to large-scale unemployment and economic uncertainty.[22]

Deindustrialization

As migrants sought to realize their new-found opportunity, a new and more repressive racial order emerged. African Americans who had fled the poverty and brutality of the south soon found new barriers erected in their wake. In 1946, the Final Report of the Fair Employment Practice Committee argued, "The entire West Coast Area is characterized by problems which in newness and intensity distinguish it from the rest of the country."[23] Black labor's remarkable gains quickly receded. The workforce employed by shipbuilders shrank from 250,000 at the war's height to 12,000 people in 1946.[24] In Oakland and south Berkeley, five short years of boom were followed by long decades of bust. Immediately after the war ended, Oakland entered a period of industrial decline and structural unemployment became a permanent feature of the local economy. By 1960, the federal government officially classified Oakland as a depressed area.[25] Despite California's thriving cold war economy, Oakland limped along. Deindustrialization had a devastating social impact on African American residents. In 1959, one quarter of the total population in Oakland lived under the poverty line and roughly 10 percent earned less than $2,000 per year.[26] Union discrimination, concentration in temporary wartime industry like shipyards, and entrenched patterns of employer discrimination, relegated much of the growing black population to secondary labor markets. Black youth remained most vulnerable to economic retrenchment, facing high rates of unemployment and repression from local law enforcement.[27]

Police Repression and "Juvenile Delinquency"

Among historians, it is well recognized that white residential and capital flight from cities was a direct reaction to black migration. In Oakland and other metropolitan areas in California, however, city and state government's postwar preoccupation with "juvenile delinquency" was an equally important development. Racial anxieties about the city's rapidly changing demographics led to an increasing integration of school and recreational programs with police and penal authorities. In this context, the discourse of "juvenile delinquency" took on a clear racial tone, leading to wide-scale policing and criminalization of black youth. While extensive police harassment and arrest of black migrants started during the population influx of World War II, it vastly intensified in the period of economic decline that ensued.[28]

In the 1950s, public service agencies fielded the cascade of disputes that followed from black settlement in white enclaves. School grounds and recreation areas became volatile flashpoints of racial conflict. White neighborhoods undergoing swift racial transition sought to obtain funds from the city council to reorganize social service agencies. When city government refused to allocate money for specific areas, groups of residents banded together to form the Associated Agencies (AA) and District Community Councils (DCA).[29] In its final form, the AA of Oakland encompassed three tiers of government responsible for youth and family services. At the local level, the AA integrated Oakland's public school system, recreation, and police departments with the county's probation, welfare, and health agencies. In turn, these local groups were linked up with the California Youth Authority, the state's largest penal authority for juvenile offenders.[30] Meetings with multiple family service and juvenile agencies allowed them to work together to identify and monitor "troublemakers."[31] The most disturbing aspect of this integration of recreational and police agencies was the tracking of youths identified as delinquent. Police monitored, and even arrested, individuals who had been identified as delinquent by school and recreational staff, despite the fact that they had no prior record. Increasingly, the category of black youth itself became defined as a social problem at best, and as a criminal presence at worst.

Local politicians used cold war metaphors of contagion and containment to describe black residents with the greatest threat emanating from the youth. Oakland city manager Wayne Thompson, a self-professed liberal, explained the preventative logic behind introducing police and penal presence into the local school system to stem the tide of "delinquency." "If you didn't stop it, it would spread into the business sections and even infect the industrial community," Thompson warned. "We had eyes and ears in those areas to alert us in advance.... Before the Associated Agencies program, it was an admission of weakness on the part of the school official, or... failure if he even let a policeman in the door.... What a change now! The first man they call is the police."[32]

In the mid-1950s, a restructuring of the Oakland Police Department (OPD) exacerbated this situation. Changes in East Bay law enforcement reflected a national trend toward "legalistic policing," characterized by modern equipment, formalized systems, and greater emphasis on juvenile detention. Oakland's new police chief dissolved local precincts, concentrated the OPD into a single headquarters, and overhauled hiring practices in favor of better educated, more affluent candidates.[33] In practice, these policies created an almost exclusively white middle-class force that resided outside the city and had little understanding or connection to the neighborhoods they served.[34] Oakland's reinvigorated police force became a constant and intrusive presence in people's lives. Systematic arrests of young offenders linked them to the web of professional services, including probation officers, judges, and child guidance clinics, further blurring the line between "authoritative" police functions and family services.[35] Given the pervasive hostility toward black migrants, this framework laid the basis for the simultaneous criminalization of black youth and long-term neglect of black families.

Black Students and the Roots of Black Power

While Black Power has often been treated as a post-Watts phenomenon, its roots in the East Bay stretch far back into the decade preceding the urban rebellions.[36] Public education became the most immediate arena in which migrant youth confronted a hostile white establishment and mobilized against it.[37] Black students entered secondary schools and universities in large numbers at a time when the

California system of higher education was undergoing a major restructuring. Faced with a mushrooming population and a conservative fiscal structure, state policy makers sought to contain costs while expanding capacity. Projections warned that student populations would increase nearly fivefold in fifteen years. In 1960, 227,000 students were enrolled in higher education, by 1975 the total reached 1,000,000.[38] California's university system, with its integrated tiers of community colleges, state, and public universities, led the nation in superior levels of funding, infrastructure, and quality of instruction. In 1960, the statewide Master Plan for Higher Education vastly increased the number and capacity of junior colleges and mandated that they admit all applicants with high school diplomas. Urban campuses greatly expanded black working-class college enrollment, and provided an institutional base for political organizing. By 1969, the San Francisco Bay Area boasted one of the highest rates of minority college completion in the nation.[39] Full access to community colleges became particularly important given racial segregation and inequalities in the city's primary and secondary schools.

The Oakland Unified School District (OUSD) consistently allocated resources to segregated white schools in wealthy areas of the city, while neglecting overcrowded schools in the "flatlands." In the early 1960s, this issue came to a head with the building of Skyline High School in the Oakland hills. Black parents and civil rights leaders charged the school board with "gerrymandering" the district and draining resources from the rapidly integrating schools in the lowlying areas of the city. Discrimination extended beyond issues of unfair financing to the racialized culture of the schools themselves. Starting in 1957, black students and their families protested low standards and achievements in West Oakland's all-Black McClymond's High School. They cited the low rate of college attendance among "Mack" graduates, and a recurring pattern of counselors and school officials discouraging students from continuing their education.[40] A Fair Employment Practices Commission (FEPC) report published several years later identified differential standards as a pervasive problem throughout the district. Principals and teachers in majority black schools repeatedly emphasized the importance of discipline, comportment, and hygiene over academic achievement.[41] In the spring of 1966, the Ad Hoc Committee for Quality Education (AHCQUE) formed to protest the school board's unfair use of resources and the school's miseducation of their children.[42] Over the next decade, flatland parents and their supporters vigorously contested the increased police presence in the schools, the failure to hire black faculty and staff, and the self-fulfilling prophecy of lowered expectations producing poor academic results.

Donald Warden and the Afro-American Association

In the San Francisco Bay Area, some of the most important battles over curriculum and social access took place at the university level. Within less than a decade, unprecedented numbers of black students entered college for the first time, and urban campuses became major sites for political organizing. In the spring of 1961, Berkeley graduate students from a variety of disciplines and a sprinkling of undergraduates from UCB and San Francisco State began to meet regularly. Donald Warden, a second year student at UCB's Bolt School of Law, emerged as the "leader" of the study group. In early March, he wrote a series of editorials to the Daily California, denouncing Roy Wilkins, the NAACP, and the civil rights strategy of integration.[43] Students debated books of immediate political relevance and hosted weekly forums throughout the Bay Area. Charter members included Henry Ramsey, Donald Hopkins, Ann Cooke, Mary Lewis, and Maurice Dawson.[44] As the group cohered, they chose the name Afro-American Association (AAA) and limited membership exclusively to people of African descent.[45] Ernest Allen, a Merritt student who later joined, described the choice as containing a "revolutionary.... sense of rebirth" paralleling the Nation of Islam's (NOI) repudiation of "slave names."[46] W.E.B. Du Bois's *Souls of Black Folk*, Carter G. Woodson's *Miseducation of the Negro*, and Ralph Ellison's *Invisible Man* numbered among their selections, however, E. Franklin Frazier's *Black Bourgeoisie* and Melville J. Herskovits's *The Myth of the Negro Past* elicited the most debate.[47] The discussion and the controversy these two volumes engendered had the greatest impact on the Association's evolving ideology. Ultimately, the AAA successfully fused Herskovits and Frazier's opposing views on African survivals to fashion its own anti-assimilationist ideology.[48]

Many of the ideas generated in the Association, including their debates about the nature of identity, African retention, and the integrationist sins of the black middle class, anticipated cultural nationalist thought of subsequent years.[49] In May 1961, Association members worked together with the UCB campus chapter of the NAACP to bring Malcolm X to speak. Soon after, a group of students began regularly attending the NOI's mosque, Temple 26B, in West Oakland. Although the Association remained secular, their rhetoric revealed the NOI's clear influence.[50] Opposition to integration, understood as forced assimilation, served as the unifying theme; their public speeches, often reserved their greatest rancor not for the dominant white society, as for the compliant "Black Bourgeoisie." Warden and others in the Association argued that while civil rights leaders spoke of desegregation and compliance with Brown, what they truly advocated was assimilation. They encouraged their members to learn Arabic and Swahili, and in the mid-1960s began manufacturing an African-inspired garment called the "Simba."[51] Ronald Everett, later known as Karenga, joined the Association in 1963, and helped establish a Los Angeles chapter. Historian Scot Brown notes that "Warden, though not specifically defining the group as cultural nationalist, set in motion many of the cultural concepts and organizing principles that Karenga utilized in US."[52]

The AAA was not content to simply remain a study group, Warden and others moved on to become integral to the East Bay's larger African American community. Association members experimented with different forms of activism, including sponsoring the "Mind of the Ghetto" youth conference at McClymonds High in West Oakland. However, Harlem-style street rallies remained the AAA's most consistent form of outreach.[53] Although street speaking had long been a staple of black nationalist political culture, the AAA adapted it to the particularities of the Bay Area. A pattern developed in which the association held rallies in San Francisco until early afternoon, before moving on to Oakland and to Richmond. The exile of Robert F. Williams prompted one of the first street-speaking sessions. Association members traveled down to 7th street, the central black business district in West Oakland, and held up the newspaper headlines, loudly proclaiming their support.[54] Looking back, Maurice Dawson remembered the uproar over Williams's exile as a turning point. The name Robert F. Williams was poised on everyone's lips. "[He] ain't scared of nothing or nobody," Dawson explained, "This was the talk of the Bay Area.... It was the genesis of the growth and evolution, frankly, of racial pride in the East Bay."[55]

In early 1963, the AAA reached the height of its powers and influence. The association offered an effective mix of black cultural nationalism and colorful display that helped mobilize a whole generation that passed through Bay Area schools. The support received by the association from different segments of the black community reflected its profound appeal. Many participants in the association later became prominent across a broad spectrum of black politics. On the electoral front, Ronald Dellums briefly attended meetings along with future Oakland Mayor Elihu Harris, and local powerbrokers Ortho Green, Henry Ramsey, and Donald Hopkins. Charter member Ann Cooke went on to publish in the groundbreaking feminist anthology, *The Black Woman;* while political radicals Ernest Allen, Cedric Robinson, Huey Newton, and Bobby Seale socialized with nationalists Ronald Karenga, Fritz Pointer, and David Patterson.[56] In sum, the Association represented a foundational stage in the evolution of black politics in California. While an older school of historiography has emphasized the divisions between civil rights and electoral politics on the one hand, and black nationalist and Black Power thought on the other, the history of the AAA clearly demonstrates how the two were nurtured together in this early student movement.

Despite the association's many accomplishments, this period of unity was short lived. The AAA soon underwent a series of splits that alienated a core portion of its more radical membership. Students interested in socialism and direct community action became frustrated by Warden's recalcitrant anti-communism and his resistance to more concrete forms of political organizing. Others questioned his political integrity and personal motivation.[57] Nevertheless, the AAA helped launch a new era of Black activism and institution building that culminated in the founding of the BPPSD.

Merritt College, Black Studies, and the Black Panther Party

While the AAA recruited throughout the East Bay, its largest following emerged at Merritt College, affectionately known to Black residents as "Grove Street." Ernest Allen explained, "The fact that it [Merritt College] was located right in the middle of a community was a historical accident, but what people made of it was something else."[58] The boundary between Merritt and North Oakland was completely porous. People passed on and off the campus, and many residents from the surrounding area hung out in the cafeteria, a major hub for debate.[59] By locating their headquarters adjacent to the school and regularly staging street rallies on campus grounds, the Association helped ignite a militant black student movement.

Until the late 1950s, African American presence on California campuses was too small and diffuse to be called a community. Although the University of California did not collect statistics on the racial breakdown of the Berkeley student population until 1966, anecdotal evidence reveals that there were less than 100 black students out of nearly 20,000. As the civil rights movement progressed, these figures began to slowly increase, until by 1966, black students, including both native born and African, breached the 1 percent barrier with 226 undergraduate and graduate students enrolled in Berkeley.[60] Although these gains were significant, the expansion of the black student body at community colleges dwarfed that of the comparatively elite University of California system. By 1965 black students made up nearly 10 percent of Merritt College's total enrollment, and within two short years, they formed more than 30 percent of the student body. A mutually reinforcing dynamic took hold in which the increase in black students fed political organizing and political organizing, in turn, attracted people who would never have considered attending college.[61]

Many of these students were not only the first members of their family to attend college, but they were also recent arrivals from the south who still retained strong cultural ties to their families' places of origin. Their intermediary status as migrants led them to look "backwards as much as forwards" and helped to provide additional motivation for seizing opportunities unimaginable to them and their families a decade before.[62] While Huey Newton was exceptional in many ways, his background typified that of the growing black student body at Merritt College. He was the child of Louisiana migrants, raised in poverty in Oakland by parents who had come to California in search of better jobs and more educational opportunity. Similarly, Bobby Seale was a first-generation migrant from Dallas, Texas.[63] In the late 1950s, Seale began taking night classes at Merritt with hopes of earning a degree in engineering. As his interest in "American Black History" grew, he shifted his emphasis from technical training toward the humanities.[64] Attending community college was the single biggest influence on their radicalization, Newton later explained. "It was my studying and reading in college that led me to become a socialist.... The transformation from a nationalist to a socialist was a slow one, although I was around a lot of Marxists."[65]

In the mid-1960s, Merritt students began organizing to have Black Studies classes included in the regular curriculum. Between 1964 and 1966, Virtual Murrell, Alex Papillion, Isaac Moore, Kenny Freeman, Ernest Allen, and Douglas Allen formed the Soul Students Advisory Council (SSAC).[66] Leo Bazille, who became president of Soul Students in 1966, described the organization as a place where "youth met and devised political involvements." The same year they changed their name to "Black Student Union," a new term at the time. One of the council's first accomplishments was a large rally at Merritt protesting the draft of blacks into the military. However, their fight to implement black history classes at Merritt and to increase the hiring of black faculty and staff became their most sustained campaign.[67]

After a confrontation with white faculty member Rodney Carlisle over the content of his "Negro History" class, Huey Newton became involved in this protracted struggle.[68] He saw it as an important chance to implement a new type of organizing. Newton proposed sponsoring a rally in support of the Afro-American History Program in which SSAC members would invite the press, strap on guns, and march outside Merritt College on Malcolm X's birthday. This type of action would enable Soul Students to mobilize not only students, but the populations surrounding the school, including the "lumpen proletariat," the key constituency for social revolution.[69] A display of armed self-defense would impress the community, call attention to police brutality, and intimidate Merritt's administrators into taking the students' demands more seriously.[70] Soul Students refused, and Newton refocused his attention on the world beyond the "the sandbox politics" of the community college.

While the BPP had its origins firmly in early student activism at Berkeley and Merritt College, Seale and Newton quickly distanced themselves from their campus roots and cultivated their image as "brothers off the block." Newton viewed the gun as a powerful "recruiting device" that would attract youth from the broader community, thereby bridging the gap between students and the grassroots. This duality, merging different strata from "college and community," remained a hallmark of the BPP throughout its history. Given the sharp spike in local college attendance, this dynamic was strongest in Oakland, but it was true for other chapters as well. In describing the Chicago chapter, David Hilliard likened their strategy to Bunchy Carter's efforts in Los Angeles, "They [tried] to forge an alliance between the two largest concentrations of Black youth—the campus and the streets."[71]

While many black nationalist and New Left groups hoped to do this, the Panthers set about achieving this broad coalition through spectacular displays challenging state violence. As Newton searched for a medium to "capture the imagination" of Oakland's black community, he turned to the law library at the North Oakland Service Center, a poverty program that employed Bobby Seale. Drawing on his training from law school, Newton pored over the California penal code and resurrected an old statute that legalized carrying unconcealed weapons. After much discussion with peers over the right to bear arms, Newton and Seale decided that they needed a concrete political program before initiating police patrols. In October 1966, in less than twenty minutes, Seale and Newton drafted the "Black Panther Party Platform and Program" in the North Oakland Poverty Center.[72]

One of the Panthers' first community actions took place on 55th and Market near the antipoverty program where Newton and Seale were working. Several pedestrians had been killed at the intersection, which had no stoplight. They attempted to get the city to put up a stop sign and made little progress with local bureaucracy. So they went out and started directing traffic; within weeks, the city installed a signal. This strategy of forcing the hand of local government through assuming some of its powers was repeated a number of times throughout the party's history.[73] Policing the police, food giveaways, and public-service actions such as the one on market, highlighted the simultaneously negligent and repressive role of government in Oakland's black neighborhoods. The implicit message was clear—either improve state services or face an armed movement of local youth.

Conclusion

Ultimately, Oakland's Black Power Movement is best understood through the historical circumstances that produced it. Large-scale migration to California, impelled first by defense industry and the inertia of chain migration—and later by the death throes of agricultural tenancy—created a displaced population that remained shut out of the major avenues of decision making. For first-generation migrants, shipyard- and defense-related employment promised a vast increase in living standards that quickly dissolved in the war's aftermath. As jobs and money flowed to the suburbs in the coming decades, the core of the migrant population found itself trapped in the familiar cycles of poverty and debt. For the young, the situation was most difficult of all—they not only faced economic uncertainty, but also the constant threat of police harassment and incarceration. As they approached college age, federal funding and an expansive network of community colleges provided newfound access to integrated higher education. Black students seized this opportunity and used it as an arena for addressing the most immediate circumstances of their lives. College campuses became major sites for political organizing, and first-generation attendees articulated the grievances of the larger community. Black Studies and student union struggles created strong networks of activists that would later venture beyond the campus into grassroots and community organizing after 1965. The AAA, US Organization, and the BPP all had origins in these campus-based struggles. Huey Newton said it best, "Everyone—from Warden and the Afro-American Association to Malcolm X and the Muslims to all the other groups active in the Bay Area at that time—believed strongly that the failure to include Black history in the college curriculum was a scandal. We all set out to do something about it."[74]

Notes

1. Huey Newton, *Revolutionary Suicide* (New York: Writers and Readers Publishing, 1973), p. 14.
2. Harry Haywood, *Negro Liberation* (Chicago: Liberator Press, 1976), p. 11.
3. Manning Marable, "Foreword" in Rod Bush's *The New Black Vote: Politics and Power in Four American Cities* (San Francisco: Synthesis Publications, 1984), p. 3; Nicolas Lemann, *The Promised Land: The Great Black Migration and How It Changed America* (New York: A.A. Knopf, 1991), p. 6.
4. Quoted by Albert S. Broussard, "In Search of the Promised Land: African American Migration to San Francisco, 1900–1945," in Lawrence de Graafe et al., eds., *Seeking El Dorado: African Americans in California* (Los Angeles: Autry Museum of Western Heritage, 2001), p. 190.
5. Charles Johnson, *The Negro War Worker in San Francisco: A Local Self-Survey* (San Francisco: YWCA, 1944), p. 1.

6. U.S. Bureau of the Census, Population by Age, Race, and Sex in Oakland, Calif. by Census Tracts: 1940.

7. U.S. Department of Labor, "Data from Census Bureau Estimates for Oakland, California," 1980 Census, Run No. 831120, p. 4.

8. For a sustained discussion of the complex relation of the Black Panther Party to the concept of Black Power, see Donna Murch, "When the Panther Travels: Race and the Southern Diaspora in the History of the BPP, 1964–1972," Conference Paper, Diaspora and the Difference Race Makes Symposium, Black Atlantic Seminar, Rutgers University, February 16, 2007.

9. Donna Murch, "The Urban Promise of Black Power: African American Political Mobilization in Oakland and the East Bay, 1961–1977" (UC Berkeley: Ph.D. Thesis, 2004).

10. After conducting extensive oral history interviews with activists in the Bay Area Black Power movement for my dissertation, I was struck by how many had served time in the California Youth Authority and other penal institutions. For representative sample, see Donna Murch, "Interview with Emory Douglas," March 7, 2002, "Leon White," August 9, 2002, "Fritz Pointer," March 12, 2002; Judith May, "Struggle for Authority: A Comparison of Four Social Change Programs in Oakland, California" (UC Berkeley: Ph.D. Thesis, 1973).

11. Newton, *Revolutionary Suicide*, pp. 110–127; Murch, "Interview with Ernest Allen," February 3, 2002; Murch, "The Urban Promise," p. 147; Paul Alkebulan, "The Role of Ideology in the Growth, Establishment, and Decline of the Black Panther Party: 1966 to 1982" (UC Berkeley, Ph.D. Thesis, 2003), p. 104.

12. Quote taken from Jeanne Theoharis, "'Alabama on the Avalon': Rethinking the Watts Uprising and the Character of Black Protest in Los Angeles" in Peniel E. Joseph, ed., *The Black Power Movement: Rethinking the Civil Rights-Black Power Era* (New York: Routledge, 2006), p. 33.

13. Murch, "Interview with Melvyn Newton," March 15, 2002.

14. Albert Broussard, Black San Francisco: *The Struggle for Racial Equality in the West, 1900–1945* (Lawrence: University of Kansas, 1993); Gerald D. Nash, *The American West Transformed: The Impact of the Second World War* (Lincoln: University of Nebraska Press, 1985), p. 17.

15. Marilynn S. Johnson, *The Second Gold Rush* (Berkeley: University of California Press, 1993), p. 30.

16. Broussard, *The Struggle for Racial Equality*, p. 192; Gretchen Lemke-Santangelo, *Abiding Courage: African American Women and the East Bay Community* (Chapel Hill: University of North Carolina Press, 1996); Charles Johnson, *Negro War Worker*.

17. According to Charles Johnson, in the 19–24 age group, women outnumbered men by 2 to 1; Johnson, *The Negro War Worker*, p. 6.

18. Lawrence B. De Graaf and Quintard Taylor, "Introduction" to *Seeking El Dorado*, p. 24; Murch, "Interview with Walter Bachemin," June 28, 1998, p. 1; William Henry Brown, "Class Aspects of Residential Development and Choice in Oakland Black Community" (UC Berkeley Ph.D. Thesis, 1970), p. 86; This dynamic was reenacted inside the state itself. Large numbers of southern migrants who first settled in Los Angeles, which had a much older and larger African American community, later chose to move north in search of a less hostile environment; Floyd Hunter, *Housing Discrimination in Oakland, California; A Study Prepared for the Oakland Mayor's Committee on Full Opportunity and the Council of Social Planning, Alameda County* (Berkeley: University of California Press, 1964), p. 14.

19. In my oral history interviews with migrants, this theme frequently emerged. See for example, Murch, "Newton," "Bachemin."
20. Donna Murch, "The Problem of the Occupational Color Line," unpublished paper, p. 15.
21. Charlers Wollenberg, *Marinship at War: Shipbuilding and Social Change in Wartime Sausalito* (Berkeley: Western Heritage Press, 1990), p. 71.
22. C.L. Dellums, International President of the Brotherhood of Sleeping Car Porters and Civil Rights Leaders, Northern California Negro Political Series, Regional Oral History Office, Bancroft Library, UC Berkeley; Robert Self, *American Babylon: Race and the Struggle for Postwar Oakland* (Princeton, NJ: Princeton University Press, 2003).
23. Committee of Fair Employment Practice, Final Report, June 28, 1946, Institute for Governmental Studies, University of California Berkeley, p. 77.
24. Oakland Police Department Report (6), p. 23, Oakland Public Library; Marilynn Johnson, *Second Gold Rush*; Murch, "The Problem of the Occupational Color Line."
25. Edward, C., Hayes, *Power Structure and Urban Policy: Who Rules in Oakland?* (San Francisco: McGraw-Hill Book, 1972), p. 48.
26. Ibid., p. 44.
27. Hayes, *Power Structure and Urban Policy*; Johnson, *Second Gold Rush*, p. 167; Gretchen Lemke-Santangelo, "Deindustrialization, Urban Poverty and African American Community Mobilization in Oakland, 1945 through 1990s," in *Seeking El Dorado*, pp. 343–376.
28. Marilynn Johnson, *Second Gold Rush*, p. 167; OPD Report (6).
29. May, "Struggle for Authority," pp. 115–117.
30. Ibid; Evelio Grillo, *Black Cuban, Black American: A Memoir* (Houston: Arte Publico Press, 2000), p. 131; Laura Mihailoff, "Protecting Our Children: A History of the California Youth Authority and Juvenile Justice, 1938–1968" (UC Berkeley, Ph.D. Thesis, 2005).
31. May, "Struggle for Authority," p. 24.
32. Ibid., p. 128.
33. Ibid., p. 130; Oakland Police Department History 1941–1955, Part 6, pp. 36–40.
34. May, "Struggle for Authority," pp. 130–135; Oakland Police Department History 1941–1955, Part 6, pp. 36–40.
35. May, "Struggle for Authority," p. 130.
36. Komozi Woodard, *A Nation within a Nation: Amiri Baraka (LeRoi Jones) & Black Power Politics* (Chapel Hill: University of North Carolina Press, 1999); Self, *American Babylon*; Peniel E. Joseph, *Waiting 'Til the Midnight Hour: A Narrative History of Black Power in America* (New York: Henry Holt, 2006). For new literature on the history of Black Studies see also Peniel E. Joseph, "Black Studies, Student Activism, and the Black Power Movement," in *The Black Movement*, pp. 251–277; Noliwe Rooks, *White Money, Black Power: The Surprising History of African American Studies and the Crisis of Race in Higher Education* (Boston: Beacon Press, 2006).
37. For a sustained discussion of the roots of the Bay Area Black Power movement in postwar struggles over California higher education, see Murch, "The Urban Promise."
38. John Aubrey Douglas, "Brokering the 1960 Master Plan: Pat Brown and the Promise of California Higher Education," in Martin Schiesl, ed., *Responsible Liberalism: Edmund G. "Pat" Brown and Reform Government in California 1958-1967* (Los Angeles, CA: Edmund G. "Pat" Brown Institute of Public Affairs, 2003), p. 86; John Aubrey Douglas, *The California Idea and American Education; Sidney W. Brossman and Myron Roberts, The California Community Colleges* (Palo Alto, CA: Field Educational Publications, 1973).

39. "Completion Levels: Percentage of High School and College 'Completers' (Aged 25 and Over) in Selected Cities, 1969," in Jessie Carney Smith and Carrell Peterson Horton, eds., *Historical Statistics of Black America* (Detroit, MI: Gale Research, 1995), p. 530.

40. Jonathan Spencer, "Caught in Crossfire: Marcus Foster and America's Urban Education Crisis, 1941–1973" (New York University: Ph.D. Thesis, 2002), pp. 361–363.

41. Jonathan Spencer quotes an article from 1952 in which the planners of the new McClymonds building described how their choice of design suited "the modified curriculum" meant to "fit the needs of the pupils in the area." Although biology was still required, McClymonds possessed a different "set of contents and set of objectives… [with] a good deal of attention… to the care of the hair, skin and feet." Spencer, "Caught in Crossfire," p. 361.

42. Spencer, p. 363.

43. Donald Warden, Letters to the Ice Box, Daily California, March 1, 1961, March 22, 1961.

44. Murch, "The Urban Promise," p. 99.

45. Lisa Rubens, "Interview with Donald Hopkins," unpublished transcript, Regional Oral History Office, UC Berkeley, September 29, 2000.

46. Murch, "Interview with Ernest Allen," July 3, 2001.

47. Murch, "Interview with Dawson," July 26, 2002; "Interview with Khalid Al Mansour," July 22, 2002.

48. Ibid.

49. Scot Brown, *Fighting for US: Maulana Karenga, The US Organization, and Black Cultural Nationalism* (New York: New York University Press, 2003), pp. 25–29.

50. Murch, "Dawson."

51. Murch, "Mansour"; Khalid Al Mansour, *Black Americans at the Crossroads–Where Do We Go From Here?* (New York: First African Arabian Press, 1990).

52. Brown, *Fighting for US*, p. 28.

53. James Edward Smethurst, *The Black Arts Movement: Literary Nationalism in the 1960s and 1970s* (Chapel Hill: University of North Carolina Press, 2005), pp. 260–262.

54. Murch, "Dawson"; Timothy Tyson, "Introduction: Robert F. Williams, 'Black Power,' and the Roots of the African American Freedom Struggle," in Robert F. Williams, *Negroes with Guns* (Detroit, MI: Wayne State University Press, 1998), p. xxvii.

55. Murch, "Dawson."

56. Murch, "Mansour."

57. Newton, *Revolutionary Suicide*, pp. 60–66; Bobby Seale, *Seize the Time* (New York: Random House, 1970), p. 21; Murch, "Interview with Mary Lewis," March 18, 2002.

58. Murch, "Allen."

59. Murch, "Melvyn Newton."

60. Gabrielle Morris, *Head of the Class: An Oral History of African-American Achievement in Higher Education and Beyond* (New York: Twayne Publishers, 1995), pp. xvii–xviii.

61. "Special Report on Minority Group Relations Presented to the Trustees," Peralta Colleges Bulletin, 5(8) (January 12, 1968), p. 2.

62. Eric Hobsbawm, *Primitive Rebels: Studies in Archaic Forms of Social Movement in the 19th and 20th Centuries* (New York: W.W. Norton & Company, 1959), p. 108.

63. Seale, *Seize the Time*, pp. 3–6.

64. Ibid., pp. 3–12.

65. Newton, *Revolutionary Suicide*, p. 69.

66. Seale, *Seize the Time*, pp. 26, 30.

67. Murch, "Interview with Leo Bazile," February 19, 2001.

68. Seale, *Seize the Time*, p. 20.

69. Ibid., pp. 30–31.

70. Newton, *Revolutionary Suicide*, pp. 108–109.

71. David Hilliard and Lewis Cole, *This Side of Glory: The Autobiography of David Hilliard and the Story of the Black Panther Party* (New York: Little, Brown and Company, 1993), p. 228; Robyn Ceanne Spencer, "Repression Breeds Resistance: The Rise and Fall of the Black Panther Party in Oakland, CA, 1966–1982" (Columbia University: Ph.D. Thesis, 2001), p. 44.

72. Newton, *Revolutionary Suicide*, pp. 115–116.

73. Murch, "Newton."

74. Interestingly, Warden distanced himself from the successes at Merritt rather than claiming credit. He described the Merritt student movement in the following words, "...that leadership tended to be what the press would call more militant, more radical, and out of that grew the Black Panther movement." Newton, *Revolutionary Suicide*, p. 72; Murch, "Mansour."

5

"W-A-L-K-O-U-T!": High School Students and the Development of Black Power in L.A.

Jeanne Theoharis[1]

> We waited a long time for those folks to do something to improve our schools, but they let us down and so we have decided to do the job ourselves.
>
> —*Jefferson High School student, March 1968*[2]

During the first week of March 1968, high school students staged a five-day walkout in six Los Angeles high schools—Garfield, Roosevelt, Lincoln, Wilson, and Belmont High Schools, all predominantly chicano schools in East Los Angeles, and Jefferson High School, a black school in South L.A. These dramatic school walkouts highlighted curriculum and dress code issues; dramatized the lack of resources and inferior schooling conditions in schools that educated black and Latino children; pressed for college prep courses and more black and Latino teachers/administrators; and demanded more community input into how the school was run. The Mexican American newspaper *La Raza* proclaimed the significance of these events, "The first 15 days of March of the year 1968 will be known in the 'new' history of the Southwest as the days of the BLOWOUT... These days became the moment of truth to many people."[3]

These student walkouts drew on the legacy of activism within the black and Latino communities around school inequality dating from the 1940s. In March 1945, five Chicano parents with the help of the League of United Latin American Citizens (LULAC) sued four California school districts for segregating their children. Judge Paul McCormick ruled in *Mendez v. Westminster School District of Orange County* that this violated the California constitution and the Equal Protection clause of the 14th Amendment. McCormick's decision was upheld by the U.S. Ninth Circuit Court and became an important precedent for the Supreme Court's 1954 decision *Brown v. Board of Education*. Parents and community activists with the National Association for the Advancement of Colored People

(NAACP), Congress of Racial Equality (CORE), the American Civil Liberties Union (ACLU), and the United Civil Rights Council (UCRC) which formed in Los Angeles in 1963 as a coalition of civil rights groups also challenged segregation and educational inequity in L.A. in the 1950s and 1960s. Throughout the early 1960s, parents and community organizers pressed hard around the issues of school resource shortages, overcrowding, hiring discrimination, biased curriculum, and the acute segregation of L.A.'s schools. They held numerous marches and meetings, engaged in hunger strikes and civil disobedience, and organized independent busing initiatives—all to demonstrate the acutely segregated and unequal nature of L.A.'s public schools and to push the Board of Education to address their concerns.[4] Students held protests at Jordan High School in 1963 and organized sit-ins at the Board of Education, exposing the inequities that were rife within L.A.'s public school system.[5] And the city steadfastly refused any systematic solution to these inequities.

Many black students in 1967 and 1968 saw continuities between the activism of the early 1960s and the struggles they were engaging in. As Jefferson High School student Lawrence Bible, one of the walkout organizers, explained, the March walkouts were part of a "pyramid" of activism that had been building for a long while. Indeed, the demands the students made in their walkouts for more black teachers, expanded black history, better facilities, and more college preparation had been key demands of the protests in L.A. in the early 1960s. Students were now taking the struggle to the next level. Many adults also saw the militancy of the walkouts as marking the gravity of the concerns that community activists had been pressing for more than a decade. Indeed, the walkouts present a more complex view of Black Power, with its young leadership and its ties to earlier civil rights activism and Chicano Power simultaneously.

Looking at the political activism of high school students provides a crucial—but understudied—window into the character and direction of the black freedom struggle. High school students had blazed the trail in many crucial battles of the civil rights movement. In 1951, high school junior Barbara Johns organized a strike of her classmates at the all-black Moton High School in Prince Edward County, Virginia, to protest the school's unwillingness to respond to black demands to address issues of poor conditions and overcrowding.[6] Her classmate recalled Johns saying, "[O]ur parents ask us to follow them but in some instances...a little child shall lead them."[7] Johns also called the NAACP to ask for their assistance. They sent lawyers Oliver Hill and Spottswood Robinson who initially aimed to caution the students against their action. But Johns and her band of 114 striking students won the lawyers over, and Hill and Robinson agreed to represent them. Their actions led to one of the five cases that formed the basis for the historic 1954 *Brown v. Board of Education* decision.

High school students joined sit-ins that swept the country in 1960 to protest downtown business segregation in Southern cities. And it was young people in Birmingham in 1962 and 1963 who formed the backbone of the Southern Christian Leadership Conference's Project C, bringing new momentum to the downtown protests. Through their sustained courage in facing Bull Connor's firehoses, dogs, and jails, these junior high and high school students captured the attention of the nation and underscored the need for a federal Civil Rights Act. High school students thus provided crucial vision and militant action to the development of the black freedom struggle. But, in the history books, they often function as walk-on players, visible in the familiar narratives of *Brown* to Selma but not treated as serious political players.

The high school walkouts of the late 1960s continued this tradition of high school activism, demonstrating the ways young people were willing to undertake dramatic action to force change in their schools. However, the brief glimpses of high school activism in the Black Power era that do appear in the historical record often focus on dress codes and hairstyles, on angry slogans and fists in the air—in short, on the appearance of Black Power. But that appearance was undergirded by a broader vision as protesting students demanded educational equity and respect (which included changes in dress codes, curriculum, facilities, and teaching staff as well as increased access to college). An examination of these student walkouts challenges the prevalent picture of urban black teenagers, particularly those living in large Northern cities such as Los Angeles, as angry, nihilistic, and uncommitted to education—and thus antithetical to the spirit of the civil rights movement.[8] Even within studies that take seriously the turn to Black and Brown Power, urban teenagers are rarely portrayed as key thinkers and strategists but more often framed as alienated youth and thus impulsive followers. Accordingly, Black and Chicano Power advocates are viewed as encouraging (or even fomenting) rebellion among young people. Embedded in this idea is the notion that teenagers do not think for themselves and were simply persuaded by radical malcontents.

What can be seen from these protests, however, is that many young people were thoughtful and organized in their politics, and that they did not conceive of these demonstrations in strict opposition to civil rights activism earlier in the decade. Although some of these protests devolved into disorganization or engaged in unplanned acts of sabotage, most were not simply spontaneous eruptions. Aware of the kind of schooling they were receiving, many students voiced their objections to the ways they were being described in the media and by school officials as anti-intellectual (and thus held responsible for the limits of their own schooling). Frustrated with the problems in their schools, these young people attempted to voice their grievances—often only to be ignored or treated like troublemakers, as were their parents—and then moved to action.

A study of these high school protests also provides new insights into Black Power on the ground. Although visual images of Black Power abound, and a growing body of scholarship has emerged on national groups such as the Black Panthers and the US Organization and on political theorists such as Stokely Carmichael, Huey Newton, and Malcolm X, we have much less of a sense of Black Power as a grassroots movement that grew out of local conditions as well as a growing national consciousness.[9] In examining these protests, although the US Organization, the Brown Berets, and the Black Panthers were certainly active participants, scholars need to dig deeper to understand the local adult and student leadership and the ways these protests evolved out of young people grappling with their own (mis)education. Black Power in school meant students demanding improvements in the quality of their education—diversifying the curriculum, having a teaching and administrative staff committed to them as people and young scholars, giving them and their parents an actual say in how the school functioned, and providing real college preparation at black and Latino high schools like that found in white high schools in other parts of the city. Indeed, although scholars have examined the movements for community control of schools that grew in cities in the late 1960s, little attention has been paid to the ways young people also spearheaded these efforts.[10]

Finally, a study of these walkouts shows the important connections between black and Chicano liberation struggles and the commonalties of discrimination blacks and Chicanos faced in the city's schools.[11] The histories of black and Chicano protest have largely been told separately in this period. Although the walkouts (or blowouts, as they were called) have become a central part of the narrative of the Chicano movement, there is no sense that walkouts are taking place at black high schools as well. The film and supporting documents for the documentary series *Chicano* and a number of historians who have written about the East L.A. blowouts mark the historical significance of these events but give little indication of black student involvement.[12] The 2006 HBO film *Walkout* directed by East L.A. native Edward James Olmos and produced by Moctesuma Esparza, who as a UCLA student helped orchestrate the walkouts, similarly pictures no black students in its moving dramatization of the March 1968 protests. The film dramatically ignores pickets in the fall of 1968 at the black Manual Arts High School—which were the opening salvo of school activism that year—or any mention of the Jefferson walkouts occurring across town at the same time as the East L.A. blowouts. Those scholars who do mention black students in their histories of the blowouts often render the actions of black students as secondary or sympathy strikes.[13] Yet notably, in 1967 and 1968, the black newspaper the *Los Angeles Sentinel*—both in its news articles and its editorial pages—and black political leaders such as Congressman Augustus Hawkins linked the struggles of black and Latino students.[14] Mainstream news sources like the *Los Angeles Times* and the *Los Angeles Herald-Examiner* as well as other school observers also noted the connections.[15] And historians such as Matt Ides and Ernesto Chavez have argued that political meeting places like the East L.A. coffee shop La Piranya which became crucial spaces for Chicano organizing attracted black activists as well.[16]

Yet while the walkouts are considered seminal in Chicano history as a founding moment of Chicano Power, they have been all but ignored by scholars of African American history, even by those studying L.A.'s black community.[17] L.A.'s Black Power story too often is told through flashpoints—the 1965 Watts riot, the shoot-out between the US Organization and the Panthers—and charismatic leaders such as Ron Karenga and Geronimo Pratt. Locating part of the impetus behind L.A.'s Black Power movement in a longstanding movement for educational equity in the city and the actions of high school students who struggled for open bathrooms, diversified curriculum, and responsive school officials gives a more everyday view of Black Power itself. It shows the ways that Black Power militancy evolved out of—rather than simply set itself against—civil rights struggles around schools earlier in the decade and from the city's decades-long refusal to deal with black demands for educational excellence. Finally it also disrupts the idea that the Black Power story can be told apart from other histories of other people of color in the city.

*   *   *

At the beginning of the school year in 1967, students, parents, and community leaders organized protests against the administration of Manual Arts High School. Constructed in 1910 as a vocational school, Manual Arts had been the third school established in L.A.; by 1967, it sat in the heart of black South L.A., was 95 percent black, dramatically overcrowded, under-resourced, and still offering a largely vocational educational program to its black student body. Frustrated by the school's unwillingness to take parent concerns seriously, community members decided to picket the school. These protests were launched by the United Parents Council (UPC, a coalition of parents' groups) and the Black Congress (including members of the US Organization and Ron Karenga) and joined by the NAACP. Formed in 1967, the Black Congress created a united front organization for black political action in the city and brought together nearly all the black groups in L.A. from the NAACP to the Black Panther Party.[18] Longtime activist Walter Bremond headed the new organization.[19]

Beginning with the start of school in September, parents and community activists demonstrated in front of the school to protest conditions at the school and called for the replacement of the principal Robert Denahy on grounds that he was "insensitive, inhuman and hates children."[20] The previous June, Denahy had initially not allowed a black student, Angela Bates, to march for graduation. Denahy subsequently relented after parents and community activists, including NAACP chapter president Celes King, protested. The previous school year, parents and community activists had also sent letters and petitions to the district protesting the poor conditions at the school and Denahy's leadership but had received little attention to their concerns. According to organizers of the September pickets, Denahy, a white man who had been principal for two years, suspended and expelled students with little cause or discussion about the problems with parents, used physical threats or coercion when disciplining students, let students sit idle at school waiting for their schedules to be assigned, looked the other way as drug and alcohol traffic went on within the school, and denied students access to bathrooms.[21] The school was dirty; roaches had been found in the cafeteria food; and there were not adequate courses available. This was not a blanket protest against white administrators at the school, however, but against those administrators—Denahy in particular—who were seen as insensitive to the students' and parents' needs.[22] Protesters highlighted the poor conditions at the school. "We're concerned with an inadequate library," explained Bremond. "We're concerned with substandard education generally for the students."[23]

One demonstration, with protesters carrying signs reading "This School Belongs to Us, not Denahy" and "We are sick of our Children being mistreated!" drew a diverse and spirited crowd, including Assemblyman Bill Greene, US founder Ron Karenga, Representative Hawkins, and Charles Thomas of the NAACP.

The Black Congress also held pickets outside the home of Superintendent Jack Crowther when he stood behind Denahy. (In a closed door meeting between school officials and community activists in the first week of school, activists believed that Crowther told them he would recommend Denahy's removal but the Board of Education meeting the next day produced no such decision.) Following a demonstration outside the school where seventeen-year-old Lester Taylor was arrested, Bremond accused the police of "intimidation" and harassment.[24]

The Board of Education initially backed Denahy as did most of the teachers who saw this as a threat to their own jurisdiction at school. Still, the pickets at Manual Arts drew attention to problems with many predominantly black or Chicano schools. Newly-elected Latino board member Julian Nava connected the problems found at Manual Arts with the "deplorable" conditions at Garfield High School.[25] In addition, African American board member James Jones who visited nearby Jefferson High School decried the "filthy" conditions at the school and recommended the appointment of community relations personnel at black and Latino schools to "avoid community tensions."[26] Two weeks later, under pressure from Assemblyman Bill Greene to "turn the controversy into something positive," the Board of Education ordered a citywide probe into narcotics and liquor trafficking in Los Angeles Unified School District (LAUSD).[27]

Gladys Loupe, whose niece was attending Manual Arts and who had been involved in organizing efforts around the school for more than a year, explained the frustration that led to the pickets. "We have tried as far as we could to communicate with these people. We went through channels.... This school has become run down in the last few years and when we tried to rise up and see that our children get a good education they call us troublemakers. We're tax-paying citizens who vote."[28] The UPC reiterated this; parents had called on the UPC when "they could not secure a meeting with the Principal. The Board of Education would not give parents a hearing."[29] Margaret Wright, the forty-five-year-old head of the UPC, underscored the importance of community input in how the school functioned: "I feel we should have a hand in picking our own principals." That did not mean that every principal and teacher should be black. "An insensitive black one is as bad as an insensitive white one," she explained. "We don't want all black teachers. It would be appalling to have all black teachers."[30]

The daily picketing continued into October. Protests continued to escalate. Demonstrations turned more explosive as people threw rocks and bottles, set small fires, and broke windows, and the police arrested and assaulted protestors. Thirty-five protesters were arrested, including Margaret Wright who had "caused a disturbance during a teacher's meeting" and was dragged down the hallway.[31] The coverage turned sensational as the *Los Angeles Times* claimed, "Youths Go on Rampage at Manual Arts High School." Still, Superintendent Jack Crowther did concede that, as picketers had highlighted, "physical conditions at Manual Arts High school are far from those of a 'normal' school."[32]

Thirty-three more protesters were arrested the next day and more than one hundred over the course of the week—as the Los Angeles Police Department (LAPD) put its force on tactical alert and stationed hundreds of officers in and around the area. Wright and other demonstrators complained of this show of police force. Teachers at Manual Arts asked the Board of Education to close the school until "intimidation of faculty by students and outside agitators was stopped." The Board of Education refused.

As a result, more than half the teachers struck and did not go into work the following Monday (the district used substitutes to keep the school open). Many teachers and administrators at Manual Arts sought to retain the prerogative to govern schools and discipline students as they thought fit without outside input. 2,100 students also stayed out of school to protest issues of security and conditions at the school. Teachers went to the Board of Education to present their list of demands. In support of the Manual Arts teachers, Joseph Brooks, executive secretary of the Los Angeles Teachers Association, threatened to shut down all L.A. schools if the teachers' demands were not met. Teachers also presented a broader list of "general problems that need immediate consideration" at Manual Arts. While the teachers presented their grievances as distinct and in opposition to the pickets, their list included inadequate library and gym facilities, insufficient materials, overworked counselors, lack of consistent programming, deteriorating physical plant, and lack of communication between administration and teachers and parents—all issues that the picketers had also been highlighting.[33]

The school sought and received more security guards as well as an injunction banning certain community members from demonstrating around the campus or entering the school without invitation. The injunction specifically named Mrs. Wright as the "prime agitator" along with fifty "John Does." Principal Denahy also blamed Wright as the main troublemaker who, he claimed, was inciting students to takeover the school: "Mrs Wright has picketed almost daily since September 1. She doesn't live near here and she has no children in this school."[34] Wright had two young children who attended a public elementary school a few miles away. Black radicals like Wright along with the US Organization were viewed by much of the school leadership and the *LA Times* as outsiders who inflamed the situation unnecessarily. Denahy sought to play down the causes of the picket, claiming, "This is all part of the big move for Black Power. A handful of people are upsetting the education of 3,700 students."[35] In an October summary of the situation at Manual Arts, the *LA Times* characterized the origins of the current struggle in revealing, if contradictory, language: "when a parents group which felt it had gotten nowhere in its protests against the general conditions of the school finally invited in black nationalist forces into the controversy." The *LA Times* portrayed the situation as violent and out of control, treating the militancy of protesters as outside the bounds of the situation. (Yet their use of the word "finally" tacitly acknowledged the longstanding nature of the complaints about the school.)

Some black leaders also disparaged the pickets. Former NAACP chapter president Claude Hudson wrote an editorial in the *LA Sentinel* criticizing the NAACP chapter (and current chapter president Celes King in particular) for getting involved in the Manual Arts protests. While claiming that Manual students "were more lax in their morals and more rowdy in their conduct," Hudson called the organizing at Manual Arts "wasted energy" since he believed that it was not a clear case of discrimination.[36] Like the Board of Education, Hudson regarded Manual Arts students with trepidation and, despite widespread acknowledgment of persistent and severe problems at the school, thought that their improved behavior would be a way to improve conditions at the school.

The protesters disagreed. One letter-petition sent to the Board of Education during the pickets from the UPC called it a "lie" that the UPC does not have strong community support and that the picket was organized to oust the white principal. They insisted on the "fact" that "[s]ince 1960, quality education for all pupils has been the rallying cry for *all* schools in the ghetto."[37] They explicitly sought to "improve the gap between the education of the poor and the middle-class." They also highlighted the aggressive tactics used by the school and the police against the protests, claiming that these tactics were what had inflamed the situation. According to historian Scot Brown, "The cover of the November 17, 1967, issue of the US Organization's newspaper *Harambee*, displays a photograph of a police officer chokeholding a black female. The police were in the process of breaking up a protest at the school. The front-page headline of the newspaper read, 'Another View of Manual.'"[38]

Challenging the way that administrators act as though "if a child fails, something must be wrong with him," the UPC stressed that actually "something is wrong with Manual Arts High School."[39] Black congressman Augustus Hawkins echoed this sentiment, decrying the lack of communication between school personnel and the community and asserting that longstanding inequities in LAUSD were driving the militant protests. "I contend that the long history of discriminatory practices that have plagued Negroes is the major contributor to the Manual Arts situation and outbursts throughout the nation."[40]

Indeed, black parents, students, and community activists had been protesting the conditions in L.A. schools for more than a decade. School segregation had worsened in L.A. after the 1954 *Brown* decision; the *California Eagle* subsequently reporting, "More Negro children attend all-Negro schools in Los Angeles than attend such schools in Little Rock." Community activists objected to the ways the overwhelming majority of black students were not tracked for college, and the curriculum reflected racial biases and "happy slave tales."[41] Contrary to prevalent belief about Northern segregation, school segregation did not simply derive from racialized housing patterns in the city. Local and state officials systematically worked to solidify residential segregation and to distribute educational resources through the creation of racially homogenous districts, gerrymandered district lines, restricted hiring, and other bureaucratic measures. During the early 1960s, the NAACP, CORE, and the ACLU pressed the Board of Education and organized local protests at schools. The summer of 1963 the UCRC organized regular marches to the Board of Education because the Board had *still* not responded to the demands of civil rights groups. Movement leaders grew increasingly frustrated with the board's inaction and national civil rights leaders—such as Martin Luther King, James Farmer, and James Forman—joined local activists to protest L.A.'s school inequities. They held protests in board meetings, conducted sit-ins, organized demonstrations at individual schools, and filed suit in court. The board remained intransigent. Despite a decade of protest, in 1966, 84 percent of the teachers and 95 percent of the principals in the city's secondary schools and 76 percent of the teachers and 91 percent of the principals in the elementary schools were white.[42] Educational equity, thus, was a key battleground in the years *before* the Watts uprising, and, tellingly, despite widespread property damage during the 1965 uprising, schools were left untouched by rioters.

LAUSD officials refused any substantive desegregation and blamed the problems of schools largely on the values and motivation of students of color and their parents. Teachers and administrators in L.A. during the 1950s and 1960s used a sociological language of "cultural deprivation" to explain educational disparities and funded programs at black schools to address "juvenile delinquency" while refusing any systematic change to eliminate resource differentials and segregated schools. Simultaneously, they built a security apparatus and introduced new forms of school discipline into district policy, including the use of expulsion, that by the mid-1960s disportionately targeted increasing numbers of black and Latino students.[43] Facing a growing desegregation movement in L.A., the Board of Education issued a report in September 1963 that placed responsibility for the problems that did exist in the schools outside the district's purview, notably "the lack of hope and motivation among some of these [black and Mexican American] families which leads them into negative attitudes toward education and the demands the school makes on their children." And Board of Education member J. C. Chambers asserted that if there was not much black history being taught in LAUSD, it was because there was "not much of it to teach."

According to Margaret Wright, the UPC had come out of this long history of protest against the segregation and inequality in L.A.'s schools. Parents sought to challenge the inadequacies of schooling their children were receiving and the ways they were often blamed for their children's educational under-attainment. This coalition of forty parent groups came together in the UPC to demand change and highlight the ways issues of discrimination and inequality were roundly ignored in a "liberal" city such as Los Angeles. Their rising militancy stemmed in part from the ways public officials and journalists, despite a 10-year movement in the city, repeatedly forgot black grievances and were surprised by black anger. Wright contrasted the attitudes in Mississippi with those found in L.A. "At least we know where we stand [there]...where they hit you over the head. This way the children know they aren't wanted. It causes scars that never heal. People wonder what's wrong with them when they grow up and throw a Molotov cocktail."[44] Favoring community control, Wright had protested to the board around a number of school-related issues, including the lack of black history in L.A. schools, deplorable conditions in many black schools, and the policy of sending students home if they wore natural hairstyles.[45] The Summer before the Manual Arts pickets, Wright had taken her family to Washington DC to protest the deficiencies in L.A.'s Schools.

The Manual Arts protests drew a great deal of media and public attention. On October 29, 1967, foreshadowing the much broader school disruptions in the spring, *La Raza* drew connections between what was happening in South L.A. and what was to come in East L.A., proclaiming on its front page,

> Garfield High School has the potential of becoming another terribly troubled school within Los Angeles, forcing Manual Arts off the front pages. The Negro community protested, and the Board of Education voted unanimously last Tuesday to provide "all possible funds and staff necessary to achieve improved education" at Manual Arts. It is over-due that the Chicano community become the "squeaky wheel" and Garfield is the obvious focus for protest.[46]

LA Raza thus noted the ways that the tactics used at Manual Arts succeeded in getting improved education at the school.

The protests at Manual lasted through much of the fall and did produce some change at the school. In mid-November, Principal Denahy went on sick leave and was ultimately reassigned to a different school for the next semester.[47] Concurrently, a number of additional teachers and other school personnel were transferred to Manual Arts, and committees and other mechanisms were set up for parents to give more input to the school. The Board of Education also established two task forces to tackle the problems of school community relations in South Central L.A. and East L.A.[48] But, the board simultaneously assigned more security guards to the school—what education historian Judith Kafka has described as "an increased presence of non-educators enforcing discipline."[49] Yet, despite criticism of the tactics and the de-legitimation of the protests as the work of "outsiders," these militant protests had succeeded in bringing some of the needed resources, staff, and attention to the school.

The Spring of the Walkouts

In 1966, young people who would play an important role assisting the East L.A. walkouts had organized the reform-oriented Young Citizens for Community Action (YCCA), shortly renamed Young Chicanos for Community Action and by 1968 reformulated to call themselves the Brown Berets. In 1967, with the help of a local priest, YCCA had opened La Piranya, an East L.A. coffeehouse for young people to meet, discuss, and hang out. Prominent civil rights leaders such as César Chávez, Reies Lopez Tijerina, H. Rap Brown, Stokely Carmichael, and Ron Karenga all visited La Piranya. They also held "Educational Happenings" to encourage and assist young people in going to college—and representatives from the UPC (including Margaret Wright) spoke. According to historian Ernesto Chavez, "The coffeehouse remained, however, a gathering for young people run by young people, with little and only nominal adult supervision."[50] Police would often harass the young patrons of La Piranya, claiming that it was a hangout for hoodlums.[51]

By early spring 1968, according to historian Ian Haney Lopez, plans for mass walkouts in the Latino high schools in East L.A. were in place. Strike committees had been organized at each high school and a central committee formulated a list of demands, which included "reduced class size, more teachers and counselors, expanded library facilities, and an end of the requirement that students contribute janitorial services. By and large, however, the demands focused on community control of the schools: the students called for bilingual education, more Mexican teachers, the implementation of a citizen review board and the establishment of a Parents' Council."[52]

On Friday March 1, 1968, to protest the canceling of the school play, students staged an impromptu walkout at Wilson High School in East L.A. The Wilson students had jumped the gun but once they had walked out, students at the other schools were committed to follow. On Tuesday March 5, a large number of students at Garfield High School (in East L.A.) and Jefferson High School (in South L.A.) stayed out of their afternoon classes "in orderly fashion."[53] The next day, students at Lincoln and Roosevelt high schools walked out as well. Simultaneously, 400 Jefferson students congregated on the bleachers instead of going to classes. Jefferson students initially walked out to draw attention to the conditions in their cafeteria but their grievances included dress code and hair-style restrictions, lack of black history in the curriculum, teacher insensitivity, poor guidance counseling and lack of college preparation, and the dearth of black administrators. For instance, black students were required to wear their natural hair no longer than two inches. Homeroom and P.E. teachers would mea-sure students' hair with a ruler, and students were sent home if their hair was too long. This physical inspection constituted a great indignity. With the growing popularity of natural hairstyles among black people of all ages, students chafed under these regulations.

Two students identified as leaders at Jefferson were Brenda Holcomb and Larry Bible. Both students in interviews they gave to the *Los Angeles Sentinel* argued that dissatisfaction about conditions at the school had been building for a while but students' grievances had not been taken seriously. So they had resolved to walk out. Indeed, as the quote from the anonymous student that begins this chapter highlights, students had grown frustrated with the ways their concerns had been brushed aside and thus decided to take matters into their own hands. Issues of class size, curriculum, hiring, and college preparation had been long-standing grievances that community activists had been pressing for years. Bible explained, "We picked up on what was already started." Inspired by Malcolm X, students had formed a Black Student Union (BSU) in 1966. At four black high schools (Fremont, Jordan, Washington, and Jefferson), students had boycotted school in May 1967 to honor Malcolm X's birthday. Moreover, as their Chicano peers were arguing across town, LAUSD's curriculum almost completely ignored the literatures, histories, and experiences of people of color. There was almost no black history of any kind taught in L.A. schools; those blacks who did appear in the curriculum were "yes sir, no sir" types rather than activists, according to Bible. Students had taken steps to educate themselves, drawing on the resources of the public library and the advice of a handful of sympathetic teachers and had engaged in study groups the previous year. "We were coming with action," Bible explained, referring to the walkouts as the "accumulation of a year and a half."[54]

Specifically, the walkouts stemmed, according to Holcomb and Bible, from the lack of guidance counselors and adequate preparation for college at black high schools such as Jefferson. Many students getting A's were not being prop-erly prepared for college and unable to pass college entrance exams. Most of the organizers were student leaders in the academic (rather than vocational) tracks. As they prepared to go to college, these students felt the inadequacies of the edu-cation they were receiving at Jefferson and objected to the ways they were not expected to be college material. A diploma from a school such as Jefferson was looked down upon by many college administrators.[55] Thus, contrary to the pop-ular notion of Black Power appealing to young people who were troublemakers turned off on school, the protests at Jefferson reveal the ways successful students, indeed student leaders, turned to militancy to demand a quality education for themselves and their peers. Jefferson had only one counselor for every 500 students. Moreover, students had little success in getting their concerns addressed by other means, Holcomb explained, because "too often teachers and administrators shrugged off student complaints or branded students who differed with them as 'troublemakers.'"[56] As Floyd Benton, a sixteen-year-old Jefferson High School student, observed, "The news media, instead of dealing with the causes, jumped on our backs. We were very orderly."[57]

At the Board of Education meeting on March 7, board members Nava and Jones raised the issue of the walkouts and expressed their desire to have the students speak to the board. Jones also praised the students at Jefferson for how "orderly" they had been. A student from Jefferson was allowed to speak. According to the board minutes from the meeting, "He wanted to set the record straight and assure the audience that there were no outside influences in control of the students. The students wanted black studies and other things to solve their problems. He told the Board Members that if the students did not get what they wanted, the students would not remain in school."[58]

The next day, teachers walked out of Jefferson, saying they "could no longer hold classes under prevailing conditions."[59] The *LA Times* explained that the teachers initially left in protest of the latitude being shown toward students, particularly in allowing "student militants" to control the campus.[60] Still, echoing one of the students' demands, the teachers also called for more black administrators at the school. The school shut down and did not reopen until the following Wednesday. School board president Georgianna Hardy and board members Ralph Richardson and Rev. James Jones met with students in the cafeteria and library—where a "spirited discussion" ensued, according to the *LA Times*, on many of the core issues of the walkout.

With the school closed and the teachers supporting student demands for black administrators, the board bowed to the pressure and three black administrators were reassigned to Jefferson High School in the positions of principal, vice principal and guidance counselor. The Board of Education acted measurably differently and moved more quickly at Jefferson than it did with the East L.A. schools. Part of this likely stemmed from the teachers' protest at Jefferson (and some administrators claimed these changes were in the works before the walkout)—but all must be seen in the context of a visible black militancy in the city, the events at Manual Arts the preceding fall, and the specter of the Watts riot.[61]

The three administrators brought to Jefferson were not new hires but black people already in other administrative positions in LAUSD who were then promoted to Jefferson. Lewis Johnson Jr. (formerly the vice principal at the new Locke High School) was appointed to be the principal of the school. The Board of Education made a commitment that black history would be taught in school and that human relations meetings would be held to improve communication between teachers and students. They also offered amnesty to boycotting students at all six high schools—a move that, apart from being more practical than expelling thousands of students, implicitly legitimated students' grievances. Students were "jubilant" and the *Los Angeles Sentinel*'s front-page banner headline trumpeted "Jefferson High Gets Negro Principal" and called the board's proposal a "victory" where "virtually all their [the students'] demands had been met."[62] At the end of March, Principal Johnson spoke publicly about the problems facing Jefferson, including a school debt because of lack of support to its athletic programs, and the need for more guidance counselors (particularly ones to work on college scholarships). But even though some changes were made such as lifting the hair restrictions, as Bible explained later, "it wasn't resolved. Just talk."[63]

Protests spread to George Washington Carver and Edison Junior High Schools, both predominantly black junior high schools. Their demands included change in cafeteria food, lowered class sizes, lifting of dress codes, and increased black history in the curriculum. After a broad-based student demonstration at Carver on March 8, 1968 where students broke windows and threw garbage, thirteen students and one young adult were arrested for loitering. One teacher explained that these junior high school students, knowing what had transpired earlier in the week at Jefferson and other East L.A. high schools, "wanted to be involved too."[64] On March 12, several hundred students left Edison at noon and 300 refused to return to class after lunch. School was dismissed at 1:30 because so many students had left class.

While school officials acted surprised, they had been aware of rising discontent among many students and their parents. L.A. County supervisor Kenneth Hahn had issued an internal memo in August 1967 cautioning that "[m]ilitant forces seem intent on trying to disrupt every university college and high school campus" and urging a countywide crackdown on young militants.[65] Ralph Richardson, one of the liberal members of the Board of Education, later admitted, "I was aware that there was frustration with the minority community...and so I knew that in a sense we were sitting on a tinderbox."[66] Indeed, in 1964, the head of the UCRC Rev. Brookins was quoted in the *Los Angeles Times* criticizing the Board of Education's intransigence—they "want to play ostrich" and saying they would have to share the blame if some civil rights organization "went off half cocked."[67] Notably, the demands made by students in terms of curriculum, hiring, and college preparation bore a striking resemblance to the demands made by the educational movement of the 1950s and early 1960s and the pickets at Manual Arts. Many adults, such as Rep Hawkins and UCRC members, made connections between these walkouts and earlier civil rights activism.[68]

As a response to the protests, the L.A. County Conference of Negro Elected Officials set up two committees to address student grievances and to look into Board of Education policies on hiring, promotion, and assignment of teachers and administrators. Black assemblyman Leon Ralph demanded that the Board of Education take real steps to address black and Chicano students, instead of token, piecemeal approaches.[69] The Board of Education agreed to investigate the issue of corporal punishment in schools—and in 1971 issued a policy banning it completely.

School protests would continue over the following year. In December 1968, students, along with a number of black teachers, walked out of Fremont High School (also 95 percent black) demanding the removal of (white) principal Robert

Malcolm, the hiring of more black teachers and administrators, and the creation of Afro-American studies courses.[70] The decision to walkout also came from students feeling like their complaints had not been taken seriously. At a faculty meeting to discuss student evaluations of teachers, 200 students showed up and took over the meeting. One student explained, "How can they know anything about students until they start listening to them."[71] Four student leaders were suspended ostensibly for using obscenities. However, Gail Van Meter, head of the Faculty Association understood the student frustrations: "I'm not condoning the take over of the meeting but the students do have very legitimate gripes that we should look into."[72] In protest of these suspensions, a two-day student strike ensued and BSU members presented their demands for black history, community screening of teachers, and a say in determining the selection of the principal at the faculty meeting. UPC chair Margaret Wright supported the striking students calling attention to the problem of "insensitive" teachers and the lack of black administrators at Fremont and in the district at large.[73]

Even more decisively than the previous years, students and their supporters sought more community control over the workings of the school. Black principal Donald Bolton was subsequently hired. The BSU, while describing Bolton as "probably the finest person we've met, and probably one of the strongest black men we have had," called for his replacement. Their boycott continued for two weeks. Students objected to the ways they did not have a hand in selecting Bolton and opposed the process of having a principal "sent down by the board."[74] They demanded the appointment of Ida Barrington, vice principal at Fremont, to the position—seeing her as the kind of positive and responsive force they wanted for the school. Barrington was symbolically appointed for one day and Bolton was then named permanent principal. The *LA Times* in a somewhat incredulous tone observed, "it was the first time that the community has demanded a direct voice in how the schools are run. The Negro community had previously lodged protests and demanded changes in schools, but never before had it dictated specifically what action should be taken."[75]

Indeed, central to these student walkouts and parent protests in South L.A. as well as East L.A. was the desire for real community control.[76] Yet limited change in governance structures resulted. As historian Donald Cooper has noted, "With reluctance, the board granted the minorities a small degree of community control through the establishment of ethnic commissions and school advisory councils to address their concerns. The board granted this form of local autonomy only to ensure the maintenance of its own power."[77] Judith Kafka framed the result somewhat differently, "Specifically, while the protests brought few new resources to minority schools, they successfully challenged the authority of school-site educators and had a lasting impact on the organization of school discipline."[78] Although the protests succeeded in getting changes in teaching and administrative personnel, the Board of Education capitulated to the demands of teachers for more security personnel on campus. These increased security measures and police presence were the targets of student protests the following spring. In March 1969, eleven black junior high schools and seven black high schools walked out to demand an end to police presence on campus.[79] And again in the fall of 1969, students walked out of Jefferson to protest over-policing at school, calling for the police to leave the campus. Disproportionate and aggressive security at schools serving students of color would continue to be a significant grievance of black and Latino community activists in the years to come.

One of the driving motivations of the walkouts and the demands for community control was to disrupt "culture of poverty" theories popular among public officials. City and state officials, often in response to charges of inequality and discrimination within L.A.'s schools, attributed the problems in schools to black and Chicano families themselves. (These theories had been given national stature in Daniel Moynihan's 1965 report for the Department of Labor "The Negro Family: The Case for National Action.") Such theories claimed that the lack of work ethic and value for education held by many black and Chicano families, the motivations of black and Chicano students, and the "tangle of pathology" in family and community organization caused black and Chicano students' school failure. Trumpeted by school officials in the 1950s and early 1960s, these sociological theories crescendoed after the Watts uprising. When the McCone Commission issued its report on the causes of the Watts riot, they largely attributed it to black pathology that had developed from the history of slavery and a "dull devastating spiral of failure that awaits the average disadvantaged child." Advocating more remedial programs, the commission blamed black students who they described as "unprepared and unready" for their own segregated schools: "the very low level of scholastic achievement we observe in the predominantly Negro schools contributes to de facto segregation in the schools.... We reason, therefore, that raising the scholastic achievement might reverse the entire trend of de facto segregation."[80] Renowned novelist Thomas Pynchon took up this strain of analysis in "A Journey in the Mind of Watts," his much-vaunted 1966 piece in the *New York Times Magazine*[81] that traveled to "the heart of L.A.'s racial sickness...the coexistence of two very different cultures: one white and one black." Such a culturalist approach treated black urban communities as a problem to be studied and helped explain the presence of racial disparities and conflict through the lens of cultural difference.

Black and Latino community activists organized walkouts and advocated for community control in part to repudiate these cultural theories. According to Larry Bible, Black Power movements in L.A.—and the walkout at Jefferson in particular—were, in part, geared to show "the intellectual side of Black people."[82] *La Raza* elaborated, "Administrators in the L.A. City School System have been crying for years about Mexican American parent participation with the schools; cries such as 'what is wrong with Mexican Americans, don't they care about their children's education?'...Ralph Cuaraon, community leader and parent of a student at Garfield High, found the answers to these questions last week...He was arrested for inquiring about the educational deficiencies that exists there and also beaten up by the ELA Sheriff Placas."[83]

Although many in the city blamed these high school demonstrations on outside agitators (such as the Brown Berets and the US Organization), a public opinion poll published in the *Los Angeles Sentinel* on March 14 took issue with the idea that the boycotts were the work of outside agitators; the black people interviewed largely thought the demonstrations were justified and genuine and not simply the work of outside forces. Rev. H. C. Ross explained, "These abuses have been going for years and are now coming to a head."[84] One student, Norman Strawder, stressed that the protests were "well-organized" and not the product of outside forces. Rep. Augustus Hawkins agreed, "The youth of our Negro and Mexican American ghettos yelled a historical note last week when they expressed frustration and disgust over the poor quality of educational services offered by the L.A. City School system. Unfortunately, the local Board of Education and the superintendent of our school district have been historically insensitive to the cry of the black and brown communities."[85]

Hawkins wrote of his "pride" in these students, hoping "the adults will not let them down." The *Los Angeles Sentinel* editorial page agreed, "To be sure, a boycott of school classes was a serious step, and it indicated how deeply committed to their cause the students at Jefferson High School were.... Students told the SENTINEL that teachers and administrators either ignored or shrugged off their attempts to talk over problems at the school. The boycott was a last resort."[86] What is clear from the *Sentinel*'s coverage (and the *Los Angeles Sentinel* was L.A.'s mainstream black newspaper) is how student militancy was framed as a continuation of a long tradition of black activism in the city around schools and showed how serious young people were about their own educations. Another *Sentinel* columnist elaborated on how the walkouts should force adults to reconsider the ways they thought about black and Chicano students. "Blackboard jungle schools in the black ghetto and the Mexican American barrio have come home to roost. Very questionable and un-called-for neglect and insensitivity to the needs and necessities of young people in these schools have created a crucial crisis in education.... The young brothers and sisters in the ghetto and barrio are more serious and more dedicated than most of us give them credit for being."[87]

Conclusion

Indeed part of the lesson to be taken from these walkouts—and from looking at local Black Power movements more generally—is to complicate our notions of the character of black and Latino student militancy. By casting Black Power either as the frustrated reaction of the ghetto or as the purview of charismatic black men, scholars unwittingly diminish the ways that disruptive politics and the rejection of racial liberalism were a considered response to decades of white resistance to educational equity in cities such as L.A. These militant school protests succeeded in drawing needed attention to the schools in ways that many early demonstrations had not and prompted some important changes in terms of hiring and curriculum. Although Congressman Hawkins was wary of Black Power and credited other activists with "doing a much better job," he still acknowledged the ways Black Power "made it easier to get things done. The immediate benefits, I think were good.... It was certainly a lot more visible than other groups and individuals who had struggled over the years."[88]

There has been a dangerous tendency in much of the scholarship around Black Power to capitulate to an underclass formulation of urban militancy, which draws a sharp delineation between the character of Black Power militants and that of civil rights protesters. Such formulations cast ghetto youth as angry and alienated and suggest that Black Power evolved out of the absence of organizing in these communities. This contributes to the misunderstanding of urban black communities as estranged from politics and possessing a separate culture and social norms of their own (a formulation that bears a striking similarity to the culturalist ideologies the Board of Education relied on to justify inferior schooling for black and Latino students). Yet these very ghetto youth, many of them top students at their schools, saw their protests in 1968 connected to earlier civil rights activism in the city around schools. They sought to challenge the ways that much of this earlier activism and their own grievances—not to mention their intellects—had not been taken seriously.

By ignoring the "seriousness and dedication" of these young people, the visions of the schooling they desired, and their willingness to use militant means to demand the education they deserved, we miss the ways that Black Power evolved at the grassroots from years of struggle around issues of schools, jobs, and housing. By overlooking the history of black high school activism, it becomes too easy today as it was forty years ago to view these young people as disruptive and dangerous and thus meriting increased school security, to treat their visions of and demands for *real* education as disaffection.[89] Students "came with action" to draw attention to the need for more guidance counselors, black history classes, responsive teachers and administrators, substantive college preparation, and better facilities—demands that sound all too relevant today. Their actions demonstrate the ways that these young people were conscious political actors who demanded a better education for themselves and future for their communities.

Notes

1. I am deeply grateful to Steve Lang whose experiences as a student at Fremont in the 1960s and as a teacher there for more than thirty years have helped me see this history in new ways. All mistakes are, of course, mine but if I have managed some fundamental truth in this narrative of high school activism, it is due in large measure to Steve's support and insights. Matthew Ides, Mark Wild, Peniel Joseph, Alejandra Marchevsky, Prudence Cumberbatch, and Komozi Woodard offered crucial insights and feedback on this work. A Rockefeller Humanities Fellowship, a CUNY Scholar Incentive award, and a Tow Travel Fellowship supported this research.
2. As quoted in Augustus Hawkins, "Inside Government: The Agonies of Social Change," *Los Angeles Sentinel* (March 21, 1968), A6.
3. Cover page photos with text, *La Raza* (March 31, 1968), 1.
4. Two race riots had flared at Fremont High School in 1941 and 1947 when black students began attending the formerly all-white school. At Compton High School in 1958, when a black student Naddie Smith was crowned Homecoming Queen, a "C" was burned outside of the school with signs that read "niggers leave Compton" and "We don't want a nigger queen in our yearbook." Brad Pye, "Compton 'Queen' Causes Row," *Los Angeles Sentinel* (October 30, 1958).

5. See Jeanne Theoharis, "Alabama on Avalon: Rethinking the Watts Uprising and the Character of Black Protest in Los Angeles," in *The Black Power Movement* (New York: Routledge, 2006) and Josh Sides, *L.A. City Limits: African American Los Angeles from the Great Depression to the Present* (Berkeley: University of California Press, 2003).

6. After some of the black male students who worked at the white high school told her and her friends how nice the white high school was, Johns remembers "thinking how unfair it was" and called for a strike.

7. Bob Smith, *They Closed Their School: Prince Edward County, Virginia 1951-1964* (Greensboro: University of North Carolina Press, 1965).

8. For further elaboration of the problematics of the North-South dichotomy, see Jeanne Theoharis and Komozi Woodard, *Freedom North: The Black Freedom Struggle Outside of the South, 1940-1980* (New York: Palgrave Macmillan, 2003).

9. See, for instance, Peniel Joseph, *Waiting for the Midnight Hour* (New York: Henry Holt, 2006) and *The Black Power Movement* (New York: Routledge, 2006); Yohuru Williams and Jama Lazerow, *In Search of the Black Panther Party* (Durham, NC: Duke University Press, 2006); Scot Brown *Fighting for US* (New York: New York University Press, 2003); Komozi Woodard, *A Nation within a Nation* (Chapel Hill: University of North Carolina Press, 1999); Nikhil Singh *Black Is a Country* (Cambridge, MA: Harvard University Press, 2004). Tim Tyson *Radio Free Dixie* (Chapel Hill: University of North Carolina Press, 1999); Charles Jones, ed., *The Black Panther Party Reconsidered* (Baltimore: Black World Press, 1998); Kathleen Cleaver and George Katsiaficas, eds., *Liberation, Imagination and the Black Panther Party: A New Look at the Panthers and Their Legacy* (New York: Routledge, 2001); Robert Self, *American Babylon: Race and the Struggle for Postwar Oakland* (Princeton, NJ: Princeton University Press, 2003).

10. See Jerald Podair, *The Strike that Changed New York* (New Haven, CT: Yale University Press, 2003); Jack Dougherty, *More Than One Struggle* (Chapel Hill: University of North Carolina Press, 2003); Wendell Pritchett *Brownsville, Brooklyn* (Chicago: University of Chicago Press, 2002). Conversely, Matthew Countryman's *Up South* (Philadelphia: University of Pennsylvania Press, 2005) and Jesse Hoffnung Garskof's *A Tale of Two Cities* (Princeton, NJ: Princeton University Press, 2007) are two works which take seriously the activism of young people in the development of Black and Brown Power.

11. The Civil Rights Congress, a black left group which in its heyday had eleven chapters in L.A., also made connections between blacks and Latinos. See James Smethurst, *The Black Arts Movement* (Chapel Hill: University of North Carolina Press, 2005), 293.

12. *Chicano!* credits the genesis of the walkouts in East L.A. to a series of meetings held by the Los Angeles County Human Relations Council in April 1966 at Camp Hess Kramer in Malibu. *Chicano!: The History of the Mexican American Civil Rights Movement, Taking Back the Schools* Tape 3 (Los Angeles: NLCC Educational Media, 1966). Although these meetings were convened for Mexican American students, they say 200 teenagers from various backgrounds attended—which makes it possible that African American students also attended. In October 1967, a similar meeting was held at Camp Hess Kramer for 150 black students though it is not clear if there were also Chicano students at that meeting. In November 1967, the Los Angeles City Schools division held human relations workshops for 400 junior high and 400 high school students on human relations. Furthermore, Jefferson High School had recently been transferred out of the southern conference with the rest of the black high schools and into the eastern conference that included these East L.A., predominantly Latino

schools. This meant that these schools were having regular contact through athletics and students likely knew each other.

13. See Rudolfo Acuna, *Occupied America, 3rd edition* (New York: Harper and Row, 1988) and *Community under Siege: A Chronicle of Chicanos East of the L.A. River* (Los Angeles: UCLA Chicano Resources Center, 1984); Ian Haney Lopez, *Racism on Trial: The Chicano Fight for Justice* (Cambridge, MA: Harvard University Press, 2003); Carlos Munoz, *Youth, Identity, Power: The Chicano Movement* (New York: Verso, 1989). Curiously, while the *Los Angeles Times* in 1968 carried ample coverage of the Jefferson High School walkout, its coverage of the 40th anniversary of the walkouts in "1968 protesters honored" locates the center of the action in East L.A.—and talks about how "the East L.A. High School Walkouts inspired similar protests at 15 additional high schools across the Los Angeles Unified School District, including...Thomas Jefferson High School." "1968 Students Honored" in The Homeroom Blog, *Los Angeles Times* (March 3, 2008). Similarly, much of the other media coverage marking the 40th anniversary of the walkouts says that Jefferson High School walked out "in solidarity."

14. Interestingly, while the *Los Angeles Times* initially covered the walkouts at Jefferson along with its coverage of the East L.A. blowouts, they begin to treat them separately. For instance, on March 17, 1968, they published "Frivolous to Fundamental: Demands Made by East Side High School Students Listed," a long article on the demands of the East L.A. walkouts where *Times* education reporter Jack McCurdy enumerates the 38 demands and evaluates their accuracy and validity. This seems to reflect the city's own strategy which is to treat the issues raised by Chicano students and community activists differently and separately than those by black students and activists.

15. Johns H. Harrington, "L.A.'s Student Blowouts," *The Phi Delta Kappan* 50: 2 (October 1968).

16. Ernesto Chavez, *"Mi Raza Primero!": Nationalism, Identity and Insurgency in the Chicano Movement in Los Angeles, 1966–1978* (Berkeley: University of California Press, 2002); Matthew Ides, "Cruising for Community: Youth, Politics, and Culture in Los Angeles, 1910–1970" (Ph.D. Dissertation, University of Michigan).

17. One exception is Scot Brown in *Fighting for US* who devotes a page and a half to the student protests. Brown could have elaborated this history further to bolster his argument around the political programs and legacies of cultural nationalism and the local conditions that gave rise to the particular direction that United States took in these years.

18. This included the Afro-American Association, the Black Panther Party, Black Unitarians for Radical Reform, CORE, L.A. County Welfare Rights, NAACP, UPC, the U.S. Organization, and Watt's Happening Coffee House, among others.

19. Most of the participating groups moved their headquarters to the Black Congress building and served on councils (much like the United Nations), which then designed action plans. Scot Brown, *Fighting for US*, 82–84. Historian James Smethurst explains, "One result of this upsurge in nationalist activity of various types...and the new status of Watts as the symbol of the new black politics and art, is that Watts became an essential stop for any African American political leader attempting to come to grips with the new political and cultural movement." (Smethurst, *The Black Arts Movement*, 301).

20. 3,700 students were attending Manual Arts, making it significantly overcrowded. Crenshaw High School was slated to open the next year to alleviate some of the problems.

21. "Parents Demand Changes," *Los Angeles Sentinel* (September 14, 1967), A1, 8.

22. For instance, protesters raised no objections to the boys vice principal who was white.

23. Joe Bingham, "Manual Arts Truce Ticks, Ticks," *Los Angeles Sentinel* (October 26, 1967), B12.

24. "Harassed by Police, Say Militants," *Los Angeles Sentinel* (September 14, 1967).

25. "School Board Sets Manual Arts Probe," *Los Angeles Times* (September 19, 1967), A8. African Americans had helped elect Nava to the board and also saw him as a potential ally in the struggle for educational justice. Numerous columns in the *Sentinel* celebrated his victory.

26. "Jeff High 'Filthy' Action Demanded," *Los Angeles Sentinel* (October 19, 1967); "School Use of Relations Experts Asked," *Los Angeles Times* (September 20, 1967).

27. "High School Dope, Booze Traffic Leads to Inquiry," *Los Angeles Sentinel* (September 21, 1967).

28. Jack Jones and Ray Rogers, "Roots of Trouble Are Deeply Embedded in Community: Manual Arts High Typifies Problems in Negro Schools" *Los Angeles Times* (October 27, 1967).

29. Robert Long Mauller "An Analysis of the Conflicts and the Community Relationships in Eight Secondary Schools of the Los Angeles Unified School District 1967–1969" (Ph.D. Dissertation, University of California, Los Angeles), 289.

30. Jones and Rogers, "Roots of Trouble."

31. Joe Bingham, "Manual Arts Truce Ticks, Ticks," *Los Angeles Sentinel* (October 26, 1967), A1, B12; Jones and Rogers "Roots of Trouble."

32. Jones and Rogers, "Roots of Trouble."

33. "Teachers Tell Manual Arts Problems," *Los Angeles Sentinel* (November 2, 1967), 8C.

34. John Dreyfuss, "Plea by Faculty to Close School Denied by Board," *Los Angeles Times* (October 20, 1967), 3.

35. John Kendall, "33 Arrested on Second Day of Manual Arts Disturbance," *Los Angeles Times* (October 21, 1967).

36. Dr. H. Claude Hudson, "Opinions on Manual Arts," *Los Angeles Sentinel* (October 12, 1967), 6A.

37. Appendix B in Mauller dissertation.

38. Brown, *Fighting for US*, 77–78.

39. Appendix B in Mauller dissertation. They also listed the community support that the UPC had amassed including the NAACP, Council of Community Clubs, BSU, and several elected officials, including Green, Hawkins, Assemblyman Charles Warren, Assemblywoman Yvonne Braithwaite, Council Billy Mills, and Councilman Thomas Bradley.

40. Augustus Hawkins, "Why Manual Arts Today," op-ed *Los Angeles Sentinel* (November 9, 1967), 6A.

41. Indeed, in an angry confrontation with a protester over demands that the curriculum include more black history, one Manual Arts teacher responded, "You want us to invent a mythology for you!" Jones and Rogers, "Roots of Trouble."

42. Judith Kafka, "'Sitting on a Tinderbox': Racial Conflict, Teacher Discretion, and the Centralization of Disciplinary Authority," *American Journal of Education* 114: 3 (May 2008), 250.

43. See Judith Kafka's, "Sitting on a Tinderbox" and her dissertation "From Discipline to Punishment: Race, Bureaucracy, and School Discipline Policy in Los Angeles, 1954–1975" (UC-Berkeley) for elaboration of this argument.

44. Tom Goff, "Negro Parents Meet Defeat in School Dispute," *Los Angeles Times* (September 16, 1966), 3.

45. The board then countered that students were allowed to wear naturals as long as they were "clean" (leaving the discretion to school officials on what constituted "clean").

46. "Garfield High Another Manual Arts?" *La Raza* (October 29, 1967), 1.

47. He was replaced by another white principal.

48. "Ex-Jordan High Principal Heads School Task Force," *Los Angeles Sentinel* (November 23, 1967), 4A.

49. Kafka, "Sitting on a Tinderbox" 254. A memo sent from Superintendent Crowther to the Board of Education listed the ways that school security was being increased, including developing a walkie-talkie system, issuing id cards for students, and assigning six additional security guards to the school, up from two previously (Mauller dissertation, 307–308).

50. Chavez, *Mi Raza Primero*, 45.

51. Ibid., 44–45. The YCCA organized demonstrations at the East L.A. sheriff's department to protest this police presence.

52. Lopez, *Racism on Trial*, 20. Lopez does not mention the organizing that occurred in L.A.'s black schools—missing the fall protests at Manual Arts and the concurrent demonstrations at Jefferson. Other historians of the blowouts who do note the actions of black students tend to characterize them as secondary or sympathy demonstrations—or in the case of historian Rudolph Acuna as inspired by the actions of Chicano students. They have, however, given detailed and nuanced accounts of what transpired in the walkouts in East L.A. Space does not permit me to reproduce them here, so I have thereby concentrated this account on the events at Jefferson High School.

53. Jack McCurdy "Student Disorders Erupt at 4 High Schools; Policeman Hurt," *Los Angeles Times* (March 7, 1968). By the early 1930s, most black students in L.A. attended Jefferson or Jordan High School; Jefferson did not become all black until after World War II.

54. Author interview with Lawrence Bible, June 12, 2006.

55. Ibid. According to Bible, he was made an example of because he was a star track athlete, subsequently suspended, and followed home by the police.

56. Bob Lucas, "'Black' Boycott Victory" *Los Angeles Sentinel* (March 14, 1968).

57. Paul Houston, "3 Negro Officials Take over at Jefferson High," *Los Angeles Times* (March 14, 1968), 3.

58. As quoted in Mauller, 111. While three people from Jefferson were allowed to speak (this student, a teacher, and an audience member), the meeting was adjourned before anyone from the East L.A. high schools who also wanted to address the board were allowed to address the meeting.

59. Jack McCurdy, "1,000 Walk Out in School Boycott" *Los Angeles Times* (March 9, 1968).

60. Interestingly, in a meeting with the Board of Education to resolve some of the student demands, Garfield High faculty chairman Ray Ceniceros explained, "We feel disturbed and ashamed that these kids are carrying out our fight. We should have been fighting for these things as teachers, and as a community. Apparently we have been using the wrong weapons. These kids found a new weapon—a new monster— the walkout. If this is the way things are done, I'm just sorry we didn't walk out." Jack McCurdy, "School Board Yields to Some Student Points in Boycotts," *Los Angeles Times* (March 12, 1968).

61. On May 31, thirteen individuals connected to the East L.A. walkouts—including the editors of *La Raza* and leaders of the Brown Berets—were arrested. That these indictments were concentrated in East L.A. is notable but perhaps not surprising considering the assassination of Martin Luther King on April 4 and the riots that followed in many cities. L.A. did not have a riot in the wake of the assassination due in part to the order that community leaders in the city, including the Black Congress, were able to maintain. As Scot Brown observes, "Violent revolts occurred in several American cities in response to King's death, but the Black Congress succeeded in directing the collective rage felt in the Los Angeles African American community away from retaliatory violence and toward a plan for organized antiracist community action," Brown, *Fighting for US*, 91. It is not clear whether fears of violence or tacit acknowledgement of the role many black leaders had played in averting an uprising factored into the decision not to indict members of the Black Congress, the U.S. Organization, or the UPC on similar conspiracy charges to their Chicano counterparts.

62. Lucas "'Black' Boycott Victory." Indeed, the *Los Angeles Times* in an editorial "School Boycotts Not the Answer" acknowledged that "the Board of Education yield to demands by pupils and teachers for appointment of a Negro principal." In contradictory form, the *Los Angeles Times* praised that "only a minority of students actually joined the 'strike.'...It can also be regarded as healthy that these young Mexican-Americans themselves are crying for the education tools that will keep them from becoming the victims of a kind of apartheid via language." "School Boycotts Not the Answer," *Los Angeles Times* (March 15, 1968).

63. Interview with Bible.

64. Ken Reich, "Principal Calm Amid Excited Carver Junior High Students," *Los Angeles Sentinel* (March 8, 1968).

65. Cited in Brown, *Freedom North*, 229.

66. Quoted in the documentary *Chicano*.

67. Paul Weeks, "L.A. Protests Threatened if Rights Efforts Stall" *Los Angeles Times* (June 19, 1964).

68. These walkouts in L.A. are part of a larger mobilization of high school students across the country. Black students in Boston formed a BSU and walked out of high schools in 1968 and 1969—as did many of their counterparts in cities like Philadelphia, New York, and Milwaukee.

69. "Negro Groups to Study Jefferson High Unrest," *Los Angeles Times* (March 16, 1968), 20.

70. Principal Malcolm had expressed surprise to the *Los Angeles Times* in 1967 about the hunger for knowledge in South L.A. "I'm amazed that these children can do so well to follow what is happening." Jack Jones, "Parents and Children Hunger for Knowledge," *Los Angeles Times* (July 20, 1967).

71. Mauller dissertation, 131.

72. Ibid.

73. "Fremont High School Explodes!" *Los Angeles Sentinel* (December 19, 1968).

74. "Fremont High Factions Want Bolton Out, Barrington In," *Los Angeles Sentinel* (December 26, 1968).

75. Jack McCurdy "Local Control Concept Wins at Fremont High," *Los Angeles Times* (January 6, 1969), A3. Assemblyman Greene called for a community meeting at Fremont similar to the one held the previous spring at Lincoln High School but this request was never supported by the board.

76. This is not to suggest that all parents were supportive of these walkouts. Many parents were not, and the walkouts caused generational gaps to widen or at least become visible, as many historians of the Chicano walkouts have noted.

77. Donald Glen Cooper, "The Controversy over Desegregation in the Los Angeles Unified School District, 1962–1981 (Ph.D. Dissertation, University of Southern California), 65.

78. Kafka, "Sitting on a Tinderbox."

79. Dial Torgenerson, "Negro Strike Forces 2-School Shutdown," *Los Angeles Times* (March 11, 1969).

80. Caughey, *To Kill a Spirit*, 29.

81. Thomas Pynchon, "A Journey in the Mind of Watts," *New York Times Magazine* (June 6, 1966).

82. Bible continued to encounter these assumptions when he went on to UCLA for college. Bible talked of the "amazement" he encountered when he said he had attended Jefferson—they "put you in a category." Bible interview.

83. "The Establishment vs. the People," *La Raza* (March 31, 1968), 5.

84. "L.A.'s School Demonstrations: Who's Responsible for Them?" *Los Angeles Sentinel* (March 14, 1968).

85. Hawkins, "Inside Government," *Los Angeles Sentinel* A6.

86. "Politico or Educator" editorial, *Los Angeles Sentinel* (March 21, 1968), A6.

87. Booker Griffin, "Crisis in Education: 'Jungle Schools' Come Home to Roost," *Los Angeles Sentinel* (March 14, 1968), D1.

88. Interview of Augustus Hawkins by Carlos Vasquez, 1988, State Government Oral History Program, California State Archives at UCLA, 177–178.

89. One fall-out of the walkouts was that teachers and administrators gained traction in their calls to intensify security and police presence at these schools. As these schools had become more overcrowded in the 1950s and 1960s, the Board of Education had increased security in these high schools (which was one of the grievances in many of these schools in these protests in 1967–1969). This form of school policing increased—or was solidified—in the late 1960s after the walkouts.

6

"We Were Going to Fight Fire with Fire": Black Power in the South

Simon Wendt

For many students of the 1960s, June 16, 1966 continues to mark the beginning of the history of Black Power in America. That day, Stokely Carmichael, the young and flamboyant chairman of the Student Nonviolent Coordinating Committee (SNCC), introduced two words that would dominate the memory of the black freedom movement in the following decades. Standing on a wooden makeshift podium in Greenwood, Mississippi, which was one stop on the Meredith March's tour across the Magnolia state, Carmichael told some 600 blacks that the "only way" to stop white racists from "whuppin'" African Americans would be "to take over." "What we gonna start saying now," he shouted, "is Black Power!" This exclamation struck a chord with his audience. It roared back in unison: "Black Power!"[1] Listening to the angry chants of Carmichael and seeing armed members of the Deacons for Defense and Justice—a black self-defense organization from Louisiana—protect the march, puzzled observers feared the dawn of a new and violent era. To many, Black Power seemed to symbolize both an abrupt rupture with the nonviolent and integrationist vision of Martin Luther King and the advent of violent upheavals in northern black communities. In the following decades many historians adopted and perpetuated this interpretation, portraying the black freedom movement's radicalization as a sudden, essentially northern, phenomenon that seemed to betray the ideals of the southern civil rights struggle.[2]

In recent years, a number of historians have begun to challenge such traditional interpretations. What these scholars have found is that the southern black freedom struggle and the Black Power movement were far from being distinct movements. Rather they frequently overlapped, stimulated each other, and shared many tactical and ideological elements.[3] "Although civil rights and Black Power activists certainly claimed unique worldviews, intellectual philosophies,

and political tactics," Peniel Joseph writes with regard to these new interpretations, "the distinctiveness of each era becomes less stark depending on where one
looks."[4] Some of the links that Joseph alludes to become more visible when we
explore local activism and black militancy in the southern freedom struggle. The
use of armed self-defense in particular—despite the fact that this form of resistance underwent significant reinterpretations in the late 1960s—calls attention
to certain continuities between the post-World War II freedom struggle and what
came to be known as Black Power. An earlier generation of historians portrayed
Stokely Carmichael's angry chants and subsequent calls for armed resistance
as an abrupt break with the "nonviolent" civil rights movement. In truth, local
activists in the South protected themselves and their communities against racist
attacks throughout the civil rights era, and the radicalization of Carmichael and
many of his fellow organizers was no sudden abandonment of King's tenets but
must be seen as the culmination of a long-simmering debate over self-defense
within the southern movement. Thus, despite conspicuous differences between
armed resistance efforts in the campaigns of southern civil rights activists and
post-1965 black nationalists, at least some of the antecedents of Black Power
can be located in the local freedom struggles that challenged Jim Crow in the
American South.[5]

As early as the 1950s, self-defense complemented nonviolent protest in the
black freedom struggle. Even Martin Luther King Jr., the acclaimed icon of
nonviolence, accepted armed protection in the early days of the Montgomery
bus boycott. After a bomb had destroyed parts of King's home, armed sentries
made sure that the young pastor remained unharmed. Bayard Rustin, a veteran
activist and member of the pacifist Fellowship of Reconciliation who arrived in
Montgomery in February 1956, later remembered that the parsonage resembled
"a virtual garrison."[6] For pacifist Rustin, the guards and the weapons scattered
across King's living room were hard to swallow. In a report, he spoke of "considerable confusion on the question as to whether violence is justified in retali-
ation to violence directed against the Negro community."[7] Together with white
minister Glen Smiley, Rustin began to tutor King in the nuances of the teachings of Indian anticolonial activist Mohandas Gandhi, but in the next few weeks
the armed guards remained in place. By Rustin's account, King reconsidered his
stance on armed protection only in March 1956, when one of the guards almost
shot a white telegram-delivery boy who approached the parsonage. After this
incident, King banned all guns from his house and began to formulate a nonviolent philosophy that fused Gandhian tenets with Afro-Christianity.[8]

While King pondered Gandhi's philosophy and its potential as a protest tactic in the aftermath of the successful bus boycott in Alabama, blacks
in other parts of the region complemented peaceful protest with organized
forms of armed resistance. In Birmingham, Alabama, African Americans
formed the "Civil Rights Guards" to protect black minister and head of Bethel
Baptist Church, Fred Shuttlesworth, the local freedom movement's leader.
Although Shuttlesworth urged his followers to remain nonviolent, he readily
accepted their efforts to protect him and his church with arms. In 1957, after
Shuttlesworth miraculously survived a bomb attack that destroyed his home,

members of his congregation formed the protective squad that guarded the parsonage and church.[9]

The same year that Birmingham's self-defense group was formed, black activist Robert F. Williams, president of the Monroe, North Carolina, chapter of the National Association for the Advancement of Colored People (NAACP), established a similarly sophisticated organization to repel attacks by the Ku Klux Klan. Born and raised in Monroe, Williams was a veteran of the U.S. Marines and had reorganized the town's defunct NAACP chapter in 1955. Inspired by the Montgomery movement, Williams and his followers organized nonviolent campaigns to desegregate Monroe. But unlike King, Williams had not adopted nonviolence as a way of life. "I had just come out of the Marine Corps," he remembered years later, "and I had been in the Army, and I didn't believe in the pacifist document." Nevertheless, Williams did believe that African Americans "should use or utilize any method that brought results." In his mind these methods included both nonviolent protest and what he termed "armed self-reliance."[10] In 1957, when trying to integrate Monroe's local swimming pool, Williams learned that what he called armed self-reliance was sorely needed. After black activists began to stage peaceful demonstrations, the revived North Carolina Ku Klux Klan launched a reign of terror, staging nightly parades through the black neighborhood and attacking black homes. Confronted with this unprovoked wave of violence, Williams and several black army veterans formed a defense organization that guarded the black community with pistols, machine guns, and dynamite. After a violent confrontation with Klansmen in October 1957, Klan harassment stopped.[11]

The significance of Robert Williams, who after 1961 was forced to live in Cuban and later Chinese exile, goes beyond his advocacy of armed resistance. As Timothy Tyson has demonstrated, his activism contained many of the elements we associate with the post-1965 Black Power movement. Through speeches and his newsletter *Crusader*, Williams disseminated a message that emphasized black pride, economic nationalism, and anticolonial internationalism. In spite of this multilayered ideology, Williams became known primarily for his ardent advocacy of armed self-defense. Together with Malcolm X, Williams had a profound impact on succeeding generations of militant black activists, among them the founders of the Revolutionary Action Movement (RAM), the Black Panther Party (BPP), and the Republic of New Africa (RNA).[12]

To suggest, however, as Tyson does, that the civil rights struggle and what came to be known as Black Power "emerged from the same soil, confronted the same predicaments, and reflected the same quest for African American freedom" exaggerates the commonalities between Williams's early advocacy of "armed self-reliance" and the radicalism that he and other activists espoused during the Black Power era.[13] Before his forced escape to Cuba in 1961, the militant North Carolinian was an ardent supporter of nonviolent integration through legal means. Williams did advocate self-defense, but he insisted on its use only if white supremacists threatened peaceful civil rights activities with violence. It was between 1962 and 1968 that he turned into a fiery advocate of revolutionary guerilla warfare and black separatism. By 1968, he rejected the idea that racial integration was feasible, arguing that whites would never relinquish white supremacy. Nonviolence, too, was no longer useful, he said. "If nonviolence for civil rights was ever going to achieve anything, we would have integration today, because we have had an awful lot of nonviolence," he told the *New York Times*.[14] Instead, as Williams repeatedly stated both in interviews with his first biographer Robert Carl Cohen and on the pages of the *Crusader*, revolutionary violence would now have to bring about radical change. In exile the NAACP maverick became one of the first black activists to redefine aggressive guerilla warfare as a justified form of self-defense, thus becoming a significant bridge figure that linked southern civil rights activism and Black Power militancy.[15]

Between 1960 and 1965, few black southerners espoused the revolutionary ideas that Williams advocated by the end of the decade, but they engaged in the same militant actions that had contributed to the activist's renown in movement circles. In July 1963, for example, NAACP activist and Korea War veteran Robert Hayling organized a black defense squad in St. Augustine, Florida. A few weeks earlier, black protestors had begun nonviolent protests to desegregate the city's restaurants, movie theaters, and other public places. Within days, the Ku Klux Klan began to attack the home of movement leader Hayling. In response, the black dentist bought a number of rifles and shotguns, taught a group of black teenagers how to use them, and stationed these guards around his house and other strategic locations in St. Augustine's black neighborhood. On July 1, 1963, Hayling's bodyguards clashed with white attackers. In the following months, tensions remained high and led to more racial violence. Two months after the first shootout, the defensive squad repelled an attack on the home of local NAACP activist Goldie Eubanks, killing one white man during the confrontation.[16] In March 1964, the arrival of Martin Luther King's Southern Christian Leadership Conference (SCLC) triggered a new wave of racist terror. By that time, Robert Hayling had quit the NAACP, after the organization's executive secretary Roy Wilkins had castigated him for warning St. Augustine whites that his guards would "shoot first and ask questions later."[17] Hayling then joined the SCLC and asked Martin Luther King to assist the St. Augustine movement. Nonviolent protest marches in May and June 1964 triggered more white violence and pressured federal authorities to intervene in the crisis. King resented the defense efforts of local blacks, but when confronted with death threats and shotgun attacks, King grudgingly consented to the deployment of armed guards to protect his life.[18]

According to civil rights activist Frank Solomon, some African American activists in South Carolina also armed themselves to confront white aggression. Solomon had left his hometown Allendale in the 1950s and later joined the army. After his discharge, he became interested in civil rights activism, and in 1962, he joined the Congress of Racial Equality (CORE), working as an organizer in the North. In December 1963, he decided to return to Allendale to assist in the town's nascent freedom movement against segregation and disfranchisement. Soon after his arrival, Solomon began to receive death threats from white residents. Tensions increased in 1964, when black teenagers staged sit-ins to desegregate a local restaurant. After an argument between Solomon and a white female voting registrar, a group of white men vowed to lynch him. Hunted by a large mob

and local police, Solomon was rescued by local blacks, who had armed themselves with shotguns and pistols.[19] After this incident, the movement turned
into an armed camp. "There was one big difference between us and civil rights
workers in other places in the South," said Solomon. African American activists "let whites know that we were not nonviolent like others. We were going to
fight fire with fire." By Solomon's account, he and his comrades slept with pistols
under their pillows and rifles stacked in their rooms. When blacks announced
that Klansmen who intended to burn crosses in the black community "would
be blown away," nightly harassment stopped.[20] Solomon finally left Allendale in
late 1964, but the militant movement that he had helped to organize continued.
Throughout 1965, Allendale blacks staged nonviolent demonstrations, demanding that white authorities prevent local officials from impeding the registration
of black voters.[21]

In North Carolina, black resistance continued as well. John Salter, a white
activist who had quit his job as a professor of sociology at Mississippi's black
Tougaloo College to work for the Southern Conference Educational Fund as a
civil rights organizer, found the northeastern region of North Carolina to be a
hotbed of Ku Klux Klan activity. In 1964, the state's hooded order was stronger
than ever, boasting several thousand members.[22] When Salter arrived in rural
Halifax County in January 1964, Klansmen immediately attempted to end his
voter registration drive around the town of Enfield with violence. Cross burn-
ings, arson, and armed parades through black neighborhoods became routine,
and local blacks responded by guarding their communities with rifles and shotguns. "The Negroes in Halifax County are now pretty well armed," Salter wrote
in July 1964, "and, in Enfield particularly, are standing night-time guards."[23]
Salter himself never left his house without a .38 caliber revolver.[24] North
Carolina Governor Terry Sanford and the U.S. Justice Department did nothing
to stop the Klan's reign of terror. Neither did the Federal Bureau of Investigation
(FBI), whose agents had shadowed the white activist for years. As in the rest of
the South, FBI agents refused to risk their lives for the safety of a white civil
rights organizer, let alone African American citizens.[25] Local police felt even less
responsibility to provide security. At times the lawmen seemed indistinguishable
from members of the Ku Klux Klan. Bulletin boards at Halifax County's police
station featured regular advertisements for local Klan rallies.[26] "Fortunately,"
Salter later recalled, "we lived in the middle of a heavily armed Black community,
with neighbors...who were protective, especially when I was away in the field
for long periods of time." In 1964, such defense efforts were not exceptional. In
Tuscaloosa, Alabama, for instance, black activists formed another sophisticated
protective squad that guarded the homes of movement leaders and watched over
the activities of local civil rights activists.[27]

Local activists tended to regard such forms of armed resistance as a pragmatic
necessity, but within civil rights organizations that assisted them in challenging Jim Crow, self-defense frequently sparked heated debates, which ultimately
contributed to the radicalization of the civil rights movement. In the summer of
1964, for instance, members of the Student Nonviolent Coordinating Committee
(SNCC) passionately discussed whether their nonviolent mission conflicted with

the use of armed force in Mississippi, where many blacks formed self-defense groups to protect their communities against attacks by racist attackers. The reaction of black men to white harassment in the town of Mayersville was typical of such protection efforts in Mississippi. Activist Unita Blackwell recounts in her memoirs how white teenagers repeatedly threw firebombs at black homes or burned crosses in the vicinity of the black community during SNCC's Freedom Summer campaign of 1964. A group of armed black men, who served as protectors of Mayersville, quickly put an end to violent intimidation. "Then three or four of our black protectors started walking the streets with guns," Blackwell remembered in her autobiography. "They didn't want to shoot the kids, but they did want to scare the hell out of them; so they came up behind their car and made a circle around it...they shot at the top back window and shattered the glass. Those white children got out of town in a hurry, and we never saw them again." Across the state, civil rights workers and journalists reported similar forms of armed resistance.[28]

At a staff meeting on June 10, 1964, in Atlanta, several SNCC organizers discussed the implications of such protective efforts for their work in the South. When student activist Willie Peacock touted a "self-defense structure" that blacks in Greenwood had organized to repel white attacks, one field worker raised the question as to whether SNCC had a right to "stop people from doing what they want to do."[29] Veteran organizer Bob Moses admitted that they were in no position to do so. "Self-defense is so deeply ingrained in rural Southern America," he explained, "that we as a small group can't affect it. It's not contradictory for a farmer to say he's nonviolent and also pledge to shoot a marauder's head off." Yet he urged his comrades to accept that staff members would not be allowed to carry guns.[30] A similarly difficult problem was the question as to how SNCC activists ought to react if caught in a situation that required armed self-defense. Charles Cobb explained his personal predicament. "We will be living on a farm with a man who has guns," he hypothesized. "What would happen if someone attacked his house and he shot back[?] If Charlie were there would SNCC stand by him, even though SNCC advocates nonviolence[?]" In the end, the organizers agreed that SNCC would support staff members who became involved in self-defense incidents, but they refused to commit themselves to an official position on armed resistance.[31]

SNCC's Freedom Summer project, which brought hundreds of white student volunteers to Mississippi to register black voters and to teach black children in independent Freedom Schools, triggered more debates and radicalized many of SNCC's field workers. In the process, some of them became strong advocates of armed self-defense. As early as June 1964, one activist told the black magazine *Jet* of being chased by three carloads of whites in the little town of Valleyview: "I had a shotgun and I'll tell you if they had come in to get me, I would have used it." While adhering to nonviolence in demonstrations, he had no objection to using the gun for protection in the face of white vigilante attacks.[32] In July 1964, a spy of the Mississippi State Sovereignty Commission reported that SNCC staff in Jackson began to advocate a "doctrine of self-defense" among local activists. "We are told that if we find ourselves under physical attack," the informer wrote to his superiors, "we may take steps to defend ourselves until we are out of danger."[33] Journalist Nicholas von Hoffman also detailed in a book on the Mississippi movement that some civil rights organizers had "stopped preaching" nonviolence and were "urging the contrary."[34] In large part this shift in SNCC's thinking was a direct result of their experience in the Deep South. In his memoirs, James Forman argued that the Freedom Summer campaign "confirmed the absolute necessity for armed self-defense—a necessity that existed before the project but which became overwhelmingly clear to SNCC people during and after it."[35] From the perspective of many activists, the fact that some communities in Mississippi experienced less white terror than others was not the result of the presence of FBI agents but of black armed resistance.[36] Following this logic, some of SNCC's field workers began to arm themselves. According to historian Godfrey Hodgson, "virtually every SNCC worker in the field was carrying a gun" before Freedom Summer was over. By 1965, an increasing number of SNCC members advocated, and on occasion practiced, armed resistance. Born out of necessity, armed black militancy in the South influenced SNCC's Black Power program in the second half of the 1960s.[37]

Among members of the Congress of Racial Equality (CORE), self-defense debates exacted a comparable effect on the organization's ideology between 1963 and 1965. Focusing most of their energies on local freedom movements in Louisiana during this period, CORE fieldworkers quickly learned that blacks who joined the movement had little respect for theories of Gandhian nonviolence. Consequently, a number of organizers voiced concerns about the increasing tendency among blacks to arm for protection. Delegates at CORE's 1963 annual convention in Dayton, Ohio, warned of an "imminent possibility of a violent racial explosion" in the South. One staffer reported that it was common to see African Americans check their guns and knives on a table outside the meeting place. Some of them even brought their weapons to demonstrations. Northern volunteers, whom CORE had recruited to assist in its 1964 Louisiana summer project, were similarly perplexed to find their black host families armed and ready.[38] As in the case of SNCC, the fact that local blacks guarded homes and civil rights meetings with rifles and shotguns provoked serious discussions within the nonviolent organization. During a staff meeting in February 1964, national director James Farmer, veteran activist Bayard Rustin, and the southern field staff discussed CORE's position on the issue. The question of white organizer Miriam Feingold whether "a violent person" was a "'traitor to our cause'" probably tormented the conscience of many. In the discussion, James Farmer made clear that CORE remained committed to nonviolence on civil rights projects, but he offered no definite policy on armed self-defense.[39]

The Deacons for Defense and Justice, a sophisticated self-defense organization that was founded in Jonesboro, Louisiana, in 1964, compounded CORE's moral predicament but ultimately convinced an increasing number of civil rights organizers that armed protection was necessary. Patrolling black neighborhoods, providing armed escorts for civil rights organizers, and occasionally trading shots with racist attackers, the Deacons became an integral part of local freedom movements in Jonesboro, a small town in southwestern Louisiana, and in

Bogalusa, a city north of New Orleans.[40] Given the nonviolent orthodoxy that characterized the nation's civil rights discourse, it came as no surprise that rights leaders and white authorities condemned the Deacons. Because of this criticism, CORE's leadership was at pains to reassure the national media that the organization's alliance with the defense squad did not affect its nonviolent commitment, but James Farmer and others clearly recognized the significance of the Deacons as a community organization that symbolized protection and black pride. Many field workers praised the defense group. Some of them even began to emulate the example of the Deacons. In August 1965, *Newsweek* reported that "some CORE workers in Bogalusa," "like practically everybody else in town,... are now carrying weapons."[41] As early as April of that year, civil rights volunteers from Berkeley, armed with pistols, had assisted the Deacons in patrolling the black neighborhood. "When their numbers grew short," one of them remembered, "I was deputized as a deacon, carrying a handgun as student volunteers from my college went door to door."[42] Few of CORE's activists had ever been committed to nonviolence as a way of life, and those who considered nonviolence a useful tactic increasingly argued that it would have to be complemented by armed resistance.[43]

In terms of armed militancy, then, it is difficult to conceive of the radicalization of SNCC and CORE in the aftermath of the Meredith March as a sudden break with the nonviolent tenets of Martin Luther King. Rather civil rights organizers' vociferous advocacy of armed resistance owed much to the example of local black activists in the South and the numerous discussions that their armed actions triggered. By 1966, many civil rights organizers had come to accept armed resistance as a simple necessity. After years of debating the pros and cons of tailoring the movement's nonviolent image to the expectations of white liberals, many grew weary of professing love for their enemy. No longer willing to preserve the movement's reputation for philosophical nonviolence, both SNCC and CORE officially endorsed armed self-defense shortly after the Meredith March. "I refuse to debate the black man's right of self-defense," Carmichael stated in September 1966. "It is inalienable, beyond debate. To ask anybody in Mississippi to be non-violent is tantamount to encouraging suicide, and I don't believe in self-destruction."[44] At CORE's annual convention in July 1966, the organization's new chairman Floyd McKissick suggested that the movement had to challenge the traditional double standards that whites continued to force upon blacks. From his perspective, the right to self-defense was "a constitutional right" that blacks would not surrender as long as white racists continued to attack African Americans.[45] This interpretation received almost unanimous support from the convention delegates. When Harlem CORE's chairman Roy Innis recommended that the group's requirement that members "adopt the technique of non-violence in direct action" be deleted, the proposal passed easily. The organization had not yet completely abandoned nonviolent protest, but the right of armed self-defense had now become CORE's official policy.[46]

Of course, black self-defense efforts and the debates that they triggered were only one among a plethora of radicalizing factors that culminated in the emergence of Black Power. For example, the failure of the indigenous and

interracial Mississippi Freedom Democratic Party to unseat the state's segregationist Democratic delegation at the party's 1964 national convention in Atlantic
City shattered the organization's trust in America's political system. SNCC's
subsequent work in Lowndes County, Alabama, where activists helped organize a black political party to wrest power from a minority of white planters,
also shaped the political program of Black Power.[47] Freedom Summer, on the
other hand, successfully convinced many black members that white participation hampered rather than aided the freedom movement. Too often, white
northern student volunteers presumptively assumed leadership positions in local
civil rights projects, failing to realize that their behavior prevented local blacks
from developing their own leadership potential. CORE too had learned that
white field workers could frequently become an obstacle to black empowerment.
Jonesboro, Louisiana, where white student Charles Fenton had helped organize
the Deacons in 1964, was a typical example. San Francisco CORE member Bill
Bradley explained in an assessment of CORE's southern projects: "In Jonesboro,
Louisiana Charles Fenton is regarded by many local Negroes as a God. He can get
local Negroes to march where no one else can." From Bradley's perspective, the
Jonesboro movement demonstrated that "the very independence we are trying to
encourage is discouraged by the presence and activity of whites." The Deacons
for Defense and Justice did represent a form of black empowerment, but their role
was mostly confined to protection duties. According to Bradley, their presence
did not translate into the kind of independent local movement that CORE had
originally envisioned.[48]

The radicalization of SNCC and CORE was also a result of the impact of
events and people outside the South. Urban unrest in the black ghettos of Harlem
and Watts in 1964 and 1965 directed attention to the growing frustration among
northern blacks over poverty, unemployment, discrimination, and police brutality. The Civil Rights Act of 1964 and the Voting Rights Act of 1965 did little to change these dismal conditions. Malcolm X's black nationalist themes of
black pride, self-defense, and Pan-Africanism coupled with the militant calls
for armed rebellion by exiled activist Robert Williams further radicalized both
organizations. Finally, the escalating military involvement of the United States
in Vietnam, coupled with the militancy of African independence movement and
the significant role of race in the cold war, led civil rights organizers to consider
the international implications of the black freedom movement.[49] In the case of
self-defense, however, homegrown black militancy at the local level was clearly
one of the most important factors that contributed to the radicalization of the
civil rights movement.

After the advent of Black Power, which tends to be associated primarily with
militant groups in the North, armed resistance efforts continued in the South. In
the summer of 1966, African Americans in Port Gibson, Mississippi, responded
to continued police harassment and racist intimidation with the formation of
a highly sophisticated protection agency. Organized by NAACP activist Rudy
Shields, the group came to be known as Deacons for Defense and Justice, although
it was never affiliated with the original Louisiana defense unit. Others simply
called them "Black Hats," alluding to the black cowboy hats that many of its

members wore in a uniform-like fashion. Like its Louisiana counterpart, the unit protected nonviolent demonstrations and mass rallies. In addition, it assisted in enforcing a local economic boycott against white merchants who refused to hire African Americans. Until the end of the selective buying campaign in 1967, the Black Hats harassed and intimidated those who had violated the boycott.[50]

Like these Mississippi groups, the Bogalusa Deacons for Defense and Justice remained active throughout 1967. Deacons continued to patrol the city's black neighborhood, escorted CORE organizers and white volunteers in and out of town, and protected those who tested white compliance with the Civil Rights Act of 1964. Peter Jan Honigsberg, a white volunteer who worked in Bogalusa for the Lawyers Constitutional Defense Committee, recalled in his memoirs that members of the defense unit usually positioned themselves in front of segregated cafes to protect him and fellow activists from white aggression.[51] The Bogalusa Deacons also maintained an impressive arsenal of weapons. According to Honigsberg, the trunk of Charles Sims's old yellow 1958 Chevy usually contained "a semiautomatic carbine that looked like a submachine gun, two shotguns, several boxes of shells, and a handful of grenades."[52] Since 1965, when the Deacons repelled several attacks by the Ku Klux Klan with gunfire, no racist terrorists had approached the black section of town, but Sims and his comrades were undoubtedly prepared for another confrontation.

One of the last civil rights campaigns in Louisiana, a nonviolent protest march from Bogalusa to Baton Rouge in August 1967, marked the end of the Deacons' activities. By that time, more and more southern towns and cities began the process of desegregation, and hundreds of thousands of African Americans had added their names to the voter rolls. In addition, the number of racist attacks on the movement waned, and state and local authorities finally began to protect black demonstrators against the attacks of those die-hard racists who still sought to stop the freedom movement with violence. With the original justification for their formation gone, the Deacons had outlived their usefulness, putting their shotguns back on the rack. The same was true for Mississippi defense organizations like the Port Gibson Deacons, which had disbanded by the end of the decade.[53] By that time, protective agencies in Alabama, Mississippi, and North Carolina also ceased activity.

After the demise of these defense groups, armed militancy in the southern freedom struggle continued but took on a different character. Like Black Power activists outside the region, an increasing number of black radicals regarded weapons primarily as a symbol of defiance and frequently blurred the boundaries between self-defense and armed self-assertion.[54] The first flares of this new type of militancy began on southern college campuses, where black students sometimes chose to display weapons to emphasize their demand for curricular and societal change. Sometimes, this strategy of martial symbolism exploded into violent clashes between students and police. In May 1967, for example, a shootout between student militants and lawmen on the campus of Texas Southern University at Houston left one police officer dead and two other officers and one student wounded. Police later explained that their attack on one of the college's dormitories was justified because students had opened fire on them after a student rally on campus.[55] In the aftermath of the assassination of Martin Luther King on April 4, 1968, the *New York Times* reported that black student radicals in Gainesville, Florida, firebombed white businesses in the black section of town and the homes of two white public officials.[56] Students were not the only ones willing to confront white authorities with guns. A month before the riot at Texas Southern University, black militants in Prattville, Alabama, fired at police officers who patrolled the black neighborhood, wounding two of them. Tensions started after SNCC leader Stokely Carmichael was arrested for allegedly threatening several policemen. During the subsequent five-hour gun battle between police and black radicals, three policemen were wounded by buckshot.[57] However, in spite of SNCC Chairman H. Rap Brown's statement that the Prattville shootout would be "the starting battleground for America's race war," such clashes were rare in the late 1960s.[58]

More confrontations between police and black radicals occurred in the early 1970s, when white authorities sought to disrupt the activities of black militant organizations in the South. In Houston, for instance, police repeatedly clashed with People's Party 2 (PP2), a group that black activists had formed to combat police brutality. Modeled after the Oakland-based Black Panther Party for Self-Defense, the PP2 intended to patrol Houston's black neighborhood to prevent unlawful arrests and harassment. On July 17, 1970, a confrontation occurred between armed members of the new group and the Houston Police Department. The PP2's martial rhetoric in the next few days exacerbated the tense situation, which ultimately exploded into violence. During the night of July 26, police officers attacked the organization's headquarters, fatally wounding PP2's chairman Carl Hampton. Although none of the black militants had fired at the police, Houston's white authorities claimed that the police officers had acted in self-defense and in accordance with the law.[59]

Southern chapters of the BPP engaged in similar confrontations with white lawmen. On January 12, 1971, policemen riddled the headquarters of the Winston-Salem, North Carolina, chapter of the BPP with bullets, claiming that two members had been involved in stealing a truck.[60] A week later, police arrested thirteen Black Panthers in Memphis, Tennessee, confiscating shotguns, rifles, and ammunition.[61] The most violent confrontation between black radicals and white authorities took place in New Orleans. After what the *Chicago Tribune* described as "a massive gun battle" between the New Orleans BPP and police officers in September 1970, one young black man lay dead, and three others wounded. As in cities outside the South, the police department appeared to interpret the party's armed militancy—the New Orleans BPP had amassed a small arsenal of shotguns, automatic weapons, and pistols—as a direct challenge to white authority. "These revolutionaries have expressed openly the desire to kill any enforcement officers and those refusing to join their revolution," explained the city's Police Superintendent Clarence Giarusso.[62] After the raid, twelve Panthers were charged with attempting to kill police officers. In August 1971, a jury of ten blacks and two whites acquitted all defendants of the charges.[63] Few scholars have probed the history of the BPP in the South, but as the examples of Winston-Salem, Memphis, and New Orleans suggest, many of the problems that plagued the original Panthers in Oakland also burdened its southern chapters. The party's provocative rhetoric resulted in similar confrontations with white authorities who resolved to infiltrate BPP chapters and disrupt their activities.[64] As historian Curtis Austin has concluded in his recent study of the Oakland Panthers, it was primarily the BPP's "early emphasis on self-defense" that "left it open to mischaracterization, infiltration, and devastation by local, state, and federal police forces."[65]

The same was true for the Republic of New Africa (RNA), a Detroit-based black nationalist organization that called for a separate and independent black nation that would consist of five Deep Southern states and a few black enclaves in northern and western cities. In the late 1960s, the RNA established a "consulate" in Mississippi. In 1971, the RNA set up its "government headquarters" and a "presidential residence" in Jackson, Mississippi. As in the case of the BPP, the RNA's militancy alarmed white authorities. On August 18 of that year, FBI agents and Jackson police officers raided these two buildings, which led to a shootout with several RNA members.[66]

But self-defense was only one aspect of Black Power, which was a complex ideology that defied overtly simplistic categorizations. In the South, as in the rest of the country, the Black Power movement stood above all for black pride, Pan-Africanism, radical internationalism, and black political power. Some southern cities became important centers of the Black Power movement. Atlanta, in particular, in the words of historian James Edward Smethurst, "became an increasingly important hub of nationalist thought and activity" in the early 1970s.[67] In the realm of culture, the Black Arts Movement blossomed at southern black colleges and universities and contributed to redefinitions of black identity. Hosting conferences and festivals that explored and celebrated black art and literature, students established important links with other black militants in the region. Students and Black Power militants also established new educational institutions, such as the Malcolm X Liberation University, which was founded in Durham, North Carolina, in 1969. These independent institutions stressed Pan-Africanism and fostered activism for the cause of anticolonialism. Seeking to create "a Black Revolutionary Ideology" by providing "a real alternative for Black people seeking liberation from the misconception of an institutionalized racist education," the independent university began to put into action Black Power at the local level.[68]

Black political power in the South was inextricably linked with the ideas about racial consciousness that the southern Black Power movement disseminated across the region. As Steven Lawson has noted, "burgeoning racial pride among African-Americans was instrumental for black political mobilization."[69] Earlier traditions of civil rights activism had toppled the most egregious forms of white supremacy in Dixie. Black Power militancy contributed to people's eagerness to use the new possibilities that the Voting Rights Act of 1965 provided. By 1970, over 700 African Americans had won political office in the states of the former Confederacy (as compared to 24 elected officials in 1964).[70] Two years later both northern and southern proponents of Black Power focused on political organizing, abandoning earlier plans to use revolutionary violence to transform

American society. The National Black Political Convention in Gary, Indiana in 1972 showcased both the possibilities of black political organizing and the schisms that continued to divide the black freedom movement in the post-civil rights era. Although the Black Power movement lost momentum in the following years, some of the militant ideas and activities that first impacted at the local level left a lasting legacy for later generations.

Notes

1. Quoted in Cleveland Sellers, *The River of No Return: The Autobiography of a Black Militant and the Life and Death of SNCC* (Jackson: University Press of Mississippi, 1973), pp. 166–67.
2. Nikhil Pal Singh, *Black Is a Country: Race and the Unfinished Struggle for Democracy* (Cambridge, MA: Harvard University Press, 2004), pp. 5–6.
3. Some of the most important examples of this revisionist literature include Peniel E. Joseph, *Waiting 'Til the Midnight Hour: A Narrative History of Black Power in America* (New York: Henry Holt, 2006); Peniel E. Joseph, ed., *The Black Power Movement: Rethinking the Civil Rights-Black Power Era* (New York: Routledge, 2006); Matthew J. Countryman, *Up South: Civil Rights and Black Power in Philadelphia* (Philadelphia: University of Pennsylvania Press, 2006); James Edward Smethurst, *The Black Arts Movement: Literary Nationalism in the 1960s and 1970s* (Chapel Hill: University of North Carolina Press, 2005); Jeffrey O. G. Ogbar, *Black Power: Radical Politics and African American Identity* (Baltimore: Johns Hopkins University Press, 2004); Nikhil Pal Singh, *Black Is a Country*; Robert O. Self, *American Babylon: Race and the Struggle for Postwar Oakland* (Princeton, NJ: Princeton University Press, 2003); Komozi Woodard, *A Nation within a Nation: Amiri Baraka (LeRoi Jones) & Black Power Politics* (Chapel Hill: University of North Carolina Press, 1999).
4. Peniel E. Joseph, "Introduction: Toward a Historiography of the Black Power Movement," in *The Black Power Movement*, p. 21.
5. For a more detailed discussion of the complexities of armed resistance in the civil rights/Black Power movement, see Simon Wendt, *The Spirit and the Shotgun: Armed Resistance and the Struggle for Civil Rights* (Gainesville: University Press of Florida, 2007).
6. JoAnn Ooimann Robinson, "Diary 6/21/64–6/26/64," entry June, 25, 1964, JoAnne Ooiman Robinson Papers, box 2, folder 1, State Historical Society of Wisconsin (hereafter cited as SHSW); Howell Raines, ed., *My Soul Is Rested: Movement Days in the Deep South Remembered* (New York: G. P. Putnam's Sons, 1977), p. 53; Adam Fairclough, *To Redeem the Soul of America: The Southern Christian Leadership Conference and Martin Luther King, Jr.* (Athens: University of Georgia Press, 1987), p. 25.
7. Bayard Rustin, "Report on Montgomery, Alabama," published by the War Resisters League, March 21, 1956, Bayard Rustin Papers, microfilm, reel 17, frame 01140, Library of Congress, Manuscript Division, Washington, D.C.
8. "Interview with Bayard Rustin, March 28, 1974," August Meier Papers, box 58, folder 4, Schomburg Center for Research in Black Culture, New York Public Library, New York.
9. Andrew M. Manis, *A Fire You Can't Put Out: The Civil Rights Life of Birmingham's Reverend Fred Shuttlesworth* (Tuscaloosa: University of Alabama Press, 1999), pp. 110, 117–18; Glen T. Eskew, *But for Birmingham: The Local and National Movements in the Civil Rights Struggle* (Chapel Hill: University of North Carolina Press, 1997), p. 141.

10. Timothy B. Tyson, *Radio Free Dixie: Robert F. Williams and the Roots of Black Power* (Chapel Hill: University of North Carolina Press, 1999), pp. 80–83; Robert F. Williams, interview by James Mosby, transcript, July 22, 1970, Detroit, Michigan, 50, Ralph J. Bunche Collection, Moorland-Spingarn Research Center, Howard University, Washington, D.C.

11. Tyson, *Radio Free Dixie*, pp. 84–89.

12. Ibid., pp. 195–196, 297–298.

13. Ibid., p. 3.

14. Quoted in "Fugitive Mapping New Africa in U.S.," *New York Times*, July 14, 1968, p. 26.

15. Robert Carl Cohen, "The Negro Che Guevara: Will He Turn the U.S.A. into Another Viet Nam?," pp. 19–21, 27, box 5, folder 3, Robert Carl Cohen Papers, SHSW.

16. David J. Garrow, *Bearing the Cross: Martin Luther King, Jr. and the Southern Christian Leadership Conference* (New York: Random House, 1986), pp. 316–317; David R. Colburn, *Racial Change and Community Crisis: St. Augustine, Florida, 1877–1980* (New York: Columbia University Press, 1985), pp. 50–55; Edward W. Kallal Jr., "St. Augustine and the Ku Klux Klan: 1963 and 1964," in David J. Garrow, ed., *St. Augustine, Florida, 1963–1964: Mass Protest and Racial Violence* (Brooklyn, N.Y.: Carlson, 1989), pp. 136–137.

17. Quoted in Robert W. Hartley, "A Long Hot Summer: The St. Augustine Racial Disorders of 1964," in *St. Augustine, Florida, 1963–1964*, p. 21.

18. Garrow, *Bearing the Cross*, pp. 317–334; Colburn, *Racial Change and Community Crisis*, pp. 84–89, 212.

19. Frank Solomon, *A Hell of a Life* (New York: Vantage Press, 1976), pp. 5–75.

20. Ibid., pp. 77, 84.

21. "Sanders Asks Race Negotiation," *Washington Post*, August 5, 1965, p. A7; "Allendale Protests Continue," *New York Times*, August 6, 1965 p. 12; "17 Jailed at Allendale, S.C. For a Protest at Courthouse," *New York Times*, August 21, 1965, p. 8.

22. Wynn Craig Wade, *The Fiery Cross: The Ku Klux Klan in America* (New York: Oxford University Press, 1987), p. 315.

23. John R. Salter Jr. to Francis Mitchell and Mandy Samstein, October 6, 1964, box 1, folder 33, John R. Salter Papers (hereafter cited as Salter Papers), SHSW; John R. Salter Jr. to Dear Folks, July 6, 1964, box 1, folder 6, Salter Papers.

24. John R. Salter, *Jackson, Mississippi: An American Chronicle of Struggle and Schism* (Hicksville, NY: Exposition Press), p. 240.

25. John R. Salter to Governor Terry Sanford, n.d., telegram, box 1, folder 22, Salter Papers; "6/14/65," 27–30, John R. Salter, Jr. FBI File 44–29407, unprocessed accessions, Salter Papers.

26. John R. Salter Jr. to Francis Mitchell and Mandy Samstein, October 6, 1964.

27. John R. Salter, "Civil Rights and Self-Defense," *Against the Current* 3, no. 3 (July–August 1988): 24. On the Tuscaloosa movement, see Wendt, *The Spirit and the Shotgun*, pp. 42–65.

28. Unita Blackwell, with JoAnne Prichard Morris, *Barefootin': Life Lessons from the Road to Freedom* (New York: Crown, 2006), p. 98. On self-defense in the Mississippi movement, see Emilye Crosby, "'This Nonviolent Stuff Ain't No Good. It'll Get Ya Killed': Teaching about Self-Defense in the African American Freedom Struggle," in Julie Buckner Armstrong, Susan Edwards, Houston Roberson, and Rhonda Williams, eds., *Teaching the American Civil Rights Movement: Freedom's Bittersweet Song* (New York: Routledge, 2002), pp. 159–173; Emilye Crosby, *A Little Taste of Freedom: The Black Freedom Struggle in Claiborne County, Mississippi* (Chapel Hill: University of North Carolina Press, 2005); Akinyele O. Umoja, "'We Will Shoot

Back': The Natchez Model and Paramilitary Organization in the Mississippi Freedom Movement," *Journal of Black Studies* 32, no. 3 (January 2002): 271–294; Akinyele O. Umoja, "1964: The Beginning of the End of Nonviolence in the Mississippi Freedom Movement," *Radical History Review* 85 (Winter 2003): 201–226; Wendt, *The Spirit and the Shotgun*, pp. 100–152.

29. "Staff Meeting Minutes June 9–11, 1964," 12–13, box 2, folder 7, Howard Zinn Papers, SHSW.

30. Mary King, *Freedom Song: A Personal Story of the 1960s Civil Rights Movement* (New York: Morrow, 1987), p. 318.

31. Ibid., p. 314; "Staff Meeting Minutes June 9–11, 1964," 14, 15; James Forman, *The Making of Black Revolutionaries* (New York: Macmillan, 1972), p. 375.

32. Quoted in "Shocking Notes on Miss. Brutality in Just One 21-Hour Period," *Jet*, July 2, 1964, p. 6.

33. "Report of Operator #79," box 136, folder 1, Johnson Family Papers, McCain Library and Archives, University of Southern Mississippi, Hattiesburg.

34. Nicholas Von Hoffman, *Mississippi Notebook* (New York: David White, 1964), p. 95.

35. Forman, *The Making of Black Revolutionaries*, p. 375.

36. Doug McAdam, *Freedom Summer* (New York: Oxford University Press, 1988), p. 32; Clayborne Carson, *In Struggle: SNCC and the Black Awakening of the 1960s*, new edn. (Cambridge, MA: Harvard University Press, 1995), p. 123.

37. Godfrey Hodgson, *America in Our Time* (Garden City, NY: Doubleday, 1976), p. 212; Carson, *In Struggle*, p. 164.

38. M. S. Handler, "Militancy Grows CORE Aides Warn," *New York Times*, June 28, 29, 1963, p. 12; Jim Peck, ed., "Louisiana—Summer, 1964: The Students Report to Their Home Towns," unprocessed accessions, box 1, folder 2, Congress of Racial Equality Papers (hereafter cited as CORE Papers), SHSW.

39. "Staff Meeting: New Orleans, La., February 14, 1964," notebook number 10, reel 2, frame 422, Miriam Feingold Papers, microfilm, SHSW.

40. On the Deacons, see Lance E. Hill, *The Deacons for Defense: Armed Resistance and the Civil Rights Movement* (Chapel Hill: University of North Carolina Press, 2004); Wendt, *The Spirit and the Shotgun*, pp. 66–99; Simon Wendt, "'Urge People Not to Carry Guns': Armed Self-Defense in the Louisiana Civil Rights Movement and the Radicalization of the Congress of Racial Equality," *Louisiana History* 45, no. 3 (Summer 2004): 261–286.

41. "The Deacons," *Newsweek*, August 2, 1965, p. 29.

42. Carl Hufbauer, "Bogalusa: Negro Community vs. Crown Colony," *Campus CORE-Lator* 1 (Spring 1965): 21, reel 17, frame 0293, CORE Papers, Addendum, microfilm, SHSW; Jeffrey M. Dickeman, "Skeleton in the Closet," *New York Review of Books*, July 5, 2001, p. 66.

43. August Meier and Elliot Rudwick, *CORE: A Study in the Civil Rights Movement, 1942–1968* (Urbana: University of Illinois Press, 1975), p. 202.

44. Quoted in Lerone Bennett Jr., "Stokely Carmichael: Architect of Black Power," *Ebony*, September 1966, p. 26.

45. M. S. Handler, "Negro Vote Bloc Pressed by CORE," *New York Times*, July 2, 3, 1966, p. 28.

46. "Minutes of Western Regional Convention of September 3 and 4, 1966," box 2, folder 12, CORE Papers—Western Regional Office Files, SHSW.

47. Carson, *In Struggle*, pp. 123–129; Hasan Kwame Jeffries, "SNCC, Black Power, and Independent Political Party Organizing in Alabama, 1964–1966," *Journal of African American History* 91, no. 2 (Spring 2006): 171–193.

48. Bill Bradley, "Our Southern Projects 'A Review,'" Allan Gartner Papers, SHSW.

49. Carson, *In Struggle*, pp. 2–3; Stokely Carmichael, with Ekwueme Michael Thelwell, *Ready for Revolution: The Life and Struggle of Stokely Carmichael (Kwame Ture)* (New York: Scribner, 2003), p. 255; Meier and Rudwick, *CORE*, p. 297.

50. A.L. Hopkins, "Investigation of a Report that a Group of Negro Males Have Organized a Unit of 'Black Panthers' in Port Gibson, Mississippi," July 11, 1966, box 139, folder 2, Johnson Family Papers; L.E. Cole, "Boycott and Civil Rights Activities in Area of Fayette and Port Gibson, Mississippi," September 30, 1966, box 139, folder 4, Johnson Family Papers; L.E. Cole, "Port Gibson, Mississippi, Claiborne County," December 30, 1966, box 139, folder 7, Johnson Family Papers. The Port Gibson Deacons, however, were only one among many "enforcer squads" that assisted local Mississippi boycott campaigns in the 1960s. See Umoja, "We Will Shoot Back," p. 271.

51. Adam Fairclough, *Race and Democracy: The Civil Rights Movement in Louisiana, 1915–1972* (Athens: University of Georgia Press, 1995), p. 374; Peter Jan Honigsberg, *Crossing Border Street: A Civil Rights Memoir* (Berkeley: University of California Press, 2000), p. 24, 33, pp. 43–44.

52. Honigsberg, *Crossing Border Street*, p. 52.

53. Letterhead Memorandum, "Deacons of Defense and Justice, Inc.," November 27, 1967; Memorandum, W.C. Sullivan to R.W. Smith, March 26, 1968, Deacons for Defense and Justice FBI File 157-2466-266. In early 1970, the FBI terminated its investigation of the group. SAC, New Orleans to Director, FBI, February 17, 1970, Deacons FBI File 157-2466-279; Emilye Crosby, "Common Courtesy: The Civil Rights Movement in Claiborne County, Mississippi," Ph.D. diss., Indiana University, 1995, p. 405.

54. For a detailed account and discussion of these changes, see Wendt, *The Spirit and the Shotgun*, pp. 153–186.

55. Martin Waldron, "Shot Kills Texas Policeman in Riot at a Negro College," *New York Times*, May 18, 1967, p. 1; "Houston Campus Riot Is Laid to 'Black Power,'" *Washington Post*, November 4, 1967, p. A4.

56. Anthony Ripley, "Black Power Unit Stirs Florida City," *New York Times*, April 21, 1968, p. 27.

57. "Violence in Alabama," *New York Times*, June 12, 1967, p. 88; "Carmichael Held, Shots Erupt in Alabama Town," *Los Angeles Times*, June 12, 1967, p. 16.

58. Quoted in "4 wounded in Alabama Gunbattle Following Carmichael's Arrest," *Washington Post*, June 13, 1967, p. A3.

59. For a more detailed account of the Black Power movement in Texas, see Brian Behnken, "Fighting their Own Battles: Blacks, Mexican Americans, and the Struggle for Civil Rights in Texas," Ph.D. diss., University of California, Davis, 2007.

60. Jim Gray, "Panther Center Shot Up in Theft Probe," *Washington Post*, January 13, 1971, p. A3.

61. "Panthers, Police Clash in Memphis," *Washington Post*, January 19, 1971, p. A2.

62. "1 Black Slain, 3 Shot by Police," *Chicago Tribune*, September 16, 1970, p. 2. See also "Police Kill Negro and Hurt Three in Shootout," *Los Angeles Times*, September 15, 1970, p. 15.

63. "Jurors Acquit 12 Panthers in New Orleans," *Los Angeles Times*, August 7, 1971, p. C14.

64. In September 1970, for example, New Orleans Panthers discovered that two undercover agents had infiltrated their organization. See Roy Reed, "Panthers 'Tried' 2 Police Agents," *New York Times*, September 19, 1970, p. 12.

65. Curtis J. Austin, *Up against the Wall: Violence in the Making and Unmaking of the Black Panther Party* (Fayetteville, AR: University of Arkansas Press, 2006), p. xxii.

66. Donald Cunnigen, "The Republic of New Africa in Mississippi," in Judson L. Jeffries, ed., *Black Power in the Belly of the Beast* (Urbana: University of Illinois Press, 2006), pp. 93–115.

67. Smethurst, *The Black Arts Movement*, pp. 319–337, 339. For recent scholarship on the Black Arts Movement, see also Lisa Gail Collins and Natalie Crawford, eds., *New Thoughts on the Black Arts Movement* (New Brunswick, NJ: Rutgers University Press, 2006).

68. Christina Green, *Our Separate Ways: Women and the Black Freedom Movement in Durham, North Carolina* (Chapel Hill: University of North Carolina Press, 2005), p. 187.

69. Steven F. Lawson, *Running for Freedom: Civil Rights and Black Politics in America since 1941*, 2nd edn. (New York: McGraw-Hill, 1997), p. 117.

70. Ibid., p. 122.

7

Empowerment, Consciousness, Defense: The Diverse Meanings of the Black Power Movement in Louisville, Kentucky

Tracy E. K'Meyer[1]

In the summer of 1967, residents of the majority African American West End neighborhoods of Louisville, Kentucky, were feeling increasingly frustrated and powerless. The local drive for open housing legislation was stalled. Despite residents' complaints, the city's Urban Renewal Authority scheduled the building of more public housing units in an already overcrowded section of the neighborhood. School officials refused to replace the inadequate, fire-trap facilities that served the children of the area. The Community Action Commission (CAC) was in the process of shifting power away from representatives of poor communities. In response to the growing sense of crisis: members of a neighborhood integrationist and antipoverty organization called the West End Community Council (WECC) hosted a workshop to consider what new strategies they might try to address the problems in the community. Approximately fifty people, a mix of black and white, attended the "Citizens' Power Conference." At the end of the all-day meeting the group made two decisions. First, they resolved that henceforth WECC "should become a force for Black Power," making it the first local civil rights organization to publicly declare its support for the rising militant movement. Then, the group voted to hire a white Episcopal priest, the Reverend Charles Tachau, as the new executive director.[2] One year later, at a time when nationalist sentiment among African Americans engendered calls for separate institutions and led to demands for blacks-only civil rights organizations, the new "voice for Black Power" in Louisville found itself at the head of a broad-based interracial coalition formed to defend six of its members accused of conspiracy that united white and black activists from across the political spectrum.

The seemingly contradictory elements of this story—a self-proclaimed Black Power organization hires a white leader and then in response to the persecution of black militants rallies an outpouring of interracial cooperation—suggest how examining the expressions of the Black Power philosophy on the local level can complicate our understanding of this part of the freedom struggle. The narrative of Black Power is often construed as part of a trajectory of the southern integrationist campaigns giving way to a northern nationalist ferment. But activists in Louisville rarely made a sharp distinction between Black Power organizing and other ideas and tactics in the broader movement against racism. Integrationists in WECC embraced black consciousness. War on Poverty organizers in the West End saw their task as empowering the black community. In short, the story of Black Power in Louisville illuminates how that philosophy and movement flowed seamlessly out of earlier organizing as part of a longer search for visions and strategies that would contribute to the ongoing project of overcoming racism.

In Louisville the Black Power philosophy manifested itself both in the work of indigenous activists like those in WECC and through local units of national organizations, such as the Black Panthers, that linked the city to a broader movement. The activities of these groups made it clear that the philosophy meant different things to different people and did not always fit into a stereotypical image of Black Power. Over time, as the Black Power movement grew, local activists focused on empowerment, pride, and community development and protection. Regardless of the diversity in the Black Power movement, however, militants shared the common aim of shifting agency into the hands of black people who would then assert their legitimate authority in, and in the interest of, their community.

But, as local African Americans began to adopt the language of Black Power and promote its expression in community programs, the rising racial tension across the nation inspired fear among white city leaders about the potential for radicalism and violence, which lead to repression of activists through conspiracy and other trumped-up charges. This in turn sparked a "fight back" campaign— also part of a broader national movement—that in Louisville united Black Power militants, white leftists, and moderate whites who saw it as a way to take a stand against racism.[3] To some extent the Black Power philosophy did cause divisions within the local freedom struggle, as older African American leaders criticized the tactics and rhetoric of the rising generation. But, those divisions were generational not racial. Instead, the reaction against Black Power and the repression that resulted provided the context for interracial organizing in the name of civil liberties and antiracism. The story of the Black Power era in Louisville, then, is a two-fold tale of the diverse ways that local people interpreted and acted on the philosophy and how the reaction to it provided the rallying point for the civil rights forces of the city.

Just as Black Power had deep roots and a gradual pattern of development nationally, it grew in Louisville slowly and from multiple sources. There were early expressions of some of the ideas that would be called Black Power in the preaching of Louisville's Nation of Islam (NOI) congregation, which existed by 1963 and which expressed both a desire "for the separation of Negroes and whites" and a rejection of integration as a "hypocritical notion" offered "by those who were trying to deceive the black people." While receiving mostly negative attention from the black press, after native son and hero Cassius Clay converted and became Muhammad Ali, younger activists expressed admiration, although the NOI never grew to significant numbers or influence in the community. More important as a root of black militancy was the rising frustration with the city's open housing movement, which climaxed in 1967, and more generally with both legislation and the mass nonviolent direct action meant to procure it. As Blaine Hudson, future Black Student Union leader, recalled, it was those younger activists who recognized "the ineffectiveness of those old strategies and the fact that we were using tools that were already worn out and that needed to be discarded" who embraced Black Power. Some of those young people gained experience in War on Poverty and social service agencies, where ideas about the need for more black community control were already gaining hold. Finally, by the late 1960s some people were recognizing that to change race *relations*, you needed to build black self-respect and promote recognition of African American culture.[4]

National politics also nurtured Louisville's Black Power movement. Bob Cunningham, who would help to launch a black workers' organization, traveled to California in the 1960s and returned mesmerized by the words of Stokely Carmichael and H. Rap Brown. Student leader Blaine Hudson credited older activists who left the city for work with SNCC and then returned radicalized. Ken Clay, a staff member of the CAC was inspired by friends in Chicago and New York to open the Corner of Jazz, a store with posters of Malcolm X and Muhammad Ali which sold African clothes and art and hosted discussions of black art and culture.[5] The experiences of these leaders, all of whom played a role in nurturing a particular organization or expression of Black Power in the city, demonstrate the ways that ideas traveled across space through personal encounters and connections, linking activists in different cities together in a national movement.

When WECC became Louisville's first major civil rights organization to embrace Black Power, internal discussions and newspaper reports immediately focused on what this meant. The council presented the shift as a natural outgrowth of their goals. The organization had been founded to keep the West End integrated and a nice place to live by promoting interracial understanding and cooperation. It seemed, however, that the members' efforts toward that goal were failing. The West End neighborhoods were becoming overcrowded, predominantly black, and relatively powerless compared to other areas. Thus, members realized that speaking for the West End now meant speaking for a black community, and seeking power for the West End meant seeking Black Power. The goal of integration had not been abandoned, however. WECC members reasoned that they could only accomplish their vision of integration if "negroes can generate enough power and leadership to force the rest of the community to grant them equal housing, job, and educational opportunities."[6] As Sister Rose Colley, the white supervisor of elementary education for the Catholic School Board who lived and worked in the West End put it, "we all want integration, and if to get integration we have to move the way Black Power is moving, then we will have to move with Black Power."[7]

A number of members questioned whether this meant that whites were no longer welcome in the council. The consensus was that white residents of the West End neighborhoods were still encouraged to participate, but that they would have to reorient their thinking about their role in the organization. As African American member and future chairman Ken Phillips declared, "It doesn't mean we are excluding whites. It means white people are going to have to reassess their relationship with Negroes" and get used to taking "something less than a leadership position."[8] From the beginning of the group's Black Power program, however, whites did continue to hold some positions of leadership. When new elections were held Eugene Robinson, an African American community organizer, was elected chair; the white wife of a Presbyterian minister was co-chair; a white nun was elected treasurer; and a black woman member of the National Association for the Advancement of Colored People (NAACP) became assistant treasurer.[9] Most significantly, the position of executive director was immediately offered to Tachau. Although he argued that whites should withdraw from all leadership positions and resisted the new position, the members pressed him, and he accepted in order to help the group weather its transition. He insisted it be temporary however and began fund-raising to hire new African American leadership.[10]

WECC's positioning of itself as a "force for Black Power" illustrates both the flexibility of the term and the way a community organization could adapt it for its own ends. When held up against the Black Panthers or the US organization, or other groups that dominate the historiography of late 1960s black militancy, WECC doesn't look like a Black Power organization. But, while rejecting separatism and showing no interest in armed self-defense members of WECC found something useful in the philosophy, specifically the idea of empowering a black community. WECC saw Black Power as an effective tool for community organizing. WECC's embrace of Black Power also belies the notion of a rigid distinction or hostility between advocates of integration and Black Power. Rather than getting caught up in such philosophical disputes, the group focused on seemingly mundane issues such as bus fare rates, night games for the local high school teams, the need for a new swimming pool, or whatever issues neighborhood residents brought to them. Two major emphases in the Black Power phase of the organization were schools and jobs. WECC publicized overcrowding and deteriorating conditions in the schools and organized parents to protest. The group also pressured employers in the West End to hire blacks, securing more than sixty jobs by 1969.[11] Finally, WECC assisted other West End activist organizations such as the Black Workers' Coalition, Louisville Art Workshop, and Welfare Rights Organization by providing publicity, a printing press, and a meeting space.[12]

WECC's most important contribution to the Black Power movement was the founding of the Black Unity League of Kentucky (BULK). Inspired by his experience in open housing and by Father James Groppi, a priest in Milwaukee, Wisconsin, who led a group of young black activists, Tachau wanted WECC to launch an organizing effort by and for black youth. In October 1967 he recruited local activist Sam Hawkins, Bob Sims of the Southern Christian Leadership Conference (SCLC), a technician who had come to town for the open housing demonstrations, and a new Volunteers in Service to America (VISTA) worker named Willie Coggins to head the effort. Initially their purpose was to "use activist methods" to "fight discrimination on issues like police and court practices and job discrimination." Within a few months, however, the young men named the group the Black Unity League of Kentucky and reoriented it to focus on promoting black consciousness. Their aim was "to teach black people to think black" and thereby to "instill identity and self-pride into Negroes." Specifically, they reached out to African American high school and college students and developed a black history curriculum to be introduced in the schools.[13]

In its first year, BULK promoted black consciousness through various programs. They used a donated building to establish a "Black House" headquarters where they hoped "black consciousness and pride can be symbolized and dramatized by the display of appropriate literature, visual art, music and so forth." BULK turned its attention to the preparation of the black culture curriculum, which included topics such as "the relation to society of black youth," the "need for unity among black people," and "the mechanics of the power structure," as well as readings about Malcolm X, slave revolts, and the origins of segregation. Meanwhile they planned workshops, recruited instructors, and negotiated with the Board of Education to get the material into the schools. They succeeded in securing an agreement from the board, although principals of individual high schools often balked. BULK also organized arts events, such as a Spring 1968 "Soul Session" featuring food, music, and dancing attended by about 300 people, followed by a larger "Black is Beautiful Festival" with "African inspired" arts and crafts. Finally, members cooperated with students at the University of Louisville, Kentucky State University, and University of Kentucky to form Black Student Unions.[14]

The prominent roles BULK leaders played in the local open housing movement, and rhetoric that linked them to the national Black Power movement, drew the attention of city authorities. Sims and Hawkins in particular were identified as potential troublemakers. The first sign of trouble came in August 1967 when they were arrested, with scant evidence, along with three others for arson. Nevertheless, the court set a high bond and they languished in jail awaiting trial in October, when Sims, Hawkins, and one other were acquitted. Tachau took up the issue, writing a series of letters and articles condemning the Louisville justice system for keeping three innocent men in jail. He charged city officials with arresting the men and holding them on the theory that the "community would be 'better off' with these men 'out of circulation' until cool weather." Tachau's campaigning on this issue led WECC to create a legal committee to investigate and take action on police relations, court practices, bail regulations, jury selection, and the lack of adequate legal aid.[15]

By this time fears of racial tension and the potential for civil strife gripped local leaders both black and white. In response to the confrontations between police and young blacks in Harlem and elsewhere, Louisvillians debated whether the same could happen there too. At first, despite some concerns over reported near riots, civil rights spokesmen repeatedly reassured white authorities that Louisville was safe from violence. Drawing on the city's self-image as a progressive leader in civil rights, black leaders argued that Louisville differed from Los Angeles and other racial powder kegs. But by late 1967, frustration over the failure of open housing demonstrations and overcrowding in neighborhoods and schools created a tinder box that would soon explode into civil disorder.[16]

In the spring of 1968, the arrest of two prominent African American professionals set off a chain of events leading to a riot and conspiracy charges against six members and associates of WECC and BULK. On May 7, police pulled black school teacher Charles Thomas over on suspicion of robbery. Manfred Reid, a black real estate agent and businessman, saw his friend Thomas with the police, and fearing he had been in an accident stopped to see if he could help. When he approached, police officer Michael Clifford demanded that Reid move back and pushed him on the chest. Reid recalled that when he knocked the officer's hand away "he grabbed me and started hitting me in the face. He hit me once with his open hand and then with his fist." Reid was arrested for breach of peace and assault and battery. No charges were brought against Thomas.[17]

For the next three weeks the atmosphere in the city became increasingly hostile as African Americans and their white allies waited to see if action would be taken against the police. Pressured by black leaders, Mayor Kenneth Schmied suspended Officer Clifford, a decision upheld by the police department's review board. Clifford's dismissal ignited a furor from the Fraternal Order of Police, however, which called on the city to reinstate him. In the midst of this, on Monday, May 20, 800 members of the Poor Peoples Campaign came through the city. During a rally of 1,000 people gathered in their honor, the police tried to disperse the crowd, touching off minor confrontations and ratcheting up tension. Three days later the Civil Service Board overturned Clifford's suspension.[18]

Beginning at about 7:30 on the evening of Monday, May 27, 1968, BULK held a rally to protest the reinstatement of Clifford at the intersection of 28th and Greenwood, the location of a small number of black-owned businesses. With no public address system, speakers stood on the hood of a car to address the crowd. According to white labor and civil rights activist Carl Braden, "police were parked in the alleys, not visible to people in the street, but maybe to those on rooftops." The speeches focused on "respecting black women and Black Power," recalled WECC leader Eugene Robinson, "nothing any of us hadn't heard day in and day out for some time." More specifically, James Cortez and Charles X of the local NOI mosque called for unity in the black community. Cortez, who claimed to be representing Stokely Carmichael and SNCC, was visiting Louisville on the invitation of Ruth Bryant, a prominent member of WECC who had met him in Washington DC. He and other speakers urged African Americans to shun association with whites, to rid the neighborhood of "honkies" and to assert black control over the community.[19]

As the speeches wound down and the crowd began to disperse, the sound of a broken bottle, the screeching arrival of a police cruiser, and general confusion combined to trigger an expanding wave of looting, confrontations with police, and riotous violence that lasted throughout the week. At 8:15 p.m. a bus rode through the intersection and some witnesses recalled bottles and rocks were thrown at it. Then, just before the speeches ended, Mervin Aubespin, an African American artist for the *Courier Journal*, the prominent daily paper, heard someone say "stick around, something is going to happen." Rumors circulated that the teenagers sitting atop some of the buildings were going to do something. A few bottles were thrown, but witnesses recall the crowd shouted "cool it" and continued to disperse. Just then, a lone police car came into the intersection with lights and sirens on. The officer jumped out of the car with his gun drawn. People who were near the intersection disagree as to whether the cruiser arrived before or after the bottles were thrown, though the general consensus is that the events were close enough in time to be simultaneous and thus the cause and effect were ambiguous. Then suddenly "bottles were hurtling everywhere," people began to rush away from the intersection, and "the police were chasing people into lots to make arrests."[20]

By the weekend the disturbance diminished and the riot was declared over. The final tally of destruction included $250,000 in property damage, 119 fires set, 472 people arrested, 52 people injured, and 2 killed.[21] During the riot, blacks in the affected areas and white sympathizers reported numerous cases of police brutality against both participants and innocent bystanders. The most serious were the fatal shootings of James Groves and Matthias Washington Browder during the night of May 29–30.[22]

The week also featured sporadic efforts by community leaders to try to quell the unrest and respond to police violence. Late on Monday night the local news ran a special broadcast with NAACP lawyer Neville Tucker, Cortez, and Reverends W. J. Hodge and A. D. King representing the NAACP and Kentucky Christian Leadership Conference (KCLC) respectively, urging people off the street for their own protection. King was the brother of Martin Luther King who had moved to Louisville in 1965 to take the pastorate at one of the largest, most prominent black churches in the city. On Tuesday during the riot, he held a press conference calling on the mayor to visit the West End, with no reply. During the day on Wednesday, KCLC successfully negotiated an agreement with city hall to pull back the National Guard and the police and let a group of young black marshals keep order. The agreement was announced at a "cool-it" rally organized by WECC chair Eugene Robinson, at which King urged people to show calm now that blacks were "patrolling the area." Other speakers at the rally showed less interest in soothing tempers, however. Hawkins accused the mayor of being "afraid of black people" and Sims declared that he hoped "the frustration is still inside of you. I hope you'll tell the white man that you won't accept any more crumbs.... I won't tell you to stop rioting. I tell you to do whatever is necessary."[23]

Meanwhile, a group of white Louisvillians organized the White Emergency Support Team (WEST) to investigate the causes and events of the riot and to provide whatever assistance they could to black victims.[24] WEST's activity soon became part of a larger movement, which included WECC, BULK, the Southern Conference Education Fund (SCEF), and others, to support victims of the riot while defending those accused of conspiring to cause it.[25] SCEF, which moved its headquarters to Louisville when the Bradens stepped into its leadership positions, soon became one of the primary organizers bringing whites into support for Black Power advocates.

While black militants and their white allies sought justice for victims of police violence during the riots, city officials examined the causes of the disorder itself. At first there were hints that police suspected BULK and its allies of starting the trouble. On May 31, the City County Crime Commission ordered an investigation into various people and groups associated with the black community, activism, and the War on Poverty. The same day Cortez was arrested and held overnight. On the morning of June 1 police and FBI agents claimed Cortez had confessed to a conspiracy to blow up the oil refineries in the West End. Sims and Hawkins were also arrested and after a hasty court of inquiry, with no witnesses for the defense or opportunity to cross-examine those against them, Judge William Colson ordered the three held on security warrants and charged Cortez with "common law nuisance." Sims and Hawkins were placed under 50,000-dollar bonds and Cortez under a 75,000-dollar one. Within a few days Mayor Kenneth Schmied announced he would form a biracial panel to investigate the cause of the disturbance, though he remarked at the time, "I think it [the rioting] was planned and set. When a known outside agitator, looter, and rioter comes to town, that's the cause of all the trouble."[26]

Civil rights advocates blasted the move and mobilized to exonerate the three militants. Moderate civic leaders such as the editors of the *Courier Journal* criticized what looked like a "scapegoat hunt" and the "dangerous manipulation of bail power" saying that it appeared the city was "making a concerted effort to have it appear that a few agitators are the root of all of Louisville's racial troubles." Almost immediately the Kentucky Civil Liberties Union (KCLU) criticized the use of excessive bail to "restrain Hawkins and Sims, who had not yet been accused of any crime." Meanwhile, BULK, WECC, SCEF, WEST, the Louisville Welfare Rights Organization, and a group of white Southern Baptist Theological Seminary students initiated an ad hoc coalition to coordinate the defense. The coalition's first action was to host a rally on June 8. A diverse slate of speakers, including a white Presbyterian minister, a black Muslim, a white peace activist, a member of SNCC, and prominent civil rights attorney William Kunstler addressed the crowd of 350 people, about one-third of whom were white. Over the next two days local leaders met with representatives from various national organizations, forging links between the Louisville case and those fighting the repression of militant activists across the country.[27]

By the end of the month a new grand jury indicted not just Hawkins, Sims, and Cortez, but a total of six local African Americans for conspiracy to destroy private property. Specifically they were charged with conspiring to damage a taxi company, dry cleaners, and the oil refineries located on the far edge of the West End along the Ohio River. In addition to the original three, the "Black Six" included Manfred Reid, Walter "Pete" Cosby, and Ruth Bryant. Cosby was included because a police officer saw him driving around town with Cortez, and Bryant because she had donated the money to bring him to town and had made the invitation. The theory behind the charges was that this group had conspired to cause the riot and the violence that followed, and had planned even greater damage in a plot to blow up the refineries.[28]

An uproar against the charges united a cross section of local activists including blacks and whites in Black Power, new left, civil rights, religious, and community organizations. Within weeks of the indictments, WECC produced a plan to defend the Black Six that included fund raising for legal expenses, hosting forums to publicize the issues in the case, writing letters to newspaper editors, visiting and delivering petitions to city officials, and calling for a U.S. Justice Department investigation. To fulfill the last goal, the group filed a complaint stating that the "constitutional rights" of the six had been violated because the law under which they were charged was "so broad that it violates" the rights of "free speech and peaceful assembly."[29]

The forums held by WECC to inform Louisvillians about the Black Six spawned an interracial coalition effort not only to defend these accused, but to oppose government repression of dissent in general. In early November 1968 the group hosted meetings in the south and east ends of the city specifically to attract white interest in the case. In the East End approximately 200 white residents attended, and the next day 150 of them formed the Ad Hoc Committee for Justice. Spokesman John Filiatreau reported that "Our members are mostly white people who have been wondering what they could do to combat racism—and now they are acting on their convictions." The new group formed committees to contact officials, spread information, and raise bail money. The statements of the group reveal that the primary consideration was the "violations of Constitutional rights in the handling of the case" specifically the "denial of the right to reasonable bail, speedy trial, and free speech," though members also spoke of the need to combat the "unjust conditions" that caused the riot rather than search for a scapegoat in black activists. Although black participants were welcome, Filiatreau stressed that members believed it was important for whites "to protest this kind of injustice against black people." Thus, the Ad Hoc Committee joined the White Emergency Support Team in representing white Louisville in a coalition with SCEF, WECC, the Welfare Rights Organization, KCLC, and BULK, among others, to defend black militants.[30]

The Black Six conspiracy trial began in late June 1970. During jury selection, demonstrators gathered outside the court house chanting "Free the Black Six." Prosecutors offered a last-minute deal: a fifty-dollar fine and reduced charge of disorderly conduct against Hawkins, Sims, and Cortez in exchange for dropping the charges on the others. The deal was rejected. In their opening statements, prosecutors promised to prove that "the riots were not spontaneous; they were planned and executed by the defendants." Twenty-two witnesses testified during the two-week trial. The most damning evidence was a report that at a meeting with the mayor, Cortez had promised "trouble" if Officer Clifford wasn't fired. But the commonwealth attorney was never able to provide evidence of the six defendants meeting let alone planning a conspiracy; and, some witnesses asserted that the violence of the riot had begun only in response to police intervention at the rally. After the prosecution rested its case, on July 7, Judge S. Rush Nicholson ordered a directed verdict of not guilty due to insufficient evidence of the charges. Although the Black Six and their supporters celebrated this much-delayed victory, they also criticized the whole affair as a frame up by a commonwealth attorney seeking reelection and pointed out that the real causes of the riots—poverty, police misconduct, and unemployment—remained unaddressed.[31]

The defense of the Black Six started the fight-back movement against government repression of black militants, antiwar demonstrators, and activists of all kinds. The fight-back campaign opposed the effort to harass and silence activists and the revival of anticommunist rhetoric and machinery to do so. It united Black Power militants, antiwar and leftist organizations, civil rights groups, civil libertarians, and whites looking for a way to oppose racism, particularly those living in the West End or inspired into action by the open housing movement. At a time when the main legislative goals of the local movement had been accomplished, and when people were beginning to question the efficacy of that approach anyway, when it was unclear what strategies would work in the continuing struggle against inequality, the fight-back campaign was one way that opposition to racism could be expressed and acted upon. Moreover, the cooperation around the Black Six and government harassment kept the lines of communication open between different groups in the city and sustained relationships between activists through a period when the combination of repression and divisions within civil rights forces had the potential to weaken the movement.

There were some signs of those divisions in Louisville by the end of the 1960s, manifesting particularly in the hostility against Black Power and its influence expressed by some older, long-time civil rights leaders. Traditional rights leaders criticized youthful militants as excessive and the local black newsweekly, the *Defender* touted integration as the best solution to racial tension. Yet, while the paper continually criticized militants, associated them with youth violence and vandalism, and declared their leadership bad for the community, it also routinely covered the activities of Black Power-oriented organizations, and came to endorse some aspects of political and economic independence.[32] Moreover, these criticisms did not keep older leaders from cooperating with militants on issues of unequal justice or repression. And, the antagonism that burst out occasionally between those now called "moderates" or "militants" did not stop either of their from organizing in their own way on their own issues. In short these divisions were often mainly rhetorical and did not greatly impact the ability to work together on problems of mutual concern.

While WECC members had embraced Black Power and given it their own distinctive spin of community empowerment, and through BULK promoted black consciousness, other small and short-lived groups formed in the community to act on their own interpretation of the philosophy. The intellectual center of the Black Power movement in Louisville involved a group of young men and women who, while the Black Six and their supporters focused on the conspiracy trial and efforts to repress dissent, created a stir on the University of Louisville campus. By the late 1960s the larger movement to reshape higher education and reform its relationship to the community, that had its roots at University of California at Berkeley in 1964, was influencing African American students at both mixed and historically black colleges. They began to seek courses reflective of their own experience and history, and to make their education in turn relevant to their community. Historian Peniel E. Joseph dates the birth of the modern black studies movement to 1967 when student unrest led to the founding of a program at San Francisco State. From there a wave of African American student activism spread across the country as newly formed Black Student Unions (BSU) used direct action to demand changes in the curriculum, the recruitment and support of black faculty and students, and outreach programs into black communities.[33]

The BSU at the University of Louisville had its roots in the efforts by a handful of African American student leaders to reach out to others through social events and informal organizing in fall 1967. Member Blaine Hudson recalled that the group more formally organized in spring 1968 as a reaction to the Martin Luther King assassination. Early leaders included undergraduates Hudson and Bobby Martin, social work student Sterling Neal Jr., and his brother Gerald, who was in law school. Initially the BSU focused on producing a newsletter and starting a tutoring program. They had some early success when in June 1968 they convinced the university to have summer school courses on the Civilizations and Cultures of Africa and the Negro in American Culture. In the fall the students grew more militant and the BSU more structured. In October the newsletter carried a formal list of "purposes and aims" that included "to instill black consciousness within our group," "to unlearn the white mind," and to "create black loyalty." While still maintaining a social program by sponsoring dances and mixers, the group spent more time studying the black consciousness philosophy. By the end of their first year they were calling on their fellow students to "bring the Black Revolution to the academic community" by resisting the myth of the "integrating power of education" and the "deceitful instruction" they received at the hands of racist professors.[34]

In March 1969 the BSU acted on these general ideas by submitting an extensive "recruiting proposal" to university administrators. The group collaborated with community Black Power organizations Our Black Thing (OBT) and Black United Brothers under an umbrella organization called the Black Coalition Association. The problem as they saw it was that the university focused on training whites, ignoring black students, and failing to prepare them for leadership positions in, or as role models for, the community. The solution they proposed was a multipronged effort to recruit students and faculty, enhance the curriculum, involve black students in the machinery of the university, and serve the community. The University of Louisville BSU proposal combined elements from similar demands being made by black students across the country; and indeed, student leader Blaine Hudson recalled "We felt we were part of this nationwide or worldwide movement." Specifically, the proposal called for enhanced efforts in recruiting black faculty and students, especially through the offer of 200 Martin Luther

King Scholarships. The BSU also demanded additional courses on African and African American history and culture, working toward the establishment of a Department of African Studies. To help black students succeed, tutoring programs would be established, with paid black students as staff. In order to create a stream of potential applicants as well as serve the community more generally, the BSU wanted to establish an outreach program. Finally, the proposal demanded that the university employ a graduate and undergraduate level coordinator to manage these programs, and that the BSU and its allies in the community have a voice in who was hired.[35]

BSU leaders met on March 4, 1969 with University President Woodrow Strickler in his office and after they read the proposal he expressed some sympathy with their goals. The president expressed reservation about the proposal's financial costs and promised that he would discuss the issues with the Board of Trustees. Two days later the group invited him to attend an upcoming rally. He declined, instead warning the students against violence—which might have surprised them since up to this point there had been no militant rhetoric or threats. After the rally on March 8, however, Strickler agreed with the proposal "in principle" and promised to begin implementing it.[36]

By the end of the next month negotiations were off and relations between the university and the BSU had soured dramatically. The point of discord was the issue of who would be hired as director of the recruiting program. The BSU wanted their own Sterling Neal as the first choice, with two alternates, Morris Jeff and Hanford Stafford. Strickler informed the group that he heard Neal was emotionally unstable, though he could not name his source and eventually admitted the opinion came from within the state government in Frankfort. To press for their choice as well as the right of the BSU and black community to have a say in the hire, the group collected letters and petitions supporting Neal. When they delivered them, however, Strickler abruptly reversed course, cut off negotiations, and declared there was no money for the implementation of the program. In response the BSU released a statement calling for one more meeting and promising "should the results of today's meeting prove unacceptable, it would be impossible for us to justify dealing through the channels of an institution whose main concern with black people is lack of concern."[37]

A week later the BSU carried out its implied threat to cease working through "channels" and take direct action. On April 30, fifteen members attempted to meet with Strickler. When they arrived at his office they found he was not there and they seized the room, in effect launching a sit-in in the administration building. They remained there for three hours, until Reverends Leo Lessor and Fred G. Sampson, as well as Morris Jeff, arrived and served as mediators. They secured from Strickler a willingness to have a short conversation and to promise no penalties for the protestors. After the confrontation was over, however, Strickler did warn that any repeat performance would result in expulsions. According to Hudson, the BSU was very much planning a repeat, indeed an escalation of actions. On the day of the action, May 1, however, many of their non-student supporters were picked up by police on a variety of charges. Hudson and others believed that officials had been tipped off by an infiltrator. Instead a smaller number of students took over the Arts and Sciences administration building. White students from Young Americans for Freedom wearing George Wallace for President stickers gathered outside the building and tried to rush the doors, but black athletes—a group that had kept its distance from the BSU up until then—formed a barricade and prevented them. The situation came to an end when riot-gear wearing police stormed the building as white students cheered them on and removed the protesters.[38]

With the end of the takeover, BSU leaders found themselves facing arrest and expulsion. When police cleared the building the students spent the night in jail and the next morning, after a hasty hearing, Judge Colson fined each of the leaders 100 dollars and sentenced them to three days in jail on charges of violating the state's antiriot law and for disorderly conduct. The students appealed and almost a year later a jury overturned the conviction. Meanwhile the university expelled eight of the leaders. Three were allowed back on probation; the BSU concluded, "In other words, the 'good niggers' were separated from the bad, at least as UL would have the community believe." The others appealed the decision to the Student Conduct and Appeals committee. That hearing took on the characteristics, in Hudson's words, of a "star chamber." A former attorney general of Kentucky acted as the "prosecuting attorney." Faculty members on the committee were selected by the administration rather than elected. The students had no time to prepare a defense, and the proceedings lasted until 4:30 in the morning. Finally, at the start of the hearing it was announced that the committee did not have the power to reinstate the students anyway. The result was a foregone conclusion: the expulsion of the five leaders. After a year of appeals to various university committees eventually all the students were readmitted. In an ironic historic twist, Hudson, the ringleader in many ways of the takeover of the administration building, reentered it more than thirty years later when he became Dean of the College of Arts and Sciences at the university.[39]

In the wake of the takeover and controversy, the university began to take some steps to implement parts of the BSU proposal. In late May 1969, as it was expelling the leaders of the group, the Board of Trustees voted to accept some of their demands. Hanford Stafford was hired as the Interim Coordinator of Black Affairs and in July the Black Affairs Program launched elementary school tutoring efforts in the five War on Poverty target areas. Also in keeping with the community outreach vision of the BSU, the university sponsored an arts festival in Shawnee Park and a junior-high summer theater school. At the same time, two representatives from the black community were put on a committee to screen African American student applications. By September there was enough success that the Louisville *Defender,* the local black newsweekly, was calling the program a "model for the Southeast" and touting the six courses, fourteen faculty members, and twelve tutors that had been secured for the new school year. A year later the school offered financial aid to 100 hundred black students and promised to teach "black awareness, black culture, and history" in an "attempt to develop racial pride and black identity." In 1973 the efforts initiated by the BSU were formally organized as a program, which in academic year 1990–1991 was expanded into the Department of Pan-African Studies.[40]

Meanwhile the BSU, even with many of its leaders fighting for readmission and then on probation, continued to agitate for its goals. The group participated in service projects in the War on Poverty target areas separate from the Office of Black Affairs. The BSU also hosted its own arts festivals. Most important, the students continued to press for the full implementation of their proposal. In their view Stafford and the Office of Black Affairs were being used to "placate the black community" and had succeeded in impressing middle-class blacks. Indeed, the *Defender* exemplified this, declaring the problems on campus solved and praising the program. The BSU and other black students organized in Blacks Getting Together (BGT) felt otherwise. Continuing problems with the shortage of black faculty and staff, insensitivity to black students, and the lack of a black-oriented campus newspaper led to renewed demonstrations and even a sit-in in the administration building in 1971. Agitation on campus continued into the early 1970s when black students at the university joined with those at nearby Bellarmine College and Jefferson Community College to form the Black Students Coalition of Louisville and called for "self-determination" for black students on area campuses.[41]

As the new decade dawned the Black Power philosophy continued to inspire a number of small nationalist organizations with overlapping memberships and agendas. The members tended to be primarily men under thirty-five associated with the university or War of Poverty and community development projects in the West End.[42] Three themes dominated the work of these militant organizations: unity, cultural pride, and protection of the community in the form of resistance to the influx of drugs into it. The first was taken up as the main goal of the local branch of the Junta of Militant Organizations (JOMO). JOMO was founded in May 1968 by Joe Waller of St. Petersburg, Florida. The organization claimed a Marxist-Leninist position, describing western whites as the bourgeoisie and non-whites as a worldwide proletariat. Their official list of positions emphasized the colonial nature of the black community, rejected all "white" law, and called on blacks to be ready to "build our own nation and separate from this brutal racist nation." Local leader Henri Williams, Jr. argued that to prepare for that time Louisville blacks needed to unify. While there was a range of black organizations "from conservative to revolutionary" in the community, JOMO saw no coalition fighting to protect the colonized. In the interest of promoting that unity JOMO first established the Institute of Black Unity in October 1970, housed in the offices of SCEF, and then organized Black Solidarity Week, during which speakers from a variety of organizations were featured, in spring 1971. JOMO made a strong beginning in the city, even winning an indirect endorsement from the *Defender*, which published several articles about its ideology and goals. It never succeeded in developing a large following, however, and according to Hudson remained a "fringe" group.[43]

A second major emphasis in the later Black Power years, as in BULK's program at the start of the period, was the need for racial consciousness and pride. One leader in this area was OBT, formed by Blaine Hudson, Sterling Neal, and others as an arm of the BSU in the community. Sterling Neal recalled that members of the group obtained permission from Reynolds Metal Company to use a house they owned in the West End as a base of operations. They moved in, called it the "Black House"—the same name BULK used for their headquarters—and painted it accordingly. From there they launched a number of outreach programs with the goal of stirring "up the awareness and the consciousness of the people about the oppression that we saw." Though they provided some social services, they became most known for the cultural events they sponsored. The first was a production of theater, poetry, and music for young people, followed by a performance and workshop by a Kent State University African culture group. Through their jazz exhibitions, rap sessions, and theater they could relate to, OBT aimed to recruit young people into the revolution.[44] It was one of the longer lived and better received of the black nationalist organizations. Even after it faded from the scene, however, the cultural emphasis was maintained by arts and cultural festivals sponsored by groups such as Burning Spear, the Kentucky branch of the World Black and African Festival, and a coalition of groups that sponsored African Liberation Day.[45]

The third common agenda for the various Black Power organizations in the city was a campaign to stem the flood of drugs into the African American community and to confront its effects. Community defense was part of the agenda of Black Power groups across the country, at times taking the form of armed neighborhood patrols to monitor the police. In Louisville there was little hint of armed self-defense, but the issue that loomed large was community control. By the early 1970s a coalition of such groups had come to believe that "dope is a way to keep blacks 'stupefied' and fighting each other" and that "the government, starting in 1960 had begun pumping drugs into the black community as a way of smoldering the social agitation that was going on at the time." In late 1971 the Black Committee for Self-Defense (BCSD) formed to educate blacks against heroin through leaflets, movies, rap sessions, and a hotline. A coalition of older civil rights and new militant organizations worked together to urge theaters to refuse to show "black exploitation films" that "condone dope, free sex, and bad race relations," demonstrating how older leaders and the new generation continued to cooperate on some issues despite their differences. The most organized and enduring program was Stop Dope Now, formed in 1969 by Sterling Neal and sixteen other black men, who incorporated as Enterprise Unlimited to do community development work. Initially Stop Dope Now launched a methadone clinic, lecture series, and radio show. Then, in the mid-1970s it was incorporated into River Region Eight, a government-funded complex of drug and alcohol programs. That success left Neal a little uneasy, however, since blacks did not fund their own antidrug efforts. Nevertheless, the work of both Enterprise Unlimited and Stop Dope Now illustrated the overlap between the community self-determination and strengthening projects of Black Power advocates and the antipoverty outreach of government programs.[46]

The Black Panthers briefly operated in Louisville. The initial effort to organize a Panther group in the city in 1969 was aborted when national party officers insisted someone go to California for training and to pick up the charter, and local organizers could not afford to go. Consequently, the Panthers were late in arriving at the city, not getting well established until 1972. At that time they emphasized community survival and social programs. Nancy Pennick Pollock, former sit-in participant and SNCC activist who had in the late 1960s been with the Panthers in Chicago, remembered her activity with the Louisville group: "If a person didn't have food we got the food, we went and bought it, took the food. If they needed something, clothes, even if they needed a pack of cigarettes or whatever, we helped them get it, or if they needed to get on social security we took them to the social security office. We were trying to serve the black community." The group set up a sickle cell anemia testing clinic, provided transportation to area medical offices, ran a shuttle bus to the state prison for family members to visit inmates, and sponsored a local version of the Panthers' well-known free breakfast program. Finally, the Panthers joined other Black Power organizations in their own version of the war on drugs.[47]

The Panthers became the target of police repression in 1972 when the night before the Kentucky Derby five members and two associates were arrested for armed robbery. Authorities alleged that the group had crashed a Derby party at Laird's tourist home and "forced a large group of people to undress and stole $8,200 in cash and jewelry." When they were arrested police confiscated from their property a list of "revolutionary readings" and of "dope pushers marked for assassination." When the trial began the judge immediately released five of the group for lack of evidence. Two men, Ben Simmons, who was leader of the Panthers, and William "Darryl" Blakemore were tried by an all-white jury. Simmons was acquitted, but one witness claimed to have seen Blakemore at the party and thus he was convicted. Police added charges of carrying a sawed-off shot gun, which guaranteed him extra jail time.[48]

Just as in the Black Six case, a defense effort sprang up around the "Louisville Seven." The Panthers called the charges against their members part of a national pattern of political harassment of the party and of a local police conspiracy to "bust" those who were fighting the drug problem. They pointed out the irony that they, who had a public position against drug pushers, were accused of robbing a known "dope house." Robert Sims, formerly of BULK and now with the African Liberation Committee, brought black nationalists into the defense coalition. And a new organization, the Kentucky Committee to Smash Repression reached out to the broader national effort to fight official persecution of activists. But, the defense effort also again rallied more moderate local activists. The Kentucky Civil Liberties Union protested the judge's behavior and Suzy Post, a white Jewish woman who was organizing for a civilian review board of the police, criticized law enforcement's "frame up" of the Panthers. Finally, a black minister, Father Joseph Bell, lent his prestige at the rallies, praising the Panthers for their antidrug campaign and their efforts to "administer to the sick." While the coalition celebrated the dropped charges and acquittal of most of the seven, it continued to challenge Blakemore's conviction. The enduring result was the formation of the Kentucky Political Prisoners' Committee, an interracial organization which was formed to work on Blakemore's case and more generally "to support brothers and sisters in prison and fight police brutality."[49]

Although the campaign to defend the Panthers spawned a local movement to defend black militants and fight police repression more generally, indirectly it also revealed the declining significance of the Black Power movement in the city. When the Panthers were arrested, their white and black allies organized to stand up for them, but, as their lawyer Bill Allison recalled, the broader community, white or black, failed to show much interest in the outcome. As he put it, "there wasn't the kind of filling up of the courtroom" that had been seen in the case of the Black Six. He attributed this to the change in atmosphere in the new decade: "By this time, the repression had set in, the war had divided people, the economy was turning down." The Panthers never recovered from the setback of having to devote their energy to the case, and no strong Black Power organization arose to take their place. Although individuals like Sterling Neal and Robert Sims showed up on lists of sponsors, the antirepression efforts, moreover, would increasingly be led by white left-wing organizations or biracial civil rights groups. Meanwhile, police brutality issues were taken up by civil rights and civil libertarian groups, particularly those working for a civilian review board. The Panthers and other small nationalist organizations did not completely disappear, however. They resurfaced in the community-wide controversy over school integration in 1975, taking their place alongside moderate civil rights groups and interracial organizations in the resistance to anti-busing forces.

Conclusion

In the public imagination and in much of what has been traditionally taught about the black freedom struggle, the mid-1960s saw a turn from the "heroic" integrationist campaigns led by Martin Luther King to the nihilistic, destructive turn of the Black Power militants. The story of the latter is dominated by images of angry gun-toting Panthers, separatists kicking whites out of SNCC and CORE, or, the less violent but as confusing to whites, blacks in Afros and dashikis rejecting their slave names and embracing their African heritage. The story continues with how these radicals led to division, antagonism, and repression and thus to the end of the civil rights movement. In recent years scholars have thoroughly debunked almost every part of this narrative, from its "beginning" in 1966 to its nature and impact. We now know that the roots of Black Power reach back into a period of nationalist organizing earlier in the century and that to a great extent the modern Black Power movement grew contemporaneously with the civil rights struggle.[50]

The story of the Louisville Black Power era, as an example of how the philosophy was acted upon on the ground in communities, contributes to this rethinking of Black Power. Put most simply, Black Power meant different things to different activists and organizations. For some it was another tool to bring about community empowerment by getting black voices heard. WECC members, who saw it this way, acted on their interpretation by organizing black residents of the West End to protest poor housing and school conditions and to demand black input into War on Poverty institutions. For most Black Power advocates in the city, a large part of the meaning was the importance of black consciousness and pride. Indeed the most visible and consistent expression of Black Power in the city were the arts and culture programs of BULK, the BSU, and others. Finally, Black Power meant community self-improvement and solidarity, whether that took the form of a specific program such as stemming the influx of drugs or a more ambiguous or undefined call for unity.

What is clear in all of this Black Power activity, however, is that it was not separate from other forms of activism in some false dichotomy between it and the civil rights or antipoverty, or even antiwar, movements of the time. Integrationists in WECC embraced Black Power as a means to an end of interracial understanding in a more equal society. White leftists, antiwar activists, and civil libertarians rallied around and with black militants to face the common enemy of the repression of dissent. Individuals like Sterling Neal got jobs in the War on Poverty and later social service agencies, demonstrating how community organizing could overlap with community empowerment. Finally, although there was some discord between older long-time civil rights leaders and the new generation, even they were able to cooperate and respect each other in the fight against the influx of drugs into the community. In short, in the interest of fighting racism or resisting common enemies, a wide variety of activists—from liberal whites new to the freedom struggle to black moderate traditional leaders to the rising generation of militants—could overcome differences and cooperate in shifting alliances that made up a larger movement. Seeing Black Power and the Black Power era in the context of this set of connections across issue, race, and generation highlights both the multiple meanings and expressions of African American militancy in the late 1960s and the lack of rigid chronological or ideological breaks in the larger struggle against racism.

Notes

1. An extended version of this chapter appears in Tracy E. K'Meyer, *Civil Rights in the Gateway to the South: Louisville, Kentucky, 1945–1980* (Lexington: University Press of Kentucky, 2009).
2. "West Enders Speak But Are Officials Listening," "Council Challenge to CAC," and "There is Need in West End for Both Parks and Schools," [reprinted from *Courier Journal*] *Voice* [newsletter of the West End Community Council], May 17, 1967; Interview with Blaine Hudson by Tracy E. K'Meyer, March 23, 2001 in the Oral History Collection, University of Louisville Archives, Louisville, KY [hereafter all interviews unless otherwise noted are in the OHC]; "James Resigns as West End Council Director," *Courier Journal*, August 8, 1967; "Hulbert James' Farewell Address to Highlight Council Workshop," *Defender*, September 14, 1967; Lawrence Pryor, "Black Power Policy Gains in West End," *Courier Journal*, September 17, 1967; "Rev. Tachau New West End Leader," *Courier Journal*, September 18, 1967; WECC [Tachau] to Reverend Charles L. Glenn, January 5, 1968, Box 2 folder 2 of the West End Community Council Papers, State Historical Society of Wisconsin, Madison, WI [hereafter cited as WECC box#:folder#]; "Council Adopts 'Black Power' but Names White Director," *Defender*, September 21, 1967.

3. Here I borrow the term "fight back" from Anne Braden, a long-time Louisville activist who used it to describe the cooperative resistance against oppression of activists of all kinds.

4. "Muslims Express Beliefs," *Defender*, July 18, 1963; K' Meyer, Interview with Blaine Hudson.

5. Interview with Bob Cunningham by Tracy E. K'Meyer, September 1, 1999; K'Meyer, Interview with Blaine Hudson; Interview with Ken Clay by Tracy E. K'Meyer, February 19, 2001.

6. WECC statement quoted in Lawrence Pryor, "Black Power Policy Gains in West End," *Courier Journal*, September 17, 1967.

7. Ibid.

8. Ibid; Anne Braden to Reverend Gilbert Schroerlucke, May 5, 1968, in box 1 folder 4 of the Anne and Carl Braden Papers, State Historical Society of Wisconsin, Madison WI [hereafter cited as Braden box#:folder#].

9. Robinson Becomes West End Community Council's Chairman, *Defender*, November 23, 1967.

10. "Rev. Tachau New West End Leader," *Courier Journal*, September 18, 1967; WECC [Tachau] to Reverend Charles L. Glenn, January 5, 1968, WECC 2:2; "Council Adopts Black Power but Names White Director," *Defender*, September 21, 1967.

11. Ongoing activity on all these issues is covered in the *Voice*. For specific cases see "Welfare Recipients Plan Action," *Voice*, December 13, 1967; "Parkway Place Residents Press Complaints," *Voice*, January 16, 1968; "West Enders Ask: Why Only One Pool?" *Voice*, June 18, 1968; "Council Works for More Black Jobs on Local Market Staff," *Voice*, December 19, 1968; "Parents Confront School Board," *Voice*, May 14, 1968. See also 63 "Given Employment in West End Job Drive," *Courier Journal*, February 28, 1969; "West End Council Wants Tenants on Housing Commission," *Courier Journal*, February 14, 1969.

12. See articles in the *Voice*, for example Pat Wagner, "Bread and Justice," *Voice*, June 14, 1967; "Welfare Recipients Plan Action"; "VISTA Ellen Barry Reports on WRO Work," *Voice*, March 12, 1968.

13. Margaret Roxga, "March on Milwaukee," *Wisconsin Magazine of History* 90 (4) (2007): 28–39; Interview with Charles Tachau by Tracy E. K'Meyer, August 16, 1999; "Youth Organizing," *Voice*, October 17, 1967; "Black Consciousness Goal of New Organizing Effort," *Voice*, February 12, 1968; Bill Peterson, "New Rights Group Urges Negroes to Think Black," *Courier Journal*, February 26, 1968; Tachau to Reverend Charles L. Glenn, Jr., February 29, 1968, WECC 2:2: West End Community Council Press Release, May 23, 1968, WECC 1:13; Charles Tachau, "Black Unity League…A Force Against Racism," *Voice*, March 12, 1968.

14. Tachau for WECC to Reverend Charles L. Glenn, Jr., February 29, 1968, WECC 2:2; [Plan for BULK Black History Program], [1968], WECC 4:1; Cecil Blye, "Black Unity League Formed to Further Black Culture," *Defender*, February 29, 1968; Bishop Marmion to Clergy of Diocese of Kentucky, July 1, 1968, WECC 4:1; "A Plea for Direct Help by the Administration," [addressed to administration of Louisville Male High School] May 28, 1968, in Social Action File 26, State Historical Society of Wisconsin, Madison, WI [hereafter cited as Social Action File #]; "A Soul Session," *Voice*, May 14, 1968; "African Topics Dominate Black Arts Festival," *Defender*, July 11, 1968.

15. "SCLC's Sims' Arrest Termed A Mistake," *Defender*, August 2, 1967; Charles Tachau, "Innocent Men Jailed Two Months," *Voice*, October 17, 1967; "Charles Tachau Criticizes Bonds in Fire-Bombing Case," *Defender*, October 26, 1967; Charles Tachau, "Most

Important Lessons for Louisville," *Voice*, December 13, 1967; Charles Tachau and Neville Tucker to [form letter], March 28, 1968, WECC 1:11.

16. Clarence L. Matthews, "New York's Youth Unrest Absent Here," *Defender*, June 11, 1964; "Police Quell Pending Racial Outburst Here," *Defender*, July 16, 1964; "West End Riot Averted," *Defender*, September 23, 1965; "Trouble Erupts in West End Over Weekend," *Defender*, August 25, 1966; "No Racial Violence Expected in Louisville," *Defender*, August 13, 1964; Clarence L. Matthews, "Civil Rights Leaders, Experts Have No Fear of Riots Here," *Defender*, September 9, 1965; Nat Tillman, "Riot Root Problems Exist Here in Louisville," *Defender*, July 27, 1967.

17. James Braden notes on tapes with Manfred Reid, Braden 16:4.

18. Morris Jeff, "Police Incident Adds to Tension," *Voice*, May 14, 1968; James Braden transcript of tape with Carl Braden, April 4, 1969, Braden 16:4; James Braden notes on tape with Eugene Robinson, Braden 16:4; Cecil Blye, "Rep. McGill Leads Protest Delegation to City Hall," *Defender*, May 16, 1968; "Police 'Strike' Talked as Civil Service Board Dockets Appeal," *Defender*, May 23, 1968; Braden, "Civil Disorders," Braden 16:2; Absence 'Sways' Civil Service Board," *Defender*, May 30, 1968.

19. Braden tape transcript with Bill Peterson; Braden transcript of tape with Carl Braden; Braden notes on tape with Eugene Robinson; Partial transcript of speeches made May 2[7], 1968; Martha Leslie Allen Papers, 1969–1977, box 1 file 8, State Historical Society of Wisconsin, Madison, WI; Peterson notes on rally (with Mervin Aubespin), Braden 16:4; Braden transcripts of tapes on riots—Jay Thomas, Braden 16:4; Jim Braden tape transcripts—Florian and Reginald Meeks, Braden 16:4; Braden transcript of tapes—Robert Kuyu [Sims], April 4, 1969, Braden 16:4.

20. Braden tape transcript—Bill Peterson, Braden 16:4; Peterson notes on rally (with Mervin Aubespin), Braden 16:4; Braden transcripts of tapes on riot—Jay Thomas; Jim Jordan tape transcripts—Florian and Reginald Meeks, Braden 16:4; Braden notes on tapes—Manfred Reid, Braden 16:4; Braden, "Civil Disorders," p. 89, Braden 16:2.

21. Braden, "Civil Disorders," p. 1, 89–137, Braden, 16:2; Braden tape transcripts—Bill Peterson; Jim Jordan transcripts—Jay Thomas, Braden 16:4; K'Meyer, Interview with Ken Clay; Cecil Blye, "West End Riot Laid to Officer Clifford's Reinstatement," *Defender*, May 30, 1968.

22. Memo to Manley N. Feinberg from Charles B. Tachau, August 3, 1968, WECC 1:9.

23. Braden, "Civil Disorders," pp. 96, 122–128; Braden 16:2; Transcript of KUAC Hearings, September 24–25, 1968, Braden 16:4; Braden transcript—Carl Braden; Braden notes on tapes—Eugene Robinson.

24. Louisville Staff of the Southern Conference Educational Fund, "Lessons of Louisville: White Community to Black Rebellion," June 14, 1968, gift to author from Anne Braden.

25. Braden, "Civil Disorders," p. 117–118, Braden 16:2; "Schmied Hears Complaint of Slain Youth's Mother," *Defender*, June 13, 1968; Cecil Blye, "Mrs. Groves Asks for FBI Help," *Defender*, June 27, 1968; Priscilla Hancock, "BULK Demands Charges Against Officer Noe," *Defender*, July 4, 1968; "Mayor Rejects Groves Plea," *Defender*, August 8, 1968; "Council in Joint Reply to Mayor Seeks Action on Killing," *Voice*, August 16, 1968.

26. Braden transcript—Carl Braden; Transcripts of KUAC Hearing, September 24–25, 1968; "City Shifts Blame for Civil Disorders: Frames Black Leaders," [1968], WECC 1:9; "A Dangerous Manipulation of Bail Power," *Courier Journal*, June 5, 1968.

27. "A Scapegoat Hunt is Not the Answer," *Courier Journal*, June 4, 1968; "A Dangerous Manipulation of Bail Power," June 5, 1968; George Gibson, "Ky. Liberties Unit Raps Colson," *Defender*, June 13, 1968; "City Shifts Blame...," WECC 1:9; Fred Hicks, "Speakers Stress Unity at West End Protest Rally," *Voice*, June 18, 1968; "National Militants to Convene in City," *Defender*, June 6, 1968.

28. Paul M. Branzburg, "West Enders to Reconsider Boycott," *Courier Journal*, October 23, 1968; Braden notes on tapes—Manfred Reid; Cecil Blye, "Mrs. Ruth Bryant Aided Black Arts and Culture," *Defender*, October 24, 1968.

29. WECC Meeting to Support the Black Six notes, October 29, 1968, WECC 1:9; West End Community Council Press Release, January 2, 1969, WECC 1:13.

30. Press Release, November 7, 1968, Braden 75:4; "Council Initiates City-Wide Action Movement," *Voice*, November 12, 1968.

31. Ben Johnson, "Black Six Jury Selected; Cortez Offers Objections," *Defender*, June 25, 1970; News from SCEF, July 5, [1970], Allen 1:14; Ben Johnson, "Directed Verdict Ends Trial of the Black Six," *Defender*, July 9, 1970; Handwritten notes on Black Six trial, June 29–July 7, 1970, Allen 1:15; "A 'Big Frame' Claimed by Sims, Reid," *Defender*, July 9, 1970; Memo to Louisville Friends from SCEF, July, 1970, Braden 75:5.

32. "Bishop Tucker Denounces Black Militants at Jackson, Mississippi Church Meeting," *Defender*, December 19, 1968; Lyman Johnson to editor, *Defender*, May 15, 1969; "Sound Advice for Anarchists," *Defender*, May 15, 1969; Lester Pope, "Memorial Rites Become Black Militancy Forum," *Defender*, April 10, 1969; Cecil Blye, "Reverend W. J. Hodge Calms Unrest at City Rites," *Defender*, April 10, 1969.

33. On the history of black studies programs and campus Black Power activism see Peniel E. Joseph, "Black Studies, Student Activism, and the Black Power Movement," in *The Black Power Movement: Rethinking the Civil Rights-Black Power Era* (New York: Routledge, 2006), pp. 251–277.

34. K'Meyer, Interview with Blaine Hudson; "Black Student Union at UofL Wins Fight for Negro Courses," *Defender*, June 13, 1968; "The Black Student Union," flyer, October 1968, Black Student Union Papers file 3, University of Louisville Archives, Louisville, KY [hereafter cited as BSU file #]; "In the Revolution," *Ahead in the Revolution*, December, 1968, BSU file 3.

35. "Recruiting Proposal to the University of Louisville," March 1969, BSU file 1; Cecil Blye, " 'Proposals' Are Wide-Sweeping," *Defender*, March 6, 1969; K'Meyer, Interview with Blaine Hudson; Anne Braden to Jim Braden, March 6, 1969; Braden 15:10.

36. "Fact Sheet," May 1969, published by the Black Student Union Community News Service, box 1 file 4b in the F. W. Woolsey Papers, University of Louisville Archives, Louisville, KY [hereafter cited as Woolsey box#:file#]; Lester Pope, "Black Students Make 16 Demands at UofL," *Defender*, March 6, 1969; Human Relations Commission Minutes, March 6, 1969, in Martin Perley Papers, Filson Historical Society, Louisville, KY; "A Good Beginning," *Defender*, March 13, 1969; "Black Coalition, University of Louisville Come to Terms," *Defender*, March 13, 1969.

37. K'Meyer, Interview with Blaine Hudson; "Fact Sheet," May 1969; Press Release, April 23, 1969, BSU Executive Committee, BSU file 1.

38. "Strickler 'Reads Riot Act'," *Defender*, May 15, 1969; "Fact Sheet," May 1969; K'Meyer, Interview with Blaine Hudson; Interview with Bob Winlock by Tracy E. K'Meyer, March 13, 2001; Joe Hoban, "The University of Louisville Crisis: Background and Analysis," May 4, 1969, Woolsey 1:4b.

39. Hoban, "The University of Louisville Crisis"; John Filiatreau, "UL Re-Admits 3 of 8 Dismissed Blacks," *Louisville Cardinal*, May 16, 1969, in box 5 folder marked Open Housing/Public Accommodations, 1961–1967 in the Ray Bixler Papers, University of Louisville Archives, Louisville, KY [hereafter cited as Bixler box#:folder name]; "Expelled UofL Students Claim Rigged Hearing, Double Jeopardy," *Defender*, May 22, 1969; K'Meyer, Interview with Blaine Hudson; Odell McCollum, "Seven Blacks Acquitted in UofL Takeover Case," *Defender*, April 16, 1970; "Expelled Black Students Are Readmitted by UofL," *Defender*, November 27, 1969.

40. Anne Braden to Jimmy Cortez, May 22, 1969, Braden 1:5; "UofL Black Affairs Coordinator Makes Big Hit with Community," *Defender*, June 12, 1969; "Black Affairs Program Begins in Five City Poverty Areas," *Defender*, July 10, 1969; "Shawnee Festival Planned by Black Affairs Office," *Defender*, July 17, 1969; "An Experience in Self-Expression," *Defender*, August 14, 1969; "Screening Committee Appointed by Black Affairs Office at UofL," *Defender*, July 24, 1969; Cecil Blye, "Black Affairs Program Model for Southeast," *Defender*, September 4, 1969; "UofL Releases Final Progress Report on Blacks," *Defender*, September 25, 1969; "UofL Increases Black Recruitment, Admissions," *Defender*, September 17, 1970; Department of Pan-African Studies, University of Louisville, Web site: http://www.louisville.edu/a-s/pas.

41. Lester Pope, "BSU Joins Park-Duvalle 'Paint Program'," *Defender*, August 7, 1969; "Black Art Festival Scheduled by BSU," *Defender*, February 19, 1970; Ray Bixler, "Psychology Head Pleads for Support of UofL's Black Student Union," *Defender*, February 12, 1970; "Bishop Tucker Denounces BSU Position," *Defender*, December 25, 1969; "Black Students Demonstrate at University of Louisville," *Defender*, April 29, 1971; Priscilla Hancock, "Black Student Unions Join," *Defender*, November 22, 1973.

42. K'Meyer, Interview with Blaine Hudson; Interview with Sterling Neal by Tracy E. K'Meyer, April 21, 2000; Interview with Howard Owens by Tracy E. K'Meyer, February 28, 2000.

43. Henri Williams, Jr., to Brothers and Sisters, [1970] Social Action 6; "14 Steps to Equality—What JOMO Believes," *Defender*, December 24, 1970; "Black Solidarity Week," *Defender*, April 22, 1971; K'Meyer, Interview with Blaine Hudson.

44. K'Meyer, Interview with Sterling Neal; "Our Black Thing Brings Kent State Drama Here," *Defender*, July 16, 1970; Priscilla Hancock, "WATU—Our Black Thing Scores," *Defender*, July 23, 1970; "Our Black Thing Presents Show," *Defender*, August 20, 1970.

45. "MOJA ENIA ODUN DUDU," Festival Program, September 28–30, 1973, in possession of Mervyn Aubespin, Louisville, KY; "African Liberation Day Scheduled for May," *Defender*, May 6, 1976.

46. K'Meyer, Interview with Sterling Neal; "Dope Program Seeks Funds to Combat Narcotics Wave," *Defender*, December 10, 1970; Susan Brown, "Bullets Deface Bldg of Com for Self Defense," *Defender*, February 24, 1972; Jason Williams, "New 'Rights' Coalition Decries 'R' and 'X' Films," *Defender*, April 4, 1974; Ron Long, "Stop Done Now Director Charges Conflict of Interest," *Defender*, October 7, 1976.

47. Cecil Blye, "Black Panthers to Organize Here?" *Defender*, February 27, 1969; Susan Brown, "Panthers Initiate Sickle Cell Clinic," *Defender*, August 3, 1972; Interview with Nancy Pennick Pollock by Tracy E. K'Meyer, September 9, 1999; Susan Brown, "Free Breakfasts Become a Reality," *Defender*, September 28, 1972; "Panthers Picket Film 'Superfly'," *Defender*, January 11, 1973.

48. "Black Panthers: Intensify Lou. Action," *Defender*, May 18, 1972; "Over 100 Protest Lou. '7' High Bonds and Nixon War," *Defender*, May 25, 1972; Press Statement on Behalf of the Louisville 7, [1972] Social Action 26; Confidential Report, September 14, 1972, in box 1 folder marked FBI Files in the Kentucky Civil Liberties Union Papers, University of Louisville Archives, Louisville, KY [hereafter cited as KCLU box #: folder name]; Meryl Thornton, "Panthers Trial Set for Monday," *Defender*, September 21, 1972; "Free Blakemore," undated flyer, Social Action 24; Meryl Thornton, "Panthers Vow to Free Member," *Defender*, October 5, 1972; Interview with William Allison by Tracy E. K'Meyer, September 21, 2001.

49. "Over 100 Protest Lou."; Confidential Report, September 14, 1972, KCLU 1: FBI Files; Thornton, "Panthers Trial Set for Monday,"; Flyer, January 1973, Social Action 24.

50. See for summary of this narrative and critique of it Peniel E. Joseph, "Introduction," in *The Black Power Movement*; on the overlap between the Black Power and civil rights movements see Timothy B. Tyson, *Radio Free Dixie: Robert F. Williams and the Roots of Black Power* (Chapel Hill: University of North Carolina Press, 1999).

8

The Black Arts Movement in Atlanta

James Smethurst

The Black Arts Movement in Atlanta had something of a paradoxical history. Given its enormous importance as a black educational center, the administrative heart (if not always the focus of grassroots activities) of the civil rights movement, and an enormously important locus of the Black Power Movement (from the Atlanta Project of the Student Nonviolent Coordinating Committee [SNCC] to the founding convention of the Congress of African People [CAP] to the Institute of the Black World [IBW]), Atlanta had an enormous national impact on the new black politics and arts of the 1960s and 1970s. Many important African American artists, writers, and cultural critics worked at the historically black colleges and universities of University Center, producing work, like Stephen Henderson's *Understanding the New Black Poetry* (an Institute of the Black World book), that had (and continues to have) a wide impact across the United States.

At the same time, despite efforts of Black Arts theaters, the journal *Rhythm*, the Black Art Center, and other cultural institutions to reach out to the grassroots African American communities of the city, the movement initially had a very hard time getting much beyond Atlanta University Center (AUC). The Black Arts activists and institutions there were also for a long time relatively detached from the movement elsewhere in the South, which was the home of the most successful regional Black Arts organization, the Southern Black Cultural Alliance (SBCA). Like other cities, cyclical crises in funding—public and private—and a lack of stable financial foundations, caused much institutional instability. Yet ultimately, perhaps nowhere else in the United States, even Chicago and Detroit, was the Black Arts Movement so successfully integrated into the cultural life of the city. In Atlanta, the Black Arts Movement ultimately reached a grassroots audience, largely through the efforts of artists, educators, activists, and political officials such as Michael Lomax, Shirley Franklin, Ebon Dooley, Toni Cade Bambara, Ed Spriggs, Alice Lovelace, Carlton and Barbara Molette, Pearl Cleage, and Andrea Frye during the administration of Maynard Jackson in the 1970s and after.

Atlanta has long had a contradictory character that distinguished it from many other southern cities. As the premiere "New South" city that emerged from the ashes of the 1864 fire and the Civil War, it became the commercial center of the region, rebuilt on Jim Crow lines. It was among the first to try to legislate residential segregation, breaking from the pattern of older southern cities where black families were scattered in virtually every ward and precinct. Though residential segregation laws were ruled unconstitutional by the U. S. Supreme Court, Atlanta would continue to enact such laws into the 1930s—and certainly housing became segregated as a practical matter, if not according to statute.

As in other southern cities, segregation of housing, education, public accommodations, public services, and so on, resulted in the establishment of many black social, religious, economic, and educational institutions. However, Atlanta became unique in the sheer number and concentration of its historically black colleges and universities. While the origins of Clark College and Atlanta University (AU) can be traced to Reconstruction, it was in the Jim Crow era that they, along with Morehouse College, Spelman College, and Morris Brown College fully matured, becoming some of the most prominent black institutions of higher education. By the 1930s these schools were located in the West End of Atlanta near the black working-class neighborhood of Vine City—with AU, Spelman, and Morehouse formally affiliating in 1929, joined by Clark a decade later.

During most of the twentieth century the political and economic elite of the city preferred to manage race relations through paternalistic consensus and cooptation rather than direct repression. However, spasms of violence (most famously Atlanta's 1906 riot) periodically wracked the city, often by vigilante groups, such as the Black Shirts and the Ku Klux Klan. Atlanta also saw episodic repression of attempts to challenge the Jim Crow order, as in the arrest of black Communist organizer Angelo Herndon in 1932 and his subsequent trial for "attempting to incite insurrection."[1] As the state capital, it also felt some contradiction between the local municipal government and state government (which was generally far less inclined toward accommodation than the city authorities) as to enforcement of segregation laws—and the relative willingness of different branches of government to tolerate organized dissent against segregation.

While there was and long continued to be a serious town-gown split between the schools of AUC and the black working-class neighborhoods that adjoined it, the 1930s saw the beginnings of black cultural initiatives rooted on the campuses that reached out into the neighborhoods, particularly after John Hope became AU's president in 1928, giving AU an increasingly high profile locally and regionally. The visual artist Hale Woodruff was hired by the new AU in 1931, basically launching the university's program in the fine arts.[2] Woodruff encouraged his students to paint subjects in Vine City and other nearby black neighborhoods as well as in the rural communities of North Georgia. This focus on workers, small farmers, and sharecroppers led to Woodruff and the circle of artists he mentored becoming known as the "Outhouse School" (named for the propensity of the artists who included outhouses in their unsentimentalized rural landscapes).

Woodruff's program became a major beachhead of the Popular Front in the South and made Atlanta a hub for black visual artists. It essentially became the regional center for the training of black visual artists and art educators—who in turn went on to do much the same work at other historically black colleges and universities. Woodruff launched the AU Annual Exhibition of African American artists, beginning in 1942 and lasting until 1969. The Annual Exhibition became a premiere (if not the premiere) show of African American artists in the United States, often highlighting such Left artists as Charles White, John Wilson, and Elizabeth Catlett—all of whom, especially Wilson and Catlett, would have a direct impact on Black Arts era writers and artists. Woodruff also worked with the WPA's Federal Arts Project, directing the painting of a four-part mural, *The Negro in Modern American Life* at a local junior high school as well as murals at the AU School of Social Work. Finally, he was a member of the faculty of AU's People's School, a progressive adult education program founded in 1942 that offered a wide range of free classes to the black community.[3] Another participant in the People's School was W. E. B. Du Bois, whom Hope brought back to AU in 1934. In 1940 Du Bois founded what was arguably the leading black intellectual journal, *Phylon*, at AU.

In 1934, a member of the Spelman faculty, Anna Cook, founded AU's Summer Theater, which would put on four plays in six weeks. While the majority of these plays were by European and white American authors, Cook (who continued to direct the Summer Theater even after she left for Hampton Institute and then Howard University) attempted to stage at least one show by a black playwright each summer. Sterling Brown, Owen Dodson, and Baldwin Burroughs were among the prominent figures who worked in the Summer Theater. Burroughs, who went on to teach at Spelman and direct the Summer Theater himself, became a central figure of black theater in Atlanta for decades.[4]

Many of the more Left artists and intellectuals, including Woodruff and W. E. B. Du Bois, left Atlanta in the mid- to late-1940s—often under the pressure of the deepening cold war that particularly intensified in the South after Henry Wallace's presidential campaign in 1948.[5] Even then Woodruff maintained contact with Atlanta University, painting the six panels of the mural *Art of the Negro* there in 1950–1952. The mid-1940s also saw the repeal of the poll tax and the end of whites-only primaries, producing a great increase of black registration, particularly in Atlanta where African Americans were a third of the population. This had the contradictory effect of giving African Americans significant, if limited, political leverage in Atlanta while galvanizing white voters to replace the liberal governor Ellis Arnall with the arch-segregationist Eugene Talmadge (who died before he could assume office and was replaced by his son Herman, another pro-segregationist who eventually had a long career in the U.S. Senate). This sort of push and pull between black advances and white backlash became a hallmark of Atlanta (and Georgia politics) through the election of segregationist icon Lester Maddox as governor in 1967 to the Fulton County "tax revolts" of the 1990s.

The 1950s were relatively quiet in Atlanta as compared with other cities in the South. As had been generally the case in Atlanta, Mayor William Hartsfield (who had held office since 1937) preferred to manage black demands for equality through cooptation and relatively small concessions. He made such gestures as removing "colored" and "white" signs from Atlanta's airport. The black community was also able to win concessions in efforts to open up new property to black residents to relieve the fierce overcrowding in African American neighborhoods hemmed in by residential segregation. Hartsfield (and his successor Ivan Allen) avoided the sort of confrontation around school desegregation seen elsewhere in the South through adopting a voluntary plan—one that initially involved only a handful of black students.[6]

Similarly, the African American arts community centered on AUC was lower keyed during the 1950s than it had been during the 1930s and 1940s, but still a substantial presence. Although many of the leading cultural figures of the 1930s and 1940s had moved elsewhere and the sort of politicized art and outreach efforts aimed at the black working class of Woodruff and the Outhouse School were little seen, AUC remained the hub of "high culture" for the black community in Atlanta with the Summer Theater and the Annual Exhibition as yearly events. Of course, other sorts of popular art thrived in black Atlanta, especially rhythm and blues music. Carlton Molette, who came to Morehouse College from Kansas City, Missouri, recalls that Baldwin Burroughs inspired in his students an interest in the process of theater, including the achievement of a high level of competency and the importance of doing things right. Molette got directly involved in the theater through a freshman roommate who was an actor. Since each role required an understudy, Molette found himself drawn into acting and eventually directing and, especially, technical design. Molette left Morehouse to pursue a graduate degree in scenic design at the University of Missouri-Kansas City and the University of Iowa, finding jobs in community theater and theater departments at Tuskegee, Howard, and Florida A & M (FAMU) before he returned to Atlanta and the Spelman theater department in 1969.[7]

Molette returned at a crucial juncture of Black Arts and Black Power in the South. Atlanta was a key site of the radicalization of the civil rights movement and the emergence of Black Power as a social formation. Atlanta was on the front lines of the civil rights movement for only a relatively short period in the early 1960s, particularly as the black student movement emerged after the 1960 sit-in by four North Carolina A & T students in Greensboro, North Carolina, engaging many students from the schools of University Center in the struggle against what Winston Grady-Willis has called the city's "petty apartheid."[8] SNCC and the Southern Christian Leadership Conference (SCLC) both headquartered there for much of the 1960s, Atlanta was the most important administrative center of the movement. It was from Atlanta that SNCC announced its opposition to the Vietnam War at the beginning of 1966. While many SNCC organizers had opposed the war and even spoken against it on occasion, and while SNCC (like Students for a Democratic Society) had refused to genuflect before the anti-Communism that the domestic cold war pressed on the civil rights movement, this was the first public antiwar statement by the organization. It was largely on the basis of this statement that the Georgia State Legislature refused to seat SNCC leader Julian Bond, son of the distinguished black educator Horace Mann Bond and a Morehouse graduate who had won a seat in the Georgia House of

Representatives the previous November. It took another victory in a special election, demonstrations, and a U.S. Supreme Court decision for Bond to assume his seat. A year later, after keeping his misgivings mostly private, Martin Luther King, Jr. (a Morehouse graduate and a resident of Vine City) spoke out forcefully against the war in a series of speeches, including a powerful sermon at Ebenezer Baptist Church in Atlanta on April 30, 1967 in which SNCC leaders Kwame Ture (Stokely Carmichael) and Cleveland Sellers were in the audience.[9]

In 1966 SNCC also began an urban organizing project in Vine City that became known as the Atlanta Project. A number of the staff members of the Atlanta Project, including Gwendolyn Robinson, William Ware, Michael Stewart, Donald Stone, and Askia Touré (Rolland Snellings), were increasingly concerned with issues of black self-determination and self-reliance. Several of the project's members, including (at least) Stone, Stewart, and Touré (a poet and one of the architects of the Black Arts Movement), were influenced by the Revolutionary Action Movement, a revolutionary nationalist cadre organization with headquarters in Cleveland and Philadelphia.[10] In addition to their day-to-day work in Vine City, the Atlanta Project also issued a series of position papers on, among other issues, black consciousness, the need for organizing in poor black neighborhoods in the urban south, community-based "freedom schools," and housing. The paper on black consciousness and self-determination argued for both a nationalist (as members of what was essentially a black nation) and an internationalist (in solidarity with black people in the diaspora and on the continent) consciousness on the part of African Americans and for the black freedom struggle to be led and staffed by African Americans. The paper suggested that white civil rights workers devote themselves to fighting racism in their own communities. The position paper on black consciousness, and the nationalist stance of the project staff, produced tremendous debate within SNCC and antagonism on the part of the group's leadership because of the disruption and confusion it perceived arising from the paper. Still, it anticipated the Black Power slogan raised by Ture and Mukasa (Willie) Ricks that same year.[11]

When the poet A. B. Spellman arrived in Atlanta from New York (where he had worked closely with Amiri Baraka and other early Black Arts activists) in 1967, he found a community of increasingly radicalized and increasingly nationalist activists, many of whom had either just arrived from, or were about to head out to, the frontlines of civil rights struggles in the South. One result of the increased radicalization of the movement, and indeed the politics of the African American community, particularly the intelligentsia, was that the black schools of Atlanta were willing to appoint radical political and cultural activists as faculty to a greater degree than had been the case since (at least) the 1930s and 1940s. Vincent Harding, for example, joined the Spelman faculty as chair of the History and Sociology Department in 1965 after several years in the civil rights movement. Abdul Alkalimat (Gerald McWhorter), one of the founders of the Organization for Black American Culture (OBAC) in Chicago, joined him a few years later. And, academics already in place at the schools became increasingly radicalized and openly sympathetic to Black Arts and Black Power as well as the emerging Black Studies movements. For example, Stephen Henderson who chaired Morehouse's English Department developed into one of the best known of Black Arts literary critics and with Vincent Harding initially brainstormed the idea of the black institute that became IBW. It should be noted, though, that the experience of activist faculty of the historically black schools of AUC in the 1960s was uneven and that there were limits to faculty activism, especially if faculty sided with students in direct political challenges to college administrations. The firings of Howard Zinn from Spelman and A.B. Spellman from Morehouse, based on their support of student activism, attest to this.[12]

While the African American arts community was comparatively small at that time, and centered on the university communities, there was a small, but significant in-migration of African American artists. Many, like A.B. Spellman had some experience with Black Arts organizations elsewhere. Black artists, intellectuals, and civil rights activists became intertwined to an incredible degree. Falling in love with and marrying the SNCC national office manager Karen Edmonds, Spellman stayed in Atlanta. Stephen Henderson hired him to be a poet in residence at Morehouse College. Musician and music scholar Bernice Johnson Reagon, who had come into SNCC during its Albany, Georgia, campaign and become a field secretary as well as an initiator of the group's Freedom Singers, founded the Harambee Singers in Atlanta in 1968. The Harambee Singers appeared at many black political and cultural events over the next few years. Skunder Boghossian, a Pan-African, surrealist-influenced painter and the leading contemporary visual artist of Ethiopia was hired as an artist in residence at AU in 1969. Kofi (Herman) Bailey (Kofi X), a Pan-African visual artist close to SNCC circles and influenced by the painter Charles White, served as a mentor to young black visual artists in Atlanta. Before his arrival in Atlanta, Bailey had been part of the Left-nationalist expatriate community in Ghana until Kwame Nkrumah's overthrow in 1966. Numerous movement posters, pamphlets, flyers, and broadsides in Atlanta featured his illustrations so that his work was practically ubiquitous in movement circles and on the street.[13] The poet Ebon Dooley, a veteran of OBAC in Chicago, moved to Atlanta in the 1969 to run the Timbuktu Market of New Africa, a Left-nationalist, black-owned bookstore (one of the very few in the South) near Vine City and AUC that Alkalimat had helped found. Dooley and Spellman in particular would be crucial to the institutionalization of Black Arts in Atlanta.[14]

As the community of local and transplanted black artists grew in Atlanta, grassroots-oriented initiatives that attempted to reach beyond University Center—and beyond the city—were established. These efforts were generally independent of the schools of AUC, but often depended heavily on the academic community for staff, financial support, and audience. Among the first of these initiatives was the Atlanta Center for Black Art. The center was staffed by the emerging community of artist-activists, including Spellman, Dooley, and Boghossian. It provided arts instruction aimed at the black community outside the campuses as well as putting on performances of poetry, theater, music, and other genres and media. For example, Dooley as director of the center in 1973 organized "The Great Black Music" series of public concerts (not unlike New York's Jazzmobile), featuring local black musicians.[15] While its funding and impact were limited, it helped prepare the ground for the Neighborhood Arts Center (NAC) that flourished under the Maynard Jackson administration.

Spellman, along with such artists and activists as Donald Stone, Ebon Dooley, and Karen Spellman, also began the journal *Rhythm* in 1970 with the idea of providing a Black Arts vehicle that would give voice primarily to local artists and activists, giving them a new visibility within and beyond the South:

> *Rhythm* is based in the southern u.s. and will focus on southern readers, writers and realities. However, we will publish any and all materials made to us which clarify in a relevant way the future, present, and past of African peoples.[16]

In fact, the writers from the Deep South who published in the journal were almost all based in Atlanta. None of the BLKARTSOUTH network in New Orleans, Houston, Miami, and elsewhere appeared in the pages of *Rhythm*. Like the Atlanta Center for Black Art, with which it was affiliated, *Rhythm* was independent of the university communities, though many of its staff, contributors, and audience had ties to the AUC schools. Its staff and contributors included Donald Stone, Amiri Baraka, the Washington, D.C. poet Gaston Neal, the Indianapolis poet, editor, essayist, and editor Mari Evans, Pearl Cleage, Michael Lomax, the musician Marion Brown, Kwame Ture, Reagon, Bailey, Dooley, and Spellman.[17] The general ideology of the journal was a sort of mixture of Left nationalism and cultural nationalism that encompassed both the Kawaidist strand of nationalism, which would dominate the 1970 founding convention of the CAP in Atlanta and Ture's more Marxist-oriented version of Pan-Africanism:

> *Rhythm* is committed to Revolutionary Pan-African Nationalism, which we broadly define as the recognition that people of African origin did not cease to be Africans because they were enslaved; that we are citizens of Africa, responsible to work with other African people, wherever they are, to build liberated zones which ultimately can merge in the new Africa of the 21st century. *Rhytm* [sic] sees African people as having no moral or legal responsibility to the west except to oversee its destruction.[18]

Dooley, Cleage, and Lomax contributed in different ways to the growth of African American arts organizations in the twenty years that followed the founding of *Rhythm*.

Spellman and Henderson played significant parts in the genesis of the most important of the early independent Black Power/Black Arts institutions of Atlanta, IBW. The first black think tank, IBW primarily focused on education and the social sciences, but especially in the beginning saw the promotion of African American culture and art as one of its primary tasks. Like other early independent Black Power/Black Arts institutions, IBW had strong connections, though not formal affiliation, with the schools of AUC. IBW was initially conceived in discussions between historian Vincent Harding at Spelman and Henderson at Morehouse. As early as 1967 they began discussing a research center inspired by W. E. B. Du Bois's early twentieth-century vision of an institute "which would develop a hundred-year study of the Black Experience" as well as help undergird the incipient Black Studies movement that was emerging from such schools as San Francisco State College (now University), Cornell University, Merritt College, Wayne State University and root Black Studies on the campuses of historically black colleges and universities.[19]

The murder of Martin Luther King, Jr. galvanized Harding and Henderson beyond speculative discussion. Initially, they imagined that the institute would be affiliated with the AUC schools. However, AU was cool to the idea because it feared that the public sponsorship of such an institute would alienate donors who would see the institute as too radical. So when Coretta Scott King asked Harding to head a Martin Luther King, Jr. "Documentation Center" to commemorate Dr. King and his work and to document the civil rights movement, Harding suggested that an "Institute for Advanced Afro-American Studies" be included as part of the memorial center. Coretta Scott King agreed with Harding's suggestion. A. B. Spellman wrote a letter in early 1969 that invited artists, educators, and activists to come to Atlanta that March to discuss IBW and consider serving on its advisory board. Harding and Henderson were then joined by Spellman, sociologist Alkalimat, political scientist William Strickland, journalist Lerone Bennett, historian Sterling Stuckey, scholar of black education Chester Davis, and sociologist Joyce Ladner as senior research fellows of the institute, now named the Institute of the Black World. Like Harding, all of these scholars had histories as political activists. Strickland, for example, had been a leader of the National Student Movement, a sort of northern analogue to SNCC. Joyce Ladner had been active in SNCC itself. IBW began running seminars in 1969: Henderson on black poetry; Davis on black children and public education; Harding on black biography; Strickland on black radical politics of the twentieth century; and Ladner on the black family and social policy. IBW issued its first "Black Paper," Bennett's *The Challenge of Blackness*, in 1970.[20]

As can be seen from the above list of seminars, the study and promotion of African American art and culture, particularly literature, were among IBW's early priorities, reflecting the prominent role of artists and literary scholars, such as Henderson and Spellman, in creating the Institute—though Spellman was forced to leave Atlanta not long after the founding of IBW due to his support of the Morehouse student takeover. Of course, both Henderson and Spellman were famously engaged with other artistic media—in fact, Spellman was probably better known nationally as a critic and historian of jazz than as a poet. The seriousness of IBW's concern with art and culture can be seen in the second point of its statement of purpose and program:

> The encouragement of those creative artists who are searching for the meaning of a black aesthetic, who are now trying to define and build the basic ground on which black creativity may flow in the arts. Encounter among these artists on the one hand, and scholars, activists, and students on the other, must be constant in both formal and informal settings.[21]

Here IBW takes up the widespread Black Art imperative to develop not only a distinct and liberated black art, but also some sort of principles or criteria through which that art might be created, evaluated, and taught. At the same time, it is worth noting that IBW did not attempt to actually define a "black aesthetic," only to foster a discussion. IBW also brought in artists, such as the poet, educator, and novelist Margaret Walker, choreographer and folklorist Katherine Dunham, and musician Marion Brown, and supported local artists, such as Kofi Bailey and Ebon Dooley. The formal opening of IBW featured a particularly stellar assemblage of older and younger, local and nationally known black artists, including Walker, Dunham, Dooley, the Harambee Singers, Haki Madhubuti, Val Gray Ward, Ojeda Penn, and the Black Image Theatre.[22]

Again, it is typical of the earlier Black Power/Black Arts institutions in Atlanta that IBW was independent of the AUC schools, in part because AU did not want to be publicly identified with Black Arts, Black Power, and Black Studies, even as those schools employed many of the key figures of the institute and as their students, faculty, and graduates provided a support community that made IBW possible. In turn, IBW not only had an important national impact, particularly on Black Studies, but also locally as a linchpin of the evolving and intertwining black political and artistic community. Even during the later years of IBW when it focused much more on education and the social sciences and far less on directly promoting black artistic production, its staff continued to interact with local artists and such national artistic and intellectual institutions as *Black World*, Third World Press (which printed a number of IBW's "Black Papers"), the *Black Collegian*, and *Black Books Bulletin*.[23]

If the independent Black Arts and Black Power organizations intersected with and relied on the AUC community in vital respects, the arts institutions and programs directly affiliated with the schools also increasingly interfaced with local community institutions, as well as with the larger Black Arts and Black Power movements. A dynamic, if somewhat shifting black theater community began to develop at AUC, particularly through the work of Carlton Molette, Barbara Molette, and Baldwin Burroughs with the Spelman drama program, the Morehouse-Spelman Players and the AU Summer Theater. The dramatic programs and institutions of AUC provided a training ground for theater workers who went on to national careers as actors and directors much as they always had, but increasingly engaged with new Black Arts theaters and dramatic works. These AUC graduates went on to start local companies and often remained tied to the Atlanta black theater community even after they attained national recognition. The Black Image Theatre was started in the late 1960s by what was essentially a group of graduates of the AUC schools. The group's performances were staples of black political and cultural events in the community and on the campus in the 1970s.[24] One of the founders of Black Image, the director and actress Andrea Frye, became a pillar of African American theater in Atlanta, often returning even after she no longer permanently lived in the city. The film star Samuel Jackson, a Morehouse drama major, began his professional career in Black Image Theatre. The writer Pearl Cleage was a Spelman graduate in 1971 and later a Spelman faculty member whose career as a playwright was significantly nurtured at AUC and took off in the 1980s. Like Frye she has remained a pillar of the Atlanta theater community. The actor Bill Nunn, another longtime

Atlanta theater mainstay, was also Molette's student at Morehouse in the 1970s and later an artist in residence at Spelman. Nunn played many film character roles, including that of Radio Raheem in Spike Lee's *Do the Right Thing*—Lee, too, was another Morehouse student in the 1970s.

Beyond the training of black actors, playwrights, and theatrical technicians, Burroughs and the Molettes did much to promote a historical and internationalist sense of black theatrical practice and a black repertoire. Burroughs made sure that the Spelman-Morehouse Players staged works by African and diasporic (outside of the United States) playwrights as well as by African American dramatists, including such local artists as the Molettes and Pearl Cleage. The Molettes, besides teaching, directing, and coauthoring plays, did much to uncover the history of the African American theater. Carlton Molette researched and compiled a bibliography of hundreds of plays written by African American authors over two centuries, dispelling the notion that black drama in the United States was a relatively new and underdeveloped tradition. One practical contribution of Molette's archival work is that it greatly increased the number and historical sweep of works by black playwrights accessible to African American theaters. Barbara Molette not only did this sort of scholarly archeology, but she was one of the chief chroniclers of the contemporary black theater scene in Atlanta for journals outside of the city, such as *Black World*.[25]

At the same time that the theater programs and institutions at AUC mentored black theater workers who would go on to have a large national impact as well as eventually anchoring local institutions outside the campus, they seem to have had little direct engagement with the regional manifestations of the Black Arts. Perhaps not surprisingly, the programs at AUC were much more connected to their counterparts at other historically black schools, particularly through the National Association of Dramatic and Speech Arts (an organization of theater workers, scholars, and educators primarily on historically black campuses founded by Sheppard Randolph Edmonds in 1936 in the face of Jim Crow discrimination and exclusion) and its journal *Encore* (edited for a time by Carlton Molette), than to community theaters and Black Arts organizations in other parts of the South. The one exception was the Free Southern Theater (FST) and its leader John O'Neal in New Orleans. The FST frequently came to Atlanta and networked with the theater community at the black colleges and universities there.[26] The Molettes frequently sought the expertise of O'Neal in the area of fundraising, and O'Neal often consulted the Molettes about technical matters.[27] Nonetheless, Burroughs, the Molettes, and the theater workers on and off campus were aware of such groups as BLKARTSOUTH (a workshop, performance group, and publisher of the journal *Nkombo* based in New Orleans) and the SBCA (an umbrella group of southern Black Arts workshops, theaters, and cultural centers that largely grew out of BLKARTSOUTH and its network), but only marginally involved with them for the most part—though one of the SBCA's annual meetings was held at Clark College.

The founding of the Congress of African People (CAP) at its first convention in Atlanta in 1970 in many respects confirmed the city as a center of the new black politics and culture. The CAP convention had been organized largely by cultural nationalists influenced by Maulana Karenga and his US group, most prominently among them Amiri Baraka. However, the convention drew a wide range of black political and cultural activists. Among the prominent civil rights veterans of SNCC and SCLC in Atlanta who addressed the meeting were Ralph Abernathy, Julian Bond (chairman of the Atlanta Host Committee for the convention), and Whitney Young, all of whom reminded their listeners of the history of struggle for civil rights and black liberation in Atlanta, particularly in the schools of AUC. While it is hard to gauge the local impact of the founding of CAP in Atlanta, the emphasis that CAP placed on the election of black officials unquestionably had a considerable consequence. While many of the most visible campaigns for public office to that point, such as Richard Hatcher's in Gary, Indiana; Carl Stokes in Cleveland, Ohio; and Kenneth Gibson's in Newark, New Jersey (which was in full swing at the time of the convention), took place in northern cities, the demographics of the African American community in the United States dictated that the greatest opportunities were in the South (where more than half of the black population was concentrated). Atlanta already had a modern tradition of successful black electoral activity as seen in Julian Bond's campaigns for the state legislature and Maynard Jackson's 1968 run for the U.S. Senate against Herman Talmadge in which Jackson lost the election, but carried the city of Atlanta.

It was in this climate of black political self-reliance and electoral possibility that Jackson, who was president of the city council, decided to challenge the white mayor Sam Masell in 1973, breaking with the tradition of consensus (and some would say cooptation) politics that dominated Atlanta for decades. Gaining overwhelming support and a high turnout from the black neighborhoods of Atlanta, Jackson won with more than 60 percent of the vote. From this point on, black politicians would exercise more power in Atlanta than in any other major city in the United States.

Jackson, who wanted to be known as the "culture mayor," decided to make the promotion of the arts a centerpiece of his administration from the very start. He saw culture as an important calling card for Atlanta. In his inaugural address he promised increased municipal attention to and funding of the arts. His first act toward this end was the establishment of an Ad Hoc Advisory Committee for the Arts, which was charged with planning a Mayor's Day for the Arts, making recommendations for future financial support of the arts, and addressing the particular immediate concerns of Atlanta's arts communities.[28] Jackson's support of black cultural and intellectual activities both helped make possible the growth of new institutions and supported the work of existing groups—for example, a grant from the city's Bureau of Cultural Affairs financed the printing of IBW's monthly report.[29] The new black political power—and the attention of the Jackson administration to the arts—also facilitated grants and donations from the private sector, including local economic giants such as Coca Cola.

Michael Lomax was the key figure in the Jackson administration in carrying out the mayor's focus on the arts. Lomax, a Morehouse graduate and a literature professor at Spelman, joined the Jackson campaign as a speech writer. He was married to Pearl Cleage at the time and had close ties to the African American arts community on and off the campus, having worked at the Atlanta Center for Black Art and *Rhythm*. Jackson appointed Lomax as the Director of Cultural Affairs in 1975. In that capacity, Lomax tirelessly supported the public funding of arts initiatives in Atlanta and was an important conduit for the funding of African American arts institutions in the city. Shirley Franklin, now mayor of Atlanta, succeeded Lomax as the head of the city's Bureau of Cultural Affairs after Lomax's 1978 election to the Fulton County Commission, the powerful legislative body of the county that includes Atlanta and with a population then almost evenly divided between black and white.

Directly and through Lomax, black cultural activists, particularly Ebon Dooley, lobbied hard to make sure that the black community got a significant share of the resources made available through Jackson's cultural focus. Dooley organized a program of the public performance of jazz in parks and public housing projects through grants from the city and the Atlanta Musicians Union. Dooley and other Black Arts activists pushed for the establishment of the Neighborhood Arts Center (NAC), the most important locus of African American arts efforts in Atlanta from its inception in late 1974 until its demise in 1990, particularly from 1975 until 1985. For most of its history, the NAC was housed in black communities, first in an old school building in Mechanicsville, a working-class neighborhood in southwest Atlanta and later on Auburn Avenue, the traditional commercial and civic heart of black Atlanta.[30] While the initial support of the NAC came from Jackson's Ad Hoc Advisory Committee on the Arts and a 1974 National Endowment for the Arts Expansion Program facilitated by Spellman (who was now working at the National Endowment of the Arts [NEA]), much of the funding of NAC staff salaries and internships was made possible through the Comprehensive Employment and Training Act (CETA), which had been enacted by the federal government in 1973.

NAC ran classes in a wide range of arts and crafts. At different times it housed the most important off-campus black theaters of the 1970s and 1980s, including Jomandi Productions (a theater that survived from 1977 into the 1990s) and the Just Us Theater as well as the Southern Collective of African American Writers founded by the poet Alice Lovelace, the fiction writer and editor Toni Cade Bambara, and Dooley. Its artists in residence included at various times Dooley, Bambara, photographer Jim Alexander, jazz musician Ojeda Penn, and actors Samuel L. Jackson, LaTonya Richardson, and Bill Nunn—Spike Lee, too, participated in its programs. It also brought artists, such as writers Gwendolyn Brooks and Maya Angelou, painter Romare Bearden, and dancer Arthur Miller to Atlanta, often under the auspices of its Paul Robeson Lecture Series in which the lectures were generally paired with some sort of performance and/or workshop.[31]

Promoting the arts as he rose, Michael Lomax continued to move up through the Atlanta political structure. In 1979 he was instrumental in passing legislation in the Fulton County Commission establishing the Fulton County Arts Council, which became a major source of arts funding in Atlanta. Black cultural activists, especially Ed Spriggs (a poet, visual artist, essayist, and Black Arts veteran who had been a founder and the second director of New York's Studio Museum in Harlem) after moving to Atlanta in 1980, gained much influence on the arts council. In 1981 Lomax went on to be the first ever African American elected Chair of the Fulton County Commission, a post he held until 1993. In that position, Lomax undertook more arts initiatives. Undoubtedly, the largest was (and is) Atlanta's National Black Arts Festival, conceived by Lomax and others in 1987 and significantly funded through the Arts Council (and other private and public money significantly facilitated through the efforts of Lomax) and inaugurated in 1988. The first ten-day festival featured a premiere of Charles Fuller's play *Sally*, performances by the Alvin Ailey Dance Company, and a musical choreographed by George Faison (who gained fame for his work on the stage versions of *The Wiz* and *The Lion King*), workshops by the choreographer Katherine Dunham, Maya Angelou, and the directors Woodie King, Douglas Turner Ward, and Lloyd Richards. There was also a reading of poetry from the 1960s and 1970s hosted by Ossie Davis and Ruby Dee. While executive director of the festival Michelle Smith optimistically hoped for an attendance of 250,000, the festival drew a half million viewers.[32] While 1988 is generally considered far beyond the end of the Black Arts era, the connection of many of the featured artists with the movement, the featured session of poetry from the 1960s and 1970s, and, obviously, the name of the festival itself attest to the desire of the event's founders to link the current moment to radical, politically engaged, and often mixed media work of the Black Arts era, asking the audience (and the artists) to revisit the earlier period. In 1988, the Hammonds House gallery opened in the former home of the anesthesiologist and art collector Otis T. Hammonds, who had been the president of the board of directors of NAC. Ed Spriggs led the efforts funded by Fulton County that eventually transformed the house into a major showcase of African American art from around the United States despite recurrent physical plant problems.[33]

One sign of the sense of Atlanta as a dynamic center of black political and cultural empowerment was the inception there of the journal *First World* by former *Black World* editor Hoyt Fuller in 1977. With tens of thousands (or perhaps even more) readers, *Black World* (originally *Negro Digest*) had been the most widely circulated periodical of the Black Arts and Black Power movements, both chronicling and significantly shaping those movements. *Black World*'s parent company, Johnson Publications (best known as the publishers of *Jet* and *Ebony*) shut down *Black World* in 1976. The ostensible justification for ending the journal was an alleged anti-Semitic article about Israel. Many observers (and participants in the debate with publisher John Johnson) suspected that the real issue was that Johnson no longer wanted to continue printing a magazine that did not make money due to its inability to sell much advertising, particularly as the Black Power and Black Arts movements splintered and declined as Marxists, cultural nationalists, and liberals bitterly feuded with each other. Even though John Johnson had a certain respect for Fuller and his staff, the contradictions of a commercial journal with a radical black editorial stance had always been considerable. After *Black World*'s demise, there were a number of meetings in Chicago and New York to discuss the creation of a new journal to replace *Black World*. *First World* was designed to be that journal, but with the important difference that it would not be owned by a company concerned primarily with the bottom line, but would instead be the collective property of the political and cultural liberation movements.

However, Fuller chose to establish the new journal in Atlanta rather than in Chicago, New York, Detroit, Philadelphia, San Francisco, Oakland, or some other northern city better known as an epicenter of Black Power and Black Arts. With the election of Jackson as mayor, and with Jackson's focus on culture, Atlanta projected a considerable optimism and sense of possibility. It was also a city in which the debates between the different factions of the movement were less virulent than was the case in the Northeast and the Midwest. Though much of the black population of the city was poor, Atlanta also seemed more economically viable than, say, Detroit or Newark. Of course, Fuller, who was originally from College Point, a small city just south of Atlanta, had family ties to the region. He was also close to Richard Long, a literature professor and founder of the Center for African and African American Studies (CAAS) at AU—Long would eventually become the executor of Fuller's papers. Still, it was not merely sentiment that drew Fuller to Atlanta. Even though the AUC schools had been comparatively slow in developing Black Studies programs, Long's CAAS and IBW, as well as the growing African American arts community and the sheer concentration of black intellectuals and students affiliated with AUC, seemed to offer a promising support community for the journal.

While its layout was somewhat different, *First World* did in fact carry on in much the same manner as *Black World*. It featured articles about national and international political issues with a particular focus on Africa. It also showcased much cultural criticism as well as fiction and poetry. Its various departments contained reviews of books, films, and plays as well as news about black cultural institutions and events across the country. While it was not particularly oriented toward Atlanta and the South, it covered black southern arts and political activities more consistently than was generally true of other national African American journals. Its list of editorial advisors included an impressive list of artists, scholars, and intellectuals associated with Black Power, Black Arts, and Black Studies—though such prominent "Third World Marxists" as Amiri Baraka, Kwame Ture, and Fuller's old OBAC comrades Abdul Alkalimat and Ebon Dooley were conspicuous by their absence.

Despite the successes of the Black Arts Festival, NAC, and African American community arts efforts, the change in the political climate during the Reagan era took a toll on the stability of African American arts institutions in Atlanta—as, indeed, on community-based arts efforts all across the United States. The rising conservative movement increasingly took aim at publicly supported art work (and the programs that funded that work), as part of what came to be known as the "culture wars" as well as of the Republican anti-tax drive. One result was increasing pressure for the National Endowment of the Arts (NEA), the National Endowment for the Humanities (NEH), Arts Councils, and other funding agencies to not fund politically engaged arts and arts institutions.

One of the first major casualties of the Reagan era in Atlanta was *First World*. Despite the broad support indicated by its board of editorial advisors, the journal had persistent funding problems and could never achieve financial stability. And the absence of the third-world Marxists from the board suggests the continuing ideological battles within the movement. After 1977 it came out sporadically with the last issue appearing in 1980. Some efforts were made to revive *First World*, but Fuller's untimely death in 1981 effectively foreclosed that possibility. The collapse of *First World* was hardly a unique event. With the exception of the *Black Scholar*, virtually every Black Arts and Black Power journal and newspaper had disappeared. Still, the end of the journal and the subsequent death of Fuller jolted radical African American political, cultural, and educational circles, locally and nationally.

CETA essentially lost its funding in 1981 and was replaced by the Job Placement Training Act in 1982. As a result, programs and institutions significantly underwritten by CETA funds, such as NAC, were thrown into crisis. Reductions in Community Block Grants that had also supported theaters and other community arts projects exacerbated the problems created by the abolition of CETA. Though NAC limped along until 1990, it never fully recovered from the financial problems caused by these cutbacks.

On both a local and national level, Republican tax cuts and the anti-tax fever characterizing the New Right that arose during the Reagan years and became even more pronounced in the 1990s also took a toll on Atlanta's African American arts institutions. In fact, Lomax's championing of the arts as Chair of the Fulton County Commission was a prime target of the Right in what became known as the "tax revolt of 1991." In this "revolt" conservatives especially rallied white voters on Atlanta's North Side as well as in many of the suburbs against Lomax's leadership of the commission. While Lomax initially survived these attacks, they undermined his leadership and forced the commission to draw back in its support of the arts. The tax revolt also contributed to Bill Campbell's solid victory over Lomax in the 1993 mayoral campaign, effectively ending Lomax's political career. The 1996 elimination of the NEA Expansion Arts Program, a program that had supported many community-based theaters, also had a negative impact on African American arts institutions in Atlanta. The 1990s saw financial crisis and even collapse of some of the most prominent black arts organizations and theaters in Atlanta, including NAC, Jomandi Productions, New Jomandi Productions, and the Black Arts Festival. While some of these institutions, such as New Jomandi and the Black Arts Festival, were able to survive their financial problems, others such as NAC vanished.[34] Of course, again, these sorts of problems were not just limited to Atlanta, but true of some of the best-known Black Arts institutions across the nation, such as New York's Negro Ensemble Company and New Jersey's Crossroads Theater. As private and public funding dried up for independent artistic and intellectual endeavors, job opportunities opened up at historically white universities leading to a considerable exodus of artists and scholars from AUC and Atlanta.

While most of the political and cultural institutions of the Black Power and Black Arts movements in Atlanta did not survive the 1990s, many of the individuals who sparked or were trained by those institutions, including the late Ebon Dooley, Ed Spriggs, Andrea Frye, Jim Alexander, Pearl Cleage, and

Stephanie Hughley, remain at the heart of black arts initiatives in the city. Even those, such as Frye, Hughley, Carlton and Barbara Molette, and A.B. Spellman, who left Atlanta for long periods of time (or even permanently) for brighter career opportunities, often returned to act in or direct plays, curate art shows, work on the National Black Arts Festival, or helped gain support for Atlanta arts initiatives. Nowhere else was public support of the arts such a grassroots issue and so prominently tied up with black political and economic empowerment (and white backlash toward that empowerment). And, as a result nowhere else have the long-term legacies (and failures) of the Black Arts and Black Power movements been so clearly displayed.

Notes

1. For a discussion of the Herndon case and the CPUSA efforts to organize the unemployed in Atlanta, see James Lorence, "Mobilizing the Reserve Army: The Communist Party and the Unemployed in Atlanta, 1929–1934," in Chris Green, Rachel Rubin, and James Smethurst, eds., *Radicalism in the South Since Reconstruction* (New York: Palgrave Macmillan 2006), pp. 57–80.
2. Donald F. Davis, "Hale Woodruff of Atlanta: Molder of Black Artists," *Journal of Negro History* 69.3–4 (Summer–Autumn 1984): p. 149.
3. Ibid., pp. 149–152; Stacy Morgan, *Rethinking Social Realism: African American Art and Literature, 1930–1953* (Athens, GA: University of Georgia Press, 2004), pp. 42–170; Oral History Interview with Hale Woodruff, Smithsonian Institute Archives of American Art, November 18, 1968.
4. Errol Hill and James Hatch, *A History of African American Theatre* (New York: Cambridge University Press, 2003), pp. 258–261.
5. Patricia Sullivan, *Days of Hope: Race and Democracy in the New Deal Era* (Chapel Hill, NC: University of North Carolina Press, 1996), pp. 249–275.
6. Clarence Stone, *Regime Politics: Governing Atlanta, 1946–1988* (Lawrence, KS: University of Kansas Press, 1989), pp. 46–50.
7. Author's phone interview with Carlton Molette, December, 8, 2006.
8. Winston Grady-Willis, *Challenging U.S. Apartheid: Atlanta and Black Struggles for Human Rights, 1960–1977* (Durham, NC: Duke University Press, 2006), pp. xvii–xviii.
9. Stokely Carmichael (Kwame Ture) and Ekueme Michael Thelwell, *Ready for Revolution: The Life and Struggles of Stokely Carmichael (Kwame Turé)*, (New York: Scribners, 2003), pp. 515–519 .
10. Author's phone interview with Muhammad Ahmad, August 20, 2002; author's interview with Askia Touré, December 2, 2000, Cambridge, Massachusetts; Grady-Willis, *Challenging U.S. Apartheid*, p. 67.
11. Turé and Thelwell, *Ready for Revolution*, pp. 567–570; Grady-Willis, *Challenging U.S. Apartheid*, pp. 79–113; author's interview with Askia Touré.
12. Author's interview with A. B. Spellman, 2000; author's interview with A. B. Spellman, November 11, 2006, phone interview; Harry Lefever, *Undaunted by the Fight: Spelman College and the Civil Rights Movement, 1957–1967*, (Macon, GA: Mercer University Press, 2005), pp. 161–164.
13. James Early, "Memory of Black Arts Spirits: Kofi Bailey and Atlanta in the 1960s," *International Review of African American Art* 15.1 (1998): 27.

14. Author's interview with Ebon Dooley, August 16, 2001, Atlanta, Georgia.
15. Letter from Ebon Dooley to Mike Clark, October 24, 1973, Vincent Harding Papers, Woodruff Library, Emory University. Box 17, Folder 5. Clark was an official at the We Shall Overcome Foundation at the Highlander Research and Education Center in New Market, Tennessee, which gave "The Great Black Music" a 500-dollar grant, apparently facilitated by IBW director Vincent Harding—though Harding's precise role is not entirely clear from his papers.
16. "Statement of Purpose," *Rhythm* 1.1 (1970): 1.
17. Author's interview with Ebon Dooley; author's interview with A. B. Spellman 2000; author's interview with A. B. Spellman, 2006.
18. "Statement of Purpose," p. 1.
19. Author's interview with Bill Strickland, November 6, 2002, Amherst, Massachusetts; Vincent Harding, "History of the Institute of the Black World," in *Education and Black Struggle: Notes from the Colonized World,* edited by the Institute of the Black World (Cambridge, MA: Harvard Educational Review, 1972), p. 145; Rachel Harding, "Biography, Democracy, and Spirit: An Interview with Vincent Harding" *Callaloo* 20.3 (Summer 1997): 691; Bill Strickland, "Critik: The Institute of the Black World (IBW), the Political Legacy of Martin Luther King, the Intellectual Struggle to Rethink America's Racial Meaning," in Green, Rubin, and Smethurst, eds., *Radicalism in the South,* pp. 168–170.
20. Grady-Willis, *Challenging U.S. Apartheid,* pp. 143–168; Vincent Harding, "History of the Institute of the Black World" pp. 146–147; Strickland, "Critik:" pp. 170–172; Rachel Harding, "Biography, Democracy, and Spirit," p. 691. For another short history of the inception and early days of the Institute of the Black World, see Stephen Ward, "'Scholarship in the Context of Struggle': Activist Intellectuals, the Institute of the Black World (IBW), and the Contours of the Black Power Radicalism" *Black Scholar* 31.3–4 (Fall–Winter 2001), 42–53.
21. Institute of the Black World, "Statement of Purpose and Program," in Abraham Chapman, ed., *New Black Voices: An Anthology of Contemporary Afro-American Literature* (New York: New American Library, 1972), p. 576.
22. *IBW: The First Year* (October 1, 1970), pp. 6–7, Vincent Harding Papers, Woodruff Library, Emory University, Box 21, Folder 10; *Celebration of Blackness* (program of the formal opening of IBW), Doris Derby Papers, Box 24.
23. Early, "Memory of Black Arts Spirits" pp. 29–30; letter from Hoyt Fuller to Vincent Harding, September 16, 1970, Vincent Harding Papers, Woodruff Library, Emory University, Box 14, Folder 6; letters from Haki Madhubuti to Sharon Bourke, February 12 and February 14, 1972, Vincent Harding Papers, Woodruff Library, Emory University, Box 15, Folder 5; letter from Sterling Plumpp to Vincent Harding, April 6, 1972, Vincent Harding Papers, Woodruff Library, Emory University, Box 15, Folder 7; letter from Kalamu ya Salaam to Vincent Harding, undated, Vincent Harding Papers, Woodruff Library, Emory University, Box 18, Folder.
24. Brochure for Black History Week at AU February, pp. 8–13, 1971, Vincent Harding Papers, Woodruff Library, Emory University, Box 53, Folder, 30; flyer for Afro-American Black Awareness Week at Georgia Tech February, pp. 18–24, 1973, Vincent Harding Papers, Woodruff Library, Emory University, Box 53, Folder 36.
25. Author's interview with Carlton Molette; Barbara Molette, "Atlanta." *Black World* 22.6 (April 1973), pp. 90–92.
26. Letter from John O'Neal to Vess Harper (of the Clark College Drama Department), February 21, 1964, Doris Derby Papers, Woodruff Library, Emory University, Box 2.
27. Author's interview with Carlton Molette.

28. "Executive Summary," Neighborhood Arts Center Archives, Auburn Avenue Library, Atlanta, Georgia, Box 1, Folder 1, 7.
29. Strickland, "Critik," pp. 176–177.
30. Author's interview with Ebon Dooley; "Executive Summary," Neighborhood Arts Center Archives, Box 1, Folder 1, 5.
31. "Tentative Programming for 1981–82," Neighborhood Arts Center Archives, Box 3, Folder 1.
32. Wendell Brock "NBAF Looks to 2000 and 'New Cadre of Artists," *Atlanta Constitution* (June 28, 1988): Arts, 11L; James Flannery, "A Black Arts Festival—And More," *New York Times* (July 31, 1998), Arts and Leisure 8, 30.
33. Catherine Fox, "Seeking an Artful Transition: Hammonds House at Crossroads as Gallery's Longtime Director Retires," *Atlanta Journal-Constitution* (August 4, 2002), Arts 1L; author's interview with Edward Spriggs, August 16, 2001, Atlanta, Georgia.
34. Author's interview with A. B. Spellman 2006; author's interview with Carlton Molette; Landon Thomas, "Saving the Black Arts Festival," *Atlanta Constitution* (August 15, 1992), A14; Tom Sabulis, "Exit of Theater Pioneer Jolts Jomandi, Community" *Atlanta Constitution* (January 5, 2001): Features 1E; Dan Hulbert, "Jomandi's JAM Black Theater's in Fight for its Life" *Atlanta Constitution* (November 13, 1994), Arts 1.

    For an example of the attack on Lomax by one of the tax revolt's leaders, see Mitch Skandalakis, "Lomax's Use of Tax Dollars to Fund Arts is Politically Motivated," *Atlanta Constitution* (April 15, 1993), A11.

    For the response of Lomax (who went on to become president of Dillard University and the head of the United Negro College Fund) to the revolt and his subsequent political defeat by Campbell, see Gary Pomerantz, "Lomax on Leaving Atlanta," *Atlanta Journal* (May 2, 1997), 02E.

9

Militant Katrina: Looking Back at Black Power

Kent B. Germany

In 1955, Louis Armstrong sang a sentimental song depicting Christmas in New Orleans as a dreamy time of praying barefoot choirs and sparkling midnight magnolias.[1] A few days before Christmas in 2007, cameras at New Orleans's city hall captured a different kind of yuletide. During the third holiday season since Hurricane Katrina, the city's centuries-old struggle over race, poverty, and exclusion erupted in plain view, producing one of the most troubling public moments since the storm. Upset over the planned demolition of approximately 3,500 units of public housing in a housing-starved city, dozens of protesters showed up to voice their outrage. Upstairs, the city council was set to vote to follow the wishes of the federal government and tear down four large public-housing developments that had been closed since Katrina. Apartments and town homes painted in pastels and spaced out to appeal to market-price renters would replace the half-century old brick buildings of Lafitte, St. Bernard, C. J. Peete (originally Magnolia), and B.W. Cooper (originally Calliope). Three of the complexes occupied over 100 hundred acres of downtown real estate and fired the imagination of developers and speculators familiar with HOPE VI projects, the initiative of the federal Department of Housing and Urban Development (HUD) to turn troubled public housing projects into mixed-income neighborhoods.[2] Over the past year, opponents formed the Coalition to Stop the Demolition, and activists linked to it were demanding that the city reverse course and allow residents to return to their former apartments.[3] On this final official day of autumn, a few public-housing activists were allowed into the council's chambers for the afternoon session, but space limitations kept most of them outdoors. Inside, anger toward this exclusion fueled a violent exchange as officers took aggressive measures to subdue several voluble protesters, all of them African American. Police and protestors tumbled across the floor as city council members, who happened to be part of the first majority white council in several decades, looked on in shock.[4] Many conservative online bloggers and commenters derided the protesters as "rent-a-rioters," "thugs," and "welfare queens."[5]

Outside, the scene was no better. At one point, industrious participants rocked open a locked gate, and protesters stepped toward the gap, clashing with the police. One protester screamed, "We gonna fight! We gonna fight!" The police responded in kind. After knocking down and subduing a middle-aged woman who walked with a cane, they regained control of the black metal gate and unleashed streams of liquid pepper and powerful electric tasers at the crowd of black and white activists. Sensing the seriousness of the situation, the police chief, Warren Riley, arrived quickly to suppress the officers, and he kept the incident from escalating. Before things were over, the police department arrested fifteen people.[6] Images from the day soon found their way to the digital world of YouTube, blogs, and emails. With one click, viewers could watch council members preside over the equivalent of a Jerry Springer talk-show-gone-wild or observe panicked police officers squirming, ironically, behind steel bars.[7] They could see protesters being put into ambulances or rolling on the ground, getting bottled water poured on their burning eyes.

These scenes revealed a city confused about its future and disturbed about its past. In addition to the frustrations surrounding the Katrina recovery, decades of distrust and suspicion had set the stage for this moment of bewilderment and rage. Attuned to issues of racial discrimination, class privilege, and political corruption, many of the protesters sensed that they were being had, that the deals had already been struck, that their voices were being left out once again. They formed a long line of such individuals in New Orleans's history, grassroots rebels with ambitious objectives and little power, except to take to the streets. The militancy of post-Katrina activism, however, pales in comparison to the last time New Orleans went through a major civic reconstruction—the era of the civil rights movement and Black Power in the 1960s and early 1970s. Set against that historical period, the grassroots reaction to Katrina has seemed relatively peaceful, tending to be defined more by litigation, logistical coordination, public relations management, and political lobbying than by direct action protest, civil disobedience, and public confrontation. With over one million volunteers donating over 14 million hours in the first two years after the storm, the overall response has been massive, but it has, for the most part, not been militant.[8] Advocacy for the various post-Katrina causes has generally not been aggressive, combative, or confrontational, but some organizations have been militant in action or outlook, and their origins lay as much in the late 1960s, early 1970s era of Black Power as it did from the hurricane.[9] This chapter is not intended as a survey of ongoing grassroots organizing, but an early attempt to draw parallels and distinctions between two key movements in the city's struggle for social justice.[10] In both periods, the responses to problems of race and poverty have been central to the evolution of the city's civic identity and to the question of what it means to be from New Orleans.

Thirty-eight years before the Christmas housing brawl, another group of New Orleans protesters riled another group of bureaucrats and police officers. In April 1969, several dozen mostly female public-housing activists physically took over the headquarters of the Housing Authority of New Orleans (HANO) and demanded that HANO lower its rents to match cuts in welfare (Aid to Families with Dependent Children or AFDC) payments, with at least one of them threatening to kill somebody. After a few hours, they left without any blood on the floor. Shortly after, the state legislature appropriated funds to offset the welfare cut.[11] Five months later in August, a group of low-income black women gathered in another building to collect groceries and clothing promised in a flier circulating in a housing project. These women found no food and no welcome. Upset, they eventually surged toward the building and smashed several windows. Some of them rushed up three flights of stairs looking for answers. Officials quickly repulsed them. A few were sent to jail, and the story disappeared.[12] Later that week black women ascended the steps of the Louisiana State Capitol, culminating a weeklong welfare rights march from New Orleans. This scene ended with less volatility but, perhaps, more reality. The governor decided it was not worth his time to show up, and the protesters returned home understanding that they had a long way to go to change the system.[13] In November, several of the same activists went to jail after a heated protest over rents charged for public housing.[14] Those incidents, however, illustrate the milder confrontations between grassroots activists and local and state authorities during this period. Several of those confrontations led to tragic violence.

One year earlier, in April 1968, New Orleans experienced several evenings of unrest following the assassination of the Reverend Dr. Martin Luther King, Jr. Almost two dozen fire-bombs were set off, and a small civil disorder emerged in the St. Bernard Housing Development, one of the projects later slated for demolition by the Christmas 2007 city council vote. The situation in St. Bernard, however, did not escalate into a large riot. Police officers cordoned off the project until they amassed a sizeable force, and then swooped in to crush any rebellion.[15] Two years later in May 1970, the Thugs United, Inc., a militant social uplift organization run by former gang members, called publicly for the killing of white police officers after witnessing an incident of police brutality. The episode created public relations troubles for the Thugs United and led to arson at one of their offices, but they still were able to secure grant funding from the federal government and fundraising assistance from the local white-controlled Chamber of Commerce. A showdown between police and Black Panthers occurred that September, this one including several shootings and beatings. The local chapter of the Black Panthers had taken up residence in the Desire neighborhood, home to the 12,000-resident Desire Housing Development, and the New Orleans Police Department (NOPD) decided to root them out. After two military-style invasions by the NOPD, two shootouts, and much negotiation, city officials quashed the Panthers' insurgence. Two years later, a few days after Christmas, Mark James Essex, a disturbed black Navy veteran, turned his rebellion into murder. Committed to an ultraviolent interpretation of black liberationist ideas, he went on a rampage that targeted whites and police officers. He killed nine people in one week and put New Orleans on the front page around the world. Some white leaders in New Orleans thought that Essex was firing the first shots in the long-anticipated race war.[16]

These episodes were part of a broad process of sorting out political power in the early years of post-Jim Crow Louisiana, and they represent important precedents that can inform the post-Katrina reconstruction. At the end of the 1960s, militant activists speeded the emergence of black political power and contributed to a new era in the city's long and complicated history of race. Partly by making it impossible to ignore inequality and injustice and partly by accelerating white flight, black-led militant organizations offered a challenge to the traditional roles played by African Americans, particularly black residents with low-incomes. Black voting strength was an outgrowth of this transformation and led to the election of a white racial liberal as mayor in 1970, the first black mayor in 1978, and a majority black city council in the 1980s, but it was only one part. The end of Jim Crow precipitated a scramble for power from the grassroots to the highest levels of local politics, as the city's residents and institutions adjusted to the new realities of black power. After Katrina, new realities had to be faced, and the old questions about the role of African Americans in local civic culture came roaring back.

In New Orleans's 1960s reconstruction, as elsewhere, local power did not stay at the grassroots. A number of groups emerged from the margins to become part of a new political establishment. Most of their members were not political radicals or black militants, and most preferred reform and access to power instead of revolution. They tended not to want to end capitalism but to make it work better for them. Led by college-educated professionals, these organizations wore the brands of their militant-sounding acronyms—Southern Organization for Unified Leadership (SOUL), Black Organization for Leadership Development (BOLD), and Community Organization for Urban Politics (COUP)—and built their machines from a meticulous mobilization of predominantly black neighborhoods. Benefiting from the proliferation of black neighborhood improvement associations and the widespread community organization efforts funded by the federal War on Poverty, the newest brokers of black political power established a durable model for managing black public influence for several decades. In the post-Voting Rights Act era, they created impressive get-out-the-vote efforts, patronage networks, and bureaucratic loyalties that leveraged access to the local and regional political table. Adept in the boardroom and the corner club, leaders of SOUL, BOLD, and COUP proved less ominous to many white leaders than their more militant counterparts, though at least initially their membership held some militants and their rhetoric often drew from Black Power thinking. They were capable of carrying on protest, but tended to do so in less public, and often more productive, settings. In contrast to militant entities such as the Black Panthers and the Thugs United, the leaders of these more mainstream organizations were less ideological, less abstract, less concerned about black solidarity, and more likely to compromise in the short-term to gain more power for themselves. Five years after the Civil Rights Act and the Voting Rights Act, these groups emerged as new incarnations of classic urban politicians, positioning themselves as liaisons to established politicians and officials in local, state, and federal government, while distributing the rewards associated with being well-fortified in the governing framework. Their ascendancy showed that the southern black challenge to white supremacy produced not a revolutionary critique of the local political economy but the incorporation of black leadership into the existing system.[17]

Unlike the more moderate and agile SOUL, BOLD, and COUP, most of the militant grassroots organizations in New Orleans did not survive the period intact. Typically, they were either crushed by law enforcement, crumbled internally from lack of bureaucratic support, or faded fitfully into near obscurity when their defining issues faded nationally. For example, the Thugs United, a collection of former convicts-turned-community-organizers, lasted barely four years, as did the Carrollton Central Steering Committee, a biracial group organized by the politically moderate League of Women Voters. The famous Black Panthers existed as a significant group for less than a year. One collective with a clearer focus, clearer targets, and fewer ideological demands, the New Orleans Welfare Rights Organization (NOWRO), had a longer run of over a half decade, but was eventually subsumed by a larger coalition. A cultural organization, the Free Southern Theater, began before all of them and kept going long after they were gone. This collection of free-spirited activist playwrights and performers were a vanguard of the Black Arts Movement and mixed their art and politics in some of New Orleans's grittiest neighborhoods. Throughout the period, their productions and their newspaper, *The Plain Truth*, served as the most consistent, identifiable voice for Black Power and militant reconstruction of local civic culture, helping spark the vigorous alternative newspaper scene of the early 1970s. Despite having little identifiable electoral power, the Free Southern Theater helped keep New Orleans's black neighborhoods saturated with a more sophisticated intellectual understanding of black nationalism.[18] Grassroots activists in these groups and in many others tried to carve out enough influence to force the state to respond to problems in the so-called ghetto and improve the options for its residents to make a better living. And in a theme that cut across all of the militant groups, they pressed relentlessly for individuals to be better able to stand on their own and be fully functioning, contributing, responsible, proud, self-aware citizens.

Each of these organizations was led by local activists who were able to tap into national organizations or trends. The Panthers and NOWRO were explicitly linked to their respective national umbrella organizations, although those larger organizations had little money and could provide only partial bureaucratic assistance to affiliate groups. The Thugs United developed ties with a loose national confederation of similar groups, receiving little more than moral support and information in the process. The Carrollton Central Steering Committee was a side project of the national League of Women Voters funded by the Ford Foundation. It brought together middle-class, mostly white, women with black activists from an area of the city left out of the War on Poverty organizing framework. Together with the Catholic Church and Xavier University, the Carrollton Committee put together programs for healthcare, childcare, early childhood education, and voter registration, while also publishing a militant community newspaper, the *Carrollton Advocate*. The Committee collapsed when one of its politically ambitious black male leaders decided he could no longer work with white activists.[19] The locals with the longest-lasting success, SOUL, BOLD, and

COUP, came away with the best blend of local and national connections—being able to use local political power to secure influence over the distribution of federal and state funding. The Thugs United, the Black Panthers, and the women of NOWRO took different routes.

The men who formed the Thugs United, Inc. are some of the least-known activists in New Orleans's history, which is surprising since they were exquisitely talented in the art of self-definition, if not self-promotion. They were gang members and convicted criminals—and proud of it—carrying around the psychological wounds from a life of crime and flaunting physical scars as relics of political authenticity. Though battered by their previous lives, they wanted everyone to know that they were still men, but had become wise men who wanted to pass on valuable lessons. To newspaper reporters, to leaders of the Chamber of Commerce, to officials at the wealthy and almost exclusively white Tulane University, they presented themselves unapologetically as the toughest of thugs and sold their knowledge of the streets as one of their greatest strengths.[20] Like other grassroots groups at the time, they operated in public/private terrain occupied by governmental bureaucrats, nonprofit organizations, and elected officials, what I have previously called the "soft state."[21] For the city's white civic and business leadership, they offered an authoritative link to black neighborhoods during the hot summers of the late 1960s.

The Thugs United leader was a teenager named Warren Carmouche, a burly, ambitious janitor and War on Poverty organizer who proudly claimed to have been a pimp for his mother when he was growing up. Carmouche developed the idea for the group in 1966 while working in the Algiers-Fischer Housing Development, a sprawling tract of low-rise apartments and a high-rise building across the Mississippi River from downtown New Orleans. After an epiphany inspired by his high school principal, Carmouche gathered young men from the neighborhood together to try to reduce violence, create solidarity, and chart paths to better education. By 1968, the idea had become the Thugs United, Inc., one of dozens of urban, gang-related organizations in the United States that sought federal funding during the War on Poverty, the most famous of which were Chicago's Vice Lords and Blackstone Rangers. Over the next year, the Thugs United expanded to three locations and included at least several hundred members.[22]

In addition to its role as a liaison between ghetto residents and civic leaders, the Thugs United served several functions. One was community uplift, partly through traditional social service relief work but primarily through administering educational programs tailored to the needs of low-income blacks and former prisoners. Another was carrying out an informal version of community policing. This included pressuring narcotics dealers to stay away from children, keeping an eye on the NOPD, and publicizing problems in the neighborhoods. Using a deeply masculine language of self-worth and personal responsibility, Carmouche tried to construct a community consciousness that could become the basis for political and economic action. That consciousness was rooted in black nationalism and black capitalism, and at least intellectually, black separatism. The impulse to embrace Black Power in spirit and rhetoric, however, conflicted with fiscal and political realities. Recognizing the need for white assistance, Carmouche and his lieutenants accepted help from a white law student at Tulane University, the white-dominated Chamber of Commerce, and the racially integrated Urban League, though never backing down from their muscular expressions of black identity and requiring that whites serve in subordinate roles.[23]

Through the help of the Urban League, they gained assistance from the Model Cities program and the Department of Health, Education, and Welfare to operate their education programs, while also operating a few small businesses. After much discussion and reluctance, the local Chamber of Commerce agreed to look past the Thugs' exhortations for black solidarity to help them raise money. This proved successful for one season, but the organization fell apart before much beneficial institutional memory could develop between the two entities. The Thugs soon collapsed amid accusations of financial impropriety, the arrests of several Thugs leaders, and the disappearance of Carmouche. An inconsistent administrative structure combined with weak finances and grand dreams could not keep the Thugs in operation beyond 1972, although Carmouche later reappeared in his Algiers neighborhood and continued a career in community organizing until an early death from heart problems at the age of forty-nine.[24]

The local tenure of the Black Panthers was even shorter than that of the Thugs United. The best-known militant activists in the United States were not around long enough in New Orleans to change calendars. The local branch of the Black Panthers was established in early 1970 and decimated by the end of the year. Huey Newton, Bobby Seale, and others attracted the national spotlight in California in 1966, and the Black Panther movement expanded for several years. By 1970, the Panthers were under debilitating pressure from law enforcement, including the FBI, and this atmosphere hamstrung the Panther's development in New Orleans. Locally, the Panthers had some reason to be optimistic that they would fare better than their comrades in Oakland, Chicago, and other cities. Maurice E. "Moon" Landrieu had been elected on a racially liberal platform with over 90 percent of the vote from the black community, and his chief of police was a professional who reached out to black leaders. The city was also home to a small, but growing, network of anti-imperial New Leftists and radicals disappointed with American capitalism and foreign policy, including an entrenched cadre of organizers with ties to the Southern Conference Education Fund (SCEF), the Student Non-Violent Coordinating Committee (SNCC), the Congress of Racial Equality (CORE), and to the American Friends Service Committee. Additionally, a militant mood was catching on in black neighborhoods as many residents were articulating concerns about police brutality and economic exploitation. Nevertheless, events proved that New Orleans was not ready for the Panthers.

The local Black Panthers consisted primarily of young, neighborhood activists with some links to the national organization. In New Orleans, they began in a Mississippi River neighborhood known as the Irish Channel, setting up office in a building owned by a white judge near the St. Thomas Housing Development (a formerly all-white project rapidly becoming an all-black complex). That judge, Bernhard "Ben" Bagert, soon initiated eviction proceedings, and the Panthers relocated to the Desire neighborhood in the city's sprawling Ninth Ward. In

Desire, they flourished. From a white frame house on Piety Street, Panthers engaged in community organizing activities and launched their signature free-breakfast program. Like other existing community organizations, the Black Panther Party highlighted police brutality, criticized capitalist inequality, and provided residents with Afrocentric visions of history and culture.[25] They did so, however, while calling for a Marxist revolution. Although their ten-point plan did not go as far as the Republic of New Africa in calling for the seizure of private lands to create a new black nation in the New South, it did set up the local Panthers as enemies of the state. When police intelligence reports (some of them from undercover officers) suggested that the Panthers were stockpiling weapons and sandbagging their offices, all while allegedly intimidating local merchants, city hall became alarmed.[26]

In mid-September, the Panthers discovered two undercover officers in their midst, Melvin Howard and Israel Fields. The Panthers held an impromptu trial and then let a mob from the local community administer justice. The two young officers escaped their beatings and fled, Howard over a fence and Fields to a small grocery. The next day, the NOPD responded with an assault force of over 100 officers with helicopter support. After an almost 30-minute shootout, the Panthers surrendered. Fourteen of them went to jail, with bail set by their former landlord Ben Bagert. That night, another shootout occurred at the grocery to which Israel Fields had gone. It led to the death of twenty-one-year old Kenneth Borden, the son of a man who, before the shooting, had been assigned as a special officer with the NOPD.[27]

Undeterred, the remaining Panthers moved into a vacant apartment in the Desire Housing Development, where they resumed organizing for another two months. After attempts to remove the Panthers failed, city hall decided in late November to send in another assault force. This time, hundreds of residents from Desire put their bodies in the way of approximately 200 helmeted officers and their urban tank nicknamed Bertha. The stalemate lasted throughout the day. When twilight came, the police left, and the community reportedly celebrated a brief victory. Tensions continued for several days. Tired of the impasse, city leaders once again took bold measures. In one, they arrested 25 militant activists on Interstate 10, traveling in cars reportedly rented by the actress Jane Fonda who had been in town giving a speech. In another, an officer dressed up as a Catholic priest and knocked on the Panthers' apartment claiming to have a donation. When the door opened, he and several other officers burst in firing, wounding a woman and taking the occupants in to custody. The tactic created an outcry among progressives, but it did effectively end the Panther's existence as a robust, functioning organization. Many of the individuals arrested during this span, though, had their day in court a year later. With support from War on Poverty-funded attorneys and others, they were declared not guilty in a trial overseen by New Orleans's first black judge in recent history, Israel Augustine.[28]

The NOWRO (and its sister organization the New Orleans Tenants Organization) proved more successful. In 1967, about the same time that the Thugs United developed from the Algiers-Fischer Housing Development, a group of mostly female activists from Algiers-Fischer and other housing developments formed what became NOWRO. Led by Clementine Brumfield, Monica Hunter, Shirley Lampton, and other mothers living in public housing, NOWRO used a combination of public protest, litigation, and community organizing to fight against cuts in AFDC payments made by the state of Louisiana. Most active from 1968 to 1971, NOWRO received assistance from the National Welfare Rights Organization, other regional tenant's rights organizations, and perhaps most important, local War on Poverty-funded attorneys. In that three-year span, NOWRO fought at least five major reductions in AFDC payments and had partial victories in four of them. Perhaps their most notable contribution came from their participation in the coalition that secured a Food Stamp program for New Orleans in 1969.[29] Throughout these battles, NOWRO displayed tendencies different from the Thugs United and the Panthers. Far from being ideological crusaders wanting to remake attitudes and identities, they were pragmatists who tended to stay on the defensive more than the offensive. NOWRO activists did more reacting to governmental officials than leading masses of individuals in a movement to force those officials to work proactively on their behalf. Instead of focusing on lofty, abstract objectives or fundamental reform goals, organizers wanted to lower the rent and to get better support from a state bureaucracy. If they tried to redefine anything, it was how low the state could go in setting minimum standards of living.[30]

NOWRO received relatively wide coverage in the local press, but they enjoyed little popular support.[31] NOWRO is significant historically because a motivated group of black women openly challenged a social policy system built by segregationists that continued to be administered by segregationists intent on maintaining as much segregation as possible. NOWRO was militant in tone, but in retrospect, their efforts seem almost traditional, fulfilling the role of a neighborhood improvement association tangling with local bureaucrats over procedures and technicalities of law. Although not welcomed openly by most local bureaucrats and politicians, NOWRO was apparently not targeted by law enforcement as extensively as other grassroots groups. This was partly because the group focused on public housing and public welfare bureaucracies instead of the police department. Although NOWRO occasionally threatened violence and engaged in minor acts of civil disorder, they did not accumulate guns or advocate a turn toward Communism. Another major reason was that NOWRO was led by mothers, not bold young black men with sunglasses and Afro hairstyles, which made aggressive policing a far less attractive option. And these grassroots women had good lawyers and a national organization capable of mobilizing pressure in Washington, D.C.

The major contribution of the Thugs United, the Black Panthers, the welfare rights activists, and other militant organizers was not their long-term institutional imprint. Their deeper legacy rests in shaping the civic and commercial identity of post-segregation New Orleans.[32] For almost 300 years, locals have engaged in a persistent process of struggle and invention to determine whose vision would rise to prominence. In the era of Black Power, the Thugs, the Panthers, and welfare activists asserted unapologetically that black residents had not only a right to equal citizenship, but also that they were central to New Orleans's culture and its history. Their demands for recognition and power helped ensure that multi-cultural tolerance became part of New Orleans's desired civic image after Jim Crow. The world-renowned Jazz & Heritage Festival (which began in 1970), the increased popularity of Mardi Gras, the revival of the French Quarter, the almost weekly national conventions, the rise of celebrity chefs, and other engines of the post-Jim Crow tourist economy emerged from cultural battles over race and individualism and civic pride at least three decades before Katrina.[33]

Katrina and Post Black Power Politics

After Katrina, that civic identity has once again been up for grabs. The central question began as "Why should we save New Orleans?" and quickly evolved to "How should we rebuild New Orleans?" Architects and urban planners and ecologists set out bold visions for land use and for a "green" city, while educators sought silver linings by seeking reform of one of the worst school systems in the United States. Others were grimmer in their answers. In one of the starkest statements, James Reiss, one of the city's wealthiest white business and civic leaders, hoped that New Orleans would be rebuilt "in a completely different way: demographically, geographically and politically.... The way we've been living is not going to happen again, or we're out."[34] Richard Baker, a Republican congressman from Louisiana, divulged a belief that Katrina had "finally cleaned up public housing," something that the government could not do, but "God did."[35] Denny Hastert, speaker of the U.S. House of Representatives, suggested, "a lot of that place could be bulldozed."[36]

In contrast, Mayor C. Ray Nagin, a cable television executive and Republican supporter who was only the fourth African American mayor in New Orleans's 290-year history, flirted with Black Power rhetoric for a moment, temporarily aligning himself away from some of his powerful white business supporters by using a metaphor popular in the 1970s. In January 2006, Nagin ran for reelection in a city that had gone from being 67 percent African American before Katrina to approximately 47 percent four months later.[37] In a speech honoring Martin Luther King, Jr. on his birthday, he declared that New Orleans *would* remain a majority black city; it would "be chocolate at the end of the day."[38] The reaction was incendiary, and at least for local politics, his "Chocolate City" comments caused many whites to see him as a radical and "racist." T-shirts and satirical online parodies turned him into a Creole Willy Wonka of the twenty-first century.[39] Nagin's injecting the issue of racial solidarity into the battle over the city's identity, whether intended or not, helped him emerge from a crowded field in the primary and then squeeze out a victory in the runoff over Mitch Landrieu, the white lieutenant governor who held more liberal credentials than the corporate-oriented Nagin and benefited from being the son of Moon Landrieu, the legendary racial liberal and last white mayor of the city. It is too early to tell if that mayoral race will end up being a defining battle for the direction of the city after Katrina—or in modern market language, the "brand" of the city—but it did highlight the peculiar power of racial identity in one of the oldest metropolises in the United States.[40] Hurricane Katrina had done more than flood 80 percent of New Orleans, it gave the once-favored candidate of white New Orleans business leaders a curious opportunity to invoke the rhetoric of Black Power and racial solidarity, then reap what he had sown.

The most popular public commentary after the hurricane, however, reflected the post-civil rights ethos of inclusion. Countless voices on the airwaves spoke nostalgically about the city's historic combining of cultures and influences from around the globe, typically expressing melancholy about all the jazz and gumbo that the world stood to lose if it lost New Orleans. In fact, the New Orleans Public Library's post-Katrina recovery plan called for the creation of branch locations celebrating food and jazz to "aggressively and adamantly depict what New Orleans is about."[41] In the years before the storm, this civic interpretation was resonant because it sold well and captured what many people have wanted the city's identity to reflect—that it is an authentic place where everybody is welcome and where the good times roll well past 2:00 a.m. That vision, however, is contrary to what seems to be another recurring theme in local history—that political power in New Orleans has been organized historically around what to keep out and how to manage the dangers posed by what was let in.

For the city's civic culture, race and poverty have been like water, things to bottle up and wall off and hope for the best. Slavery and then Jim Crow dictated those processes and set up the long-term dilemmas of civic power that were still being worked out when Hurricane Katrina collapsed the levees. From this perspective, New Orleans's celebrated culture seems to come less from the rolling good times than the permanent values debate that flares into open warfare every few generations. In that sense, the political and civic identity of New Orleans before Katrina was forged as much from black-led challenges to long-held notions of white privilege and white supremacy as it was from the mythic mixing of diverse cultures. The militancy of the 1960s and 1970s was part of an old local tradition of African American and Afro-Creole protest and resistance.[42] After the Civil War, black activism produced one of the most progressive Reconstruction efforts in the South, including integrated public schools. In the 1890s, local activists led the fight against legalized segregation represented by the ultimately unsuccessful litigation of *Plessy v. Ferguson.* That setback was devastating, but it did not deter a number of locals from creating one of the most active branches of the National Association for the Advancement of Colored People (NAACP) in the early twentieth century or from administering one of the most important labor unions for black workers in the United States, the local International Longshoreman's Union. Those efforts made possible the post-World War II freedom movement and the bold expressions of Black Power. In August 2005, Hurricane Katrina created the conditions for another movement in this long narrative of race, class, and water.

Militant Katrina

In the aftermath of Hurricane Katrina, New Orleans experienced a level of grassroots activity unseen since the Black Power era. The enormity of Katrina's destruction, the extensive media coverage of the desperation, and the widespread sense of governmental failure set the context for the establishment of new local organizations and the transformation of many existing ones. Association of Community Organizations for Reform Now (ACORN), the Industrial Area Foundation's Jeremiah Project, neighborhood associations, and a variety of religious organizations focused on local people to chart out solutions to seemingly endless problems.[43] Local universities joined in, particularly, the Loyola University Law Clinic, headed by one-time mayoral candidate Bill Quigley. Out of necessity, new organizations sprang up. Some of the most productive ones were led by affluent local women. Women of the Storm pushed for systemic reforms and lobbied for hurricane recovery funds in Congress and the highest echelons of local and national politics. Marshaling resources through their positions of privilege, they proved brilliant at using public relations to bring political pressure, going to Washington, D.C., to hand-deliver invitations to Congress to come down to Louisiana for a tour of the devastation. Over fifty senators and 120 representatives took them up on the offer, and as historian Pamela Tyler suggests, their visits helped build support for an additional appropriation of $4.2 billion for the recovery. Citizens for 1 Greater New Orleans led the fight to reform the almost sacrosanct local system for overseeing the levees, one of the most dramatic changes to come from Katrina. The Katrina Krewe targeted the mounds of garbage that went uncollected after the storm, attracting national attention and thousands of volunteers.[44] Each of these groups acted with a level of militancy, but it is a stretch to call them militants in the way one would think about the 1960s-era forbearers.

So far, no equivalents to the Thugs United or the Black Panthers have emerged from Katrina, but at least two organizations have come close, both in spirit and in leadership. The Common Ground Collective and the People's Hurricane Relief Fund and Oversight Coalition (PHRF or People's Fund) developed in the immediate aftermath of Katrina to address the material needs of residents who seemed to be forgotten by the Red Cross and/or the Federal Emergency Management Agency (FEMA). In both cases, the groups' links to the region's militant past were more than a product of historical imagining. It was literally an outgrowth of 1960s radicalism. Common Ground's co-founder, Malik Rahim (formerly known as Donald Guyton, Sr.), was a former New Orleans Panther involved in the confrontations with the NOPD in 1970.[45] The People's Fund was co-founded by Curtis Muhammad (formerly known as Curtis Hayes), a civil rights activist who had been a key organizer for the SNCC in the 1960s and a longtime community activist.

In 2005, Rahim was living in the Algiers section of New Orleans, a place where he had grown up almost forty years earlier. For the past decade or so, he had become a local political figure with the Green Party and had kept up a campaign seeking the release of the "Angola 3," three Black Panthers who had been incarcerated in solitary confinement at Louisiana's Angola State Prison since the early 1970s. Rahim survived Hurricane Katrina and witnessed the desperation of the weeks after it. Upset by the lack of basic care for survivors in the Algiers area, he, his partner Sharon Johnson, and Scott Crow, an anarchist activist from Austin,

Texas, who had been involved in the Angola 3 campaign, pooled together $50 and formed what became Common Ground. Joining them was another Austin anarchist, Brandon Darby. A few days later with the help of volunteers making their way into the city, this collective began providing aid and primary health care. Based on past organizing experience, including Rahim's involvement with the free breakfast program of the Black Panthers, they established a kitchen to provide meals. The group soon grew, as its anti-authoritarian spirit and good-Samaritan agenda attracted a wide range of activists. Common Ground's most prominent contribution was its free medical clinic, which became the focus of numerous stories in the media, helping to feed interest in the group and to make the organization a magnet for thousands of volunteers which served almost 50,000 people in the first four months after Katrina.[46]

Soon after the storm, Common Ground became a kind of humanitarian relief and recovery general store. In addition to feeding and doctoring people in some of New Orleans's most devastated areas, it became a hub for wireless communications and computing, for home gutting and cleanup, for housing opportunities, for fixing bicycles, for dispensing legal advice, for cleaning up toxic soil, and for carrying out dozens of other relief activities.[47] Its success was celebrated in the media, and perhaps unexpectedly even among conservatives who looked past the dreadlocks, body art, and alternative lifestyles of many Common Grounders to admire their success when government failed or to point out these radicals' acceptance of the concept of private property.[48] Although the decentralized, free-flowing nature of Common Ground was one of its greatest strengths, it also has kept it from maintaining its cohesion. The original organization has split into several different entities, the Common Ground Health Clinic, the RUBARB Bike Project, and Common Ground Relief.[49]

From its inception, members of Common Ground were unapologetic for their political viewpoints, reflected in its slogan "Solidarity Not Charity" and its icon, a Black Poweresque fist clenching a hammer. Nevertheless, they did not promote their organization as one with political ambitions. Its training manual for volunteers stated unequivocally that Common Ground was a relief organization whose members were "in it for the long haul" and were not attempting "to assume leadership or decision-making power." This narrow definition of politics, however, obscures the broader objectives of a group that clearly sought a shift in local power, whether by pressing for economic development, ecological sustainability, or reforms of housing rules or law enforcement. At one level, all relief work after Katrina had some part to play in the reconstruction of power at the street level, and by consequence, at other levels. Common Ground may have been a relief organization, but it was one equipped with the language and historical outlook to inject a level of militancy and confrontation into that relief. They let potential volunteers know that they were committed to "the front line work of clean up" and of "relief," but were also equally dedicated to defending "against police harassment and evictions and what we see is the largest gentrification project in US history." Embodying the spirit of civil rights and antipoverty activists from the 1960s, they demanded that Common Ground volunteers put local people first. To be in "true solidarity," volunteers had to "listen to their voices, respond to their needs, and defer to their wishes." To help volunteers orient themselves to the complicated world of New Orleans, Common Ground provided instruction on Louisiana's racial history, explaining that "not all blacks were slaves, not all whites were in the Klan, but regardless of race, all people have had to deal with white supremacy, racial and class violence, and economic and political empowerment."[50]

Curtis Muhammad, the co-founder of the PHRF or People's Fund, developed a relief organization with far more direct political purposes. Drawing heavily from being an organizer for over forty-five years, Muhammad mobilized several other activists who had been part of a small, preexisting group, the Community Labor United (CLU). On September 8, 2005, about the same time as Common Ground, Muhammad and the CLU established the People's Fund as an organization dedicated to providing relief and making it easier for evacuated residents to return. They were determined to have the post-Katrina recovery be led by "poor, working class black people" impacted most by the storm. Committed to bottom-up organizing techniques, the PHRF drew heavily from the civil rights movement of the 1960s, particularly SNCC. As such, all of its activities were intended to build power locally.[51] In addition to the guiding vision of Muhammad, the People's Fund grew out of grassroots efforts of people who remained in New Orleans after Katrina. One of them, Diane French Cole, better known as "Mama D," served as a one-woman force from her home in New Orleans's Seventh Ward, gathering and distributing supplies while pleading to the outside world for assistance for poor black residents.[52]

Reflecting the militant activism of the 1960s, the People's Fund in its early days took bold steps. A few weeks after Katrina, on September 22, 2005, Muhammad and Common Ground's Malik Rahim left New Orleans to participate in an anti-war rally in Washington, D.C., linking the oppressive conditions in New Orleans to U.S. policies overseas. Then, in another nod to the 1960s, Muhammad and others with the PHRF headed to Penn Center, the famous civil rights movement gathering place on St. Helena Island, South Carolina.[53] The highlight of the PHRF's early activities was its National State of Emergency Conference on December 8–9 in Jackson, Mississippi. This event brought together 450 New Orleanians spread across the country (although a core in PHRF thought the event was dominated too heavily by national organizations instead of voices from the grassroots).[54] The PHRF articulated several objectives at the conference. One of the goals was to create plans for "black people to fortify themselves" against future calamities and to "link today's demands for reparations and self-determination to the historical and future struggle of black people and other oppressed populations." Most important, they wanted to "rescue" black people and other "oppressed people" from "their dependency on racist and incompetent governments." They demanded the "right to return . . . with dignity and without poverty," reparations for losses suffered "before, during and after Katrina," and the prosecution of government officials for "crimes against humanity" surrounding Katrina. At the conclusion of that meeting, People's Fund organizers returned to New Orleans to lead a march of approximately 1,500 to highlight continuing problems for the poor in New Orleans.[55] A month later, some of the members of the PHRF took an even more controversial step. Under a new PHRF affiliate known as the New Orleans Survivors Council, a small delegation went to lobby for help in Venezuela, the South American country ruled by the contentious Hugo Chavez. They returned with an agreement to bring leftist organizers to New Orleans to assist with recovery efforts.[56]

Partly because of its uncompromising posture, the People's Fund lasted only seven months. In April 2006, a dispute over the direction of the organization and a struggle to control its finances led its Interim Coordinating Committee to push out the New Orleans Survivor's Council, a more militant group who wanted to continue an active, grassroots organization controlled by the poor in the community. Curtis Muhammad joined this departing New Orleans Survivor's faction and helped create a separate organization known as the People's Organizing Committee, with the slogan "Nothing about us without us is for us."[57] This dispute was not insignificant because the organization had reportedly raised over $1 million through the web and through a speaking tour by Curtis Muhammad. After the dispute, Muhammad reflected that the words of his "comrades" had been "empty," that those allies were committed only to their "various organizations and their own egos." PHRF's efforts to "institutionalize bottom-up had led instead to a coalition of opportunists," and Muhammad was particularly upset about criticism he had received from the leadership of ACORN.[58]

On the second anniversary of the storm, a frustrated Curtis Muhammad announced his farewell to the progressive community. Writing at the same time that the splinter PHRF group, the People's Hurricane Fund, was holding its International Tribunal in New Orleans, he related how his experiences with the People's Fund movement had affirmed his beliefs about the ways that militant civil rights organizers had been marginalized in the 1960s and 1970s. "Our movement has been successfully divided into thousands of groupings, non-profits and NGOs," he lamented, "and the left has been rendered ineffectual. It is not an accident that, for forty years now, the movement has been so totally reformist, or that those who want to be revolutionaries are so isolated as to be irrelevant." His sense of "hopelessness" about progressive politics in the United States was so pervasive that he planned to abandon it to go organize internationally. Not leaving a forwarding address, he recommended that anyone seeking him should "look among the youth, the poor, and the struggling masses trapped in slave-like conditions throughout the world, for I am no longer available to an opportunistic and racist left. I NOW SEEK REFUGE AMONG THE POOR."[59]

One of the aspects of life after Katrina that had given hope to men like Muhammad and Rahim were the vast number of volunteers that streamed into and out of New Orleans. Common Ground and the People's Fund thrived from the spirit they brought, with Common Ground counting over 13,000 volunteers that passed through its system.[60] This supply of labor and energy gave militant organizations the opportunity to last longer because they could survive on less money and suffer fewer bureaucracy-building demands. Hurricane Katrina created such an epic outpouring of sympathy that George W. Bush made that sentiment a central part of his administration's recovery plan, hoping for "armies of compassion" to descend on the Gulf Coast.[61] Organizations at the local, national, and international levels were able to channel that spirit into one of the most intense volunteer efforts in recent U.S. history. Since late August 2005, hundreds of thousands of people have spent time in New Orleans helping to clean and rebuild, spawning a popular new phenomenon called "voluntourism." This interest has been inspiring, but as historian Lawrence Powell has asked, "Can the methods of a nineteenth-century barn raising drag a twenty-first-century disaster area from the mud and the muck?"[62] In addition to college students on break or people taking a civic-minded holiday, politicians, journalists, and filmmakers came to try to make sense of a city that had surrendered to the sea for almost a month. John Edwards, the Democratic vice presidential candidate from 2004, began and ended his unsuccessful bid for the 2008 Democratic presidential nomination from the Lower Ninth Ward. *This Old House,* the popular home improvement show on PBS, devoted a season to two homes in the area. The documentary film circuit bulged with mesmerizing stories of loss and outrage and resilience.

Thousands of others came to the city seeking their fortune, or at least in the hope of better work. From contractors to trash collectors to day laborers, individuals with mercenary intentions sought a piece of the Katrina marketplace created by public and private recovery spending. The most visible of them were Latinos who became key parts of the local workforce and led to a five-fold increase in Latino residents as a percentage of the local population.[63] They were at the bottom of the system, trying to coax wages from employers who almost always held the upper hand. At the other end of the spectrum, well-positioned corporations reaped sizeable benefits from the storm. For example, from September 2005 until June 2006, the federal government awarded $9.7 billion for a wide variety of recovery tasks such as housing, garbage collection, roof repair, and construction, almost all of it in contracts of over $500,000. According to the congressional Committee on Government Reform, 70 percent of those contracts were granted without "full and open competition," ostensibly because of the need to move quickly.[64] An analysis of some of those early awards by the *Washington Post* found that only 2.8 percent of the first $2 billion went to companies located in Louisiana, with 90 percent going to enterprises located outside Louisiana, Mississippi, and Alabama, the three states most directly affected by the hurricane.[65] One well-respected Louisiana corporation ended up doing quite well in the competition for Katrina funds. The Shaw Environmental Group of Baton Rouge took on a number of tasks including pumping out Katrina's waters after the storm.[66] Another more controversial series of contracts, though, involved approximately $1 billion to provide temporary housing. Shaw, like several other major companies with powerful state and federal political ties (including Bechtel National who received a $517-million housing contract), were beneficiaries of "cost plus fixed fee" arrangements that guaranteed them a profit for their hurricane work.[67]

This post-Katrina scenario was classic New Orleans history, a moment so full of confusion and contradiction and possible corruption and conspiracy that it is hard to imagine it occurring any other way. Hurricane Katrina had brought out the best and the worst in a place where the impulse for altruism and reform has always collided with the need for immediate action and the lure of economic opportunity. In that sense, the situation was not terribly different from the end of the 1960s, where militant activists were moved by the spirit of the times to try to change their neighborhoods and their government, while at the same time were being disconnected from the bureaucratic power and upper-level decision structures that would determine the political and economic future. Since the Katrina reconstruction is still unfolding, making comparisons between it and the reconstruction of the 1960s can only be tentative. Hurricane Katrina was an epic natural disaster, not a political movement emerging from local and national struggles over many decades. Katrina revealed problems with race and inequality, but it did not spring forward from those problems. In short, in September 2005, the storm created the activism; in the 1960s, the activism created the storm.

Despite these fundamental differences, the era of Black Power provides some general points to consider regarding grassroots activism and the Katrina reconstruction. First, political and business leaders should take very seriously the civic visions of marginalized citizens. In the 1960s and early 1970s, struggles over differing designs for the city's future fueled the most violent episodes of political conflict. Local residents generally did not put their lives on the line to reconstruct the city for some vague, easily digested corporate conception of New Orleans, but for *their* New Orleans, their neighborhood, and their sense of self and community. At the end of the 1960s, militant activists typically wanted more from their efforts than better governmental services and more responsive bureaucratic management. They wanted a new world with new institutions and new power for the masses. They did not get those things, but they did make it easier for others in better positions to get ahead.

Second, most of those activists disengaged from politics in the 1970s, leaving the sorting out of bureaucratic rewards to career professionals. This seems to have been happening again with Hurricane Katrina. The Katrina activists that have had the most impact are those who have established bureaucratic legitimacy and made politicians take notice. Militant neighborhood activists—and even those temporary citizens on "volun-tours"—must establish sustainability and must become more active parts of the political process, articulating grievances from the grassroots and lobbying for neighborhood-level control of recovery dollars. These activists have valuable experiences that should help define the direction of public policy. Although that political process lacks the virtue and clarity of volunteerism and activism, it is where the future lies, and most important, it is where influence over the billions of federal and state dollars lies. If activists on the ground do not inject themselves formally into advocacy for problems—as Malik Rahim did in his 2008 run for Congress under the Green Party—affecting the grassroots, then who will? In the later 1960s, too many civil rights and antipoverty activists chose to remove their voices from the public square and made it easier to erode the gains they helped achieve. In New Orleans in particular, committed militant activists practiced what they preached in their ideology, and their lifestyle served as a model for those who lived around them. Their overall influence, however, affected far fewer people than the efforts of the political brokers with the SOUL, BOLD, and COUP political organizations. Although leaders of those groups did surrender some of their ideological purity and some of them proved to be corrupt, they were able to package Black Power and black solidarity as a means to secure power instead of critiquing it. They became the distributors of the Black Power inheritance. Militants made white segregationists and businesspeople take notice, but the benefits of that attention went to black leaders who could turn it into bureaucratic and electoral influence. While New Orleans was certainly a racially divided city, power there could not easily be separated into white and black. In short, what mattered more than race and racial solidarity were contracts, recurring revenue, and reliable votes. Without them, even the most ideologically cohesive organizations faltered. At the end of the 1960s, economic growth and profit imperatives trumped Black Power and black solidarity. Grassroots militants did not get consistent funding or get people elected, and they became remnants of the post-Jim Crow reconstruction.

New Orleans has a long history of politicians who have chosen power over purity—surviving long enough to prolong their influence over governmental budgets and bureaucratic rewards. Mayor Ray Nagin is the latest manifestation. By effectively reconciling appeals for racial solidarity with an agenda of market-driven, pro-business economic development, he pulled off a surprising victory, yet another politician who used the spirit of Black Power to secure immediate power. Only time will tell which constituencies will keep his attention (not to mention the attention of those who succeed him) and what post-Katrina vision will define the future of New Orleans. Can the fragmented, decentralized, ad hoc grassroots efforts of the first three years after the storm make a fundamental, long-term contribution? How will they contribute to the market of the recovery?

Post-Katrina political activism came mostly from bad weather whose time had come. The storm encouraged over a million volunteers to engage in some form of activism, whether in advocacy for housing, environmental protection, levee improvement, public works funding, or manual labor. Despite the presence of volunteers from across the globe, the direct impact of that activism stretches mostly from New Orleans to Mobile, Alabama, and then back west to Houston, Texas. By necessity, post-Katrina activism has largely focused on filling in for inadequate governmental services, addressing a severe housing crisis, fighting crime, and rebuilding school systems, healthcare systems, and physical infrastructure. That activism—much of it by "outsiders," that category of people so feared during the civil rights movement—has been inspiring, but it has derived most of its energy from compassion rather than rights. It has not been a movement creating constitutional crises. So far, Katrina activism has largely not been about revising notions of individualism and the civic contract between self and society, but about the politics of reinforcing levees and keeping the lights on for another day. Grassroots groups without clear access to Congress or even to the city council—and without clear streams of revenue—will, like their predecessors from the 1960s, probably either disappear or remain on the margins, left to ponder the implications of another Christmas in New Orleans.

At the beginning of 2007, the future of militant activism for the poor looked about as dim as it had in the mid-1970s, except for the possibilities offered by the new world of online organizing and the continuing stream of volunteer labor. The local movement gaining the most attention was the effort to prevent the destruction of public housing units, but it seemed to be fading to a glimmer at best, partly because the reputation of public housing in the city had been so low for so long that not even a hurricane could generate much support for it. Stop the Demolition's broad coalition of public housing activists, public interest lawyers, and preservationists benefited from some of the work done by the PHRF, Common Ground, ACORN, the Loyola Law Clinic, and other entities to stop the city from bulldozing condemned private property. Their work regarding the public housing projects had some success in stalling the redevelopment of the projects, but time ran out. Soon after the Christmas 2007 incident at city hall, workers began dismantling the B.W. Cooper, C.J. Peete, and St. Bernard complexes. The Lafitte development's architecture gave it a brief reprieve, but a week after spring began in 2008, Mayor C. Ray Nagin ordered most of it to come down, readying this part of the so-called Chocolate City for its future as a pastel dreamscape.[68]

Notes

1. "Christmas in New Orleans," Lyrics by Richard Sherman and Joe Van Winkle, performance by Louis Armstrong and Benny Carter's Orchestra, Decca Records, 1955.
2. Examples of similar redevelopment include the complexes of Desire, Florida, Algiers-Fischer, and St. Thomas, the latter involving a condo developer, Wal-Mart, HUD, and the city government. Brod Bagert, Jr. "HOPE VI and St. Thomas: Smoke, Mirrors, and Urban Mercantilism," M.A. Thesis, London School of Economics, September 2002; James R. Elliot, Kevin Fox Gotham, and Melinda J. Milligan, "Framing the Urban: Struggles Over HOPE VI and New Urbanism in a Historic City," *City and Community* 3 (December 2004), pp. 373–394.
3. This group resembled a spring 1970 coalition, Building Our Better Uptown Area Committee (BOBUAC), that led marches and a petition drive that forced the construction of a new Mississippi River bridge out of an Uptown neighborhood and next to an existing bridge downtown. Oretha Haley, chairperson of BOBUAC, to New Orleans City Council, March 19, 1970, Folder Central City Housing Development Corporation, Box 3, Administrative Subject Files, City Demonstration Agency Collection, Louisiana Division, New Orleans Public Library [the Louisiana Division, New Orleans Public Library hereafter cited as NOPL]; "Here Come De' Bridge! 3,000 Blacks to Go!!" *The Plain Truth*, January 22, 1970, "Stop the Bridge," March 20, 1970, *The Plain Truth*; "The Bridge All Power to the People" *The Plain Truth*, May 1, 1970, in Political Ephemera Collection, Tulane University Libraries [hereafter cited as TUL].
4. Michael DeMocker, "Housing Debate Turns Violent in New Orleans," Nola.com, December 20, 2007, http://blog.nola.com/tpvideo/2007/12/housing_debate_turns_violent_i_1.html; "Photos: Housing Debate Heats Up," Nola.com, December 20, 2007, http://www.nola.com/news/index.ssf/2007/12/photo_council_debates_housing.html. These versions also appeared on Youtube.com, and as of mid-April 2008, one had been viewed over 34,000 times and another almost 20,000 times. See http://www.youtube.com/watch?v=5jvhp4iZFd0&feature=related and http://www.youtube.com/watch?v=0CYYPV8Nlek, respectively.
5. Michelle Malkin, "The 'Shut up, white boy!' woman is the 'slum' dweller with a 60-inch TV," [including message board comments], December 22, 2007, http://michellemalkin.com/2007/12/22/the-shut-up-white-boy-woman-is-the-slum-dweller-with-a-60-inch-tv/; article comments posted for http://blog.nola.com/tpvideo/2007/12/housing_debate_turns_violent_i_1.html and http://www.nola.com/news/index.ssf/2007/12/photo_council_debates_housing.html.

6. Cain Burdeau, "Battered N.O. OKs Razing Public Housing," Associated Press, December 20, 2007.

7. Jerry Springer lived in New Orleans while an undergraduate at Tulane University, graduating in 1965.

8. According to the Corporation for National and Community Services, the institution that oversees Americorps, over 1.1 million people volunteered for Katrina work in 2006 (550,000) and 2007 (600,000). Corporation for National and Community Services, "Number of Volunteers in Year 2 of Katrina Recovery Exceeds Historic 1st Year," http://www.nationalservice.gov/pdf/07_0820_katrina_volunteers_respond.pdf.

9. Borrowing from the broad dictionary definition of *militant*, this chapter views militant activism as organized action and protest that involves aggressive confrontation with established civic authorities, in this case closely identified with advocacy for racial and social justice.

10. One group of Katrina activists has identified 29 "grassroots racial justice organizations" engaged in post-Katrina organizing and/or civic activity. "A Katrina Reader: Readings by and for Anti-Racist Educators and Organizers," http://www.cwsworkshop.org/katrinareader/view/org_listing.

11. J. Gilbert Scheib to HANO Board, May 19, 1969, Folder HANO (2), Box 5, 1969, Mayor Victor Schiro Collection, NOPL.

12. "State Office Building Closed during Welfare Demonstration," *New Orleans States-Item*, August 9, 1969.

13. "Welfare Protest March Attracts Fewer than 100," *New Orleans States-Item*, August 5, 1969; Bill Niekirk, "Welfare March Halted at State Capitol Building," *New Orleans Times-Picayune*, August 12, 1969; *The Plain Truth*, August 20, 1969, PEC, TUL.

14. *The Plain Truth*, November 1, 1969; Shirley Lampton letter, December 18, 1969, Folder HANO, Unprocessed Box 22, CSC.

15. "Police Clear Housing Area: St. Bernard Project Is Quieted by Officers," *New Orleans Times-Picayune*, April 8, 1968; Robert Richardson, "Every Black Man Is My Brother," *New Orleans* 2 (June, 1968): 21+; David Snyder, "Police Ready—In Case: Militants Willing to Talk—Good Sign for Summer," *New Orleans States-Item*, June 14, 1968.

16. Kent B. Germany, *New Orleans After the Promises: Poverty, Citizenship, and the Search for the Great Society* (Athens, GA: University of Georgia Press, 2007), pp. 211–223, 275–285, 287–294.

17. On incorporation and its limits, see Adolf Reed, "Sources of Demobilization in New Black Political Regimes: Incorporation, Ideological Capitulation, and Radical Failure in the Post-Segregation Era," in *Stirrings in the Jug: Black Politics in the Post-Segregation Era* (Minneapolis, MN: University of Minnesota Press, 1999), pp. 117–161; Germany, *New Orleans after the Promises*, pp. 246–270.

18. In addition to Thomas C. Dent, Richard Schechner, and Gilbert Moses, (eds.), *The Free Southern Theater: A Documentary of the South's Radical Black Theater, with Journals, Letters, Poetry, Essays, and a Play Written by Those Who Built It* (Indianapolis: Bobbs-Merrill, 1969), some of the best primary documents on the Free Southern Theater are in the Free Southern Theater Collection at the Amistad Research Center in New Orleans and in runs of *The Plain Truth* in Tulane University's Political Ephemera Collection. See also Clarissa Myrick Harris, "Mirror of the Movement: The History of the Free Southern Theater as a Microcosm of the Civil Rights and Black Power Movements, 1963–1978," Ph.D. dissertation, Emory University, 1988; Ellen Louise Tripp, "Free Southern Theater: There Is Always a Message," Ph.D. dissertation, University of North Carolina at Greensboro, 1986.

19. CCSC, "Carrollton Central Steering Committee Work Program," n.d., Folder 43, Box 8, League of Women Voters Collection, TUL [hereafter LWV, TUL]; Betty Wisdom to LWVNO Board, March 1970, Folder 45, Box 8, LWV, TUL; "Background of the Carrollton Project," after July 1969, Folder 39, Box 8, LWV, TUL; Robert McFarland, "Gert Town Needs 'Community Control,'" *Carrollton Advocate,* April 29, 1970, Folder 48, Box 8, LWV, TUL.

20. Lucien Salvant, "'We Are Thugs'...Who Help People," *Clarion Herald,* May 8, 1969; Betsy Halstead, "Good-Guy Thugs," *Dixie Roto (New Orleans Times-Picayune),* June 15, 1969; Warren Carmouche to Sir, n.d., [1969], Folder Proposals, Box 5, City Demonstration Agency, NOPL; J. Lunsing, et al., "Thugs United, Inc." [unpublished typescript report], n.d., 1970, Folder Thugs United, 1970, Stanton Collection, University Archives, TUL.

21. Germany, *New Orleans after the Promises,* pp. 14–17, pp. 141–149.

22. Thugs United, *Progress,* 1969, Folder Thugs United, Stanton Collection, University Archives, TUL.

23. The Black Eye, "Thugs United the Answer to Our Problems," *Street Scene Community Newspaper,* February 1971.

24. Jack Davis, "Ripping Off the Poverty Program," *Figaro,* March 24, 1973; *Star and Crescent* (New Orleans), August 1973; Obituary, Warren Carmouche, *New Orleans Times-Picayune,* April 4, 1998.

25. Transcript, WTUL Interview with Malik Rahim and Ahmad Rahman, March 13, 2000, reprinted at http://minorjive.typepad.com/hungryblues/2005/09/malk_rahim_on_b.html.

26. Joseph I. Giarrusso, police superintendent, to Moon Landrieu, confidential memorandum, July 17, 1970, Black Panther File, Addendum, Human Relations Committee Collection, NOPL.

27. Transcript, September 15, 1970, Black Panther File, Addenda, Human Relations Committee Collection, NOPL; Transcript, Moon Landrieu and Joseph Giarrusso Press Conference, September 15, 1970, Human Relations Committee Collection, NOPL; "'We Have Never Used Our Guns to Go into the White Community to Shoot Up White People. We Only Defend Ourselves," *NOLA Express,* November 1970, Panthers Louisiana File, Political Ephemera Collection, TUL.

28. Barry Portman, to Members of the NOLAC Board of Directors, December 1, 1970, Folder 15, Box 2, John Nelson Collection, Amistad Research Center, New Orleans, Louisiana; Orissa Arend, "Aftermath of the Panthers in Desire," *The Louisiana Weekly,* June 16, 2003; Orissa Arend, "Trio Ignited Controlled Revolution in the '70s," *The Louisiana Weekly,* May 26, 2003; Roy Reed, "A Police-Panther Confrontation Ends Peacefully in New Orleans," *New York Times,* November 20, 1970; David Snyder, "La. Police, Militants Clash," *Washington Post,* November 20, 1970; Roy Reed, "Panthers Freed in New Orleans," *New York Times,* August 7, 1971.

29. Germany, *New Orleans after the Promises,* pp. 230–238.

30. Lampton to organizations concerned about public housing tenants, February 27, 1970, Folder 13, Box 21, FST, ARC; and Desire Welfare Rights Organization, "'To Gain These Rights,'" Folder Desire Area Community Council, Box 3, Administrative Subject Files, CDA.

31. This issue of popular support was a bit of a shift from a notorious episode involving welfare in 1960 when the local Urban League-led Operation Feed the Babies after the state of Louisiana used "suitable home" tests to purge 22,000 children from the welfare rolls. *Lampton, et al., v. Bonin,* et al., 299 F. Supp. 336, April 15, 1969; Lisa Levenstein, "From Innocent Children to Unwanted Migrants and Unwed Moms: Two Chapters in

the Public Discourse on Welfare in the United States, 1960–1961," *Journal of Women's History* 11 (Winter 2000): 10–33.

32. For a larger argument about laws promoting civic exclusion as organizing principles, see Rogers M. Smith, Civic Ideals: Conflicting Visions of Citizenship in U.S. History (New Haven, CT: Yale University Press, 1997), pp. 470–506.

33. The role of tourism in New Orleans history is the subject of a growing body of literature. See J. Mark Souther, *New Orleans on Parade: Tourism and the Transformation of New Orleans* (Baton Rouge, LA: Louisiana State University Press, 2006); Anthony Stanonis, *Creating the Big Easy: New Orleans and the Emergence of Modern Tourism* (Athens, GA: University of Georgia Press, 2006); Kevin Fox Gotham, *Authentic New Orleans: Tourism, Culture, and Race in the Big Easy* (New York: New York University Press, 2007).

34. James Reiss, as quoted in Christopher Cooper, "Old-Line Families Escape Worst of Flood And Plot the Future" *Wall Street Journal,* September 8, 2005.

35. *Wall Street Journal*, September 9, 2005.

36. "Hastert Questions Proposed Efforts to Rebuild," Associated Press report, September 1, 2005, http://www.msnbc.msn.com/id/9164727/.

37. Greater New Orleans Community Data Center, "Census Population Estimates 2000–2007 for New Orleans MSA," http://www.gnocdc.org/census_pop_estimates. html; Elizabeth Fussell, "Constructing New Orleans, Constructing Race: A Population History of New Orleans," *Journal of American History* 94 (December 2007), p. 854.

38. Manuel Roig-Franza, "New Orleans Mayor Apologizes for Remarks About God's Wrath," *Washington Post,* January 18, 2006, http://www.washingtonpost.com/wp-dyn/content/article/2006/01/17/AR2006011701353_pf.html

39. Arnold Hirsch, "Fade to Black: Hurricane Katrina and the Disappearance of Creole New Orleans," *Journal of American History* 94 (December 2007), pp. 752–761. Some examples of parody are http://willynaginfactory.ytmnd.com/.

40. Hirsch, "Fade to Black," pp. 752–761.

41. John Pope, "Branching Out," *New Orleans Times-Picayune*, March 18, 2008, http://www.nola.com/timespic/stories/index.ssf?/base/library-144/1205818224256570.xml&coll=1

42. Karyn Cossè Bell, *Revolution, Romanticism, and the Afro-Creole Protest Tradition in Louisiana, 1718–1868.* (Baton Rouge, LA: Louisiana State University Press, 1997).

43. Lawrence N. Powell, "What Does American History Tell Us about Katrina and Vice Versa?" *Journal of American History* 94 (December 2007), p. 872.

44. Pamela Tyler, "The Post-Katrina, Semiseparate World of Gender Politics," *Journal of American History* 94 (December 2007), pp. 780–788.

45. Transcript, WTUL Interview with Malik Rahim and Ahmad Rahman by Brice White, March 13, 2000.

46. After the Republican National Convention in 2008, Common Ground activists learned that Brandon Darby had been an FBI informant, although Darby claims that Common Ground was not a target of his government work, which focused primarily on protests of the Republican Convention. His story was the subject of an episode of the National Public Radio program *This American Life*. Common Ground Relief, *Common Ground Relief Volunteer Handbook*, January 2006, pp. 4–6; Orissa Arend, "Birth of the Common Ground Health Clinic," http://cghc.org/history.html; Billie Mizell, "Fifty Dollars and a Dream," AlterNet, March 2, 2006, http://www.alternet.org/katrina/32978/?page=entire. "Turncoat," *This American Life*, WBEZ Chicago, May 22, 2009, http://www.thisamericanlife.org/Radio_Episode.aspx?sched=1300; David Winkler-Schmit, "Brandon Darby- FBI Informant & Common Ground

co-founder," *Gambit Weekly* (New Orleans), January 26, 2009, http://bestofnewor-leans.com/gyrobase/Content?oid=oid%3A49882;

47. Bob Wing, "In Interview with Malik Rahim: Finding Common Ground in New Orleans," Counterpunch.org, May 25, 2006, http://www.counterpunch.org/wing05252006.html.

48. Emily Chamlee-Wright and Daniel Rothschild, "Government Dines on Katrina Leftovers: Eminent Domain Becomes a Potent Threat," *Wall Street Journal*, June 15, 2006, http://www.opinionjournal.com/cc/?id=110008518; Neille Ilel, "A Healthy Dose of Anarchy: After Katrina, Nontraditional, Decentralized Relief Steps in Where Big Government and Big Charity Failed," *Reason Magazine*, December 2006, http://www.reason.com/news/show/116789.

49. Orissa Arend, "Birth of the Common Ground Health Clinic.".

50. Common Ground Relief, p. 6–9, http://www.commongroundrelief.org/images/Volunteer_handbook_1-9-06.pdf.

51. People's Organizing Committee, "A Timeline of Organizing in New Orleans after Katrina," March 2007, http://www.peoplesorganizing.org/survivors.html#tono.

52. People's Hurricane Relief Fund and Reconstruction Project, "Media Alert," September 19, 2005, email from Becky Belcore in possession of the author; "Mama D and the Soul Patrol," vignette in *Falling Together in New Orleans*, DVD, directed by Farrah Hoffmire (2007; Charleston, SC: Organic Process Productions, 2007).

53. Community Labor United, "Group Demands Oversight of Recovery and Reconstruction," September 26, 2005, email from Becky Belcore in possession of the author.

54. People's Organizing Committee, "A Timeline of Organizing."

55. People's Hurricane Relief Fund and Oversight Coalition, Press Release for "From Outrage to Action!!!," November 29, 2005, email from Becky Belcore in possession of the author; Muhammad goodbye letter; PHRF, "Update: The People's Hurricane Relief Fund and Oversight Coalition (PHRF), From Outrage to Action: The People Must Decide" December 23, 2005, email from Becky Belcore in author's possession.

56. People's Organizing Committee, Press Releases, "New Orleans Survivor Council Turns to Venezuela for Support" and "An Emergency Appeal to the People of Venezuela from the New Orleans Survivor Council," March 2, 2006, email from Becky Belcore in author's possession.

57. The POC's web presence became www.peoplesorganizing.org instead of the PHRF's www.peopleshurricane.org. People's Organizing Committee, "The Work Continues! If We Don't Think It, It Ain't for Us," May 13, 2006, email from Becky Belcore, in possession of the author.

58. People's Organizing Committee, "A Timeline of Organizing"; Curtis Muhammad, "A Farewell Letter on the Second Anniversary of Katrina: A Message from an Organizer to the Left and Progressive Forces Inside the USA," August 28, 2005, email from Becky Belcore in possession of the author (also found at http://www.peoplesorganizing.org/breaking_news.html#nov; Wade Rathke, "41 Days in Exile: Kuala Lampur," http://chieforganizer.net/index.php?id=57&no_cache=1&tx_eeblog[sword]=curtis%20muhammad&tx_eeblog[showUid]=659; Curtis Muhammad, "Invitation to Face to Face Meeting," October 18, 2005, email to SNCC-List listserv, in possession of the author.

59. Curtis Muhammad, "A Farewell Letter on the Second Anniversary of Katrina: A Message from an Organizer to the Left and Progressive Forces Inside the USA," August 28, 2005, email from Becky Belcore in possession of the author (also found at http://www.peoplesorganizing.org/breaking_news.html#nov).

60. This figure was used by Rahim in his 2008 Green Party bid for Congress representing the 2nd congressional district. http://www.votemalik.com/.

61. "Address to the Nation on Hurricane Relief," September 15, 2005, *Public Papers of the President*, transcript by the American Presidency Project, www.presidency.ucsb. edu.

62. Lawrence N. Powell, "What Does American History Tell Us About Katrina and Vice Versa?" *Journal of American History* 94 (December 2007), p. 874.

63. Elizabeth Fussell, "Constructing New Orleans," pp. 846–855.

64. U.S. House of Representatives Committee on Government Reform—Minority Staff, Special Investigations Division, *Dollars Not Sense: Government Contracting under the Bush Administration*, June 2006, http://oversight.house.gov/ documents/20061211100757-98364.pdf.

65. Griff Witte, Renae Merle, and Derek Willis, "Gulf Firms Losing Cleanup Contracts: Most Money Going Outside Storm's Path," *Washington Post*, October 4, 2005.

66. "History: The Shaw Group," http://www.shawgrp.com/about/history.

67. For a breakdown of one of Shaw's contracts, an $816 million cost plus fixed fee, no competition contract from FEMA, see Contract ID: HSFEHQ05D0573 in the Center for Public Integrity's database, http://www.publicintegrity.org/katrina/ContractDetail.a spx?cid=HSFEHQ05D0573&agency=7022.

68. Kate Reckdahl, "Nagin OKs Demolition of Lafitte Housing Complex," *New Orleans Times-Picayune,* March 25, 2008.

10

The Pursuit of Audacious Power: Rebel Reformers and Neighborhood Politics in Baltimore, 1966–1968

Rhonda Y. Williams

On February 27, 1966, Rep. Adam Clayton Powell spoke at a Fourth District Democratic Organization's $15-a-plate fundraiser held in the ballroom of the Lord Baltimore Hotel. The black organization was a major political club in west Baltimore's predominantly black Fourth District. Alongside criticizing middle-class black people for being more concerned with cotillions, sipping martinis in suburban homes, and distancing themselves from their "deprived black brothers and sisters," the black New York congressman told the 1,000 attendees at the posh affair, "If there is one thing in which I believe, it is the pursuit of audacious power.... I would urge black people in America to pursue audacious power—the power to make decisions which control the affairs of your city and your state."[1] Dressed in a blue suit and chain-smoking, Powell continued, "All my life I have pursued audacious power...and it has upset many of my good white friends...you see, very few white people can accept us when we move out of our prisons of shoe-shuffling, head-bowed, Uncle Tomism."[2]

At another political event four months later in July, black grassroots activists descended upon Broadway and Gay streets in east Baltimore. There, at Knox Presbyterian Church, the Congress of Racial Equality (CORE) held its twenty-third annual conference—just one month after civil rights workers "marched along inhospitable Mississippi highways...chanting 'black power.'"[3] From July 1 through July 4, CORE conventioneers celebrated the achievements of "Freedom Now" and outlined its next objective—"black power" or "self-sufficiency and an end to dependence on the white community."[4]

At the east Baltimore church—as in the downtown Baltimore hotel and on the Mississippi highways—melding "black" and "power" together drew public attention and provoked debates.[5] Black freedom activists, politicians, and the media questioned CORE's change of policy specifically and the new direction of black liberation struggles broadly. In their coverage of the conference, local newspapers printed articles and editorials under headlines such as "Black Power Top Issue," "Black Power," and "C.O.R.E.'s New Policy"—presciently, but likely unknowingly, anticipating scholarly discussions about the definitions, cadences, manifestations, and effectiveness of the slogan.[6] An editorial in the *Baltimore Morning Sun* on July 6 suggested that black power "at heart seems simply to be a fresh dedication to a classical course followed by many other ethnic groups in this country in their rise upward from poverty."[7] On the same day, a *Baltimore Evening Sun* editorial that referred to black power and "defensive 'violence'" read:

> The fact remains . . . that the definitions are something less than clear and exact and the slogans are capable of being given different meanings in different contexts. In the long run the important thing will be how they are understood and how they are applied in specific circumstances.[8]

Clearly, black power in Baltimore, as throughout the country, evoked excitement, trepidation, uncertainty, and criticism from within and outside black activist circles and black communities.

The CORE conference set off another barrage of definitional questions and pragmatic concerns. "What is black power? What is non-non-violence? Whatever they are, are they good or bad?"[9] Was black power the organizing "of the poor, both black and white, so they can participate in the democratic process of this country," as maintained by Robert Curvin, a vice-president of CORE and Newark activist? Was it black government, which is "the only honest government that could come to power in the future," as held by George Raymond Jr., the director of Mississippi CORE? Was it the hiring of "black policemen, black landlords and black judges," as Jesse Gray, the Harlem rent strike leader, ventured? Could it incorporate the vision of a guaranteed annual income, as Richard Cloward, a professor of social work at Columbia University, tried to discuss with conference delegates, half of whom walked out before his speech began?[10] Did black power "mean 'self-determination by men of color in their own areas'"?[11] Was nonviolence in a violent society "unmanly"?[12]

This chapter explores how black power shaped neighborhood politics and activism in Baltimore from 1966 to 1968. In 1966 CORE not only held its national convention there, but in shifting its battle lines to black inner cities, CORE designated Baltimore its first "target."[13] This time period, from 1966 when Baltimore became a Target City to 1968 when that target erupted in riots after Martin Luther King Jr.'s assassination, were crucial years in the development of a multivocal black power politics that "inflected the political context in which people lived and organized."[14] Black power meant shoring up black manhood, advocating self-defense, seeking self-determination, exercising political power, attacking discrimination in education, employment, housing, and welfare, challenging entrenched white and black leaders, and mobilizing poor black people to transform society. Underneath black power's multiplicity of meanings, debates, formations, and alliances was an evocation of community—whether defined by race, gender, economics, geography, or ideology—that served as a basis for challenging unjust and unequal power relationships. Understanding these community struggles for power requires unveiling how the politics of place and the character of local politics have shaped cities, neighborhoods, and residents' lives.[15] Documenting which "Black Power" materialized when and to what end exposes how its multifaceted character emerged out of, as well as reflected, local people's creative responses to inequality and oppression.

Way Up-South

The northernmost border city below the Mason-Dixon Line, Baltimore became a staging ground, like many inner cities, for the competing politics of more militant black activists, white segregationists, municipal and state officials, and establishment civil rights leaders. But Baltimore, at least according to Herbert O. Edwards, was tame. "Baltimore's Negroes are less likely to resort to violence," claimed the executive secretary of the Maryland Interracial Commission, and in his view that is probably why national CORE chose Baltimore as its Target City.[16] Why did he think this? Edwards maintained that "compared with Chicago, New York, Cleveland and Los Angeles, there is probably more apathy among the Negro leadership [in Baltimore] and it goes down to the Negro masses."[17] "Fewer transients" and black middle-class aspirations in this southern border city known for its racial parochialism, Edwards argued, had moderated the potential for militancy and racial conflagrations. Although Baltimore's geographical location and political culture arguably may have thwarted fiery conflicts and physical melees similar to those occurring in other cities, Baltimore did experience its share of racial unrest well before exploding in April 1968.

The border city of Baltimore has had many nicknames, including the Charm City. However charming Baltimore might have been to some, when it came to race and community relations, charm did not quite fully capture Baltimore's character. Other descriptions convey the fraught politics of the place better— descriptions such as progressive *and* conservative, good *and* bad, schizophrenic, complicated, and a racist backwater. As early as the 1920s, the black poet Countee Cullen depicted Baltimore as a place where white children at very early ages were readily socialized in racist rhetoric and manners. In his poem entitled "Incident," Cullen wrote: "Once riding in old Baltimore,/ Heart-filled, head-filled with glee,/ I saw a Baltimorean/ Keep looking straight at me." The second verse continued: "Now I was eight and very small,/ And he was no whit bigger,/ And I smiled, but he poked out/ His tongue, and called me, 'Nigger.'"[18]

Baltimore's native son Thurgood Marshall, a U.S. solicitor general who became a U.S. Supreme Court justice, once described Baltimore as "Way-up South," meaning it was "decent and even occasionally progressive in many of the official forms of race relations in the last 20 years, but patrician and aloof in their substance."[19] Walter P. Carter, a Baltimore CORE activist who later became director of the community organization staff for Baltimore's Model Cities Agency in 1968, described the city as complicated. "It's not like New York. Here, you can have the Ku Klux Klan in full regalia on one corner and the same guy on another corner in a gray flannel suit. You have to get the feel of this town."[20] Credited by one biographer with insinuating Gandhian "nonviolence into the heart of the black freedom struggle," Bayard Rustin harbored a dislike for the complicated, way-up South, Charm City.[21] Carter continued, "Bayard Rustin used to say when he came here, 'Take me back to de bus station.' You got to be militant but you got to be smart. You got to operate on soul feeling. Your goal's got to be liberation, not integration."[22] When asked in April 1966 during CORE's announcement of Baltimore as its target city whether the city had the worst civil rights record, national CORE director Floyd B. McKissick responded, "If it's not the worst, it is very close to it."[23] Other national CORE members were not so diplomatic in their assessments; Baltimore was CORE's target, because the city was "a segregationist, racist backwater."[24]

In June 1966, *Baltimore Afro-American* columnist George W. Collins agreed—at least to a degree. Collins portrayed Baltimore and its political culture as schizophrenic, having a split personality, and clinging to the past and "unworkable customs" while on occasion "making an honest effort to address itself to the critical issue of the closing half of the 20th century."[25] This split personality naturally affected race relations. In his column entitled "Baltimore Civil Rights," Collins continued:

> While in some areas of the city attitudes toward such matters as equality of employment opportunity, public accommodations, equal education, fair housing, etc., are as modern as today's space exploits, in other areas these subjects trigger reactions comparable to those in the most backward areas of the Deep South.[26]

Collins explained how the white racially liberal Republican Mayor Theodore R. McKeldin "often found himself locked in a bitter struggle with the reactionary wing of the City Council, which is impowered [*sic*] to give life and essence to the mayor's government's philosophy in the area of human relations."[27] While recognizing the lasting problems, Collins argued, "No objective analysis of the triumphs and failures of civil rights in Baltimore can be attempted without the admission that progress has been made."[28]

From the 1930s through mid-1966, Baltimore's black civil rights organizations, such as the National Association for the Advancement of Colored People (NAACP), had pushed for equal teacher salaries, engaged in Don't Buy Where You Can't Work campaigns, targeted segregation in public accommodations, challenged restrictive covenants, fought for low-income black housing, and successfully fought to integrate the University of Maryland Law School. In 1942, 2,000 people marched to Annapolis to protest police brutality. In the early to mid-1950s, the NAACP also led campaigns that resulted in the integration, for instance, of municipal parks and swimming pools. In other words, local black civil rights leaders did have numerous successes in their efforts to legally dismantle Jim Crow. They secured jobs, access to public accommodations, as well as government appointments in the 1950s under then Governor (and in 1966 Mayor) McKeldin. Baltimore CORE activists also held antisegregation protests long before the idea of something called a Target City emerged; the Baltimore

CORE chapter formed in 1953. Between then and the early 1960s, local CORE activists challenged Jim Crow by participating in the early 1960s' Freedom Rides and desegregation efforts along Interstate Route 40.[29]

Undoubtedly and unsurprisingly, racial and economic oppression still existed after the demise of legal segregation and the achievement of civil and voting rights. While desegregation came to Baltimore's public schools officially in 1954, "freedom of choice" policies and residential segregation meant that a majority of students still attended all-white or all-black schools. Poor police relations, employment discrimination, and fair housing continued to be volatile issues in the Charm City. In fact, the city council's refusal to pass an open occupancy ordinance three times in two years provided CORE with a sound rationale for targeting Baltimore and ultimately holding its convention there to publicize ongoing segregation and inequalities.[30] Desiring to achieve economic and political power in black ghettoes and envisioning black power as a reckoning against entrenched white or black "power structures," more militant local and national CORE leaders joined together. In April 1966 Baltimore CORE chair James Griffin joined McKissick in New York City for the Target City announcement.[31]

However, other local black leaders, particularly those of more moderate civil rights organizations, seemed flustered by the Target City announcement. They should not have been. In January 1966, local CORE leaders, including Walter Carter and James Griffin, had publicly criticized established civil rights organizations as well as professional black people for their lack of financial support for the "public fight" CORE waged against inequality. Promising a new militancy, Baltimore CORE leaders charged the "colored middle class" with "trying to escape the reality of the rampant segregation" through "the illusory comforts of private success."[32] Despite this early criticism, however, established civil rights leaders disputed what they deemed national CORE leaders' dismissal of civil rights advances in Baltimore as well as "their disregard of 'protocol' in coming into Baltimore without contacting the established organizations."[33] For instance, Juanita Jackson Mitchell, president of the Maryland State Conference of the NAACP, maintained, "You know, you can be militant with humility. You can use a 'loving' nonviolence—and it doesn't mean you have to be an Uncle Tom."[34] In addition to "marked legislative progress," Mitchell argued that Baltimore "has had its history of militancy—and in days when it was most unpopular."[35] Eventually, local black civil rights leaders agreed to cooperate—or at least not interfere—with CORE's Target City efforts after attending a local "summit" in Baltimore weeks preceding CORE's national convention there. The Interdenominational Ministerial Alliance (IMA) proffered its support, as long as the alliance agreed with CORE's plans. An IMA leader, the Rev. Marion C. Bascom even maintained "if it means going to jail I stand ready to go to jail with them."[36] Ultimately, this cooperation, uneasy at times, provides an example of the concrete links between civil rights and black power politics and local efforts and national campaigns in Baltimore.

McKeldin, too, initially took umbrage at descriptions of Baltimore as a racist backwater with a woeful civil rights record, but he also made peace with the presence of CORE Target City organizers, though not the concept of black power. McKeldin told a *Baltimore Evening Sun* reporter in words that revealed hurt and a hint of paternalism, "I don't know why we should be the target...why we should be picked on. We've been battling for these things before these people were born. It's an unusual way to treat your friends."[37] McKeldin continued, "The situation's bad all over the country....We've done every possible thing. If anyone has fought harder for the interests of Negroes than I—I've been vilified because of my interest in them."[38] Despite being perturbed at the outset, McKeldin decided to work with CORE in his effort to prevent a long, hot summer of unrest. At CORE's July convention, where the call for black power gained strength, McKeldin gave the organization a $30 donation, the key to the city, the city and state flags, and a copy of his book *No Mean City*. While acknowledging the need to address black people's political exclusion as well as their disparate, often desperate, material conditions, McKeldin preferred a politics of moderation, negotiation, and amelioration that favored measured steps to achieve racial progress—definitely not militant or potentially incendiary confrontations. During these hot years, McKeldin aimed to manage potential racial crises, and in that vein, he expressed surety—or maybe it was closer to hope—that, if CORE activists and city officials worked together, they would not only "achieve some of the goals we have been working toward," but also keep Baltimore "the safest city in the United States this summer."[39]

Non-nonviolence and Riotous Behavior

The Target City announcement generated more media coverage about urban and racial inequality in Baltimore. Just as national CORE was shining its light on the city, Baltimore CORE's drives for open housing intensified—and so did white segregationists' counter-responses. In May 1966 the *Baltimore Afro-American* reported that "For the first time in recent history Klansmen and Klanswomen, in full regalia, came to town Sunday to counter-picket CORE."[40] For three Sundays, starting April 17, 1966, local CORE members demonstrated outside of Horizon House at Calvert and Chase streets to challenge the luxury apartment building's whites-only residential policy.[41] On Sunday, May 1, approximately twenty-five Ku Klux Klan (KKK) members, with German Shepherd dogs, yelled racial epithets at seventy CORE demonstrators and promised to return in greater numbers the next Sunday.[42]

Walter Brooks, the thirty-three-year-old Target City project director, vowed to "do our utmost to maintain order," arguing that "when actions are taken against civil rights people, we have been successful in maintaining our coolness with violent people."[43] Even so, Baltimore CORE director James Griffin "warned Mayor McKeldin of potential violence caused by the presence" of white segregationists and asked that the mayor's office assert pressure "so that regrettable incidents may be avoided."[44] Baltimore state attorney Charles E. Moylan Jr. and acting police commissioner Major General George M. Gelston promised to investigate whether having dogs and yelling epithets at rallies constituted incitement of rioting and violated existing statutes. Almost two weeks after that demonstration,

Baltimore Supreme Bench judge, Charles D. Harris, signed an injunction prohibiting CORE from picketing on weekdays. CORE and its supporters protested the injunction, while KKK spokesperson, Lahton C. Braun Sr., putting on his "red Klan hood with a green lining and blue tassle on the peak" in court, praised the injunction as "wise and just."[45] By the end of May, the picketing protests would result in McKeldin and Gelston calling a meeting at city hall with owners of nine luxury apartment buildings; that meeting led to an agreement by owners to rent to black tenants.[46]

In the same May 7 issue of the *Baltimore Afro-American* that reported on the escalating tensions at Horizon House, news articles documented two other incidents that similarly revealed the growth of black militancy, as well as attempts to navigate potential racial violence, in the border city of Baltimore. On Monday, May 2, 1966, at Morgan State College, a panel on the "Negro Revolution" featured several speakers including Walter Brooks and Julius W. Hobson, a former chair of D.C.'s CORE who was expelled in 1964 because of his growing militancy and belief that "white participation and funds...bred a moderate, meeker stance in the fight against discrimination."[47] The founder of Association Community Teams (ACT), a militant black nationalist group in D.C. "left of CORE," Hobson threatened racial upheaval, saying, "We will pepper this land with Wattses. There are going to have to be some riots and violence, and we are going to have to get nasty."[48] Walter Brooks of Baltimore's Target City, however, maintained that "Those who talk the most about violence and revolution are always the least likely to do anything about it."[49] Brooks urged such rhetoricians to stop making "beautiful speeches" and engage in what he deemed real revolution—"put your bodies on the front line" with neighborhood residents to organize for social change and political strength.[50] Interestingly, at the time, Hobson was doing more than talking; ACT was engaged in a federal lawsuit to depose the entire D.C. school board. As Morgan's student government president, Warren Howe, who moderated the panel, maintained in his summation—a summation clearly applicable to the broader palette of black power politics—"there certainly has not been a meeting of the minds tonight."[51]

The *Baltimore Afro-American* also reported on another event later that week. Three days later, on Thursday, May 5, police ousted Charles Luthardt, a white segregationist and self-proclaimed gubernatorial candidate, from a school board meeting. Police escorted Luthardt from Eastern High School's auditorium when he began lashing out against racial intermingling. Raging against integrated schools, Luthardt suggested a replacement plan—the "Luthardt Plan." He proclaimed, "White children and colored children (would not be) forced to dine, swim, shower and engage in bodily contact sports."[52] Obviously upset at being expelled from the meeting, Luthardt grumbled on his way up the aisle and out of the building, "You try to talk and they turn your juice off. Now look, I'm going to charge police brutality."[53]

While city officials and mainstream media expressed concern about CORE's calls for black power, its willingness to use violence in self-defense, and the increased number of rallies and demonstrations, the immediate threat to public civility and safety did not come from black power activists. Reflecting the reality of Walter P. Carter's description of Baltimore as "not like New York," imminent trouble came from white supremacist leaders—some in the KKK, but just as many, if not more, self-described segregationists and white hate-mongers in suits and ties from Maryland and elsewhere.

In late July, just weeks after CORE's convention in Baltimore and after CORE began implementing plans to attack unemployment, low wages, poor housing, inadequate education, and other forms of discrimination, segregationist organizers responded. This time, the National States Rights Party (NSRP) held three rallies in four days at Patterson Park and made plans for a fourth rally at Riverside Park.[54] After the second rally on July 27, Mayor McKeldin held a press conference at which he condemned the racist remarks and "disclosed that Patterson Park residents bombarded him with phone calls" to urge the prevention of future meetings. According to a *Baltimore Evening Sun* news article, McKeldin explained that the mostly white residents who called "are not in favor of integration, but they are opposed to this kind of meeting. I am a thousand percent free speech, but we have to re-examine this whole thing."[55]

At the third rally held on Thursday, July 28 at 7 p.m., NSRP leaders tossed around the word "nigger" and other anti-black and anti-Jewish obscenities wantonly and freely. Described by NSRP fliers as "America's most exciting racist speaker," fifty-three-year-old Charles Conley "Connie" Lynch talked for 11 minutes to over 1,000 mostly young white people.[56] Lynch was born in Clarksville, Texas, one of ten children of a poor cotton farmer. With a ninth grade education and no seminary education, Lynch was ordained a minister by the General Assembly of Jesus Christ in California where he lived. Alongside the plentiful epithets and critiques of Baltimore's mayor at the rally, Lynch denied inciting the crowd to violence, saying instead he was "inciting" them "to victory."[57] The NSRP Maryland coordinator, Richard Berry Norton, shouted, "If a riot comes, you all have guns" and, at some point that evening, he even thrust a clenched fist in the air—a sign that seemed to threaten white violence in contrast to Baltimore CORE's and CORE Target City's public avowal of self-defense.[58]

While not all white Baltimoreans rallied around such extremism, several gangs of white male youth, obviously invigorated by the racist diatribes, left the rally that night, drove through east Baltimore black neighborhoods, and heckled and attacked black people they saw on the streets. They called black residents who sat on their steps "niggers" and even cornered a sixteen-year-old black boy in an alley. Aware of the melee, police officers outfitted in riot gear intervened to halt and arrest white teenagers and prevent an all-out riot.[59] After all, unlike other major cities, including Watts which local officials were quite aware of, Baltimore had escaped the full-scale rebellions of the early and mid-1960s.

That Thursday night, some black residents did react to the roving white gangs, but compared to other cities what happened in Baltimore represented a skirmish. Black citizens rained bottles on cars driven by white interlopers. According to one news article, "It was more than an hour before a special squad of Negro plainclothesmen could talk the residents out of their anger."[60] While ostensibly the black police officers succeeded, this did not ensure that black residents would not retaliate if white gangs reappeared. The next day, civil rights activists even warned city officials "that white forays into Negro neighborhoods could easily incite counter violence by Negroes, some of whom, they said, are arming themselves."[61]

City officials responded. Under Gelston, who was praised by the Maryland Interracial Commission for his efforts to improve police-community relations, the police moved quickly to maintain law and order.[62] City council president and future mayor, Thomas D'Alesandro III lauded the police and asked the public "not 'to panic'."[63] Deputy city solicitor, Ambrose T. Hartman, announced the revocation of the NSRP's permit for the fourth rally; a Circuit Court judge enjoined the party from further rallies in public parks and streets; and a grand jury indicted several NSRP party leaders, including Lynch, Norton, and Joseph Carroll, on riot charges.[64] Carroll, a nineteen-year-old white youth leader for the Maryland NSRP, thought that segregating black people was simply not enough; instead he dreamed of seeing "every nigger hang from a lamp post."[65] In November, Carroll, Lynch, and Norton, an advertising writer who had attended William and Mary College and the University of Maryland, received two years imprisonment and a fine of $1,000 on riot charges.[66]

Preventing major disturbances in Baltimore had been a preoccupation of city officials since 1964. Now with CORE's Target City and its call to militancy and black power, and the counter-response it elicited, city officials committed themselves anew. In June 1966, Mayor McKeldin established the Task Force on Civil Rights to develop plans and programs to deal with racial inequality and discrimination. McKeldin counseled city officials to take citizenry complaints seriously, and not as insults. He also counseled listening and responding justly and quickly to legitimate concerns, as he himself did in 1967 when he provided hundreds of summer jobs in response to civil rights leaders' demands. McKeldin continued to view his measured political approach as the most effective way to avoid urban turmoil and would reiterate this in his October 1967 testimony before the presidential commission on civil disorders, more popularly known as the Kerner Commission. McKeldin maintained (mirroring his own shift) that while black militancy can cause offense, "you cannot allow yourself to be insulted.... These people have legitimate complaint, and you must hear them out. You must accept their cause as your cause."[67]

During 1966 and 1967, Baltimore's moderate black civil rights leaders, such as Juanita Jackson Mitchell, Baltimore Urban League executive director Dr. Furman L. Templeton, and even more militant local and national CORE organizers, lauded McKeldin's willingness to listen, dialogue, and act. But, they all emphatically stated that Baltimore was not immune to riots. If the city was to remain riot free, especially in the wake of the rising expectations of the black masses and increased community organizing, substantive advances had to be made.[68]

During the summer of 1966, Baltimore city officials and established leaders were simply relieved that they had managed to prevent a potentially explosive situation. But Baltimore liberals did express trepidation, particularly in the wake of explicit demands for race-based power. The Rev. Marlin Ballard, pastor of Universal Christian Church, passed out a leaflet in the Riverside Park area where the fourth rally had been scheduled. It said, "This saiith [sic] the Lord—Not black power, not white power, but God's power."[69] The leaflet echoed the stance of Mayor McKeldin who, while welcoming CORE and its potential positive effect on keeping Baltimore calm and improving race relations, had told convention-eers in July "that their cause would not be won by 'black power' or 'white power,' but 'it's going to be saved not by any power except by the power of God.'"[70]

Black Power Approaches

Who had power, however, was clearly an issue. And quite frankly, black power had its allure as a potential antidote not simply against the terror of white extremists, but also mainstream segregationists and even elected officials who privileged caution over confronting inequality. After all, Baltimore City Council's willful refusal to pass an open occupancy ordinance had ostensibly legitimized white intransigence, including that of homeowners, the real estate industry, and land-lords of rental property like Horizon House.[71] Whether they wanted to or not, now city officials and leaders, black and white, would have to navigate the "new direction" of more militant black activists and Baltimore's emboldened inner-city residents.

In the aftermath of CORE's convention, some local black organizations publicly debated the black power slogan, wrangled over its meaning, and even accepted it in principle as a good thing—as long as it did not devolve into a poli-tics of hatred and violence. For instance, on July 7, three days after the convention ended, the IMA vowed to continue its support of CORE despite "reservations about the concept of 'Black Power' and the new attitude towards non-violence."[72] The IMA's caution illustrates how black civil rights leaders mediated and mod-erated black power politics in Baltimore. Expressing concern about how peo-ple on the street would interpret "black power," the alliance, which supported CORE financially as well as from the pulpit, made its position clear: "Black Power which advocates black supremacy or black nationalism is as totally objectionable as is the power which supports white supremacy." A powerful network of black churches, the alliance even met with CORE representatives to discuss what was meant by black power, according to Rev. Bascom, pastor of Douglas Memorial Community Church on Lafayette and Madison avenues, but "they are as ambig-uous as we are." Even so, the Rev. Frank L. Williams, alliance president and pas-tor of Metropolitan Methodist Church, revealed that many of his parishioners who asked him about both CORE and black power "seemed favorably impressed by the concept." Williams continued, "For many this idea has filled a vacuum created by the death of Malcolm X.... CORE has done a good thing by bringing these ideas out in the open.... The grassroots people are talking about them."[73]

Organizing around the daily concerns and igniting the political passions of everyday people, particularly the most forgotten and demonized, were critical goals of activists who harnessed black power politics. These particular activ-ists adopted militant civil rights approaches that viewed black power in terms of equal access to housing, jobs, and public institutions, recognized the ballot as a source of political strength, and refused to disavow violence if needed to counterattack belligerence and aggression. They were what Robert Allen might call "rebels-for-reform" in that they did not accept the social structure as it was, but they also did not call for its complete dismantling and creation anew.[74] For instance, in May 1966—after CORE announced Baltimore as its Target City and before its convention publicly announcing their "new 'black power' approach to civil rights"—black male activists focused on integrating neighborhood taverns as well as the more upscale adult bars on "the Block, a street of B-girls, prostitutes, pimps and exotic nite clubs."[75] Although Baltimore had public accommodations laws that desegregated restaurants, bars and taverns were exempted if over half their profits came from the sale of alcohol.[76] In this case, the integration of whites-only businesses operating in black communities was a necessary precursor to achieving self-determination.

On July 11, 1966, another local civil rights organization, the Civic Interest Group (CIG), publicly endorsed black power and "announced it would no longer avoid violence in cases of 'self-defense'."[77] While CIG leadership acknowledged that black power might turn white liberals away from civil rights causes, "they denied that it should be equated with 'black supremacy'."[78] Initially founded at Morgan State College in 1960 and involved with integrating public accommodations including a shopping center, restaurants, department stores, and movie houses in Baltimore, CIG members had shifted their primary focus to forcing slum landlords to address housing code violations in west Baltimore. Now CIG sought to use the block clubs, established to fight slum housing, to promote voter registration and increase black electoral power, including among the most down-and-out residents of the city. At its press conference at St. Peter Claver's Catholic Church, CIG also "announced it would start a voter drive and disclosed plans to organize Pennsylvania Avenue's 'junkies'."[79] Vernon Conway, CIG director, believed that "narcotics addicts are voters and human beings"—a statement echoed about two weeks later in congressional hearings that featured discussions about urban problems and inner-city living.[80] At those hearings, Arthur Dunmeyer, a friend of Claude Brown (the black author of the 1965 fictionalized autobiography *Manchild in the Promised Land*), "proposed that the government find 'all the numbers runners and dope peddlers and use them, see what they had to offer to society.'"[81]

Black power organizers of this ilk envisioned such integrationist and voter registration campaigns as a means to an end—arousing poor inner-city residents and transforming their weakness into political strength. They wanted to establish viable centers of insurgency and power. While such efforts between May and December 1966 garnered organizers significant publicity, they also provoked criticism from white officials and moderate black civil rights leaders, who viewed such protests as episodic, if not misguided. While CORE organizers publicly recognized that sometimes such neighborhood protests did not rile the masses to sustained action as they had hoped, they argued that organizing residents required more time and persistence.

CORE also opened Freedom Schools, picketed discriminatory landlords, and initiated boycotts of stores and employers that upheld policies of racial inequality. Target City and Baltimore CORE organizers worked with working-class black women who had established the Maryland Freedom Union (MFU) months before they affiliated with the civil rights black power group. Former nursing home workers who walked off their jobs in February 1966 to protest poor wages and working conditions, Vivian Jones and Ola Mae Johnson served as president and secretary, respectively. Ola Mae Johnson and ten other women, who worked at the Lincoln Nursing Home at 27 North Carey Street walked out when their employer fired some employees, arguing he could not afford to pay them the $1 minimum wage passed by the city council. Vivian Jones, a nurse's aide at the Bolton Hill Nursing Home on Lafayette Avenue and John Street, said while she knew about "the Movement" and "it was a fine thing what they were doing," she had to overcome her fear "of the violence, of people getting smashed and being killed. I was scared of the power structure."[82]

After affiliating with national CORE workers who were in town making preparations for its summer Target City effort, the union expanded its base to include retail workers and replaced its strike tactics with boycotts and picketing of employers to secure bargaining rights and better job contracts.[83] Assigned to MFU, Michael Flug, a white twenty-one-year-old majoring in anthropology at Columbia University in New York, advised the group, which focused on unorganized workers making poverty wages. National CORE's shift to an official black power stance did not result in the immediate expulsion of white people from its ranks; it took a little more time in Baltimore. Neither did the call for economic power result in a revolutionary anticapitalist agenda. Instead activists sought to change the labor and business practices that marginalized and excluded black working-class and poor people.

Conflict emerged quickly as a result of MFU's campaigns. MFU's attempts to mobilize the power of the black working poor upset employers and established unions, such as the American Federation of Labor-Congress of Industrial Organization's (AFL-CIO) mostly white Retail Clerks union. MFU members assured the Retail Clerks union that they had no interest in raiding their membership and argued that mostly black organizers would do a better job organizing black workers along Pennsylvania Avenue, a main shopping hub of black west Baltimore.[84] MFU's picketing campaigns, unlike strikes, allowed low-wage workers to preserve their jobs, while activists, union members, and consumers did the work. Such demonstrations, which included black consumers and activists from CORE, CIG, and MFU, were successful, according to Flug, because "the civil rights movement has built up a momentum over the past five or six years. Now is the time to use that momentum, use that black power to win something."[85] MFU activists saw economic justice and the struggle for jobs as central to their vision of black power.

Despite early successes, black power did not win over everyone. Reservations still abounded. Some local black middle-class leaders, particularly those members of more traditional national organizations, distanced themselves from the new slogan and rejected black power activity as unproductive or noninfluential. In response to national CORE director Floyd McKissick's claim that black power helped to defeat a racist white gubernatorial candidate in Maryland, local

NAACP leaders, including the state president Juanita Jackson Mitchell and her mother, Lillian Carroll Jackson, president of Baltimore's NAACP, disavowed any link between "Black Power" and the defeat of George P. Mahoney, who had firmly rejected open occupancy. Instead, Spiro T. Agnew, a political conservative and a racial liberal compared to Mahoney, won the election. The two Mitchells, along with other signatories, sent telegrams to U.S. senators Abraham Ribicoff and Robert F. Kennedy "to correct the wrong and misleading assertion made by Floyd McKissick before your sub-committee and the nation that CORE's 'black power' activity was responsible for the Nov. 8 defeat of George Mahoney." They distinguished their efforts from those of the new black militants and in the process reasserted their belief in racial liberalism: "The truth is that the colored voters of Maryland, under-girded by the clergy, the AFRO-AMERICAN Newspapers, and the NAACP, repeated the mature performance they gave in May, 1964, when they combined with fair minded white citizens" to defeat presidential candidate George Wallace in Maryland's primary in 1964.[86]

As 1966 came to a close, numerous city officials continued to express empathy for CORE's activities and praised it for helping to defuse potential violence. D'Alesandro III, then city council president, described the group as a "catalytic agent" that "refresh[ed] the minds of public officials, like myself, with their constant calls for help in the areas of housing, public accommodations and fair employment that have been made to us over the years by our own civil rights groups." He continued, "It's a shame we couldn't have listened to our local leaders. They have acted responsibly."[87] McKeldin also remained positive and complimentary. He credited CORE and its Target City with achieving integration in public accommodations, spurring the appointment of 200 citizens to local task forces, and "helping to avert a violent reaction during the period when our city was invaded by elements bent upon spreading hate" rather than being the source of disorder as initially feared.[88]

Nevertheless, public officials remained worried about the unpredictability of white segregationist groups and activists—NSRP, Luthardt's Fighting American Nationalists (FAN), the Maryland branch of the United Klans of America, and the splinter Interstate KKK. On December 26, 1966, a small group of representatives from the Maryland Klan including Carroll, NSRP, FAN, and the Ad Hoc Committee for Sound Government picketed the potential integration of a white public-housing complex, O'Donnell Heights, in southeast Baltimore.[89] On December 29, 1966, the Interstate KKK, clearly responding to CORE's activities, named Baltimore its "target city." The Imperial Wizard, Frances Xavier Edwards announced the movement of KKK's headquarters from southern Maryland to Ellicott City and "warned the civil rights organizations to leave the State."[90]

Utilizing 'Concentration Camps' in 1967

On January 16, 1967, at the invitation of Union for Jobs or Income Now (U-JOIN), SNCC national chair Stokely Carmichael delivered a speech before a crowd of 1,400 at Rev. Williams's church in Baltimore. Earlier in the day, Carmichael, renowned for raising the chant of "Black Power" in Greenwood, Mississippi, in 1966, had addressed 1,400 students at Morgan State College to much applause and joyous laughter.[91] At the church, two local black women activists preceded him at the podium—both of them directors of U-JOIN-affiliated organizations—Irene Lee of Tenants for Justice and Margaret McCarty of Rescuers from Poverty. U-JOIN had a hybrid philosophical and organizational strategy of "responsible radicalism" that drew on civil rights, New Left, and black power politics.[92] Committed to grassroots activism and black women's leadership, U-JOIN helped mothers on welfare to organize Rescuers from Poverty, the city's first welfare rights group, and started Tenants for Justice, which fought against slum landlords and pushed for rent escrow legislation. Walter Lively served as its director. After Lee and McCarty urged political unity and the maximization of the black vote, Carmichael took the stage.

In his excited and lilting clip, Carmichael told black listeners perched in the church pews that they must establish new institutions and a new political party. He lambasted black powerbrokers—or those middle-class black leaders deemed part of the power structure—such as Morgan State College's president, Dr. Martin D. Jenkins, for attacking black power as "stupid," "poor psychology," "black racism," and violent, while "he encourages institutionalized violence by compulsory R.O.T.C."[93] And tapping into the recent history of Germany's and the United States' sordid corralling of minorities (Jewish and Japanese people, respectively) during World War II, Carmichael urged the audience to beware the white power brokers: "They're setting up concentration camps for black people all over the country."[94] With rhetorical flourish, then, Carmichael attacked the existence and seeming maintenance of black ghettoes as internal colonies suffering under the weight of poverty, police brutality, and political marginalization. After his lectures, Carmichael left Baltimore, according to a staff member, because "this is a hostile town."[95]

Although it is impossible to chart a direct path, it is clear that some local Baltimore activists deployed idioms that mimicked those of more strident and nationally known black power activists such as Stokely Carmichael whose fiery speeches unsettled conservative and liberal white officials as well as numerous black civil rights leaders. Describing the urgency of black struggle in late 1960s' Baltimore, the local Target City director Danny Gant maintained, "It's no longer a thing of wrong and right—it's black and white. We're talking about the whites got it and the black got to get some."[96] Gant continued, "Ten years ago we were good little boys. Now we're angry black men. We're not asking. We're demanding.... A revolutionary force is growing. Those concentration camps are gonna be utilized."[97]

Becoming assertive men was a frequent refrain of numerous national and local male black power activists. In 1967, Baltimore Target City organizers established a youth training program at an east Baltimore gas station with a $121,000 U.S. Department of Labor grant, and they envisioned male leadership as central to this "centerpiece for progress."[98] Milton L. Holmes, the project director, maintained, "The 'Negro male...is still a developing concept among these ghetto youths. For that reason all nine project staff workers are Negroes, and all, except for one secretary, are male. We want them to respond to male leadership...and be males themselves."[99]

Similarly, in a CORE Target City newsletter, *Black Dispatch*, the editor Norman Carroll stated a critical "aim"—"upgrading the image of the black man in unity."[100] The issue's lead editorial, titled "Genocide (Mass Murder) American Style" and written by Carroll, targeted the Vietnam War and family planning centers as methods of "whitey and his power structure...to exterminate the Black people."[101] Talking to "Black Sisters," Carroll wrote, "Your main funtion [sic] in Life, is to mate with the male of your choosing...as the fruit of the seed bears child, whose future, have no boundaries. They will represent you, your family, centuries after you are dead physically, but your richly inspired traditions as a Black Mother, will forever live on."[102] On another page, the *Black Dispatch* asked "brothers and sisters"—"Are you ready?"—and then listed a series of "To..." responses.[103] They included the following: "To...TAKE YOUR PLACE AS MEN AMONG MEN?"; "To...respect your women as precious BLACK PEARLS?" and "To...our Sisters, inspiring your mates to total achievments [sic]?"[104] The kicker phrase at the end of the list, which also encouraged harnessing black "pride and dignity," "solidarity and unity," and "gainful econmics [sic]," was "Black Power."[105] At least in this iteration of black power politics authored by CORE Target City, black women, while seen as integral, did not escape the traditionally conceived familial, reproductive, and organizational roles gendered female.

Assertions of black manhood and male leadership represented only part of Baltimore's black power politics—and only for some organizations and activists. Of course, respect and dignity were critical goals for black female grassroots organizers, such as Rescuers from Poverty, but mating and bearing babies were neither articulated as the main function in their lives, nor as a primary item on their welfare rights activist agenda.[106] Other grassroots advocates vigorously promoted consolidating the black vote as a way of mobilizing inner cities—or urban concentration camps—to secure greater representation at the municipal and state level. In 1967, Clarence Davis, a twenty-four-year-old Morgan State College law student who was running as a Second District council candidate, removed himself from the political race to avoid ticket-splitting. The president of the east Baltimore Action Association, a group of college students, and co-chair of CORE-affiliated Northeast Community Project, Davis envisioned black power "not [as] the violence described in newspapers," but as the only way to achieve full equality and economic and political power. Nor did he view a hatred of whites as inherent to black power, saying "he has 'nothing against whites except the conditions I live under.' "[107]

Economic opportunities and fair housing remained hot button issues. The city council faced the introduction of a fourth open occupancy bill, the welfare department's rent subsidy program, the antipoverty agency's self-help housing program, and a parks and recreation bill that sought to include taverns in the public accommodations law.

Seeking Power in Model Cities

Black power influenced activist organizing around government programs as well. Local strife over leadership and control over the programs of the Demonstration-Model Cities Agency provides a prime example of how black power demands, particularly for community control, shaped efforts at restructuring neighborhoods and city spaces. The Model Cities program was passed in 1966—after much wrangling at the federal level. White conservative politicians feared the program would be used to dismantle racial segregation in schools and neighborhoods, but were appeased when Congress in passing the law "specifically forbade Weaver from using [Model Cities] to promote integration."[108] Liberal politicians also questioned the program, claiming it would not do enough because it was woefully underfunded. In fact, Senator Robert F. Kennedy described the Model Cities program as "just a drop in the bucket for what we really need."[109] But for black community activists, this "drop in the bucket" program was worth fighting over in cities confronting poverty, a disintegrating infrastructure, and substandard housing and schools. Echoing the sentiment of maximum feasible participation and community control, these local black leaders demanded leadership roles in government programs administered in cities and control over desperately needed resources.

In an effort to secure a Model Cities planning grant, Baltimore officials began preparing a proposal to submit to the Department of Housing and Urban Development (HUD), the program's federal sponsor. The HUD program emphasized the "social, economic and physical renewal of blighted neighborhoods," and according to Robert C. Weaver, the black secretary of HUD, an attempt "not to patch up the community but to uncover and deal with the root causes of its deficiencies."[110] Baltimore officials focused their attention on the central city areas of east and west Baltimore, which incorporated 103,000 people (45 percent of whom received public assistance), and boasted a 10 percent unemployment rate, a crime rate double that of the entire city's, as well as disproportionate substandard housing, infant mortality, and premature birth rates.[111]

Poor people and their representatives in U-JOIN quickly and publicly demanded a substantive say—or "policy power"—in structuring Baltimore's Demonstration-Model Cities proposal. In March 1967, U-JOIN director, Walter Lively told a *Baltimore Afro-American* reporter, "The group has had its fill of programs 'twisted by local politicians' until they bring nothing but more 'frustration to people who had been disappointed so many times in the past.'"[112] In a U-JOIN letter, activists expressed fear that the lack of representation by poor people would result in "nothing more than a junk heap of shattered hopes, broken promises and another grab bag for governmental big shots and traditional government agencies."[113] McCarty of Rescuers from Poverty declared that if poor people's ideas were not incorporated, they did not want the program. They also demanded that the Baltimore demonstration program include a formal mayoral and city council promise to abolish segregation in housing, employment, education, and public facilities, and a focus on employment and welfare alongside housing.[114] Nine months later, in November 1967, with the newly elected mayor Thomas D'Alesandro III in office, Baltimore became one of 63 cities (out of an original 193) to receive a Model Cities planning grant (worth $204,000 to Baltimore), and city officials announced that poor people would be involved in the process—"a marked shift from the committee of city officials which prepared Baltimore's application for the Federal funds."[115]

What role poor people would play exactly and how much control they would have in the Demonstration-Model Cities program remained a point of contention in Baltimore and elsewhere, including St. Louis and Rochester, New York.[116] In February 1968, a HUD report criticized Baltimore officials "for failing to meet standards for citizen participation."[117] Within ten days of learning about the report, a newly established coalition of about twenty civil rights, black power, and neighborhood organizations formed a "take-over" committee and demanded control of the local Model Cities Agency. It was not simply a matter of race—the director, Edgar M. Ewing, was black—but of class, representation, and neighborhood control. The coalition included U-JOIN, Activists for Fair Housing Inc., Rescuers from Poverty, SNCC, and CORE—all predominantly black organizations, many of which advocated poor and working-class people's interests in inner city neighborhoods.[118] Two former Baltimore CORE members, Walter P. Carter and Sampson Green, started Activists Inc. to press for fair and affordable housing. Green chaired the coalition's takeover committee.

The coalition held three meetings in three days with the mayor at the CORE Target City office on North Gay Street, located in the Model Cities program area. At the second meeting, coalition representatives demanded that D'Alesandro give the group "complete control over the appointment of salaried officials, the naming of community representatives and the establishment of all policy."[119] They warned that if the mayor denied their requests, the member groups would withhold their support and participation—a necessary requirement of HUD. When D'Alesandro refused to accept the coalition's terms and forty-five minutes turned into a ninety-minute meeting, CORE Target City director Danny Gant stormed out of the building, got into his car, yelled "we don't want it; we're going to destroy the program," and then threatened to go to Washington, D.C. to meet with HUD officials. An unidentified woman echoing the desire for poor black people to take control said to a white reporter in attendance, "We've tried it your way 400 years."[120]

The next day, D'Alesandro met with coalition leaders for the third time. By the end of this meeting, the parties reached an acceptable compromise. The mayor agreed to allow representatives of the poor to hire crucial personnel and to let the Baltimore coalition control the agency's community organizing division. D'Alesandro also proposed the formation of a policy steering board made up of representatives of Model Cities' neighborhood residents, community organizations, and city officials. This policy steering board would approve the agency's plans before submitting them to HUD. D'Alesandro stated, "I want to emphasize that the committee is to strive for the maximum participation of the poor at every phase in the planning of the Model Cities program."[121] Not quite a month later, Edgar Ewing even endorsed black power before a student audience at Johns Hopkins University in east Baltimore, but only so long as it "separate[s] itself from violence and separatism."[122] Ewing also stated in his speech—in which he also criticized colleges and universities for not helping to solve urban problems— that black power had "creative possibilities" such as promoting "self-help" and "self-respect."[123]

By September 1968, Baltimore became known, at least among some black power activists, as one of those cities where local community people successfully fought for control of its Model Cities program. At the Third International Black Power Conference in Philadelphia, Robert "Sonny" Carson declared that "Model Cities Programs, where Blacks are not in control of the policy-making apparatus, cannot effectively address themselves to the problems of the black community."[124] A radical CORE leader from Brooklyn, New York, Carson argued "that Black Power advocates did not 'want anything to do with the white power structure as it is now. I believe that capitalism has to be destroyed if black people are to be free.'"[125] In his statement during the conference, Carson continued, "Where federal, state, and local programs cannot be controlled, these, as well as other programs must be blocked. We have applauded the efforts of Black people in Newark, Bronx, Rochester, Baltimore, Philadelphia in their successful attempts at stopping all white model cities programs."[126]

Garnering local citizenry input and control over the Model Cities program, however, did not end the debates and disagreements in Baltimore. Even follow-ing the initial compromise that established the policy steering board and after the federal government's approval of a five-year Model Cities implementation program grant in January 1969, black activists and Baltimore officials, including Mayor D'Alesandro and city council president William D. Schaefer, continued to struggle over who ultimately should control the program as well as its direction. Edgar Ewing would leave the agency in January 1969 to manage an Inner Harbor redevelopment project, and Walter P. Carter (known as "Mr. Civil Rights" and a diehard advocate for poor people's representation, economic rights, and political power) already had become the Baltimore Model Cities agency's chief commu-nity organizer. Through all these changes, however, a crucial question remained: "Who is to run the program: City Hall or the people." In other words, "who will be working for whom?"[127]

1968

As governor and mayor, respectively, McKeldin and D'Alesandro had approached black power with relative composure, measured responses, and a willingness to sometimes relent to citizens' demands, of course, without fully ceding munic-ipal power. Spiro T. Agnew, who succeeded McKeldin as Maryland's governor, however, responded with brashness and harshness to black activists' assertive demands, particularly expressing disdain for black power activists (no matter their particular definition of black power) and anyone who seemed to consort with them.[128]

In 1968, Agnew's civil rights coordinator, Dr. Gilbert Ware sent the gover-nor a memo titled, "Your Image in Negro Community." Highlighting Baltimore activists' critical concerns such as welfare allowances, taverns, housing, and "your (to the militants) impersonality," Ware encouraged Agnew "to pay personal ostentation-free, visits to the ghetto."[129] The memo continued,

> Of the utmost importance is the Negro's, especially the black militant's, conceptualization of you as friend or foe. To this point, he has considered you to be his foe. Right or wrong, that is how it is, and we can expect hostility toward you to grow, especially in view of the recent newspaper articles which suggest that you overstated the case against Rap Brown.[130]

Apparently taken aback by Ware's assessment, Agnew sent his memo with a handwritten question on it to his Staff Steering Committee. "There is absolutely no way to overstate the case against Rap Brown. What is your analysis?"[131] Agnew had taken to frequently lambasting H. Rap Brown, head of SNCC, for a speech he had given in Cambridge, Maryland, in July 1967—following upon the heels of an NSRP rally. After Brown "called for an escalation of black liberation politics, explicitly sanctioning guerilla warfare as a political tactic," the crowd applauded feverishly.[132] That night in Cambridge, tensions mounted, resulting in a shooting, Brown leaving town, and fires burning down two city blocks while white firefighters, upon the orders of the police chief, watched from their trucks in a nearby shopping center. Agnew was appalled by Brown's fiery rhetoric—but apparently not the firefighters' and police chief's dereliction of duty—and blamed the SNCC leader and black power advocate for upsetting peace in his state. Agnew's staff committee told the governor that apparently Ware did not have a "clear understanding of the extent to which you are willing to recognize or work with the Negro militants."[133] They suggested Agnew meet with Ware to discuss Ware's performance, to clarify Agnew's views, and to tell Ware "if he has strong feelings in given areas, he should...present them in such a fashion as to suggest alternate courses of action for your consideration."[134]

A month later, in the wake of the 1968 rebellion, which exploded in Baltimore two days after Martin Luther King Jr.'s assassination, Agnew unashamedly publicized his venom, not just at lawlessness, but at what he viewed as the black power roots of that lawlessness. He called out the National Guard and asked for federal troops. Then Agnew called a meeting with 100 black leaders, many of whom had been walking the streets trying to keep order. At the meeting, Agnew did not acknowledge the black leaders' peacekeeping efforts, but instead expressed his intense dislike of black radicalism and political confrontation.

Before Parren J. Mitchell, the former executive director of Baltimore's community action program and the city's first black elected Congressman, arrived at the meeting, he already knew what Agnew had planned to say. "The Press people had alerted me and I was frantic with calling people, saying, look get to him tell him to change that, drop it all together."[135] According to Mitchell, "Here you have the governor flanked by [Gelston] representing the military power, flanked by whoever the police chief was...and this great stage setting which was really interpreted by me and others as saying, 'I've got the might and the power.' That was the first thing that rubbed me wrong."[136] Sitting next to Rev. Marion Bascom,

Parren Mitchell listened disgustedly, and when Agnew used the word "coward" to describe the assembled black leaders, Mitchell stood up and left. "Nobody calls me a coward, I don't care who it is. So at that point I was the first one up, out of the room."[137]

Agnew argued that "the looting and rioting which has engulfed our City during the past several days did not occur by chance. It is no mere coincidence that a national disciple of violence, Mr. Stokely Carmichael, was observed meeting with local black power advocates and known criminals in Baltimore on April 3, 1968—three days before the Baltimore riots began." Agnew did not address how this supposed meeting on April 3—a full day before King's unexpected assassination on April 4—resulted in "no mere coincidence" when the dismay and outrage of Baltimore residents exploded in rebellious turmoil.[138] Agnew also described Carmichael and Brown as "twin priests of violence" and "agents of destruction" and compared them with white supremacists and their organizations.[139] "They will surely destroy us if we do not repudiate them and their philosophies—along with white racists such as Joseph Carroll and Connie Lynch—the American Nazi Party, the John Birchers, and their fellow travelers."[140] He then called for black leaders to help, but told them "your help will be of little value if you did not know and subscribe to the objectives for which I seek it. We can do much together— little apart."[141] Agnew moved toward closure of his speech with the following words: "Let us promptly and publicly renounce any who counsel or condone violence."[142]

Moderate black civil rights leaders, who Agnew summoned to hear his speech while excluding others such as Walter Lively, fumed at the way Agnew talked down to them as if they were children. Outside Rev. Marion Bascom's Douglas Memorial Church, where black leaders met to devise a collective response, an unidentified minister said, "He's forcing us all to become militants.... We are the moderates who strove for a continuing dialogue for unity. I know for a fact, Agnew has not conferred with his own liaison man (Dr. Gilbert Ware) for over a month."[143] In their collective statement, leaders expressed "shock" at Agnew's "tone and fervor," his "audacity and temerity at directing such remarks to those assembled," and his attempts to "deliberately...divide us. We are all militantly against the continuation of a system which denies and demeans black people."[144] The statement called "upon all people of goodwill, black and white, to let the governor know that he failed to demonstrate enlightened and concerned leadership today and that he failed to divide the black community."[145] Looking back on the incident, Parren Mitchell stated, "I think that temporarily that Agnew confrontation provided the platform on which a much tougher, militant Black group, Black leadership could become...Had he not done this, and I'm not saying that it was right or wrong for that new tough Black militant group to emerge, but he provided a forum for it."[146]

Agnew's public statements erased the multivocal and multiorganizational character of Baltimore's black power politics through his public renderings of black militancy as singular, national, vile, and reactionary—a national politics for him akin to white extremism. He did not acknowledge the role that local black power activists and civil rights leaders played in stemming violence in Baltimore—in the past or present. He did not distinguish between the utterances of national and local black power activists. Nor did he differentiate among the politics of moderate black leaders and their more militant counterparts—even though black activists themselves often did. Agnew's public outrage and vilification of black militants would make him the darling of the Republican Party and the Richard M. Nixon presidential campaign.

By 1968 the seeds of black power activism were firmly planted and fertilized alongside rights struggles in Baltimore. CORE Target City, Baltimore CORE, welfare rights activists, U-JOIN, CIG, IMA, as well as the animated Black Panther Party mobilized with varying degrees of vigor in the city throughout the 1960s and into the early 1970s.[147] And yet, while 1968 became a year popularly remembered for tumult in cities, in fact, an examination of how urban residents' material realities, the roots and concrete activist manifestations of movement ideologies, and the unexpected historical turns coincided reveal 1968 not only as a "year" many years (and arguably decades) in the making, but also as a fulcrum for grassroots and national political campaigns in the years to come.

Notes

I would like to thank the following people for reading this chapter in its entirety and offering invaluable advice: David Goldberg, Peniel E. Joseph, Premilla Nadasen, and the participants of the Colgate 1968 conference.

1. Daniel Drosdoff, "Powell Bids Negroes Aid One Another," *Baltimore Morning Sun* (*BMS*), February 28, 1966, Folder: Problems—Negro Housing, 1965–1966, Box 5, Series VII, Citizens Planning Housing Association Papers (CPHA), University of Baltimore Archives (UBA), Baltimore, Maryland.
2. Ibid.
3. Richard H. Levine, "Black Power Top Issue," *BMS*, July 5, 1966, Folder: July–December 1966, Box 128 (Negroes) Series VI, Commission on Government Efficiency and Economy (CGEE), UBA.
4. "Black Power," *BMS*, July 6, 1966, Folder: Civil Rights, 1966, Box 3, Series VII, CPHA, UBA.
5. Yohuru Williams makes this very point in his article discussing Roy Wilkins and Black Power politics, writing, "Interestingly, it was not necessarily the term *power* but the use of the word *black* before it that made Wilkins uneasy. To be sure, Wilkins understood the implications of Black Power. Following Harry Truman's 1948 presidential victory, secured with robust Black electoral supports, Wilkins had commented, "The message was plain: White power in the South could be balanced by black power at the Northern polls. Civil rights were squarely at the heart of national politics." See, Yohuru Williams, "'A Red, Black and Green Liberation Jumpsuit': Roy Wilkins, the Black Panthers, and the Conundrum of Black Power," in Peniel E Joseph, ed., *The Black Power Movement: Rethinking the Civil Rights-Black Power Era* (New York: Routledge, 2006), p. 172. Also see, Robert L. Allen, *Black Awakening in Capitalist America: An Analytic History* (New York: Doubleday and Company, 1969), p. 19.
6. Levine, "Black Power Top Issue," *BMS*, July 5, 1966. Also, "Black Power," *BMS*, July 6, 1966, and "C.O.R.E.'s New Policy," *Baltimore Evening Sun* (*BES*), July 6, 1966, both in Folder: Civil Rights, 1966, Box 3, Series VII, CPHA, UBA. Also see Clayborne Carson, *In Struggle: SNCC and the Black Awakening of the 1960s* (Cambridge, MA: Harvard University Press, 1981), pp. 215–228.

7. "Black Power," *BMS*, July 6, 1966.

8. "C.O.R.E.'s New Policy," *BES*, July 6, 1966.

9. Bradford Jacobs, "Gray Power," *BES*, July 8, 1966, Folder: July–December 1966, Box 128 (Negroes) Series VI, CGEE, UBA.

10. Daniel Drosdoff, "C.O.R.E. Move Against War Is Expected," *BMS*, July 4, 1966, Folder: Civil Rights, 1966, Box 3, Series VII, CPHA, UBA.

11. "C.O.R.E.'s New Policy," *BES*, July 6, 1966.

12. Levine, "Black Power Top Issue," *BMS*, July 5, 1966.

13. CORE News Release, April 21, 1966, Folder 369—CORE, Box 499, S26, RG 9, BCA.

14. Rhonda Y. Williams, "Black Women, Urban Politics, and Engendering Black Power," *The Black Power Movement*, p. 84.

15. Numerous scholars have begun the work of documenting the tenor of Black Power struggles at the local level. See, for instance, essays in *The Black Power Movement*; Matthew Countryman, *Up South: Civil Rights and Black Power in Philadelphia* (Philadelphia, PA: University of Pennsylvania Press, 2006); Robert O. Self, *American Babylon: Race and the Struggle for Postwar Oakland* (Princeton, NJ: Princeton University Press, 2003); Yohuru Williams, *Black Politics/White Power: Civil Rights, Black Power, and the Black Panthers in New Haven* (New York: Brandywine Press, 2000); Winston Grady-Willis, *Challenging U.S. Apartheid: Atlanta and the Black Struggle for Human Rights, 1960–1977* (Durham, NC: Duke University Press, 2006); Komozi Woodard, *A Nation within a Nation: Amiri Baraka (LeRoi Jones) & Black Power Politics* (Chapel Hill: University of North Carolina Press, 1999). Also see, Robert O. Self and Thomas J. Sugrue, "The Power of Place: Race, Political Economy, and Identity in the Postwar Metropolis," in Jean-Christophe Agnew and Roy Rosenzweig, eds., *A Companion to Post-1945 America* (Malden, MA: Blackwell, 2002, 2006), pp. 20–43.

16. Jonathan Cottin, "City Seen Chosen for Rights Drive Because Negro Riot Not Likely," *BES*, April 28, 1966, Folder: January-June 1966, Box 128 (Negroes) Series VI, CGEE, UBA.

17. Ibid.

18. Countee Cullen, "Incident," in Dudley Randall, ed., *The Black Poets* (New York: Bantam, 1971), pp. 98–99. I thank David Goldberg for bringing this poem to my attention.

19. Ben A. Franklin, "Baltimore Vexing to CORE Campaign," *New York Times* (*NYT*), June 12, 1966, Folder: 1967, Box 128 (Negroes), Series VI, CGEE, UBA.

20. James D. Dilts, "The Warning Trumpet," *Baltimore Sun Magazine*, December 1, 1968, Folder: Congress of Racial Equality, MDVF, EPFL.

21. John D'Emilio, *Last Prophet: The Life and Times of Bayard Rustin* (Chicago: University of Chicago Press, 2004), p. 1.

22. Dilts, "The Warning Trumpet."

23. "C.O.R.E. Selects City as Target," *Baltimore News Post*, April 15, 1966.

24. Ben A. Franklin, "CORE'S 'Target City' Program in Baltimore Now Hailed for Its Moderation," *NYT*, April 16, 1967, Folder: Congress of Racial Equality, MDVF, EPFL.

25. George W. Collins, "Baltimore Civil Rights," *BAA*, June 18, 1966.

26. Ibid.

27. Ibid.

28. Ibid.

29. George H. Callcott, *Maryland & America: 1940 to 1980* (Baltimore: Johns Hopkins University Press, 1985), especially Chapter 7; Karen Olson, "Old West Baltimore: Segregation, African-American Culture, and the Struggle for Equality," in Elizabeth Fee,

Linda Shopes, and Linda Zeidman, eds., *The Baltimore Book: New Views of Local History* (Philadelphia, PA: Temple University Press, 1991), pp. 57–78; Andor D. Skotnes, "'Buy Where You Can Work': Boycotting for Jobs in African-American Baltimore, 1933–1934," *Journal of Social History*, 27(Summer 1994): 735–761.

30. CORE News Release, April 21, 1966.
31. "C.O.R.E. Selects City as Target," *Baltimore News Post*, April 15, 1966.
32. Ray Abrams, "CORE Lashes Community, Plans New Fight Tactics," *BAA*, January 8, 1966.
33. Richard H. Levine, "C.O.R.E. Chief Here to Heal Rights Rift," *BMS*, June 18, 1966.
34. Ibid.
35. Ibid.
36. Ibid.
37. Alan Lupo, "'Why Us?' for C.O. Target, Officials Ask," *BES*, April 15, 1966, Folder: Civil Rights, 1966, Box 3, Series VII, CPHA, UBA.
38. Ibid.
39. "Mayor Says Target City Could Be Summer's Safest," *BAA*, July 5, 1966.
40. "CORE to Ignore Any Court Ban against Pickets," *BAA*, May 7, 1966.
41. While these desegregation protests focused on luxury apartment buildings, the integration of low-income public housing also drew the ire of anti-black, pro-segregationists. In the latter case, CORE provided protection and legal support for black pioneer tenants moving into the all-white Brooklyn Homes in 1967. Rhonda Y. Williams, *The Politics of Public Housing*, pp. 118–119.
42. "Judge Jails 2 CORE Pickets," *BAA*, May 14, 1966.
43. "CORE to Ignore Any Court Ban against Pickets," *BAA*, May 7, 1966.
44. Ibid.
45. "Judge Jails 2 CORE Pickets," *BAA*, May 14, 1966.
46. Franklin, "Baltimore Vexing to CORE Campaign," *NYT*, June 12, 1966.
47. Black Biography, Julius W. Hobson, Answers.com, at http://www.answers.com/topic/julius-hobson. Accessed January 11, 2009. Also see "Guide to the Papers of Julius Hobson," District of Columbia Public Library, http://dclibrary.org/dcpl/cwp/view.asp?A=1264&Q=567171. Accessed January 11, 2009. In an August 14, 2008 conversation, historian David Goldberg, whose research focuses on black power, employment, and labor organizing, shared with me that Julius Hobson played an instrumental role in Washington D.C's school desegregation case and in gaining black access to contracts and jobs.
48. "Race Violence Seen by Morgan Panelist," *BAA*, May 7, 1966.
49. Ibid.
50. Ibid.
51. Ibid.
52. "Luthardt Ousted at School Hearing," *BAA*, May 7, 1966.
53. Ibid.
54. Lupo, "'Why Us?' For C.O.R.E. Target, Officials Ask," *BES*, April 15, 1966. Also, "Officials Meet on Ways to Stop New Rally-Riot," *BES*, July 29, 1966, Folder: July–December 1966, Box 128 (Negroes), Series VI, CGEE, UBA; Kenneth D. Durr, *Behind the Backlash: White Working-Class Politics in Baltimore, 1940–1980* (Chapel Hill: University of North Carolina Press, 2003), pp. 131–134.
55. "City to Request Racist Rally Cancellation," *BES*, July 28, 1966.
56. "Racist Party is Forbidden to Use Parks," *BMS*, July 30, 1966, Folder: July–December 1966, Box 128 (Negroes), Series VI, CGEE, UBA.
57. Ibid.

58. Ibid.
59. "Officials Meet on Ways to Stop New Rally-Riot," *BES*, July 29, 1966, "Racist Rally Ignites Angry Outbursts," *BMS*, July 29, 1966, "Racist Party is Forbidden to Use Parks," *BMS*, July 30, 1966.
60. "Racist Party Is Forbidden to Use Parks," *BMS*, July 30, 1966.
61. "Officials Meet on Ways to Stop New Rally-Riot," *BES*, July 29, 1966.
62. "Gelston Praised for Rights Work," *BMS*, June 22, 1966, Folder: January–June 1966, Box 128 (Negroes), Series VI, CGEE, UBA.
63. "Officials Meet on Ways to Stop New Rally-Riot," *BES*, July 29, 1966.
64. "Racist Party Is Forbidden to Use Parks," *BES*, July 30, 1966.
65. George J. Hiltner, "States' Rights Aims Outlined," *BMS*, August 11, 1966, Folder: July-December 1966, Box 128 (Negroes), Series VI, CGEE, UBA.
66. George J. Hiltner, "Leaders Get 2 Years for Racist Rally," *BMS*, November 22, 1966, Folder: July–December 1966, Box 128 (Negroes), Series VI, CGEE, UBA.
67. Adam Spiegel, "McKeldin Testifying at D.C. Riot Inquiry," *BES*, October 5, 1967.
68. Wilbur Pinder Jr., "Negro Leaders See Quiet Summer," *BES*, April 19, 1967; John E. Woodruff, "Mayor Seeks to Cool Off Hot Summer," *BMS*, June 14, 1967; Robin Frames, "Rioting Here Is Doubted by Church, Rights Leader," *BES*, July 22, 1967; Oswald Johnston, "State, City Act to Head Off Violence," *BMS*, July 27, 1967; "Mayor Hopeful on Return of Racial Peace," *BES*, October 2, 1967; Philip Potter, "Mayor Tells of Means to Prevent Riot," *BMS*, October 6, 1967, all in Folder: 1967, Box 128 (Negroes), Series VI, CGEE, UBA.
69. "Racist Party Is Forbidden to Use Parks," *BMS*, July 30, 1966.
70. Drosdoff, " C.O.R.E. Move Against War Is Expected."
71. For a similar story on the evolution of black power politics in Los Angeles, see Jeanne Theoharis, "'Alabama on Avalon': Rethinking the Watts Uprising and the Character of Black Protest in Los Angeles," *The Black Power Movement*, pp. 27–53. In this essay, Theoharis discusses how the school board's inaction throughout the 1940s and 1950s in desegregating schools, and its passage of Proposition 14 that overturned the city's 1963 Fair Housing Act in 1964, made L.A. ripe for increased protests in the 1960s, including Watts in 1965. She argues that "Indeed, Black Power in Los Angeles evolved out of a genealogy that includes, rather than reacts to, what is often deemed 'civil rights protest'—out of mounting critique of racial liberalism by community activists in the city over three decades and an activist politics of confrontation that long preceded the uprising."
72. "Concerned Ministers Still Back CORE," *BAA*, July 9, 1966.
73. Ibid.
74. Allen, *Black Awakening in Capitalist America*, p. 40.
75. Franklin, "Baltimore Vexing to CORE Campaign."
76. Ibid. Also see Richard H. Levine, "Five-year Rights Campaign Contemplated by C.O.R.E.," *BMS*, October 7, 1966, Folder: July-December 1966, Box 128 (Negroes), Series VI, CGEE, UBA.
77. "Black Power Idea Backed," *BMS*, July 12, 1966, Folder: July-December 1966, Box 128 (Negroes) Series VI, CGEE, UBA.
78. Ibid.
79. Ibid.
80. Ibid.
81. Wendell E. Pritchett, *Robert Clifton Weaver and the American City: The Life and Times of an Urban Reformer* (Chicago: University of Chicago Press, 2008), p. 297.
82. "Union for Poor Led by Women," *BAA*, April 30, 1966.

83. Horace Ayres, "Md. Freedom Union Is a Different Kind of Labor Group," *BES*, July 22, 1966, Folder: Maryland Freedom Union, MDVF, EPFL.

84. Ibid.

85. Ayres, "Md. Freedom Union Is a Different Kind of Labor Group," *BES*, July 22, 1966. Also see, "Freedom Union Wins New Recognition," *BAA*, July 5, 1966; "Bargaining Stalled; MFU Returns to Street," *BAA*, August 6, 1966.

86. "Election role of 'Black Power' Hit," *BAA*, December 13, 1966.

87. Daniel Drosdoff, "City-C.O.R.E. Cooperation Now Believed a Possibility," Baltimore Sun, October 5, 1966, Folder: Congress of Racial Equality, MDVF, EPFL.

88. "Mayor Praises CORE on Target City Role," *BAA*, October 4, 1966.

89. "Racists Picket Housing Units," *BES*, December 27, 1966.

90. "K.K.K. Names Baltimore as 'Target City,'" *BES*, December 30, 1966.

91. George Rodgers, "Carmichael Calls for Black Power," *BES*, January 17, 1967.

92. James D. Dilts, "Organization Man for the Other America," *Baltimore Sun Magazine*, June 16, 1968, Folder: Poverty Program, 1963–1969, Box 5 Series VII, CGEE, UBA.

93. Daniel Drosdoff, "Carmichael Asks Black Struggle," *BMS*, January 17, 1967, Folder: 1967, Box 128 (Negroes), Series VI, CGEE, UBA.

94. Ibid. For Martin Jenkins' views on black power, see George Rodgers, "Educator Raps 'Black Power' Slogan," *BES*, September 30, 1966, Folder: Folder: July–December 1966, Box 128 (Negroes), Series VI, CGEE, UBA.

95. Rodgers, "Carmichael Calls for Black Power," *BES*, January 17, 1967.

96. Dilts, "The Warning Trumpet," *Baltimore Sun Magazine*, December 1, 1968.

97. Ibid.

98. Gene Oishi, "C.O.R.E.'s Centerpiece for Progress," *Baltimore Sun*, May 4, 1967, Folder: Congress of Racial Equality, MDVF, EPFL.

99. Ibid.

100. "Aim: For the Upgrading of the Image of the Black Man in Unity," *Black Dispatch*, no date, circa mid-1968, Folder 369: CORE, Box 499, Series 26, RG 9, BCA.

101. "Genocide (Mass Murder) American Style," *Black Dispatch*, no date, circa mid-1968.

102. "Aim: For the Upgrading of the Image of the Black Man in Unity," *Black Dispatch*, no date, circa mid-1968.

103. "Are You Ready?" *Black Dispatch*, no date, circa mid-1968.

104. Ibid.

105. Ibid.

106. See Williams, *The Politics of Public Housing*, chapter 6; "Black Women, Urban Politics, and Engendering Black Power," in *The Black Power Movement*; "Nonviolence and Long Hot Summers: Welfare Rights Struggles in the 1960s" for *Borderlands E-Journal*, 4, no. 3, 2005. Access at: http://www.borderlandsejournal.adelaide.edu.au/vol4no3_2005/williams_welfare.htm; "We're Tired of Being Treated Like Dogs: Poor Women and Power Politics," *The Black Scholar*, Special Edition on *Black Power Studies: A New Scholarship*, Fall/Winter 2001, 31–41. Also see, Premilla Nadasen, *Welfare Warriors: The Welfare Rights Movement in the United States* (New York: Routledge, 2004); Annelise Orleck, *Storming Caesars Palace: How Black Mothers Fought Their Own War on Poverty* (Boston: Beacon Press, 2005).

107. Thomas Edsall, "Black Power Consolidation Urged," *BES*, August 10, 1967, Folder: 1967, Box 128 (Negroes), Series VI, CGEE, UBA.

108. Pritchett, *Robert Clifton Weaver*, p. 314.

109. Ibid., p. 296.

110. James Macnees, "Baltimore Chosen for U.S. Cities Aid," *BMS*, November 17, 1967, Folder: 1967, Box 123 (Model Cities), CGEE VI, UBA.

111. Ibid.
112. Roger Nissly, "Poor Demanding Role in 'Demonstration' Project," *BAA*, March 18, 1967.
113. Ibid.
114. Ibid.
115. James Macnees, "Baltimore Chosen for U.S. Cities Aid," and quote from Stephen J. Lynton, "Poor to Help with Aid Plan," both in *BMS*, Nov. 17, 1967, Folder: 1967, Box 123 (Model Cities), CGEE VI, UBA.
116. Linda Dunn, "Model Cities Plan is Criticized," *BMS*, December 12, 1967, Folder: 1967, Box 123 (Model Cities), CGEE VI, UBA.
117. James D. Dilts, "Disputes Stymie Model Cities Agency," *Baltimore Sunday Sun*, July 7, 1968.
118. Stephen J. Lynton, "Negroes Ask Model Cities Control," *BMS*, February 21, 1968, Folder: Demonstration City—Model Cities, 1966–1969, Box 3, Series VII, CPHA, UBA.
119. Ibid.
120. David Runkel, "C.O.R.E. Walks Out on Mayor in Row Over Model Cities," *BES*, February 21, 1968, Folder: Demonstration City—Model Cities, 1966–1969, Box 3, Series VII, CPHA, UBA.
121. David Runkel, "Rights Coalition Accepts Mayor's Compromise," *BES*, February 22, 1968, Folder: Demonstration City—Model Cities, 1966–1969, Box 3, Series VII, CPHA, UBA
122. "Black Power Concept Gets Ewing Backing," *BMS*, March 15, 1968, Folder: Demonstration City—Model Cities, 1966–1969, Box 3, Series VII, CPHA, UBA.
123. Ibid.
124. Robert "Sonny" Carson, "Third International Conference of Black Power, Economics," Philadelphia, PA, August/September, 1968, The Black Power Movement, Part 3: Papers of the Revolutionary Action Movement, 1963–1996, Muhammad Ahmad, Ernie Allen and John H. Bracey, eds., Reel 11(Bethesda: Lexus/Nexus, 2003). I must thank David Goldberg for providing me with this information and citation. For more detail on local activism in Philadelphia and Model Cities, see Countryman, *Up South*, pp. 300–307.
125. Matthew C. Whitaker, *Race Work: The Rise of Civil Rights in the Urban West* (Lincoln, NE: University of Nebraska Press, 2007), p. 187.
126. Robert "Sonny" Carson, "Third International Conference of Black Power, Economics," Philadelphia, Pa., August/September, 1968.
127. Quote is from James D. Dilts, "Disputes Stymie Model Cities Agency," *Baltimore Sunday Sun*, July 7, 1968. Also see, Naomi S. Rovner, "Baltimore Model Cities Plan Approved," *BMS*, January 18, 1969, both in Folder: Demonstration City—Model Cities, 1966–1969, Box 3, Series VII, CPHA, UBA. With the change in the presidency from Lyndon Johnson to Richard Nixon, approval of Baltimore's Model Cities Program was temporarily withdrawn and reapproved in June 1969. See, "Model Cities Get Final O.K.," *BES*, June 26, 1969. By the end of 1969, the Nixon administration began cutting appropriations to Model Cities, thereby hampering the effectiveness of an already financially strapped program. See Pritchett, *Robert Clifton Weaver*, p. 322.
128. On April 4, 1968, 450 Bowie State students marched on the State House to demand campus improvements, and Agnew called out the state police on the nonviolent protestors. The state police arrested 227 students, and then closed down the campus and ordered all students to leave. See, George H. Callcott, *Maryland & America: 1940 to 1960* (Baltimore: Johns Hopkins University Press, 1985), pp. 164–165.

129. State of Maryland Executive Department Memo to Governor from Staff Steering Committee, March 21, 1968, Folder: Civil Rights—Part V, Box (19037) 14, Governor's Files, MDSA.

130. Ibid.

131. Ibid.

132. Peniel E. Joseph, *Waiting 'Til the Midnight Hour: A Narrative History of Black Power in America* (New York: Henry Holt & Company, 2006), p. 188.

133. State of Maryland Executive Department Memo to Governor from Staff Steering Committee, March 21, 1968.

134. Ibid.

135. Parren Mitchell Interview, 1973, Folder: Mitchell, Parren; Mondale, Box 36, Series III: Equality Series, Transcripts, Kotz Papers (Unprocessed), Wisconsin Historical Society, Madison, Wisconsin.

136. Ibid.

137. Ibid.

138. Opening Statement by Governor Spiro T. Agnew, April 11, 1968, Folder: Civil Rights—Part I, Box 14, Governors Records, MDSA.

139. Ibid.

140. Ibid.

141. Ibid.

142. Ibid.

143. "Angry Leaders Walk Out on Agnew," *BAA*, April 20, 1968.

144. Ibid.

145. Ibid.

146. Parren Mitchell Interview, 1973.

147. For a brief discussion on the Black Panther Party in Baltimore, see Rhonda Y. Williams, "Black Women, Urban Politics, and Engendering Black Power," pp. 89–91. For a first-person account, see Steve D. McCutcheon, "Selections from a Panther Diary," in Charles E. Jones, ed., *The Black Panther Party [Reconsidered]* (Baltimore: Black Classic Press, 1998).

Contributors

Peniel E. Joseph is professor of history at Tufts University and the author of the award-winning *Waiting 'Til the Midnight Hour: A Narrative History of Black Power in America* (2006); *Dark Days, Bright Nights: From Black Power to Barack Obama* (2010). He is the editor of *The Black Power Movement: Rethinking the Civil Rights-Black Power Era* (2006). Joseph is a frequent national commentator on civil rights, race, and democracy issues and his work has appeared in the *New York Times*, *The Chronicle Review*, *The Journal of American History*, and *The Washington Post*. He has received fellowships from Harvard University's Charles Warren Center, the Woodrow Wilson International Center for Scholars and the Ford Foundation. During the 2008 Democratic and Republican Conventions, Professor Joseph served as a historian for PBS's NewsHour.

Kent B. Germany is assistant professor of history and African American Studies at University of South Carolina and author of *New Orleans after the Promises: Poverty, Citizenship and the Search for the Great Society* (2007).

Patrick D. Jones associate professor of History and Ethnic Studies at the University of Nebraska-Lincoln. He is the author of *The Selma of the North: Civil Rights Insurgency in Milwaukee* (2009).

Tracy E. K'Meyer is associate professor of history at the University of Louisville and is the author of *Civil Rights in the Gateway of the South: Louisville, Kentucky, 1945–1980* (2009).

Clarence Lang is assistant professor of African-American Studies and History at University of Illinois at Urbana-Champagne and is the author of *Grassroots at the Gateway: Class Politics and Black Freedom Struggle in St. Louis, 1936–75* (2009).

Donna Murch is assistant professor of history at Rutgers University. She is completing a book about the Black Panthers.

James Smethurst is associate professor in the W.E.B. Du Bois Department of Afro-American Studies at the University of Massachusetts-Amherst. He is the author of *The Black Arts Movement: Literary Nationalism in the 1960s and 1970s* (2005) and co-editor, with Bill V. Mullen, of *Left of the Color Line: Race, Radicalism, and Twentieth-Century Literature of the United States* (2003).

Jeanne Theoharis teaches political science at Brooklyn College. She is co-author of *These Yet to Be Free United States: Civil Rights and Civil Liberties in America since 1945* (2002) and co-editor, with Komozi Woodard, of *Freedom North: Black*

Freedom Struggles outside the South, 1940–1980 (2003) and *Groundwork: Local Black Freedom Movements in America* (2005).

Simon Wendt teaches history at the University of Heidelberg. He is the author of *The Spirit and the Shotgun: Armed Resistance and the Struggle for Civil Rights* (2007).

Rhonda Y. Williams is associate professor of history at Case Western University. She is author of the award-winning *The Politics of Public Housing: Black Women's Struggles against Urban Inequality* (2005) and co-editor with Julie Buckner Armstrong, Susan Hult Edwards, and Houston Bryan Roberson, of *Teaching the American Civil Rights Movement: Freedom's Bittersweet Song* (2002).

Index